Encyclopedia of Family Life

Encyclopedia of Family Life

Volume 1
Abandonment of the family – Community programs for children

Editor

Carl L. Bankston III
University of Southwestern Louisiana

Project Editor

R. Kent Rasmussen

SALEM PRESS, INC.
Pasadena, California   Hackensack, New Jersey

Managing Editor: Christina J. Moose
Project Editor: R. Kent Rasmussen
Manuscript Editor: Robert Michaels
Development Editor: Wendy Sacket
Research Supervisor: Jeffry Jensen
Acquisitions Editor: Mark Rehn
Photograph Editor: Karrie Hyatt
Production Editor: Joyce I. Buchea
Design and Layout: James Hutson
Indexer: Robert Michaels

Frontispiece: James L. Shaffer

Library of Congress Cataloging-in-Publication Data

Encyclopedia of Family Life / editor, Carl L. Bankston III; project editor, R. Kent Rasmussen.
p. cm.
Includes bibliographical references (p.   ) and index.
ISBN 0-89356-940-2 (set)
ISBN 0-89356-941-0 (vol. 1)
1. Family—North America—Encyclopedias. 2. Domestic relations—North America—Encyclopedias. 3. Family services—North America—Encyclopedias. I. Bankston, Carl L. (Carl Leon), 1952-   . II. Rasmussen, R. Kent.
HQ534.E53 1999
306.85'097'03—dc21   98-42491
                                                                                                        CIP

First Printing

Publisher's Note

Old definitions of what constitutes "family" no longer work in North America. Indeed, the very word "family" has become politically charged, as have a multitude of other, once familiar, words, such as "marriage," "childbirth," "motherhood," and "paternity." At the same time, new terms have entered the language: "parenting," "blended family," "serial monogamy," "dysfunctional families," and many more. With the family in a greater state of flux than ever before, and many people both bewildered and alarmed by its changes, there is a clear need for calm, authoritative, and up-to-date information on every aspect of family issues.

Encyclopedia of Family Life brings together in five volumes up-to-date discussions of the full range of family issues that confront modern society in Canada and the United States. The set offers 452 alphabetically arranged essays addressing family subjects from a variety of perspectives. Essays define terms, discuss controversies, and cover historical trends and events, health concerns, laws, court cases, people, organizations, and much more.

Individual essays range in length from 250-word articles on court cases, persons, and definitions to 4,000-word articles on core subjects. These latter include "Aging and elderly care," "Art and iconography," "Child rearing," "Childhood history," "Children's literature," "Communities," "Educating children," "Family: concept and history," "Genealogy," "Holidays," "Literature and families," "Love," "Marriage," "Parenting," "Puberty and adolescence," "Religion," "Sexuality and sexual taboos," and "Work."

Another 96 essays that are 2,500 words in length cover such topics as "Acquired immunodeficiency syndrome (AIDS)," "Adoption," "Birth control," "Child abuse," "Child care," "Child support," "Childbirth," "Children's rights," "Dating," "Death," "Divorce," "Family demographics," "Family law," "Fatherhood," "Grandparents," "Health problems," "Heredity," "In-laws," "Kinship systems," "Motherhood," "Poverty," "Retirement," "Schools," "Siblings," "Single life," "Stepfamilies," "Support groups," "Tax laws," "Teen mothers," and "Weddings."

Every essay opens with a few lines that identify the most relevant family issues and summarize the topic's significance to family life in general. Articles on individual persons, organizations, laws, and court cases provide additional ready-reference information, particularly dates. Boldfaced subheads throughout the articles are designed to guide readers through the texts of the essays, most of which are illustrated with photographs, charts, tables, and maps.

Essays of 1,500 or more words in length—which constitute more than half of all articles—end with specialized bibliographies; these collectively list nearly 3,000 relevant books and articles. Bibliographical entries in articles of 2,500 to 4,000 words are annotated, as are the entries in the general bibliography that can be found at the end of volume 5. That volume's appendix section also contains an annotated listing of support organizations, as well as a lengthy chronology of legislation and court decisions, a general time line, and an extensive glossary.

A variety of features are designed to help readers find the information they seek quickly. Subjects of most essays should be easy to find because essays are arranged alphabetically under straightforward headings, ranging from "Abandonment of the family" to "Zero Population Growth movement." Further help is provided in the List of Subjects by Category located at the end of volume 5. It organizes essay subjects under 28 broad categories, listing most under at least three headings. At the end of every essay is a list of an average of 10 cross-references to related articles. Finally, the comprehensive index at the end of volume 5 will direct readers to all the topics discussed in the set, whether they are subjects of essays or not.

The editors of Salem Press wish to thank the more than 240 scholars who contributed their time and expertise. A complete list of their names and affiliations appears in the front of volume 1. Line art for medical topics was provided by Hans & Cassady, Inc., of Ohio. We also particularly wish to acknowledge the expertise and advice of the project's editor, Professor Carl L. Bankston III of the University of Southwestern Louisiana.

Introduction

The ancient Greek philosopher Aristotle described human beings as social creatures. As social creatures, they depend on relationships with other people for their survival and for the satisfaction of all their needs and wants. Family relationships are the oldest, most enduring, and most important of human ties. The biological make-up of human beings makes some kind of family necessary. The upright human posture makes the human pelvis narrow compared to the pelvises of other animals. At the same time, large human brains require large heads. People, therefore, must be born at relatively early stages of physical development in order to pass through the narrow pelvis before the head grows too large. Much of the childhood development of humans, therefore, takes place outside the womb, and helpless children need other people who devote years to care and feeding.

Even after children may be physically able to care for themselves, they require constant attention from adults. Humans have large brains because they adapt to their environments by learning. This means that they must be taught how to live in the world by others. Moreover, when they learn, they do not simply learn how to do things in order to keep themselves alive; they also learn who they are and develop their own identities from those around them. The people who teach children tend to be the same ones who take care of them in the earliest years. Strong attachments between parents and children are needed so that parents can devote time and effort to caring for children and teaching them. Attachments between adults are essential if they are to manage this enormous job.

It would be meaningless, then, to ask what human beings were like before they had families. Families had to come into existence first in order for humans to evolve, and there are no known societies that do not have some form of family. Moreover, much of early human life appears to have been based on the family. Most anthropologists maintain that the earliest human societies lived by hunting and gathering. On the basis of evidence from contemporary hunting and gathering societies, anthropologists argue that these economic activities were organized around family relations. Men and their grown sons hunted animals, an activity requiring the ability to travel substantial distances from home. Since women gave birth to children and nursed infants, women's mobility was much more limited, and mothers, daughters, and small children took charge of gathering plant foods.

It is believed that larger social groups developed around families as clusters of people related by ancestry or marriage. In clan groups, decisions were made by elders. Therefore, families served political as well as biological, emotional, educational, and economic purposes. All of the social activities of human beings and all of the complex relationships in which human beings engage seem to have grown out of family life. Although modern complex societies, such as one finds in the United States and Canada, have families that are in many ways quite different from those in clan-based societies, modern social relationships and organizations often continue to be rooted in the family.

Importance of the Modern American Family. Very few people in modern North America make a living by hunting and gathering, and modern Americans do not live in family-based clans. Some have argued that the family has become less important as a social institution as many of the functions that once belonged to the family alone have been taken over by child-care centers, public schools, businesses, and government. Nevertheless, it is evident that even in our complex society, the family continues to be central to almost every aspect of life. Despite the development of new technologies such as fertilizing human eggs in test tubes, mothers still give birth to children. Although some radical critics of the family have argued that child care should be socialized and that children should be raised by the state, children continue to receive their earliest and most essential care and training from one or more parents.

It is probably true that Americans are more individualistic and in some ways less family-oriented than people in many other cultures. In many Asian societies, for example, family relationships are taken as models for all human relationships, so that even unrelated people are addressed as "grandfather," "grandmother," "uncle," "aunt," "older brother," "younger brother," "older sister," and "younger sister." Americans, by contrast, tend to think about their connections to other people as work or friendship relations, rather than as family-type ties. Parents in India often either choose the marriage partners of their children or strongly influence their children's marriage decisions. This kind of parental influence would be unthinkable among Americans, who might react strongly if their parents attempted to interfere in their adult personal lives. In Thailand and Laos, youngest daughters are expected to remain in their parents' home, even after they marry. American children are expected to leave home as soon as they become adults and to return only for occasional visits. Despite the individualism of modern Americans, however, the family remains, in its own fashion, at the core of nearly every aspect of American life.

As in other societies, the family is the center of most persons' emotional life in North America. Most people marry, and many of those who do not form bonds similar to those that unite married couples. The closest ties between adults are those of marriage or marriage-like relationships. For children, the most intense emotional connections are to siblings and parents.

Most Americans consider formal education to be the job of educational institutions, such as schools, training institutes, and colleges or universities. The family, however, is critical to the education of family members. Families prepare their members for schooling. How well persons do in schools and how many years of schooling they complete are generally influenced more by family background than by anything else.

Families continue to be even economically important. Although very few people in the United States or Canada live on family farms or work in family-owned businesses, the family remains the primary unit for the distribution of income and wealth. Parents work in order to bring home income to their families, and most spending is on family needs such as homes, automobiles, food, and clothing. Economic inequality is largely a matter of inequality between families; thus we speak of upper-class, middle-class, working-class, and poor families. Moreover, social-class position tends to be passed from parents to children, because families in different social classes enjoy varying resources to support their children's education, have differ-

ing ambitions for their children, have different sets of social networks for setting up job contacts, and pass differing amounts of wealth on to children through inheritance.

Although most people do not generally consider the family a political unit, the modern North American family has important political functions. When people in representative democracies vote, issues that affect their families are frequently uppermost in their minds. In addition, political attitudes and loyalties, like social class, tend to be passed along family lines. Moreover, if we consider all decision making small-scale politics, it is evident that families are political in character, since families make decisions every day and each family has its own system of authority for making decisions.

Families and Problems. The fact that the family is central to virtually every aspect of human life does not mean that families always make desirable contributions to the lives of people. In fact, the very importance of families means that they can be sources of some of the greatest problems faced by individuals and by society at large. For example, sexual and emotional intimacy between partners, whether formally married or not, can have many undesirable consequences. The more demands persons place on one another, the more their relations can cause pain as well as comfort. Police officers report that responding to reports of domestic violence is one of their most common daily activities. Criminologists say that one of the most frequent forms of murder is the killing of one spouse or lover by another.

Since families must make decisions for their members, power is a part of every family relationship. Parents take care of their children, but they also have power over their children. In a two-parent family, one parent usually has more power than the other. Even in a childless family, one partner tends to wield more power than the other. Typically, men hold more power in families than women. The imbalance in power, together with the intimacy of families, means that families can be quite oppressive, even when they meet the basic emotional and physical needs of their members. The abuse of women and children is all too often a product of family relations.

Families can easily fail at their tasks because they have so many of them. It can be difficult for two continually changing people to satisfy each other's sexual and emotional desires and expectations over the course of many years. Caring for children and preparing children for happy and productive adult lives are demanding tasks even for concerned, well-informed parents, and there are always parents who lack concern or information. Many of the personal and social problems that people face may be rooted in inadequate or abusive child care. The family is not only the most central institution of our society, it is also the cause of some of our most serious problems.

Family Change. Although families continue to be basic to our lives, they have changed greatly over the course of history and they continue to change. In North America, people have always tended to live in nuclear families containing parents and children. However, in the nineteenth century most nuclear families lived close to extended family members, such as grandparents, uncles, aunts, and cousins. These relatives provided support networks and also made demands on their members. By 1920, however, most Americans lived in cities, and urban life made it difficult for them to maintain ties with a large number of relatives. After World War II, Americans in increasing numbers moved to suburbs, where each nuclear family lived in a house in a block of other houses containing nuclear families, all of whom were unrelated to one another. By the late twentieth century, Americans routinely moved away from the regions where they had been born, making extended family ties difficult to maintain.

As ties to relatives outside the family have dwindled, the numbers of persons in families themselves have also decreased for many of the same reasons. On the farm, large numbers of children were an advantage. Children could help out on the farm, and later in life they could support aging parents. Nuclear families living in suburbs must support children who usually can make no economic contribution for many years. Because education has become critical to placing people in jobs, parents generally need to support their children until they graduate from high school. In many cases, parents contribute to the vocational training or college education of children after high school, making child rearing extremely expensive and time-consuming. Upon reaching adulthood, children often move far from their parents' homes and may not contribute greatly to parents' support or well-being unless the latter become unable to care for themselves in very old age. Over the course of the twentieth century there was a steady trend toward fewer children in American families.

Families in North America have become less permanent as they have become smaller. Divorce was once a rare occurrence. After the divorce rate increased gradually from 1900 to 1960, it grew rapidly throughout the 1960's and 1970's and remained more or less constant throughout the 1980's and 1990's. Most people who divorced remarried, leading some scholars to observe that the marriage system in North America had become one of "serial monogamy": a system in which each person could have a series of mates, one at a time. The temporary nature of American families meant that persons were more likely than their ancestors to live in several families over the course of a number of years and that they were more likely to live in families with only one parent, usually their mothers.

More and more Americans did not enter into a traditional family system at all. Both in the United States and Canada, growing numbers of people in the late twentieth century began cohabiting—living together without being married. The percentage of women who had children out of wedlock skyrocketed dramatically, especially in the United States.

In addition to undergoing rapid changes in family structure, American families changed their styles of child rearing and the nature of relations among family members. Most experts on the family agree that child rearing became more permissive in the years following World War II, with greater freedom and power accorded to children. With the women's rights movement, the increasingly temporary nature of marriage, and the large-scale entry of women into the full-time labor market, the power of women in families also increased. By the 1990's, although women were not yet fully equal partners in many American families, the old family ideal of the benevolently authoritarian family ruled by the father had been largely replaced by a more democratic ideal of a parental partnership that paid considerable attention to the desires and wishes of children.

The Study of the Family. The central part played by the family in individual life and in society, the seriousness of family problems, and the changing character of modern families all make the family a critical subject for study from a wide range of perspectives. The study of the family, therefore, involves professionals in many disciplines. Historians look at families in past times, at practices and beliefs relating to sexual practices, gender roles, and child care. Psychologists study how individuals are shaped by their families, the developmental stages undergone by people in families, and the types of family situations that produce interpersonal conflicts and psychological problems. Sociologists concern themselves with how families are related to other social institutions, such as the economy or education; they concern themselves with the social causes and consequences of social change and with social relations among family members. Anthropologists tend to focus on the family as a part of a culture and on variations in families among cultural groups. Demographers trace changes in family size, age, structure, and educational and income characteristics. Political scientists are often interested in how family background affects political involvement or attitudes and in the ways in which politically powerful people are often connected by family networks. Criminologists study how family background affects the likelihood that individuals will engage in criminal behavior or how family characteristics in an area may be related to crime rates.

Since the study of the family is so complex and multifaceted, it is difficult to identify any major trends in this study across all disciplines. Nevertheless, it is possible to identify some concerns that have tended to predominate at different times. Psychological concern with the family intensified in the early twentieth century with the work of the Viennese psychoanalyst Sigmund Freud (1856-1939), who identified relations between parents and children as the key to the human personality and to human emotional disturbances. The theoretical writings of the American sociologist Talcott Parsons (1902-1979) drew attention to the family as a social system, in which family members interact to serve one another's needs and the needs of the larger social system containing the family. Both the Freudian and the Parsonian views tended to assume the universality and the desirability of the two-parent, nuclear, father-dominated family.

During the 1960's and 1970's the study of the family became more critical. Beginning in the 1960's child abuse became a major concern, and many researchers became interested in how the American family led to the abuse of children. In the 1970's, as the women's movement emerged, the topics of wife abuse and the systematic exploitation of women moved to the forefront of family studies. Some researchers began characterizing the marriage license as a "hitting license," and a few radical students of the family called for its abolition.

By the 1980's many questioned earlier assumptions about the family and there were debates about what constituted a family. The 1980's and 1990's also saw something of a backlash in the study of the family, as some theorists and researchers became concerned about rapid changes in family style and structure. The decline of the long-term marriage and the two-parent family made family values and family relations primary issues among scholars as well as among members of the general public. Disagreements over cohabitation between unmarried people and proposals for the recognition of marriage between homosexuals made it clear that among students of the family and within the American public in general there existed fundamental differences in definitions of the family. For some, the family was chiefly two or more people bound together by ties of emotional intimacy. For others, the family was a legal and economic arrangement for sharing property. Those who defined the family in either of these ways tended to support the recognition of adult partners, heterosexual or homosexual, as parts of a family. However, other persons tended to define the family as an institution devoted to producing and caring for children or as a relationship created by religious or spiritual beliefs. For those who viewed the family as essentially concerned with child rearing or as a matter of religious commitment, cohabitation, out-of-wedlock births, and homosexual partnerships or marriage all represented the decline of the American family and not simply changes in its character.

Critical approaches to the family and the concern over changes in the family gave rise to controversy over what kinds of families were desirable, as well as to debates over how to define the family. Critics of the traditional family viewed ready access to divorce as a positive development. Without divorce, couples would be forced to remain in unhappy marriages and this unhappiness would also affect children. These critics pointed out that women in two-parent, husband-dominated marriages bore an unequal and unfair burden of household labor and were sometimes subject to psychological and physical abuse. While women and children in single-parent families did suffer, the critics maintained, these sufferings were generally economic in character. Women had lower earnings than men and many divorced husbands did not pay child support. Poverty resulting from inequality between men and women, and not the decline in the virtues of the traditional family, was the cause of the problems of family change in America.

In response, many defenders of traditional families argued that family structure is more than just an income relationship. They argued that it is difficult for one person to do the job of two. They noted the negative emotional and developmental impact of divorce on children who are already undergoing increasing stress in today's world. They also maintained that family change, especially the growth of one-parent families, tended to weaken parental authority and to lead to discipline problems among children. The debate between those who favored change in American families and those who felt that it was important to recapture the qualities of traditional families was likely to continue to be a major line of cleavage.

Family Professionals. While the family has been a focal point of scholarly interest in the social sciences and a matter of debate among scholars and activists, it has also been the occupational concern of many human services professionals. Social workers, family therapists, and marriage counselors all work with families that have problems. Police officers must deal with domestic violence and other family issues almost on a daily basis. Educators work with students who come from a wide variety of family backgrounds and must prepare students who will have families of their own. Members of the clergy are deeply involved in family life. Even loan officers at banks or financial-aid officers at colleges are often called upon to be family professionals because they must have knowledge of family budgets and spending practices. As more families become two-earner families, there is a greater need for day-care workers. The aging of the American population means that more people can be expected to work with the elderly in a variety of capacities.

The family, then, is not only a primary academic topic; it is also a concern to people in their jobs and in their personal lives. Ready access to accurate, in-depth information on the family can therefore be of use to everyone.

A Family Reference. The present work is a response to the needs of students, professionals, and general readers for a reference on the different aspects of the central and rapidly changing social institution of the family. This work concentrates on the past and present of families in North America. It seeks to present material in a clear, readable, and accessible manner, avoiding specialized language and technical jargon. It will be useful to high school students writing reports or to parents looking for reliable information about child-care or child-rearing practices. It is both fairly comprehensive in its scope and convenient in its organization. Its alphabetical structure makes it easy to find information on specific topics. A system of cross-references enables readers to find related topics readily, so that an issue can be investigated in as much detail as a reader requires. A brief heading explains the significance of each entry to family life in America.

Since the family is such a broad subject, entries approach it from many different perspectives: family psychology, problems faced by families, sexuality and the biological bases of family life, families in different American cultures, the relationship between the family and other social institutions, legal issues, and demographics. Most textbooks or books about family life tend to approach the matter from a single point of view or a single theoretical approach. Thus, a work such as this one, intended to pull a broad array of theories, problems, and facts together in a single place, can make connections that textbooks may miss. Those seeking information about a specific issue, such as abortion, will have immediate access to basic facts. Those who are interested in more general topics, such as family change, can read the entries on "Alternative family types" or "Single-parent families," following cross-references to assemble an overview that is as broad or as narrow as required.

Each entry has a list of identifiers of relevant issues, enabling the reader to place the entry in context. Readers who are interested in gerontology or in the elderly, for example, will find articles on "Aging and elderly care," "Alzheimer's disease," "Grandparents," "Retirement," "Retirement communities," "Senior citizen centers," and "Widowhood," as well as entries on specific issues related to the elderly such as the "Older Americans Act."

The identifiers themselves indicate the broad scope of this work. They include Aging, Art and the media, Children and child development, Demographics, Divorce, Economics and work, Education, Health and medicine, Kinship and genealogy, Law, Marriage and dating, Parenting and family relationships, Race and ethnicity, Religious beliefs and practices, Sociology, and Violence. Some of the topics under these identifiers are theoretical in nature. For example, entries on the "Family life cycle" and "Freudian psychology" introduce readers to psychological theories of family

life. Other entries deal with current problems or controversies related to the family, such as "Abortion," "Child abuse," "Corporal punishment," "Fatherlessness," and "Marital rape." Other articles are devoted to a variety of family-related organizations, such as Al-Anon, Alateen, Big Brothers and Big Sisters of America, and Mothers Against Drunk Driving. Readers seeking information about historical events and practices, such as bundling or antimiscegenation laws, will find entries devoted to these questions. Demographic trends in family life are treated in a general discussion of family demographics and in essays that investigate particular demographic issues, such as "Family size" and "Baby boomers." A glossary in volume 5 will help answer questions readers may have about terminology used in the entries, while providing additional information on the material covered in the entries. —*Carl L. Bankston III*

List of Contributors

Richard Adler
University of Michigan, Dearborn

Patricia A. Ainsa
University of Texas at El Paso

M. J. Alhabeeb
University of Massachusetts, Amherst

Davia M. Allen
Western Carolina University

Craig W. Allin
Cornell College

Emily Alward
Independent Scholar

Deborah Bass Artis
Independent Scholar

Sally Ashbach
Santa Rosa Junior College

Bryan Aubrey
Independent Scholar

H. C. Aubrey
Independent Scholar

Cynthia Semlear Avery
University of Delaware

Sue Bailey
Tennessee Technological University

Barbara Bair
Duke University

Robin E. Baker
Grand Canyon University

Ann Stewart Balakier
University of South Dakota

Mary Pat Balkus
Radford University

Carl L. Bankston III
University of Southwestern Louisiana

Karen L. Barak
University of Wisconsin, Whitewater

Susan Green Barger
Idaho State University

Amanda Smith Barusch
University of Utah

Lessie L. Bass
East Carolina University

Susan E. Beers
Sweet Briar College

Richard S. Bell
University of South Carolina at Sumter

Frances R. Belmonte
Loyola University, Chicago

Janet C. Benavente
University of Guam

Alvin K. Benson
Brigham Young University

Milton Berman
University of Rochester

Cynthia A. Bily
Adrian College

Margaret Boe Birns
New York University

Patricia Bishop
Independent Scholar

Barbara G. Blackwell
Augusta State University

Janice Bacino Bodet
Delgado Community College

Steve D. Boilard
Western Kentucky University

Harold Branam
Savannah State University

Holly E. Brophy-Herb
Michigan State University

Mitzie L. Bryant
St. Louis Board of Education

Robert D. Bryant
Georgetown College

Fred Buchstein
John Carroll University

Evelyn M. Buday
University of Illinois at Chicago

Stephanie G. Campbell
Mesa Community College

Edmund J. Campion
University of Tennessee

Glenn Canyon
Independent Scholar

Richard K. Caputo
Barry University

Brenda E. Reinertsen Caranicas
Fort Berthold Community College

David Carleton
Middle Tennessee State University

Russell N. Carney
Southwest Missouri State University

Jack Carter
University of New Orleans

Christine R. Catron
St. Mary's University

Karen Chapman-Novakofski
University of Illinois

Kathleen A. Chara
Independent Scholar

Paul J. Chara, Jr.
Loras College

Jo Carol Chezem
Ball State University

Robert Christenson
California Polytechnic State University

Shawn L. Christiansen
Pennsylvania State University

Lawrence I. Clark
Independent Scholar

Vanessa E. Cobham
University of Queensland

Alan J. Coelho
Eastern Washington University

Tom Cook
Wayne State College

James A. Crone
Hanover College

Rochelle L. Dalla
University of Nebraska at Omaha

Bruno J. D'Alonzo
New Mexico State University

Eddith A. Dashiell
Ohio University

Robert C. Davis
Pikeville College

Kathryn Dennick-Brecht
Robert Morris College

Brian de Vries
San Francisco State University

Thomas E. DeWolfe
Hampden-Sydney College

M. Casey Diana
University of Illinois at Urbana-Champaign

Kegan Doyle
Independent Scholar

Joann Driggers
Mt. San Antonio College

Joyce Duncan
East Tennessee State University

Miriam Ehrenberg
John Jay College, City College of New York

John W. Engel
University of Hawaii

L. Fleming Fallon, Jr.
Bowling Green State University

Marianne Ferguson
Buffalo State College

Alan M. Fisher
California State University, Dominguez Hills

Gloria Fulton
Humboldt State University

Keith Garebian
Independent Scholar

Phyllis B. Gerstenfeld
California State University, Stanislaus

Irene N. Gillum
Maine Hospice Council

Gerard Giordano
New Mexico State University

Kristin L. Gleeson
Presbyterian Historical Association

Michael Haas
University of Hawaii at Manoa

Marian Wynne Haber
Texas Wesleyan University

Irwin Halfond
McKendree College

Richard A. S. Hall
Methodist College

Sharon K. Hall
University of Houston, Clear Lake

Timothy L. Hall
University of Mississippi Law School

Susan E. Hamilton
Independent Scholar

Maurice Hamington
Western Oregon University

Roger D. Haney
Murray State University

James G. Hanson
Grand View College

Roger D. Hardaway
Northwestern Oklahoma State University

James M. Harper
Brigham Young University

Karen V. Harper
West Virginia University

Carol D. H. Harvey
University of Manitoba

Robin C. Hasslen
St. Cloud State University

Robert M. Hawthorne, Jr.
Independent Scholar

Celia Ray Hayhoe
University of Kentucky

Edwin James Heimer
State of Wyoming Family Services

Peter B. Heller
Manhattan College

Diane Andrews Henningfeld
Adrian College

Jacques M. Henry
University of Southwestern Louisiana

Steven R. Hewitt
University of Saskatchewan

David H. Holben
Ohio University

Betsy B. Holli
Dominican University

Thomas B. Holman
Brigham Young University

Katherine H. Houp
Midway College

Eril Barnett Hughes
East Central University

Áine M. Humble
University of Prince Edward Island

Mary Hurd
East Tennessee State University

Raymond Pierre Hylton
Virginia Union University

John Quinn Imholte
University of Minnesota, Morris

Bron B. Ingoldsby
Ricks College

Danielle Irving
Independent Scholar

Charles C. Jackson
Augusta State University

Robert Jacobs
Central Washington University

Jeffry Jensen
Independent Scholar

Bruce E. Johansen
University of Nebraska at Omaha

Barbara E. Johnson
University of South Carolina, Aiken

Rebecca Strand Johnson
Independent Scholar

Jane Anderson Jones
Manatee Community College

Virginia W. Junk
University of Idaho

Mathew J. Kanjirathinkal
Texas A&M University, Commerce

Laura Duhan Kaplan
University of North Carolina at Charlotte

Max Kashefi
Eastern Illinois University

Robert Kastenbaum
Arizona State University

AnnMarie Kazyaka
Niagara University

Mara Kelly-Zukowski
Felician College

Gregory E. Kennedy
Central Missouri State University

Cassandra Kircher
Elon College

Philip E. Lampe
University of the Incarnate Word

Ralph L. Langenheim, Jr.
University of Illinois at Urbana-Champaign

Eleanor A. LaPointe
Ocean County College

Calvin J. Larson
University of Massachusetts at Boston

Sander M. Latts
University of Minnesota

Robert E. Lee
Michigan State University

Thomas T. Lewis
Mount Senario College

Jian Li
Southern Methodist University

Joe E. Lunceford
Georgetown College

Margaret Ann McCarthy
Eastern Kentucky University

Nancy E. Macdonald
University of South Carolina at Sumter

Grace McEntee
Appalachian State University

Thomas K. McKnight
Southwest Virginia Community College

Paul D. Mageli
Independent Scholar

Carolyn S. Magnuson
Lincoln University

Scott Magnuson-Martinson
South Dakota State University

Robin Sakina Mama
Monmouth University

Mary Beth Mann
Southwest Missouri State University

Jo Manning
University of Miami (Florida)

Elizabeth Maret
Texas A&M University

Richard M. Marshall
University of Indianapolis

Charles E. Marske
St. Louis University

Sherri Ward Massey
University of Central Oklahoma

Dyan E. Mazurana
University of Wyoming

Steve J. Mazurana
University of Northern Colorado

Michael E. Meagher
University of Missouri, Rolla

Linda Mealey
University of Queensland

Diane P. Michelfelder
Utah State University

Baukje Miedema
University of New Brunswick

Andrea E. Miller
Independent Scholar

Randall L. Milstein
Lansing Community College

Lisa Mize
Stephen F. Austin State University

George A. Morgan
Colorado State University

Hildegarde S. Morgan
Independent Scholar

Brian K. Morley
The Master's College

Nancy Nason-Clark
University of New Brunswick

Cherilyn Nelson
Eastern Kentucky University

Joseph L. Nogee
University of Houston

Deborah Harris O'Brien
Trinity College

Gwenelle S. O'Neal
Rutgers University

David E. Paas
Hillsdale College

Maria A. Pacino
Azusa Pacific University

Rob Palkovitz
University of Delaware

Gowri Parameswaran
Southwest Missouri State University

Ty Partridge
Wichita State University

Robert L. Patterson
Armstrong Atlantic State University

Cheryl Pawlowski
University of Northern Colorado

Nis Petersen
Jersey City State College

Alvin M. Pettus
James Madison University

Erika E. Pilver
Westfield State College

Nancy A. Piotrowski
University of California, Berkeley

John Powell
Pennsylvania State University, Erie

Carol A. Radich
West Chester University of Pennsylvania

P. S. Ramsey
Independent Scholar

Lillian M. Range
University of Southern Mississippi

Michaela Crawford Reaves
California Lutheran University

Paul L. Redditt
Georgetown College

William L. Reinshagen
Independent Scholar

Wendy E. S. Repovich
Eastern Washington University

Gregory P. Rich
Fayetteville State University

Betty Richardson
Southern Illinois University, Edwardsville

Douglas W. Richmond
University of Texas at Arlington

Carl Rollyson
Baruch College of the City University of New York

John Alan Ross
Eastern Washington University

Teresa J. Rothausen
Texas A&M University

Wendy Sacket
Coastline Community College

Bibhuti K. Sar
University of Louisville

Marie Saracino
Stephen F. Austin State University

Kathleen Schongar
May School

John Richard Schrock
Emporia State University

Jay D. Schvaneveldt
Utah State University

Larry Schweikart
University of Dayton

Rebecca Lovell Scott
College of Health Sciences

Aristide Sechandice
University of Georgia

Rose Secrest
Independent Scholar

Heather M. Seferovich
Brigham Young University

Kenneth R. Shepherd
Henry Ford Community College

R. Baird Shuman
University of Illinois at Urbana-Champaign

Donald C. Simmons, Jr.
Mississippi Humanities Council

Jamie Sinclair-Andersen
University of Nebraska at Omaha

Genevieve Slomski
Independent Scholar

Jane Marie Smith
Butler County Community College

Roger Smith
Independent Scholar

David R. Sobel
Provosty, Sadler & deLaunay

Celia Stall-Meadows
Northeastern State University

Barbara C. Stanley
Independent Scholar

Glenn Ellen Starr
Appalachian State University

Roger James Stilling
Appalachian State University

Leslie Stricker
Park College

Irene Struthers
Independent Scholar

Charlotte Templin
University of Indianapolis

Terry Theodore
University of North Carolina at Wilmington

Brian G. Tobin
Lassen College

Julia C. Torquati
University of Nebraska at Lincoln

Kenneth R. Tremblay, Jr.
Colorado State University

Paul B. Trescott
Southern Illinois University

Anna Sumabat Turner
Bob Jones University

Robert D. Ubriaco, Jr.
Spelman College

Tamara M. Valentine
University of South Carolina, Spartanburg

Shela R. Van Ness
University of Tennessee at Chattanooga

William T. Walker
Philadelphia College of Pharmacy and Science

Kimberly A. Wallet
Lamar University

Annita Marie Ward
Salem-Teikyo University

John C. Watkins, Jr.
University of Alabama

Robert P. Watson
University of Hawaii at Hilo

Mark B. White
Auburn University

Richard Whitworth
Ball State University

Lee Williams
Independent Scholar

Jenifer Wolf
Independent Scholar

Kathleen M. Zanolli
Kansas University

Nillofur Zobairi
Southern Illinois University at Carbondale

Contents

Encyclopedia of Family Life

Abandonment of the family

RELEVANT ISSUES: Divorce; Law; Parenting and family relationships

SIGNIFICANCE: Society's attempts to deal with the problem of adults who desert spouses and dependent children have met with only limited success

Abandonment of the family occurs when adults leave spouses without notice and without spouses' consent. In many cases dependent children are left behind as well. Abandoning spouses usually attempt to hide from their abandoned families, although some contact may still exist in the form of letters or phone calls. Abandonment of the family is distinguished from child abandonment,

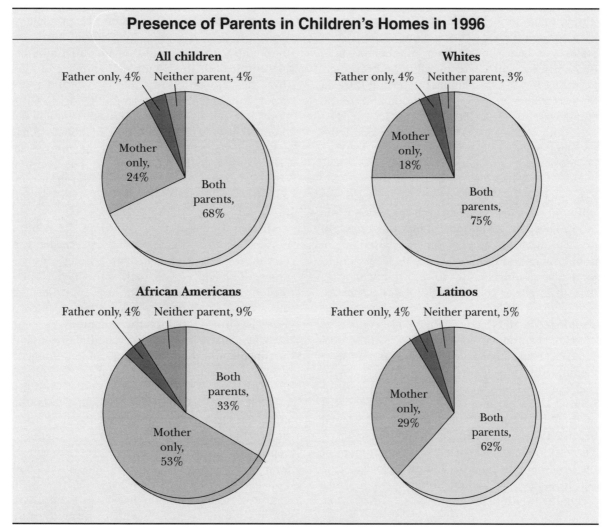

Presence of Parents in Children's Homes in 1996

All children
Father only, 4%　Neither parent, 4%
Mother only, 24%
Both parents, 68%

Whites
Father only, 4%　Neither parent, 3%
Mother only, 18%
Both parents, 75%

African Americans
Father only, 4%　Neither parent, 9%
Both parents, 33%
Mother only, 53%

Latinos
Father only, 4%　Neither parent, 5%
Mother only, 29%
Both parents, 62%

Source: U.S. Bureau of the Census, *Statistical Abstract of the United States: 1997.* Washington, D.C.: GPO, 1997.
Note: Percentages are rounded to the nearest whole number.

which generally refers to situations in which children are forced out of families. It is also distinguished from running away, which usually refers to children who voluntarily leave their families without the consent of their parents.

Abandonment of the family has been a problem for society since the earliest days of civilization. More than four thousand years ago the ancient civilizations of the Middle East formulated laws dealing with husbands who deserted wives. In the colony of Rhode Island laws were enacted to deal with this problem in 1685.

Abandonment of the family was a particular problem in the early twentieth century, when millions of European immigrants arrived in the United States. Many immigrants were husbands who left families behind in Europe, promising to earn enough money to bring them to the United States at a later time. A large number of these husbands were unable or unwilling to keep their promises. In 1911 the National Desertion Bureau, the first agency dealing with abandonment of the family, was founded in New York City. This marked a turning point in society's attitude toward the problem. No longer was abandonment of the family strictly seen as a personal problem; it was now known to be a problem for society as a whole.

In the United States abandonment is considered sufficient cause for divorce and the awarding of alimony. However, abandonment may be difficult to prove until a long period of time has passed. Abandoned spouses and children have no legal right to force abandoning spouses to return, but they do have the right to collect child-support payments. Enforcement of child-support payments awarded to abandoned families has been a particular concern of the U.S. government since the 1970's, when it became clear that large payments made under Aid to Families with Dependent Children (AFDC) went to such families. Collection of child support payments from abandoning spouses remains a serious part of the "deadbeat dad" phenomenon, so named because the vast majority of such spouses are male. The economic cost to society of abandonment of the family and the financial and psychological damage to abandoned families remain major issues facing the twenty-first century.   —*Rose Secrest*

See also Aid to Families with Dependent Children (AFDC); Child abandonment; Child support; Desertion as grounds for divorce; Displaced homemakers; Gangs; Homeless families; Orphans; Poverty.

Abortion

RELEVANT ISSUES: Health and medicine; Law; Parenting and family relationships

SIGNIFICANCE: Parent-child and spousal relationships, the well-being of mothers, and the rights of members of families and potential families are all significantly impacted by the availability of abortion

After 1973, one of the most divisive social issues in the United States became the availability of abortion—the deliberate termination of a pregnancy. On one side of the issue, "pro-choice" advocates have emphasized the rights of potential mothers to control both the timing and number of children they choose to bring into the world. On the other, "pro-life" advocates stress the right of unborn children to have safe passage through the prenatal period. The question of abortion has generated vigorous debate, involving complex social, political, and religious issues. The eventual outcome of this debate will have a significant impact on the size and nature of families throughout the world.

Historical Perspective. Abortions have been performed since the beginning of recorded history in diverse cultures through a variety of techniques. The Hippocratic oath of the medical profession banned abortions, an indication that the morality of an abortion was a matter of concern several centuries before the common era. The early Christian church condemned abortion and infanticide and therefore significantly influenced how Western societies formulated public policies toward abortion for centuries to follow. Both historically and cross-culturally, the greater the influence of religion, the lower the incidence of abortion has tended to be. The end of the twentieth century continued to witness this trend, as can be seen in clerical states such as Ireland, where abortion has been banned or is rare. Conversely, in countries where religion has been suppressed, abortions have been frequent. In formerly communist Romania, for example, approximately 75 percent of pregnancies in 1990 were reported to

Abortion protesters confront pro-choice advocates in New York City in 1995. (Hazel Hankin)

end in abortion. The percentage of pregnancies resulting in abortion in countries such as the United States (approximately 26 percent) and Canada (approximately 21 percent) has historically fallen between these two extremes.

Until 1859 the acceptability of abortion in the United States was based on "quickening": Before mothers could feel fetal movements, it was considered that a human life had not begun and that women thus had a right to abort, usually with the help of herbal concoctions. In 1859 the American Medical Association argued that life begins at conception rather than at quickening, initiating a period of state control restricting abortion access. By the middle of the twentieth century the American landscape was a mosaic of individual state abortion laws, with access ranging from open to severely restricted.

The defining moment in the American abortion debate came on January 22, 1973, with the U.S. Supreme Court decision known as *Roe v. Wade*. This judicial decision struck down all state laws prohibiting abortion within the first three months of pregnancy. The Court centered the abortion debate on the issue of viability, stating that unborn children become able to survive outside the womb only after six months of pregnancy. States were permitted to regulate or even prohibit abortions in the last six months of pregnancy, except in cases where the life or health of the mother was jeopardized. What "health" meant was clarified in a companion case, *Doe v. Bolton*, rendered at the same time as *Roe*. Health was defined to include all factors, including psychological and familial, that are relevant to prospective mothers. Thus, women unwilling to have additional children would be sufficiently justified in having an abortion, according to *Doe*. With *Doe*, the availability of abortion became a central issue in family-related issues.

Abortion Demographics and Statistics. Studies by the Alan Guttmacher Institute and the National Abortion Rights Action League (NARAL) have provided a picture of the types of women and families most affected by abortion in the United States. According to data gathered in the 1990's, approximately 60 percent of abortions were obtained by white and 40 percent by African American and nonwhite Americans. Abortion patients are most likely to have never been married (approximately 85 percent), while about half never had a live birth. Approximately half of all women

having abortions came from families with an annual income less than $30,000, and about a third of all abortion patients reported that they were unemployed at the time of the abortion. Women between the ages of twenty and twenty-four years with a high school or college education, liberal political beliefs, and little religious involvement fit the profile of the typical woman who sought an abortion. The numbers of abortions have ranged from approximately 600,000 in 1972, the year before *Roe*, to approximately 1.4 million in 1992. An estimated 50 million abortions had been performed worldwide at the close of the twentieth century.

Prenatal development can be divided into three periods: the germinal period, which lasts from

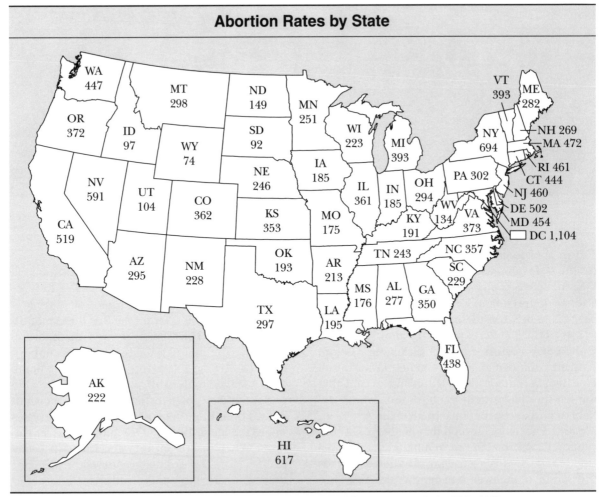

Abortion Rates by State

Source: U.S. Bureau of the Census, *Statistical Abstract of the United States: 1997.* Washington, D.C.: GPO, 1997.

Note: Figures show ratios of abortions to live births in each state in 1992. The ratio for the United States as a whole was 379 abortions per 1,000 live births during that year.

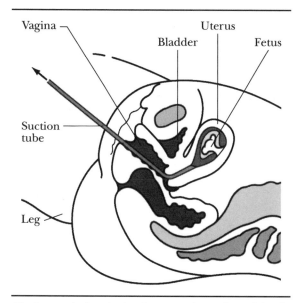

Elective or induced abortions can be performed in the first trimester using a simple suction technique; after the third month, much riskier and more complex methods are required.

conception until full implantation approximately two weeks later; the embryonic period from two to eight weeks after conception, in which all internal organs develop; and the fetal period, which lasts until birth. Since human chorionic gonadotropin, the hormone detected by pregnancy tests, is not produced until after implantation, abortions sought during the germinal period are infrequent. According to findings published in 1996 by the U.S. Centers for Disease Control (CDC), abortions are divided fairly evenly between the embryonic and fetal periods. The most likely abortion technique depends upon the stage of prenatal development. Embryonic abortions are most likely to be performed by suction-aspiration or dilation and curettage, a scraping procedure. The CDC reported that 99 percent of all abortions were performed using these techniques. Since the chosen technique is mentioned in only about a half of all reported abortions, the frequency of other techniques has been a continuing source of debate. While suction-aspiration or dilation and curettage can be used in the early fetal period, other approaches must be used for later fetal abortions. Such techniques include the injection of a poisoning saline solution into the am-

nionic fluid that surrounds the fetus; a hysterotomy, in which a cesarean section is performed and the fetus is allowed to die by neglect; and evacuation procedures such as the "partial-birth abortion," in which the fetus, except for its head, is partially delivered in the breech position and then the head is collapsed by suctioning the brain in order to allow for its passage. This technique generated considerable political debate in the late 1990's, with President Bill Clinton vetoing a congressional bill that would have banned it on the grounds that it inadequately provides for the health of the mother—a direct reference to *Doe v. Bolton.*

Impact of Abortion on Mothers. The principal focus of the abortion debate has been the degree to which a woman should have control over her pregnancy. The physiological and psychological well-being of mothers is of great concern in addressing this issue. The most important physiological concerns regarding pregnant women are life-threatening conditions. An abortion to save the life of the mother is seen by most people as the most justifiable reason for an abortion. Part of the impetus behind *Roe v. Wade* was the potential life-threatening danger posed to women by illegal abortions performed under suboptimal conditions. In the decades following *Roe,* pro-choice advocates continued to voice concern that any restrictions on women's access to abortion could have harmful effects. The Rebecca Bell case in 1988 has been used to illustrate the danger of compromised accessibility to abortion. According to Planned Parenthood, seventeen-year-old Rebecca Bell, unwilling or afraid to consult with her parents about her pregnancy, sought to circumvent the parental notification law in Indiana by having an illegal abortion. She died a few days later in Indianapolis of what was described as "septic abortion with pneumonia." This incident has been used extensively by pro-choice advocates to illustrate the dangers of restricted abortion access. Yet, the autopsy performed on Bell's body by Jesse Giles found none of the complications related to septic abortion (for example, uterine or pelvic inflammation or infection), and the autopsy report cast doubt on whether Bell actually died from a botched abortion.

Pro-life advocates have argued that abortions can cause women many physiological problems,

Religious Affiliations of American Women Who Have Had Abortions, as of 1993

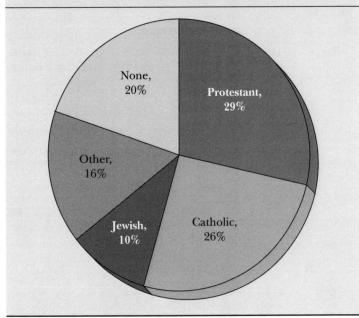

None, 20%

Protestant, 29%

Other, 16%

Jewish, 10%

Catholic, 26%

Source: *The Janus Report* (1993)
Note: Percentages are rounded to the nearest whole number.

especially if they subsequently wish to become pregnant. Ann Speckhard and Vincent Rue, in an article published in 1992, reported that women having abortions have an increased risk of endometriosis, breast cancer, tubal pregnancy, premature birth, and miscarriage. Those in the prochoice camp have countered that such complications arising from abortions are incurred by only a small minority of women and that the reports of such dangers are grossly exaggerated. The full extent of such physiological consequences has generated considerable scientific debate.

The psychological impact of abortion on pregnant women can be divided into two critical periods: the decision to abort and the adjustment period after aborting. In 1996 NARAL stated that approximately three million women a year face unwanted pregnancies and about half of them have abortions. It has been argued that greater emphasis on sex education and family planning is needed to address this high number of unwanted pregnancies. The decision to abort can be a very difficult and stressful one. It is thought by many on both sides of the issue that more education on the

consequences of getting pregnant will result in fewer unwanted pregnancies.

The existence of post-abortion syndrome is a subject of heated debate. The American Psychological Association concluded in 1989 that such a syndrome—manifested by symptoms such as depression, guilt, anniversary reactions, and other psychological disturbances—is rare. Critics have charged that since the association voted that same year to be a prochoice organization, their conclusions were biased. Research studies have varied greatly as to the extent of post-abortion syndrome. Nevertheless, opportunities for women to receive post-abortion counseling greatly increased in the 1990's.

Impact on Family Members. One of the earliest controversial legal issues involving a woman's right to abortion was the role of fathers. The most important Supreme Court decision concerning this role was rendered in 1976. In *Planned Parenthood v. Danforth*, the Court struck down a Missouri law that required a husband's consent before a woman could have a first-trimester abortion. Since then there have been numerous attempts by husbands to stop their wives' intended abortions through such means as temporary restraining orders. All such attempts have ultimately been rejected by the courts.

Research in the 1980's described the psychological impact of abortion on fathers, children, and grandparents. Family members have reported many of the same traumatic reactions that women experiencing post-abortion syndrome have described. Relations between women who have abortions and their partners, children, parents, and grandparents are likely to become strained when there is strong disagreement over the women's choice to abort. The sense of powerlessness that family members feel when women decide to abort can elicit many negative feelings and emotions, straining family ties.

Notification and Consent Laws for Minors. The access to abortion by minors (persons under the age of eighteen) has been the subject of intense debate and political action. In 1996 NARAL asserted that any laws restricting minors' access to abortion do nothing to reduce teen pregnancies and can lead to increased late-term abortions and unsafe alternatives. NARAL has contended that good family communication cannot be legislated and that many teenagers avoid involving their parents because of fear of physical or psychological abuse. The National Right to Life Committee disagreed. The committee pointed out that since minors need parental notification and consent for such minor activities as having their ears pierced or going on school trips, a major decision such as having an abortion is best made by minors in consultation with those who raised them. Both sides agree that when states enact parental involvement laws, the initial result is usually a reduction in the numbers of teen abortions. For example, according to the Missouri Department of Social Services, the number of teen abortions dropped 27.5 percent between 1983 and 1987.

Parental involvement laws can be divided into two basic types: notification and consent laws. Parental notification laws require parents, and in some cases guardians or grandparents, to be informed if a minor is seeking an abortion. Some of these state laws permit physicians to waive notification under certain circumstances. The Supreme Court tackled the constitutionality of a parental notification law in the 1981 *H. L. v. Matheson* decision. In this case the Court upheld a Utah statute requiring a physician to notify the parents or guardians of unemancipated, dependent minors before performing abortions. Subsequent Supreme Court decisions involving parents, such as *Hodgson v. Minnesota* (1990) and *Ohio v. Akron Center for Reproductive Health* (1990), and involving spouses, such as *Planned Parenthood of Southeastern Pennsylvania v. Casey* (1992), have upheld the constitutionality of state notification laws. By 1996 fifteen states had established notification laws.

Consent laws require parents, legal guardians, or, in some cases, grandparents or other adult family members to grant permission to minors who seek abortions. The Supreme Court has had an inconsistent record in judging the constitutionality of state consent laws. While it decided in *Ohio v. Akron Center for Reproductive Health* (1983) to strike down a parental consent law, it upheld a parental consent law in *Planned Parenthood of South-*

eastern Pennsylvania v. Casey. By 1996 thirty-one states had established consent laws requiring the permission of one parent (or a specified substitute), and five states had enacted laws requiring the permission of both parents (or specified substitutes) when applicable. Twenty-nine of those states provided a means of circumventing parental consent through a judicial decree.

Legislative and judicial action continues to shape the nature and extent of abortion regulations. The extent of such regulations will continue to have a significant impact on family relationships. —*Paul J. Chara, Jr.*

BIBLIOGRAPHY

Garrow, David J. *Liberty and Sexuality: The Right to Privacy and the Making of Roe v. Wade.* New York: Macmillan, 1994. Presents the history of the judicial system's review of sexual privacy cases.

NARAL Foundation. *Who Decides? A State-by-State Review of Abortion and Reproductive Rights.* 6th ed. Washington, D.C.: National Rights Action League, 1997. Compendium of executive, legislative, and judicial action regarding abortion across America.

Petchesky, Rosalind Pollack. *Abortion and Woman's Choice: The State, Sexuality, and Reproductive Freedom.* Rev. ed. Boston: Northeastern University Press, 1990. Feminist perspective examining the history of abortion and the ideology of the pro-choice position.

Reardon, David C. *The Jericho Plan: Breaking Down the Walls Which Prevent Post-Abortion Healing.* Springfield, Ill.: Acorn Books, 1996. Examines the effects of the aftermath of abortion and how to recover from them.

Schaeffer, Francis A., and C. Everett Koop. *Whatever Happened to the Human Race?* Old Tappan, N.J.: Fleming H. Revell, 1979. Discussion of the impact of abortion on the value of human life and its links to infanticide and euthanasia by a noted philosopher and a former surgeon general.

Wilke, John C. *Why Can't We Love Them Both?* Cincinnati, Ohio: Hayes, 1997. Compilation of the basic facts about abortion and its societal implications.

See also Birth control; Infanticide; Motherhood; Pregnancy; *Roe v. Wade.*

Acquired immunodeficiency syndrome (AIDS)

RELEVANT ISSUES: Children and child development; Health and medicine; Parenting and family relationships

SIGNIFICANCE: AIDS, a fatal disease caused by the human immunodeficiency virus (HIV) and transmitted between persons via bodily fluids during sexual contact, the sharing of intravenous needles, or blood transfusions, has had a devastating effect on individuals and families alike

AIDS, or acquired immunodeficiency syndrome, has been in the news almost every day since the early 1980's. By the late 1990's the number of new AIDS cases in the United States each year had begun to level out at approximately 60,000. In other parts of the world the situation was worse as the number of people with AIDS relentlessly continued to increase. The information people have about AIDS is usually incomplete at best and incorrect at worst. AIDS continues to pose a major threat to the health and well-being of the populations of the United States and the world. Until a cure is discovered, all people with AIDS will eventually die from the disease. However, AIDS is preventable. This disease has serious consequences for families.

How the Disease Is Transmitted. The virus that causes AIDS is the human immunodeficiency virus (HIV). Individuals who carry this virus are referred to as being HIV-positive. HIV is transmitted through intimate contact, including by heterosexuals and homosexuals, the sharing of hypodermic needles during drug use, and transfusions of HIV-contaminated blood. Since the middle 1990's the most common mode of transmission for HIV has been through heterosexual contact. HIV-negative couples cannot contract HIV as long as they do not engage in unprotected extramarital sex or otherwise come into contact with body fluids contaminated with HIV. In the early 1980's a number of children who received blood products also received the HIV. Many hemophiliacs who received blood products between 1978 and 1985 developed AIDS and died. AIDS can be transmitted through the exchange of HIV-infected body fluids, such as blood and genital mucous secretions. Contact may occur through genital and anal sex, cuts in the skin, and accidental punctures by contaminated needles or knife blades. AIDS starts with the adults in families and may be transmitted to children before birth. Most neonates exposed to HIV are born HIV-positive.

Normal day-to-day contact with HIV carriers involves virtually no risk. As long as persons exchange no blood or semen, transmission of AIDS is unlikely. It was previously thought that urine, tears, and breast milk could transmit the virus. Recent epidemiological studies, however, have not supported this supposition. There is no evidence that the virus is transmitted by air, insect bites, sneezing, sharing drinking glasses, sitting on toilet seats, touching doorknobs, or living in the same household with infected persons. Neither handshakes nor kisses on the cheek transmit HIV. Breathing, coughing, and sneezing are not intimate activities. Insects do not transmit AIDS, nor can HIV survive in plain water. HIV can usually survive outside the body for less than a minute.

Physiological and Epidemiological Effects. HIV attacks persons by infecting and gradually weakening their immune systems. Without immune system protection, persons can contract common and not so common diseases. HIV invades and cripples white blood cells, which are part of the body's immune system and the body's means for identifying and killing foreign materials. The result is that ordinary pathogens, which most persons' bodies can easily destroy, cause serious diseases in HIV-positive persons, causing them to contract AIDS.

The number of AIDS patients has increased every year since the first case was reported in 1979. Worldwide, the number of cases can only be estimated, but they run into the millions. The human immunodeficiency virus was first identified in 1981. The first case in the United States was reported in the medical literature in 1982 and the 200,000th a decade later. The Centers for Disease Control (CDC) estimate that well over a million people have been infected in the United States. The World Health Organization (WHO) estimates that more than 100 million people may be infected with HIV by the year 2000. More than $6 billion have been spent on AIDS research in the United States for most of the 1990's, more than three times the amount spent on cancer research.

A woman wearing an AIDS awareness sign pickets New York city hall, demanding greater government support of AIDS research. (Betty Lane)

AIDS Deaths in the United States, by Age, 1982-1995

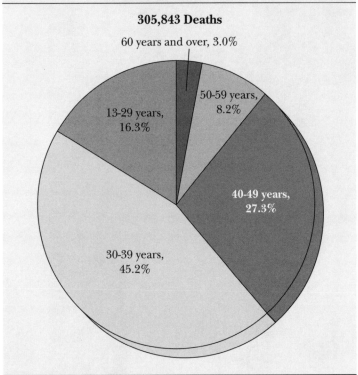

305,843 Deaths

60 years and over, 3.0%

50-59 years, 8.2%

13-29 years, 16.3%

40-49 years, 27.3%

30-39 years, 45.2%

Source: U.S. Bureau of the Census, *Statistical Abstract of the United States: 1997.* Washington, D.C.: GPO, 1997.

Most AIDS sufferers are between the ages of fifteen and twenty-five. Older Americans have also been infected at increasing rates. The greatest number of AIDS cases have been diagnosed in urban areas. While this may be related to prostitution and intravenous drug use, it may also be due to the lack of reported cases in rural areas or simply to greater population densities in cities.

AIDS and Families. AIDS places stress on family relationships, increasing the difficulties of maintaining healthy families and affecting children's lives. If parents become HIV-positive, develop AIDS, and die, family life can become truly tragic. If one family member has AIDS, the entire family is affected. Initially, families react with denial to the news that a loved one has a fatal illness and is going to die. Anger typically develops in families for three different reasons. Families feel frustrated because there is no cure for AIDS, which has agonizing consequences when health deteriorates

with the progress of the disease. Families also feel angry because of the way in which AIDS was contracted. Nonusers of illegal, recreational drugs often have little tolerance or respect for those who do use them. At best, they are willing to ignore family members' drug use, considering it a personal decision that has no effect on other family members. However, family members cannot easily ignore relatives' behavior, such as drug use or extramarital sex, when it has led to contracting HIV and AIDS. Family members also experience anger when faced with the consequences of HIV infection in the family. Aside from the ultimate death of persons with AIDS, families must often pay for care, which in the final stages of the disease can easily exceed $100,000.

Family Caregiving. Terminally ill persons require intensive support and care. At home they often require nursing services around the clock. If these services are obtained from outside agencies, families may not have to be the sole caregivers. However, they usually have to bear the economic cost of such services. More typically, families cannot afford outside agencies and must provide care themselves. Persons with AIDS can become debilitated for several months before death occurs. These are trying times for families, as they wrestle with grief over the impending deaths of loved ones and feel anger over the activities that caused AIDS.

HIV-positive persons are often parents. In the early stages of the disease, persons can function successfully. However, as their health wanes, they must seek outside help. The diagnosis of AIDS in a partner often splits families and leads to divorce. This places a difficult burden on children. If custodial parents subsequently develop AIDS, their children may become orphans. However, AIDS is not restricted to traditional families with two parents. More often, individuals who engage in behaviors that lead to AIDS are single. They may have children while they continue to pursue risky lifestyles.

Single persons often turn to their parents for support and assistance, which may bring some families closer together. However, the need for parental help can also create resentments, dividing familial generations. When single parents die of AIDS, courts may force reluctant grandparents to assume custody of their deceased children's minor offspring. Grandparents who assume responsibility for their grandchildren often live on fixed incomes. While many grandparents successfully raise their grandchildren, the demands on them are great.

After the initial denial associated with an HIV diagnosis has dissipated, it is often replaced by a renewed positive outlook on life. As family anger subsides reconciliation often occurs. Sometimes, persons who have separated because of differing values overcome their differences. Although this aspect of AIDS is positive, it is a sad commentary that death must be the catalyst. Families have the advantage of a built-in support system. If more dialogue and communication occurs before persons engage in dangerous behavior, such behavior may be preventable.

AIDS as a Political Issue. AIDS is a medical issue. However, it has also become a political issue. The earliest clusters of cases were diagnosed among gay males. The public associated AIDS with homosexuality. This led to an increase in discrimination against gay men. Gays reacted by organizing and engaging in political activity. Because of the perception that AIDS was a disease of homosexual men and because such individuals felt discriminated against, laws to protect persons from discrimination were enacted. Such laws protected some persons' civil rights at the cost of silence surrounding some aspects of the disease.

The next clusters of AIDS cases were found among intravenous drug users. This discovery reinforced negative feelings about AIDS among

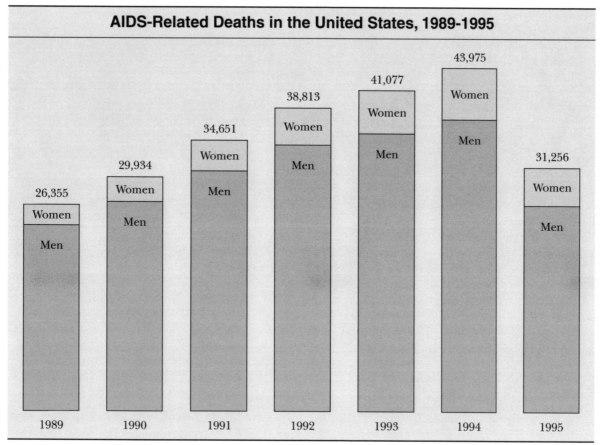

AIDS-Related Deaths in the United States, 1989-1995

Source: U.S. Bureau of the Census, *Statistical Abstract of the United States: 1997.* Washington, D.C.: GPO, 1997.

many persons in the mainstream of society and further stigmatized those with the disease. More negative myths developed. The net effect of these myths and the laws enacted to protect civil rights, such as privacy, have been to place roadblocks in the way of public health professionals who seek to control the disease.

The debate over how a medical phenomenon became political and the subsequent lost opportunity to contain the disease at an early stage remains unresolved. The reality is that AIDS is neither a gay disease nor a disease exclusively of intravenous drug users. It is present among these population subgroups, but it is also present in the heterosexual population.

Treatment and Prevention. Although there is no known cure for AIDS, drugs exist that attenuate or alter the course of the disease. Other drugs are used to relieve some of the symptoms. Experts work to develop vaccines and other drugs to treat AIDS. Whereas HIV-positive children through much of the 1990's died in their early teens, in the late 1990's it was possible to prolong their lives through therapies involving a combination of drugs. In some of the children who have undergone such drug treatments HIV has disappeared.

Participants in the national AIDS quilt project, which began in 1985 to commemorate victims of AIDS. (James L. Shaffer)

Such children, therefore, have become HIV-negative. Because it has not been possible to conduct long-term studies of children who have become HIV-negative, it is not known how long they will remain so. However, the majority of children who have undergone drug treatments remain HIV-positive, even if they do not develop AIDS as rapidly as those who have not undergone such treatments.

Preventing the transmission of AIDS is relatively easy in theory but difficult in practice. Some political and religious figures have proposed sexual abstinence as a means to prevent the spread of AIDS. However, this is unrealistic for most people. To prevent its spread through sexual contact, persons should use condoms at all times. Condoms and spermicide stop the spread of AIDS. Modern marketing practices have increased the availability of condoms. Pharmacies, grocery stores, department stores, and convenience stores commonly stock them on shopper-accessible displays. They can also be obtained by mail. Despite near-universal agreement that condoms are important for preventing the spread of AIDS, many persons think that they may be exempted from using them. While some persons complain about embarrassment associated with the purchase of condoms, others report that condoms are uncomfortable to use. Properly fitted and worn, condoms should cause minimal physical restrictions and discomfort.

HIV Testing. HIV can be detected in blood by several different tests. The Food and Drug Administration has approved a screening test for HIV that can be done at home. One problem with this test is that it can take up to six months for HIV to be detectable. A negative test result during this period may therefore be a false negative. Even if the HIV level is not great enough to be detected by the test, persons can still infect others with the virus. In the event of positive test results, the test should be repeated using a more sensitive test. Such tests are performed by doctors and at public health clinics. Laboratories and blood banks use a more sensitive screening process. Whereas negative test results may be false within the first six months after a person's initial exposure to HIV, positive tests are repeated using a highly sensitive test known as the Western Blot. It is only after HIV is confirmed by the Western Blot that physicians inform patients that they are HIV-positive. Such persons will eventually develop AIDS, although they will not feel sick for the first few years. During this period they pose the greatest hazard to others.

—*L. Fleming Fallon, Jr.*

BIBLIOGRAPHY

Barth, Richard P., Jeanne Pietrzak, and Malia Ramler, eds. *Families Living with Drugs and HIV: Intervention and Treatment Strategies.* New York: Guilford Press, 1993. Details the problems associated with drug use and HIV infection in families and discusses how medical professionals treat the virus.

Cohen, Felissa L., and Jerry D. Durham, eds. *Women, Children, and HIV/AIDS.* New York: Springer, 1993. Book dealing with women and children who have contracted HIV and have become ill with AIDS.

Corey, Lawrence, ed. *AIDS: Problems and Prospects.* New York: Norton, 1993. An excellent source of bibliographical material for lay readers.

DiClemente, R. J., ed. *Adolescents and AIDS: A Generation in Jeopardy.* Newbury Park, Calif.: Sage Publications, 1992. Discusses issues relevant to young people, such as drug use and sexuality.

Jewett, J. F., and F. M. Hecht. "Preventive Health Care for Adults with HIV Infection." *Journal of the American Medical Association* 269 (1993). Interesting review of evidence supporting medical interventions for HIV-infected individuals.

Kelly, Patricia, Susan Holman, Rosalie Rothenberg, and Stephen Paul Holzemer, eds. *Primary Care of Women and Children with HIV Infection: A Multidisciplinary Approach.* Boston: Jones and Bartlett, 1995.

Lemelle, Anthony J., and Charlene Harrington. "The Political Economy of Caregiving for People with HIV/AIDS." In *The Political Economy of AIDS*, edited by Merrill Singer. Amityville, N.Y.: Baywood, 1998. Outlines many of the HIV/AIDS issues women encounter and caregiving needs of persons living with AIDS.

Rogers, M. F. "Epidemiology of HIV/AIDS in Women and Children in the USA." *Acta Pediactrica Supplement* 421 (1997). Reviews the spread of AIDS among women and children.

See also Adultery; Alcoholism and drug abuse; Death; Disabilities; Health of children; Health problems; Pediatric AIDS; Sex education; Sexual revolution; Sexuality and sexual taboos.

Addams, Jane

BORN: September 6, 1860, Cedarville, Ill.
DIED: May 21, 1935, Chicago, Ill.
AREAS OF ACHIEVEMENT: Children and child development; Economics and work; Education; Sociology
SIGNIFICANCE: Founder of the Hull House settlement in Chicago, Addams was a prominent leader in Progressive reform

Growing up in rural Illinois, Jane Addams was strongly influenced by the example of her father, a state senator and civic leader. After excelling at Rockford Female Seminary, she decided to reject traditional paths of domesticity and motherhood and instead dedicated her life to public service.

Inspired by Christian socialism and England's Toynbee Hall, Addams and her close friend Ellen Gates Starr founded the Hull House settlement in 1889. Located in Chicago's Nineteenth Ward—a slum neighborhood inhabited mainly by immigrants from Italy, Russia, and Eastern Europe—Hull House provided a broad range of services to the immigrant families who lived nearby. It also became an important organizing center for reformers.

Addams believed that much social change could begin with the improvement of children's lives. Under her direction Hull House offered nursery and day-care services; sponsored art, music, and craft classes; and established recreation and sports programs for youth, including summer camps and boys' and girls' clubs. Addams supported the development of urban parks and playgrounds and was an advocate of the kindergarten movement, which stressed the importance of early childhood education. She strongly backed urban and labor reform campaigns that sought to improve the status and well-being of poor women and children. These included inspections and regulation of sweatshops and factories, prohibitions against child labor, the limitation of working hours for women, and efforts to improve sanitation and reduce crowding in tenement housing. She worked with city officials in the formation of a juvenile justice system, with educators promoting school attendance, and with labor organizers demanding fair wages and better working conditions. She also worked to reduce alcoholism, domestic violence, and prostitution—vices that she believed compromised women's safety while eroding family life.

Hull House provided an alterna-

Jane Addams around the time she founded Hull House. (University of Illinois at Chicago, The University Library, Jane Addams Memorial Collection)

tive, utopian family structure for its residents, most of whom were unmarried, middle-class, college-educated women who wanted to participate in its experiment in collective living and direct activism. Addams established close friendships there with many women who went on to prominence in public life, and she developed a rewarding personal partnership with resident Mary Rozet Smith.

Addams published widely on child welfare, civil liberties, and women's issues and was a founder and first president of the Women's International League for Peace and Freedom. In 1931 she was awarded the Nobel Peace Prize.

The kinds of services and studies of immigrant family life Addams helped pioneer at Hull House became standardized in the emerging field of professional social work. Many of Addams's ideas regarding government responsibility to alleviate poverty and to regulate urban and workplace conditions were institutionalized in the Progressive era in city agencies and federal legislation. They were further realized in the New Deal policies of the 1930's and the modern welfare state.

—*Barbara Bair*

See also Childlessness; Children's Bureau; Hull House; Juvenile courts; Lathrop, Julia C.; Settlement houses; Social workers; Watson, John B.

Adoption issues

RELEVANT ISSUES: Children and child development; Parenting and family relationships
SIGNIFICANCE: Modern adoption practices have challenged conventional beliefs about who should adopt, how society can adopt more children, and what types of family environments are most suitable for adopted children

By the mid-1990's, increased rates of birth control, abortion, and mothers choosing to keep their babies born out of wedlock were creating a shortage of healthy infants available for adoption in the United States. The higher value placed on adoption of infants over older children has led parents to resort to new methods of bearing children. These have included surrogacy, embryo transfer, and other advances in reproductive technology related to infertility, in vitro fertilization, and artificial insemination. Meanwhile, growing numbers of children living in foster homes may

be legally adopted. These children have experienced abuse and neglect and have not had the option of being reunited with their biological families. Most of these children are between six and twelve years old.

To address both of these trends, a variety of adoption practices has been developed to ensure that all children have the opportunity to live and grow up in families. These have included independent, stepparent, intercountry, and older-child adoptions. Nearly half of the American adoptions undertaken during the 1990's involved children adopted by a stepparent. Approximately 25,000 infants and children are adopted into families through independent adoptions. Since 1990 there have been increasing numbers of intercountry adoptions of children—particularly from China, Vietnam, Russia, Guatemala, and South Korea. In 1996 U.S. families adopted approximately 11,316 children from other countries. These practices have led to an increase in the total number of children being adopted each year. In 1992, for example, U.S. families adopted 127,441 children. However, these practices have also countered traditional and conventional views about adoptions, raising moral and ethical questions for which there are no simple answers.

Historical Overview. Even before the first state regulation of adoptions began in 1851 in Massachusetts, traditional adoption practices concentrated on finding healthy infants for couples who were unable to have children. Infants were selected to match their adoptive parents' race, ethnicity, religion, and physical characteristics. Infants' births were not disclosed, birth records were sealed, and birth and adoptive parents did not exchange information with one another. Traditional, or closed, adoptions and the associated sealing of birth records provided adoptees as well as their birth and adopted families with some protection, anonymity, and secrecy. This practice was considered important for the promotion of psychological bonding between adoptees and their adoptive parents. It also accorded with the values and beliefs of the time that disapproved of out-of-wedlock pregnancies, of mothers offering up their children for adoption, and of children knowing that they were adopted.

Traditional adoptions worked well in meeting the needs of couples who wanted the chance at

Adoption is one of several ways to build families. (James L. Shaffer)

parenting healthy infants. However, it was a less successful approach to meeting the needs of children who were orphaned, abandoned, abused, physically disabled, or emotionally or behaviorally troubled. Many of them spent their childhoods in orphanages or other institutions or they drifted in and out of foster care without the opportunity to live permanently with a family.

Nontraditional adoption practices grew out of the need to find permanent homes for children considered hard to place and unadoptable. Adoption practices were reconceptualized as a process that recruited families to meet the unique needs of children rather than as a means of finding children for infertile couples. Private adoption agencies, which emerged between 1910 and 1920, were the first to implement this philosophy by arranging adoptions of older children in 1949, transracial adoptions in 1950, and special-needs adoptions beginning in the early 1970's. Federal legislative and funding support for this shift came in 1980 with the passage of the Adoption Assis-

tance and Child Welfare Act. This act provided financial subsidies to families who adopted hard-to-place children or those with special needs.

However, the appropriateness of some nontraditional adoption practices, especially transracial adoption, did not go unchallenged. In 1972 the National Association of Black Social Workers declared transracial adoption to be detrimental to the survival of the African American family and formally opposed the practice. Responding to pressures from Native American groups, the U.S. Congress passed the Indian Welfare Act, which President Jimmy Carter signed into law in 1978 to prevent the unwarranted removal by adoption of Indian children from their homes and tribes. Beginning in the 1980's, however, the number of minority children waiting to be adopted had increased faster than the number of same-race adoptions. To encourage the adoption of minority children by nonminorities, the U.S. Office of Civil Rights declared in 1991 that adoption decisions made solely on the basis of race violated the civil rights of minority (particularly African American) children. Three years later the Howard M. Metzenbaum Multiethnic Placement Act, signed into law by President Bill Clinton, shortened the time that children of color had to wait for adoption and prevented discrimination on the basis of race, color, or national origin.

These government policy and legal changes have been responses to the changing demographic characteristics of children available or waiting for adoption. They have brought into debate the question of whether it is more important for children to have permanent families than to live with people from their own cultural backgrounds. It seemed likely that other policies and legal rulings would follow, as surrogacy, open adoptions, transracial adoptions, and intercountry adoptions continued to shape the composition of adoptive families.

Adoption Through Surrogacy. In a surrogate mother contract, the birth mother is paid a fee to bear a child whom she gives up completely to the adoptive parents. Such agreements often require the adoptive parents to accept financial responsibility during the pregnancy to ensure the well-being of the birth mother. Difficulties occur when one or both parties do not comply with the terms of the contract. One well-known example of this was the famous Baby M case, in which a woman named Mary Beth Whitehead signed a contract with William Stern to bear him his child through artificial insemination and to give up all parental claims to that child in exchange for a fee of $10,000. After the baby was born, however, Whitehead changed her mind and decided to keep the child. Stern filed suit for breach of contract. In the ensuing court action, Stern was awarded custody of the child because its best interests, the court said, would be served by Stern. Whitehead was awarded limited visitation rights. In this case, surrogacy contracts were ruled to be unenforceable and invalid.

Surrogacy raises many issues: Is it a form of buying and selling babies? Does it place the needs of adults over the welfare of the children they create? Is it a form of exploitation of women? What are the long-term effects on children born in surrogate arrangements? Should a price be placed on a human life?

Open Adoption. Open adoption permits adoptees to continue to have contact with members of both their immediate and extended birth families. It has been argued that members of the adoption triangle—birth parents, adoptees, and adoptive parents—all benefit by continued contact with each other. Prospective adopters benefit by having the opportunity to know and obtain from the birth parents vital historical and medical information about their adopted children and their birth families. Birth parents benefit from knowing and having a role in selecting adoptive parents for their children. Children benefit by being allowed to maintain relationships with birth and foster fami-

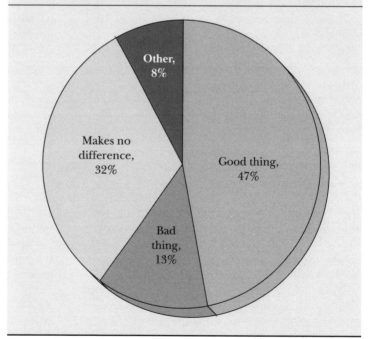

Women's Attitudes Toward Adoptees Seeking Their Natural Mothers in 1998

Other, 8%

Makes no difference, 32%

Good thing, 47%

Bad thing, 13%

Source: The Pew Research Center (1998)

Note: A cross-section of American women were asked if the trend of more adopted persons seeking their birth mothers was a good or bad thing for society.

lies, as well as other past caretakers. They are not forced to declare loyalties or choose sides. Continued contact with previous caregivers provides a resource for coping with life tasks and transitions from childhood to adulthood. On the other hand, it has been argued that continued contact with birth family members may interfere with a child's bonding with the adoptive family. Adoptive families may not feel fully entitled to their children. The ultimate fear is that birth parents may change their minds and legally request to get their children back.

In the celebrated Baby Jessica case, for instance, a couple named DeBoers adopted Jessica in 1991. Jessica's mother had placed her with the DeBoers without her biological father's knowledge. Soon after Jessica's birth, her birth parents wanted her back. As a result of the court action that followed, Jessica was returned to her birth parents.

In a another much publicized incident, the Baby Richard case, a couple's 1992 adoption of Richard was ruled illegal, and he was returned to his birth parents, because his natural father had not consented to the adoption and had been told by his mother that he was dead. In both instances, the children and adoptive parents had psychologically bonded to one another and physically lived with one another for several years. In both situations, courts ruled that the rights of the biological parents had been compromised.

These legal rulings have raised some questions about rights in open adoption. Should birth parents' rights be valued over the rights of adoptive parents? Should birth and adoptive parents have the right to go back on their agreement to participate in open adoption?

Transracial Adoptions. Transracial adoption is the adoption of a child of one race by parents of another. The North American Council on Adoptable Children in 1995 estimated that 40 percent of the 30,000 to 50,000 children available for adoption in the United States were African Americans. At the same time, the number of white families seeking to adopt was increasing. Transracial adoption affords opportunities for white parents and minority children to come together as members of the same family. Proponents of transracial adoption believe that giving children a sense of permanency and belonging is more critical than ensuring same-race placements. Furthermore, such

A Week for Thanksgiving

The week of the traditional U.S. Thanksgiving holiday in late November is also National Adoption Week. Sponsored by the National Council for Adoption, which is based in Washington, D.C., the annual event celebrates the success of infant, special needs, and intercountry adoptions.

adoptions give white parents the opportunity to know and interact firsthand with the culture and ethnic background of their child.

Opponents of transracial adoption believe that children will miss out on experiencing their own cultural heritage, traditions, and ways to cope with being members of a minority in a majority culture. It has been argued that different-race adoptive parents cannot effectively teach their adopted children about their ancestral cultures and that they cannot provide the children with the skills and techniques they will need for coping with the racism they will encounter in their lives. In addition, it has been argued that transracially adopted children must cope with multiple losses: loss of parents, loss of family, and loss of culture. Consequently, the confusion about who they are may place them at greater risk of experiencing problems in adolescence and adulthood around issues such as peer group affiliation, dating, and mate selection.

If minority children living in majority-culture families fail to develop positive identities, they may be at risk of identity confusion and developing negative self-concepts. They may grow up feeling alienated from the minority culture while suffering rejection from the majority culture. Similar concerns have been echoed by opponents of intercountry adoptions.

Popular Culture. Adoption issues and themes have increasingly become part of television programs and motion pictures. In the film *Flirting with Disaster* (1996), before an adult adoptee can name his own four-month-old boy, he makes a trek to the West Coast and back to find his birth parents. In *Mighty Aphrodite* (1995), an adoptive father searches for the birth mother of his adopted son. In *Losing Isaiah* (1995), a crack-addicted black mother comes back after her recovery to reclaim her son from the white parents who adopted him. The plots of these motion pictures reflect issues and questions that adoptees, adopters, birth parents, and the general public are grappling to answer. What types of adoptions are in the best interests of children? Is the openness in adoption proper? Should parents utilize any means possible to attain a healthy child? Should race, ethnicity, and culture have a place in adoption decision making?

—*Bibhuti K. Sar*

BIBLIOGRAPHY

Caplan, Lincoln. *An Open Adoption.* New York: Farrar, Straus & Giroux, 1990. Description of the experiences of a birth mother and adoptive parents coming together to carry out an open adoption and plans on maintaining contact throughout the child's life.

Gabor, Ivor, and Jane Aldridge, eds. *In the Best Interests of the Child: Culture, Identity and Transracial Adoption.* London: Free Association Books, 1994. Essays exploring transracial adoption as a solution for children of color in need of permanency.

Grabe, Pamela V., ed. *Adoption Resources for Mental Health Professionals.* New Brunswick, N.J.: Transaction Publishers, 1990. Resource guide examining social, emotional, and psychological issues faced by adoptive families and children.

Munson, Ronald, ed. *Intervention and Reflection: Basic Issues in Medical Ethics.* 4th ed. Belmont, Calif.: International Thomson Publishing, 1992. Documents the legal, moral, and ethical issues raised by surrogacy and the Baby M case.

Pecora, Peter J., Anthony Maluccio, and James K. Whitaker. *The Child Welfare Challenge.* Hawthorne, N.Y.: Aldine de Gruyter, 1989. Overview of policies, programs, and services for children and families who encounter the welfare system.

Rosenberg, Elinor B. *The Adoption Life Cycle.* New York: Free Press, 1992. Identifies and discusses the developmental tasks and life-cycle issues faced by birth parents, adoptive parents, and adopted children.

See also Adoption processes; Children born out of wedlock; Family: concept and history; Fertility and infertility; Foster homes; *In re Baby M*; Interracial families; Orphans; Reproductive technologies; Surrogate mothers.

Adoption processes

RELEVANT ISSUES: Children and child development; Law; Parenting and family relationships

SIGNIFICANCE: Adoption creates legal relationships between parents and children who are not biologically related, whereby the adoptive parents obtain exclusive legal custody of the children and the biological parents relinquish it

Adoption, whereby persons acquire all the rights and responsibilities of parents by making other persons their own children, has existed since ancient times. Founded on broad humanitarian principles, its primary purpose is to give children a permanent, stable environment, to protect their interests and welfare, and to promote stable family relationships.

In the United States only married couples who meet restrictive age, income, and educational criteria have been traditionally permitted to adopt children. However, adoption is now available to more people than previously. Usually, any adult resident of a state, married or unmarried, is eligible. Agencies consider applicants' social history, financial situation, moral fitness, religious background, and physical and mental health. In some jurisdictions, homosexuality has continued to be a basis for denying persons the right to adopt children.

Some states permit persons to adopt only minors, while others specifically allow adult adoption. Generally, states have prohibited the adoption of adults for fraudulent purposes, such as to make them heirs. Most courts reject applications from persons who wish to adopt their heterosexual or homosexual partners, arguing that they violate public policy. When adult adoptions are permitted, they have the same legal weight as child adoptions, without establishing guardianship.

Types of Adoptions. In cases of agency adoption, natural parents grant all rights to their children to adoption agencies. These biological parents usually do not know the identities of adoptive parents. In open adoptions, which are illegal in some states, natural mothers select their children's adoptive parents. All adoptions must conform to state laws and must be legalized through court orders.

In cases of private adoption, biological parents relinquish their children directly to the adopting parents, who pay for agency and legal fees and for biological mothers' medical care and living expenses. The biological parents retain legal custody of their children until a final judgment has been rendered. One drawback of private adoptions is that biological parents may object to the adoptions any time before a final judgment has been reached, even if they have given up physical custody.

Intrafamily adoptions, often involving stepparents or grandparents, are very common. Most states have expedited adoption procedures. The consent of both biological parents is usually necessary, but fathers who have not complied with court-ordered child support obligations may forfeit their right to object.

"Black market" adoptions, which put children up for adoption without state authority, are illegal and subject to criminal penalties in order to prevent the buying and selling of children. However, while states prohibit payments of money to biological parents or intermediaries who arrange adoptions, they permit payments for medical bills and reasonable legal fees.

The number of international adoptions, usually from developing countries, has increased: Americans adopted between 7,000 and 12,000 foreign children yearly during the 1990's. Although few newborn children have been adopted, many of the adoptees have been quite young—often only three to six months old. The advantage to adopting foreign children is that the waiting periods are shorter and the availability of children greater than in the United States. However, international adoptions, costing between $15,000 and $30,000, involve complex paperwork and multiple legal systems. Federal laws govern the admission of children to the United States and their citizenship status. Although the laws of a child's country of origin govern adoptions, the laws of the adoptive parents' state govern the legal relationship between the adopters and the adoptee. In some countries, international laws take precedence over national laws.

Adoptive parents must satisfy the legal requirements of the involved countries and complete paperwork for the Immigration and Naturalization Service (INS), which grants

Foreign-born Children Adopted in the United States in 1996

Country	Percent
China	29.3
Russia	22.4
Korea	14.0
Romania	4.9
Guatemala	3.7
India	3.4
Vietnam	3.1
Colombia	2.3
Paraguay	2.3
Philippines	2.0
Other	12.6

Percent

Source: *Newsweek* (June 16, 1997)
Note: Americans adopted approximately 11,000 foreign-born children in 1996 from these countries.

Most adoptive parents cease to think of their children as adopted by the time they get them home. (James L. Shaffer)

adopted children immediate status as permanent residents. In order to admit children to the United States without placing them on an immigration list, adoptive parents must verify that the children are orphans and furnish certified copies of the foreign adoption decrees. Nevertheless, foreign-born children do not automatically become U.S. citizens; they must be formally naturalized, either administratively or though the courts.

International adoption agencies, licensed in the United States, must conduct home studies and determine if prospective parents qualify to adopt children. Some countries, such as South Korea, do not require that adoptions actually take place in their country. Others, however, require not only that adoptions take place in the country of origin

but also that both parents be present at the time of adoption. Finally, adoptive parents must pay to transport adopted children. Although most states recognize foreign adoption decrees, parents may want to readopt their children in their states of residence.

General Procedures. Regardless of the type of adoption, prospective parents must meet statutory requirements and follow state or national procedures. Adoption starts with completing an agency application, followed by a home study. There is usually a pre-adoptive placement for about six months. The states or adoption agencies determine if petitioners are eligible and qualified to adopt, if prospective children are eligible for adoption, and if the adoptions are in the best interest of the children.

Adoptions usually take place in closed court, but the natural parents must be notified of the proceedings and granted the right to be heard if they have not consented. Usually, petitioners must be residents of the states in which the proceedings are held, and both spouses must be present. However, if the best interests of the children are served, one spouse may cease to be a petitioner without causing the proceedings to be dismissed. Completion of the legal process finalizes adoptions.

Considerations After Adoption. Adoptive parents become adopted children's legal parents, obtaining all rights, obligations, and exclusive custody. Adoptions may also have other legal consequences, such as changes in the children's surnames, changes in their right to pension benefits, workers' compensation and dependent-children benefits, and changes in their right to bring survival or wrongful death actions for injuries to or death of their adoptive parents. Adoptions also affect inheritance rights. In some jurisdictions, adopted children may inherit from both their biological and adoptive parents; if their first adoptive parents should die and they are adopted a second time, they can inherit from both sets of parents. Furthermore, adoptees' children are considered grandchildren of the adoptive parents for inheritance purposes.

In determining access to adoption records, courts consider the interests of all parties. Closed records usually provide only physical and historical information on biological parents and are opened only under exceptional circumstances, such as for medical reasons. If state statutes restrict access, hearings must be held to determine good cause, and the biological parents must be notified. Courts usually reject challenges on due process and other constitutional grounds. Access to adult adoptees or third parties, such as siblings, may be permitted, denied, or allowed restrictively.

Constitutional Considerations. States play a dual role in the adoption process. Courts act not only as protectors of children but also as guardians of parental rights to the extent that parental rights do not conflict with the paramount interests of the children. States normally require parental consent for adoption, but there are exceptions. Because adoptions are usually irrevocable, consent must be voluntary and given with full knowledge of the consequences. In extreme cases, such as if the parents are found to be unfit to care for their children, states may terminate parental rights and put the children up for adoption without the parents' consent. The Fourteenth Amendment of the U.S. Constitution guarantees that both unwed mothers and fathers have equal protection of their parental rights, so that they may prevent the adoption of their children by withholding their consent. However, if unwed parents have not developed a substantive relationship with their adopted children, they cannot be assured of constitutional protection. Some courts consider the personal, financial, custodial, and legal relationship of parents to their children before terminating parental rights.

—*David R. Sobel*

BIBLIOGRAPHY

Adamec, Christine. *There Are Babies to Adopt.* New York: Kensington, 1996.

"Adoption." In *American Jurisprudence.* 2d ed. Vol. 2. Rochester, N.Y.: Lawyers Co-operative Publishing Co., 1994.

Askin, Jayne, with Molly Davis. *Search: A Handbook for Adoption and Birthparents.* 2d ed. Phoenix: Oryx Press, 1992.

Bartholet, Elizabeth. "International Adoption: Propriety, Prospects and Pragmatics." *Journal of the American Academy of Matrimonial Lawyers* 181 (Winter, 1996).

Elliott, H. Wayne. "International Adoptions: Step by Step." *S.C. Lawyer* 37 (1995).

Lindsay, Jeanne Warren, and Catherine Raschal Monserrat. *Adoption Awareness: A Guide for Teachers, Counselors, Nurses and Caring Others.* Buena Park, Calif.: Morning Glory Press, 1989.

Liu, Margaret. "International Adoptions: An Overview." *Temple International and Comparative Law Journal* 187 (Spring, 1994).

See also Adoption issues; Family: concept and history; Family law; Orphans; Parenting; Unwed fathers.

Adultery

RELEVANT ISSUES: Divorce; Marriage and dating
SIGNIFICANCE: Infidelity and adultery are forms of sexual behavior that have been considered im-

moral in the United States according to the prevailing Judeo-Christian heritage, are illegal according to state and military laws, and are unacceptable according to social norms

Sexual behavior is a natural and essential part of nature. Among humans, two common sexual desires are found: one for enduring sexual relationships (a basis for marriage) and the other for sexual variety (the basis for infidelity). In the United States, as in virtually all of the Judeo-Christian world, monogamy is the only socially approved and legally sanctioned form of marriage, and spouses are considered to be exclusive and permanent sexual partners. As with other social norms, however, persons sometimes pursue deviant behavior, and not all persons limit their sexual behavior to their spouses. Infidelity may indicate problems in relationships that require partners to undergo counseling. Loss of trust is a common result of adultery.

Prohibition Against Adultery. Virtually every society has at least some established guidelines regarding sexual behavior. Although societies differ in the scope and specific content of such guidelines, most societies regulate certain types of sexual behavior that may in some way be seen as affecting the well-being of the community. Two of the most universally prohibited types of sexual behavior are incest and adultery. Incest taboos, which prohibit sexual intercourse between persons too closely related to be legally married, may be viewed as an attempt by society to increase and extend group unity by forcing members of one family to establish close ties with other families through the bond of marriage. The prohibition against adultery may be seen as an attempt to preserve group unity by preventing divisive conflicts from arising among families because of unacceptable sexual relationships. Relevant to this is the observation of the sociologist Kingsley Davis that a sexual custom is accepted by a society to the degree that it is perceived as supporting the social institutions of marriage and family. In addition, the prohibition against adultery has often been perceived as an extension and exercise of property rights, wherein women are viewed as the property of men.

Social Reactions. There appears to be no single universal reaction to adultery. Cross-cultural data reveal a wide variety of beliefs and practices. Acceptance of adultery, at least in certain situations, is found in some parts of the world. In some societies husbands have the right to offer their wives' sexual favors to male visitors. An example of this custom, sometimes called "wife hospitality," is found among certain Eskimo groups. In these same societies, however, wives do not have the right to volunteer themselves to males.

Severe sanctions against adultery have been found to prevail in other parts of the world. Under Muslim law, husbands of wives discovered to have committed adultery have been allowed to kill their wives with impunity. Similarly, during the colonial period some American colonies had laws under which adultery could be punishable by death. The Native American tribes of North America exhibited a variety of attitudes toward adultery, ranging from acceptance to rejection.

At times, a society's reaction to adultery has depended upon the social status of one or both of the sexual partners involved. For example, the Hebrews considered a married woman to be guilty of adultery if she had sexual intercourse with any male other than her own husband. A married man, however, was guilty of adultery only if he had intercourse with another man's wife.

Protection Against Adultery. Just as attitudes toward adultery and treatment of adulterers have been surprisingly diverse, so too are the methods various cultures have used to protect against adultery. The most common methods are the establishment of social mores and the punishment of offenders under religious, civil, and criminal laws. In addition to such regulatory measures, some societies have adopted more concrete measures that rely less on the acceptance and conformity of individuals and more on the prevention of seductive situations. Examples would include the physical separation of the sexes and the use of clothing and veils to completely cover women from view. Such practices are found in some parts of the Muslim world. Another common tactic, found in some Hispanic countries, has been the use of chaperones, often members of girls' families. In ancient Persia and China, the more affluent members of society employed eunuchs to guard wives, whereas the medieval European husband going off to war sometimes had his wife locked into a chastity belt.

Stanley Kowalski (played by Marlon Brando) commits adultery when he sexually attacks his sister-in-law, Blanche DuBois (Vivien Leigh), in the 1951 film Streetcar Named Desire. *(Museum of Modern Art, Film Stills Archive)*

Other approaches to prohibiting adultery have relied on internal controls that are developed during the socialization process. The two most commonly recognized internal controls are guilt and shame. Guilt, which is identified with the conscience, is internal discomfort ranging from mild to unbearable, which results from the violation of internalized standards of behavior. Shame is internal discomfort that is a reaction to others' real or imagined criticisms of one's behavior. The United States is a society that relies heavily on guilt to restrict adulterous behavior, although the anthropologist Ruth Benedict expressed the opinion that the United States in the mid-twentieth century was in the process of changing from a guilt culture to a shame culture. One of the reasons given for this change was a relaxation of morals.

Different Nomenclature. Although the term "adultery" is commonly used by the general public, it is not common among social scientists, because the term has had a long tradition of usage in religious thought, including in the Ten Commandments, in which it is specifically condemned. The word comes from the Latin *adulterare*, which means to go beyond the limits, to corrupt or ruin, to pollute. Consequently, the term is inextricably related to a moral judgment in the minds of most people. Social scientists also avoid other popularly used terms, such as "infidelity," "cheating," and "unfaithfulness," because of their similarly judgmental nature. Because scientists attempt to be objective and nonjudgmental, they prefer to use neutral terminology to refer to adultery, such as "extramarital relations," "extramarital sex," and "extramarital affairs."

There are also terms which refer to specific types of adultery, such as "swinging," "swapping," and "open marriage." Swinging and swapping refer to mutually supportive adultery, in which husbands and wives meet other couples to exchange sexual partners temporarily. Such adulterous behavior may also be called "comarital sex," particularly if the spouses agree that both have sexual experiences with specified others at the same time and place and that these sexual experiences take place within an organized network instead of spontaneously. Marriages in which there is an agreement between husbands and wives allowing one or both spouses to engage in sexual activity with others is sometimes referred to as sexually "open marriages"; persons in such marriages argue that they are not being unfaithful, since their behavior is known and approved by their spouses.

Studies of Adultery. Most early studies of sexual behavior were conducted by physicians, psychologists, and psychiatrists, and adultery was not the exclusive or even main focus of inquiry. These studies tended to share the same basic weakness: They were relatively small, nonrandom samples of self-selected, white, middle-class individuals who were often patients of the researchers.

The largest and most ambitious early study of sex was published in 1929 by the U.S. Bureau of Social Hygiene. The study was conducted by the sociologist Katharine Davis of 2,200 women for the stated purpose of providing more adequate data on the physical and mental aspects of the sex lives of normal individuals. Results indicated that 24 percent of the respondents believed that adultery by husbands was sometimes justified, while 76 percent believed it was never justified. Respondents gave similar responses regarding adulterous wives, as 21 percent stated that such adultery was sometimes justified and 79 percent stated that it was never justified. Justifiable reasons included unsatisfactory relations between husbands and wives, separation or divorce, unobtained divorce when divorce was nonetheless desired, love for other persons, and the unsatisfied desire to have children.

In 1948 the zoologist Alfred Kinsey published the first of his famous studies, *Sexual Behavior in the Human Male*. This study, together with its 1953 companion study, *Sexual Behavior in the Human Female*, is generally considered to be a watershed work. Kinsey found that 37 percent of the respondents admitted to committing adultery, but he believed that the actual figure was probably closer to 50 percent. His findings revealed that men are more adulterous than women, that individuals who engage in premarital sex also engage in more extramarital sex, and that devout church members are far less likely than inactive members to engage in adultery. The greatest differences, however, were related to socioeconomic status, particularly as measured by formal education. Males with little education were found to have the most premarital and extramarital sexual experience. In attempting to explain his findings, Kinsey theorized that males are more adulterous than females because of certain physical, psychological, and social differences.

A decade after the publication of the last of the Kinsey reports there was a general increase in both the number and quality of studies dealing with adulterous sexual relations. By the end of the 1960's there was a growing body of relevant research, as studies began to focus exclusively on adultery. Changes had occurred in society that allowed for a deeper, more extensive investigation of adulterous behavior. Among these changes were revised divorce laws; changes in the frequency and explicitness of the sexual materials to which the public was exposed through cinema, television, books, magazines, and even school courses; a weakening in the strength and unanimity of organized religions' moral pronouncements; greater numbers of married women in the workforce and the increased time they spent outside the home; increased personal mobility, which served to weaken community control; and the increasing spirit of individualism and the felt need for personal fulfillment. Conditions were favorable not only for the collection of information on extramarital sexual information but also for its dissemination, as state laws making adultery illegal were either abolished or unenforced.

A 1993 national survey conducted by the psychiatrist Samuel Janus and the physician Cynthia Janus found that approximately one-fourth of the women and one-third of the men questioned indicated that they had been unfaithful. However, 83 percent of all respondents believed that infidelity seriously affects marriage.

Based on research, a number of typologies have been developed attempting to explain adulterous behavior. One example was developed by the sociologists John Cuber and Peggy Harroff, who identified five distinct types of marriages. In their model, conflict-habituated marriages are characterized by tension and intermittent conflict, whereby adultery may be nothing more than another outlet for hostility. Devitalized marriages are previously full, happy, close relationships that have became lifeless and apathetic. In such marriages, one or both spouses may commit adultery in an attempt to recapture a spirit or mood that is no longer present in the marriage. Passive-congenial marriages are marked from the beginning by a lack of vitality and romance. As a result, one or

both spouses may commit adultery to break the boredom and routine of an empty, mechanical conjugal relationship. Vital marriages exhibit genuine sharing and togetherness, resulting in feelings of mutual satisfaction. In such marriages, adultery may occur because of the emancipation of the spouses or as a source of mutual, yet vicarious, gratification. Total marriages are the most satisfying and are based on important shared values and interests. Nevertheless, adultery may also occur in these marriages.

Because of the rich and deep relationships found in both the vital and total marriages, deception and insincerities are more likely to be detected by spouses than in the other types, and reactions may be more serious. Such partners may seek divorce if they are unwilling or unable to accept anything less than the full, deep, complete partnership that had existed from the beginning of their marriage.

A typology of adulterous relationships was later presented by John Cuber. Type I adulterous relationships supply, compensate, or substitute for what are seen to be defective marriages. Sometimes adulterous relationships are similar to good marriages in terms of their psychological dimensions. Type II adulterous relationships result from the temporary physical separation of spouses. Such relationships tend to be short-lived, somewhat meaningless relationships and are not considered to pose a real threat to marriage. Type III adulterous relationships are the result of what is called a bohemian mentality, in which one or both spouses refuse to accept a completely monogamous relationship.

Studies in the last quarter of the twentieth century have found two attitudes regarding sexual behavior that indicate a lack of understanding. Most Americans indicate that they accept premarital sex, at least in certain cases, but that they reject extramarital sex in all cases. While it may appear that these are two unrelated practices, research has revealed that they are actually related. Previous studies have shown that individuals who engage in premarital sex are more likely to engage in extramarital sex after they marry. It appears that once individuals separate sex from marriage so that sexual intimacy is acceptable with someone other than a spouse, it is difficult to change that perception after marriage.   —*Philip E. Lampe*

BIBLIOGRAPHY

Buss, David. *The Evaluation of Desire.* New York: Basic Books, 1994. Psychological approach to the study of love and sexuality that uses examples from the animal world and extensive cross-cultural data to explain that the basic concern of men in relationship to women is access to their reproductive capacity, while women want access to men's resources.

D'Emilio, John, and Estelle Freedman. *Intimate Matters: A History of Sexuality in America.* New York: Harper & Row, 1988. Extensive discussion of attitudes and behavior concerning sexuality from colonial times through the mid-1980's. Explains differences in sexuality based on gender, race, and socioeconomic status and that previously private sexual matters became an accepted part of public culture.

Fisher, Helen. *Anatomy of Love: The Natural History of Monogamy, Adultery, and Divorce.* New York: W. W. Norton, 1992. Explores the nature of humans' romantic lives, compares data on adultery from forty-two cultures and divorce data from sixty-two, and compares modern human behavior with that of birds and nonhuman mammals as well as primitive societies, leading to a general theory of the evolution of human sex and family life.

Janus, Samuel, and Cynthia Janus. *The Janus Report on Sexual Behavior.* New York: John Wiley & Sons, 1993. First broad scientific national survey since Kinsey, in which experts from the fields of psychiatry, sociology, psychology, medicine, anthropology, law enforcement, and history deal with a wide range of sexual attitudes and behavior, including adultery.

Lampe, Philip, ed. *Adultery in the United States: Close Encounters of the Sixth or Seventh Kind.* Buffalo, N.Y.: Prometheus, 1987. Objective presentation by professionals in the fields of law, biology, literature, philosophy, and sociology of data concerning adultery that examines the roots of American attitudes toward adultery and contains a review of major studies conducted in the United States as well as a summary of consistent findings.

See also Cruelty as grounds for divorce; Divorce; Love; Marriage counseling; Marriage laws; Midlife crises; No-fault divorce; Open marriage; Sexual revolution; Sexuality and sexual taboos.

Advertising

RELEVANT ISSUES: Children and child development; Parenting and family relationships
SIGNIFICANCE: Advertisers often try to reach consumers by targeting specific family members, especially children

Advertisers know that the best time to air a television advertising "spot" for sugary breakfast cereals is late on weekday afternoons or early on Saturday mornings. Couples set on buying a nice, comfortable sedan often decide suddenly that they really need a minivan. McDonald's restaurants are strongly associated with popular culture. All three statements are true for the same reason: target marketing.

Because of television and radio audience research, advertisers know who is watching and listening to what and when. In other words, they know that children spend most of their time watching television after school and on Saturday mornings. They also know that children lobby for vehicles that will accommodate their needs—their bikes, sports gear, and friends. McDonald's has proved to be a champion of marketing; most of its advertisements are aimed not at parents but at children, sometimes even very young children.

Advertisers use family images to sell all kinds of things. The images are present in all media but are much stronger in television. While watching daytime television, for example, persons see a number of products aimed at women but geared to family use. Cleaning products are often shown as necessary for cleaning up after children or pets. Products for babies are rarely advertised on television after the dinner hour, because the target audience—primarily young mothers—tend to watch television during the day. The image of the family as a bustling unit of individuals was popular during the 1990's. One common theme was family members' striving for common meal times. Precooked, packaged foods—including waffles, pasta dinners, and hamburger casseroles—were heavily advertised during breakfast and dinner hours, when family members think about what to eat.

Cable television changed the approach, although not the rules, of target marketing. For example, Lifetime Television is a cable network aimed at women. Thus, advertisers on this network are not limited by time in the same way as advertisers on the traditional networks. The same holds true for Music Television (MTV), whose audience of teenage viewers changes little during the day. The sports network, ESPN, caters primarily to men, and features advertisements for sports drinks, athletic shoes, and expensive cars. Men are not ignored as influences on the buying habits of families, but advertisers believe that women and children wield much power in this area.

The Influence of Children. Throughout the 1990's advertisers began to take advantage of the fact that children could influence their parents' spending habits. They did so not only for such products as food and toys but also for more expensive items. Automakers targeted children in television advertising and print direct-mail campaigns. Television spots showed children enjoying spacious minivans with backseat cupholders and stereo speakers. In 1995 Chrysler mailed 250,000 cardboard pop-up books promoting their Voyager minivans to families and pediatricians' offices. In their efforts to reach children, Nissan handed out

insulated water bottles with the car maker's logo stamped on them. Local car dealers hired entertainers, set up play areas, and offered free food to catch the attention of families.

As the number of parenting on-line web sites grew, advertisers sought new ways to reach mothers, the primary users of such sites. Advertisements for such things as children's products and household items appeared at the bottom of the computer screen. Although on-line advertising for children continued to grow, the television market remained robust. By the end of the 1990's advertising expenditures for children's television were around $700 million a year. Most of the advertisements, appearing on the Fox Children's Network or on Nickelodeon, were for toys, electronic games, videos, fast foods, and snacks.

Advertising researchers emphasized the importance of decreasing the range of target audiences, avoiding such broad groups as two- to eleven-year-olds. Two- or three-year-old children are not influenced by the same types of advertisements as ten- or eleven-year-olds. Advertisers realized that

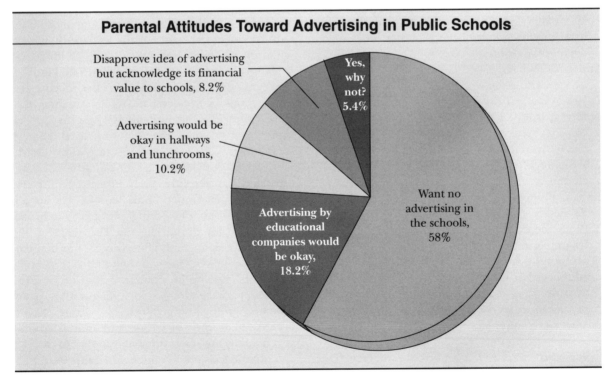

Parental Attitudes Toward Advertising in Public Schools

Disapprove idea of advertising but acknowledge its financial value to schools, 8.2%

Advertising would be okay in hallways and lunchrooms, 10.2%

Yes, why not? 5.4%

Advertising by educational companies would be okay, 18.2%

Want no advertising in the schools, 58%

Source: Moms Online website (1998)

Note: In early 1998 Moms Online conducted an informal poll among visitors to its website, asking them whether they approved the idea of public schools permitting on-campus advertising to raise money. This chart summarizes the responses.

children in the 1990's lived in a society that differed greatly from that of thirty or forty years earlier. No longer did parents make all the purchasing decisions for families. The media, changes in family structure, and changes in parental work habits all influenced children's attitudes and buying power.

Industry Regulation. Throughout the 1970's federal regulators became increasingly concerned about how many commercials children were seeing on television. For a number of years, the Federal Communications Commission (FCC) had expressed concern over advertisers' attempts to reach family buyers through children. In 1974 the FCC implemented restrictions on the amount of commercial time that could be aired during children's programs. Moreover, in 1974 the National Advertising Division of the Council of Better Business Bureaus, Inc. established the Children's Advertising Review Unit to monitor the advertising industry's attempts to self-regulate children's advertising. On October 2, 1990, the House of Representatives and the United States Senate approved the Children's Television Advertising Practice Act, which set a ceiling of ten and a half minutes per hour for commercials during weekend children's television programming. A ceiling of twelve minutes per hour was established for weekday programming. Some networks such as Nickelodeon continued to regulate themselves by restricting commercials, especially those aimed at very young children, to before and after programs.

Critics and federal regulators' arguments centered on the idea that young children had trouble distinguishing between commercials and television shows. The FCC instituted a policy restricting "host selling"—that is, the use of program characters in advertisements aired during or adjacent to programs in which such characters are featured.

Children are exposed to a wide variety of advertising forms from an early age. (Long Hare Photographs)

For example, a Bugs Bunny cartoon could not be closely associated with a commercial featuring Bugs Bunny and a commercial for Flintstones vitamins could not be shown alongside a Flintstones cartoon. Host selling, tie-ins, and other practices involving the use of program characters to promote products were barred as part of the Children's Television Advertising Practice Act.

Another FCC policy required that advertisers depict products designed for mealtime in a way that shows how such products fit into a balanced

Many advertisers use family themes to attract customers. (James L. Shaffer)

diet. Thus, cereal advertisers display their products along with juice and toast or include such voice-overs as "This cereal is part of a balanced breakfast."

Joe Camel. The idea that cigarette and alcohol advertisements, especially those aimed at children, should be banned or closely regulated is not a new one. Broadcast advertising of cigarettes was banned in January, 1971. Opponents of this ban have argued that it is unconstitutional to ban true, nondeceptive advertising for legal products. One of the biggest controversies has involved Joe Camel, the advertising spokesanimal for R. J. Reynolds tobacco company. The camel character, who always has a cigarette in his mouth and is depicted as "cool," became the subject of a series of studies reported in the *Journal of the American Medical Association* in the 1980's. According to these studies, preschoolers recognized Joe Camel as readily as they did Mickey Mouse. Illegal sales of Camel cigarettes to minors skyrocketed during the late 1980's.

Regulation inside and outside the advertising industry will not change the fact that experienced marketers know how to reach an audience. As long as advertisers understand the relationships between children and their parents and the different influences affecting children of different ages, they will have few problems selling minivans to people who set out to buy sedans.

—*Sherri Ward Massey*

BIBLIOGRAPHY

Boutilier, Robert. *Targeting Families: Marketing to and Through the New Family.* Ithaca, N.Y.: American Demographics Books, 1993.

Fox, Roy. *Harvesting Minds: How TV Commercials Control Kids.* Westport, Conn.: Praeger Books Inc., 1996.

Guber, Selina. *Marketing to and Through Kids.* New York: McGraw-Hill, 1993.

Lont, Cynthia. *Women and Media.* Belmont, Calif.: Wadsworth Publishing, 1995.

Seiter, Ellen. *Sold Separately: Children and Parents in Consumer Culture.* New Brunswick, N.J.: Rutgers University Press, 1993.

Wilson, Stan Le Roy. *Mass Media/Mass Culture: An Introduction.* New York: McGraw-Hill, 1993.

See also Children's magazines; Entertainment; Family demographics; Family economics; Gender inequality; News media and families; Sexual revolution.

Affinity

RELEVANT ISSUES: Kinship and genealogy; Parenting and family relationships

SIGNIFICANCE: A key concept in classifying family relationships, affinity distinguishes relatives by marriage from those by blood

"Affinity" refers to family relationships formed through marriage. Relatives by marriage are affinal kin, in contrast to consanguinal, or blood, kin.

Therefore, in-laws are classified as affinal kin by marriage, while persons who are related biologically—such as parents, siblings, aunts, uncles, and cousins—are consanguinal kin.

In the North American kinship system, relationships are based on two principles: the order of biology and the order of law. Because affinity concerns relationships formed through marriage, people linked in this fashion are thus affines by law.

The concept of affinity was first defined and illustrated by the American ethnologist Lewis Henry Morgan in *Systems of Consanguinity and Affinity of the Human Family* in 1871. Although this concept is used to distinguish relatives by marriage from those by blood, legal definitions of affinity based on marriage are by no means universal. For example, in matrilineal societies, in which family genealogy is traced on the mother's side, a father's sister is considered to be an affine, while a mother's sister is regarded as a direct, lineal family relative. In English, both women are called "aunt"; in matrilineal societies they are called by different names. Social definitions of affinity differ from one society to another and can vary from person to person.

The distinction between affinal and consanguinal relationships is not always clear. Divorces and remarriages create families with stepparents and stepsiblings. According to social convention in the United States, parent-child and sibling relations are the most basic and direct family relationships. According to the formal rules of kinship terminology, however, stepfathers or stepmothers should be classified as affines: relatives by marriage to one's mother or father, but not a blood relation. The same logic applies to stepsiblings, who are affines if they are born to different parents.

—*Jian Li*

See also Consanguinal families; Genealogy; In-laws; Kinship systems; Marriage; Matrilineal descent; Nuclear family.

African Americans

RELEVANT ISSUES: Children and child development; Kinship and genealogy; Parenting and family relationships; Race and ethnicity; Religious beliefs and practices

SIGNIFICANCE: Although African Americans have faced numerous challenges, from slavery to poverty and unemployment, the African American family unit has emerged as a powerful, adaptive, and ever-present force in the lives of African Americans

African American families are characterized by a vast assortment of family structures. Slavery, freedom, and modern issues have all combined to shape the history of African American family life. For example, a unique branch of African American families is a relative who has been coined as "fictive kin," alternately termed by some as a "play mother, brother, sister, aunt, uncle, or cousin." These "relatives" are not blood relations but are "appropriated" family members who are seen as a uniting force within the African American community. Andrew Billingsley's *Climbing Jacob's Ladder* (1992) describes the African American family as "an *intimate association* of persons of African descent who are *related to one another* by a variety of means, including blood, marriage, formal adoption, informal adoption, or by appropriation. . . ."

The Influence of African Culture. In *The Negro Family in the United States* (1966) sociologist E. Franklin Frazier argued that African culture did not have any meaning for African Americans because it was eradicated by slavery. Some scholars have refuted this claim, noting that most modern African Americans are descendants of West African peoples and that the structure and value of family life among African Americans are similar to those of previous West African societies. These similarities include the importance of extended family members, the significance of motherhood, the importance of roles within the family, and lineage or blood relations, which is the strongest part of the African American kinship system.

In West African culture and among modern African Americans, marriage is a valued and strongly desired custom. Marriages in Africa were not a simple joining of two people, but a joining of two groups of families, an idea still shared by many African American families. Some modern African American couples have borrowed the old African custom of "jumping the broom" at the end of the marriage ceremony. This custom symbolizes couples' leaving their old, single life and beginning a new life together. Although marriage no longer requires parental consent, it is customary to treat marriage as an event involving the blessing and support of both families.

There were various types of households in West African society, but the two main ones were the nuclear family, composed of a married couple and their offspring, and the extended family, which could consist of a married couple, children, siblings, their children, and others. Both men and women were valued for their contributions to the family, but women were more highly esteemed because their reproductive functions served to further the family lineage. The extended family was responsible for the upbringing of the children, and older family members were held in the highest regard, much as grandparents and great-grandparents of modern African Americans are cherished and respected.

The Impact of Slavery. Although slavery was certainly a disruptive force in the African American family, it did not destroy it, as some noted scholars have claimed. Even though marriage between African slaves was not recognized by white slaveowners, many slaves had marriage ceremonies and lived as married couples. Long-term slave marriages were documented in slave narratives and plantation records. Even after the sale of slaves forced families to separate, family members often tried repeatedly to reunite. However, slavery forced an end to cohabitation with extended family members because of the limited size of slave quarters. The family relationship most affected by slavery was parenting. Parents did not have a true voice when it came to the future of their children, for they were powerless to prevent their children's sale and their authority could be overruled by the slavemasters. During slavery, the primary caretakers of children were older slaves or older siblings, resulting in children becoming more self-reliant than they were before slavery. A new type of household, the female-headed household, also began to emerge during slavery, developing in large part because of the death or sale of husbands. Other female-headed households were formed as unmarried women had children out of wedlock.

The end of slavery changed the dynamics of the African American family. Although the African American family remained primarily nuclear in construction, the extended family became increasingly important. The extended family could pool

During the late twentieth century African Americans became increasingly inclined to acknowledge and study their African heritage. (James L. Shaffer)

its monetary resources and share child-care duties and other responsibilities. Another factor affecting the African American family was migration. Although many families searched for better opportunities and attempted to migrate north as family units, migration was often impossible because of poverty and other circumstances. In such cases, individual family members left the family and the oppressive conditions in the South in search of better opportunities in the North. After

Church membership plays an especially strong role in African American communities. (James L. Shaffer)

they had saved enough money, additional family members followed them.

African Americans and Church Life. Along with their African culture, Africans also brought their art, music, and religion to the United States. West Africans practiced what is known as traditional religion. They believed that there was one creator and different spirits that watched over people. While enslaved, the slaves were introduced to Christianity, which they adapted to the cultural

survivals of their ancestors. For example, funerals in Africa are very important rituals. Dancing, music, and eating figure prominently in funeral services, which usually last more than one day. African American slaves held similar ceremonies to honor their dead. The church became extremely important to the slaves, as it offered them an opportunity to join family and friends in a nonhostile environment and represented the hope that God would help them to find true freedom.

After slavery, churches within African American communities served different purposes. Some were used as schools during the week while others acted as charitable organizations by helping the community's needy. After the destruction of slavery, Christianity became a dominant religious force in African American life. The majority of modern African Americans are Baptists, Methodists, Pentecostals, and Presbyterians. During slavery, approximately 150,000 African Americans were Baptists and about 20,000 belonged to African Methodist Episcopal churches. After slavery was abolished, the number of Baptists swelled to about 500,000 and the number of African Methodist Episcopalians to nearly 200,000. About 70 percent of modern African Americans belong to a church.

Family Reunions. Although reunions have been an enduring feature of African American family life, the generation of the 1980's and 1990's has changed the face of the African American family reunion. There are several reasons for this: Many African Americans who lived in northern cities thought of their southern hometowns as oppressive places that were best left in the past, in both a physical and a spiritual sense. However, as segregation eased, it was somewhat easier to make the journey south. After reading Alex Haley's *Roots: The Saga of an American Family* (1976) or watching the subsequent television miniseries, many African Americans were eager to learn more about their own "roots," leading to the rebirth of family reunions.

At the core of the African American family reunion is the belief that families should share their blessings with one another to strengthen, empower, and encourage each family member's identity. Some families have given their reunions a loose organizational structure by publishing family newsletters and starting family chapters, while others have formed quasicorporate organizations by electing family officers, enacting bylaws, and holding conferences to discuss fund-raising plans for scholarships and opening credit unions to sup-

Three generations of women in a Brooklyn, New York, family. (Hazel Hankin)

port small business ventures. This more structured type of African American reunion has attracted the interest of corporate America. Coca-Cola and the Coors brewing company have expressed an interest in these reunions, while the National Council of Negro Women has sponsored an annual Black Family Reunion Celebration since 1986.

The Fourth of July holiday is a time of many annual African American family reunions. Relatives from neighboring northern states often rent vans or buses and travel "down South" together. Upon arrival, T-shirts sporting family names and the reunion year may be handed out to family members. Adults and children play games and enjoy a variety of home-cooked foods.

Family Gatherings and Kwanza. Sunday dinners have played an important role in the African American family unit for many years. After attending church services, families often go home or visit extended family members to enjoy typical Sunday dinners. Sometimes these meals consist of dishes such as yams and collard greens and traditional soul food (the term used to characterize certain dishes that African Americans frequently cook using recipes that have been handed down for generations). Sundays may be the only time during the week that all family members spend together for a meal. It is a time when families may discuss important happenings in their lives—but most of all it is a time to enjoy family.

Each year many African American families celebrate their heritage and roots by observing the seven-day festival of Kwanza, which means "first fruits of the harvest" in the East African language of Swahili. Created by the black nationalist Maulana Karenga during the 1960's, Kwanza centers on seven principles: unity, self-determination, collective work and responsibility, cooperative economics, purpose, creativity, and faith. Although Kwanza is celebrated from December 26 through January 1, it is not a substitute for Christmas, as many African Americans celebrate both holidays.

Modern African American Family Life. Although marriage is valued and desired among many modern African Americans, the increasing

Kwanzaa

Observing Kwanzaa has deep meaning for African Americans who participate in the celebration. The celebration centers on a *kinara*, or candleholder, with seven candles. One black candle symbolizes black people; three green candles represent hope and the abundant landscape of the African Motherland; three red candles symbolize the struggle and blood shed by black people. Each day for a week a candle is lighted and one of the seven principles of Kwanzaa is discussed. Other important elements of the celebration include *vibunzi* (ears of corn, each of which represents a child), *kikombe cha umoja* (the unity cup, symbolizing oneness), and *zawadi*, or gifts. On the sixth day a *karamu*, or feast, is held. Gifts are usually exchanged the following day.

divorce rate has forced many families to become single-parent units. As of 1990 the majority of African American families were single-parent families headed by women. African American families often face economic and racial barriers that constantly challenge the lifeblood of the family. The emotional support supplied by members of the family unit have given families strength and determination to overcome these disadvantages. African American families have taught their children to value themselves, thus increasing their self-worth to counteract the negative effects of racism, such as low self-esteem. The African American family passes on traditions and customs that are uniquely its own, traditions and customs handed down from one generation to the next that have preserved its culture and sustained African American family institutions.   —*Andrea E. Miller*

BIBLIOGRAPHY

Billingsley, Andrew. *Climbing Jacob's Ladder: The Enduring Legacy of African-American Families.* New York: Simon & Schuster, 1992.

Gutman, Herbert G. *The Black Family in Slavery and Freedom, 1750-1925.* New York: Pantheon Books, 1976.

Jones, Jacqueline. *Labor of Love, Labor of Sorrow: Black Women, Work, and Family from Slavery to the Present.* New York: Basic Books, 1985.

Logan, Sadye L., ed. *The Black Family: Strengths, Self-Help, and Positive Change.* Boulder, Colo.: Westview Press, 1996.

Willie, Charles Vert. *A New Look at Black Families.* 2d ed. New York: General Hall, 1981.

See also Family gatherings and reunions; Haley, Alex; Slavery.

Age of consent

RELEVANT ISSUES: Law; Marriage and dating; Violence

SIGNIFICANCE: The age of consent, the legal age at which persons may engage in sex of their own free will, has been upheld by family values advocates as protecting children and criticized by those who argue that it infringes on personal rights

The age of consent is defined traditionally as the age at which females agree of their own free will to engage in sexual intercourse (consensual sex). As established by state law, this age varies from fourteen to eighteen. (A digest of state laws, such as that found in the *Martindale-Hubbell Law Directory*, gives up-to-date statutes for each state.)

Statutory rape, commonly defined by law as sex with a minor female who is under the state-specified age of consent, is a serious crime in the United States and Canada. The concept has drawn sharp criticism from some highly vocal legal experts. Such critics believe that the concept of statutory rape has failed to keep pace with modern

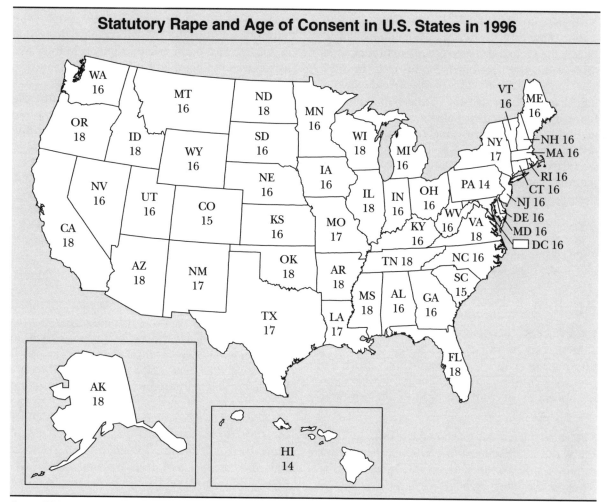

Statutory Rape and Age of Consent in U.S. States in 1996

Source: *USA Today* (Mar. 28, 1996)

Note: Sexual intercourse, even if consensual, is considered to be "statutory rape" when a female is below the age of consent. Age of consent varies among the states. Moreover, the severity of the crime is typically higher when it involves younger girls or older men.

sexual and social norms. They have raised the question of whether the concept of age of consent infringes on the right of young persons to make choices. Critics have also questioned whether individuals who have consensual sex with underage persons are necessarily guilty of committing a violent criminal act.

Statutory rape cases have often involved celebrities and well-known public figures. Film star Charlie Chaplin was found innocent of violating the Mann Act (transporting a minor across state lines for immoral purposes) but was ruled the father in a paternity suit brought against him by Joan Barry, an aspiring actress. In March, 1977, film director Roman Polanski was arrested by Los Angeles police on charges that he drugged and raped a thirteen-year-old model, ostensibly during a photo session. Free on bail after his arraignment, Polanski left the United States to complete filming on a project and did not return for his trial. In 1997 news media broke the story of a sex scandal involving Michael Kennedy, son of the late Robert F. Kennedy, and a teenage baby-sitter who cared for his children. A study involving underage girls who became pregnant by men at least five years their senior has again raised the issue of prosecution for statutory rape. The state of California began actively pursuing the prosecution of such cases.

—*Jo Manning*

See also Abortion; Children's rights; Civil marriage ceremonies; Cultural influences; Dating violence; Marriage laws; Sexuality and sexual taboos.

Ageism

RELEVANT ISSUES: Aging; Art and the Media; Economics and work

SIGNIFICANCE: Ageism, discrimination against the elderly, affects families in that it reduces the opportunity for older people to achieve their potential

The term "ageism" was coined in 1967 by Robert N. Butler, director of the National Institute on Aging. Unlike racism and sexism, ageism victimizes everyone who reaches normal life expectancy. Ageism refers to discrimination or unfair stereotyping based on age and directed at elderly or even middle-aged persons. It is widely known that people over the age of sixty face discrimination in health care, the workplace, and the media. Elder abuse may be the most extreme form of ageism.

Older persons are seen as less desirable workers than younger persons. While they may be fully capable of doing their jobs, employers often perceive them as no longer projecting a desirable image or may prefer to hire younger workers at lower wages or part-time employees. Those who have left the labor force, or are retired, are often seen as less valuable human beings. In American culture and in Western culture in general a person's identity is profoundly shaped by participation in the labor market. Such participation is often viewed as a prerequisite for social worthiness. To be too old to work or to have ceased working for a salary or a wage marks individuals as having less than full dignity. Many people who have retired from the labor force have decreased income or face other related changes in their material circumstances, and this reinforces the view that they have less value as human beings.

It should be noted that the beliefs that underlie ageism are often myths. Older people are often seen as frail or sickly, incapable of demanding work, lonely, and unhappy. In reality, many enjoy good health and are fully capable of the concentrated effort needed for most paid labor. Some research has shown that older people tend to be less lonely than middle-aged and young persons. Older people who live alone can be as satisfied with their quality of life as those who live with others.

One force that perpetuates ageism is the mass media. Television and newspapers depict old people as rigid, foolish, meddlesome, and sexless. Old people are often seen as living a second childhood and thus made to appear ridiculous. Advocates for the elderly believe that efforts are needed to change media representations of older people. It is possible that demographics may make ageism less of a problem when the baby-boom generation reaches retirement age.

Older women are especially victimized. Older men with gray hair are typically seen as worth more than older women. Women often dye their hair, use makeup, and dress to disguise their age. Many older women deplore the pressures that force them to attempt to present themselves as younger than they are and believe that advanced age should be accepted and respected.

—*Charlotte Templin*

Outraged by her forced retirement at age sixty-five, Maggie Kuhn and several friends founded the Gray Panthers in 1970 to lobby against age discrimination. (AP/Wide World Photos)

See also Aging and elderly care; Displaced homemakers; Elder abuse; Intergenerational income transfer; Life expectancy; Midlife crises.

Aging and elderly care

RELEVANT ISSUES: Aging; Health and medicine; Parenting and family relationships

SIGNIFICANCE: The graying of the world population, which has drastically altered society internationally, has added new dimensions to family life and particularly affected industrialized societies, in which both husbands and wives often work full time

The average life expectancy in pre-Christian Greece and Rome was between twenty and thirty years of age. Average life expectancy for males born in the United States in 1900 was just under forty-eight years and for females slightly under fifty-one years. By 1984, American males had an average life expectancy of about seventy-two years of age, while females were expected to live an average of nearly seventy-nine years. By the year 2050, average American life expectancy will exceed eighty years. Such an increase in the life spans of most people in industrialized societies has already had a profound effect on family life, particularly because in many families both partners must work outside the home when their aging parents are most likely to be in need of care and attention.

Aging Process in Humans. The aging process begins with conception and continues until death.

Scenes similar to that of this group of Tennessee farmers fit a traditional image of retired people as having little more to do than sit around and watch the world go by. (AP/Wide World Photos)

It is a natural process involving continual change, change that is so gradual that it is barely noticed.

As humans grow older, the aging process is accelerated by organic changes, illness, environmental exposure, lack of mental stimulation, and a feeling of uselessness that overtakes some retirees. The outward manifestations of aging differ greatly between individuals. As changes in circumstances occur, many people fill their lives with the sorts of physical, mental, and social activities that help them retain physical well-being and a youthful outlook. Their activity seems to be directly linked to making the aging process one in which they remain functioning members of their families and society.

Defining Old Age. The term "old age" is relative. Five-year-old children consider people in their twenties to be old. Active and optimistic seventy-year-olds might view the terms "old age" or "senior citizen" as an affront. Society as a whole thinks of old age as that period in which people cease to do productive work on a regular basis—that is, when they cease to hold regular, full-time jobs. In the United States, many people reach this point at the age of sixty-five, the age at which full Social Security benefits are payable. Given the financial pressures facing the United States, Canada, and other nations, however, the retirement age may soon push toward seventy. In the United States, Social Security recipients are financially penalized for earning more than a stipulated amount prior to the age of seventy-two, at which time they may earn as much as they can without penalty. In official terms, therefore, the onset of old age seems to fall somewhere between sixty-five and seventy-two. Whereas many organizations, including most public school systems, colleges, and universities, traditionally mandated that the retirement age fell between sixty-five and seventy, recent legislation has forbidden most organizations from setting such limits. However, they continue to exist for police officers, firefighters, and airline pilots, who often face compulsory retirement with full benefits at earlier ages.

The best definition of old age relates to how well people continue to function as they get older. With aging—a constant throughout life—physical, mental, and social changes take place. For many people, however, the ability to function physically, mentally, and socially continues well into the eighth decade of life or beyond. "Senescence" is the term used to describe the aging process that occurs among mature adults. "Senility," a term that medical and gerontological circles have ceased to employ, has conventionally been used to describe the state in which people's ability to function productively and to care for themselves has diminished to the point at which they require custodial care.

Providing this care usually places a considerable physical, financial, and emotional burden upon family members, who are necessarily forced into the roles of caregivers by being either directly involved in caring for the physical needs of older persons or indirectly involved by arranging for their care by outside agents or agencies. This generates pressures that can be particularly disruptive to traditional families in which both partners work.

Life Expectancy. Historically, families were often large in countries in which the birth rate was high. However, a large proportion of all infants died before their first birthdays, while many of those who survived beyond infancy did not live past the age of five. With the advent of better pre- and postnatal care, infant mortality has declined precipitously. In the United States, for example, while one hundred of every thousand infants born in 1915 died before their first birthdays, by 1991 this rate had fallen to 8.9 infant deaths per thousand. The statistics for Canada are similar. Obviously, this change in infant mortality has affected life expectancy.

At the same time, the average age of death in industrialized societies has increased dramatically, a change largely due to advances in medicine and pharmacology, the more widespread availability of medical care, growing environmental controls, and the increased accessibility of low-cost medical treatment through private insurance plans, Medicaid for the indigent, and Medicare for the elderly. By the late twentieth century the health-care net had encompassed much of the U.S. and Canadian populations, so that most families enjoyed cradle-to-grave, readily available medical care. However, millions of poor families in the United States still lacked any form of medical insurance.

Definitions of old age and statistics on life expectancy may change dramatically in the future. Plagues such as the Black Death in fourteenth

Increasing longevity has meant that many North Americans who see themselves as old are helping to care for their even older parents. (Dick Hemingway)

century Europe, the influenza epidemic of 1918, or the polio epidemics of the 1930's and 1940's—all of which wiped out or disabled enormous populations—can now be prevented through the intervention of modern drugs offered free of charge or at low cost by public-health agencies. Many forms of cancer, if detected early, have become curable, while AIDS has increasingly been treated as a chronic disease that, while still incurable, is almost as manageable as diabetes. By the late twentieth century both AIDS and diabetes had become, in most cases, controllable diseases and may, in the more distant future, be preventable and curable.

When Is a Person Old? It is not easy to determine when a person is old. Many wrinkled octogenarians have ideas and outlooks similar to those of young adults. Because they look old, they are considered old. Many physically and mentally active young people are socially withdrawn, but they are not defined as old people. The philosophical outlooks of large numbers of people under the age of forty are highly traditional and conservative, whereas their parents or grandparents may have the innovative, liberal philosophical and political outlooks often associated with young people.

The simplest way to determine who is old is by establishing chronological age. Such a facile determination, however, is generally misleading. It is necessary to remember that one might be old physically or socially and young mentally or that one might be mentally and socially old but still be young physically. Old age is probably most accurately determined by how well people function and how well they can control the physical, mental, and social aspects of their own lives. For most, old age has more to do with a person's outlook than with how long he or she has lived. People's outlooks can be altered by various forms of intervention, social and pharmaceutical. Isolated people in their seventies or eighties may lose both physical and mental functions simply because of their isolation. When they are able to share living arrangements with family and friends or even strangers, they may regain much of the physical and mental tone they lost because of their social isolation.

Intergenerational families embracing three or more generations are less common in modern Western societies than previously. Such families

are more prevalent in Asia and Africa than in Europe or North America. The older members of intergenerational families in societies where such families are commonplace often occupy positions of honor and respect that older people in Western societies seldom command. Whereas in most early and in many modern societies the care of the elderly within the family structure was naturally assumed, in modern Western cultures such care is more often institutional than familial.

Where and How the Elderly Live. In 1993, 74 percent of all older Americans lived in metropolitan areas, 30 percent directly in cities and 44 percent in the suburbs. Among older Americans between the ages of sixty-five and seventy-four, 1 percent lived in nursing homes, a rate that increased to 6 percent for those between the ages of seventy-five and eighty-four years and 24 percent for those eighty-five years and older. About 5 percent of adults over sixty-five change residences upon retirement. Affluent people often move to retirement havens in the Sunbelt after retiring. Half of the U.S. population over the age of sixty-five years has been concentrated in nine states: California, Florida, New York, Pennsylvania, Texas, Illinois, Ohio, Michigan, and New Jersey.

Many single elderly adults close to the poverty level reside in a shrinking pool of single-occupancy rooms in run-down hotels or motels. As these establishments have given way to urban development projects, many of their occupants have been forced into homelessness, because even their dependable, steady pensions are not sufficient to cover their rent. The United States has an estimated two million homeless people, 25 to 30 percent of whom are more than sixty-five years of age.

Among adults more than sixty-five years of age, some 75 percent live in homes they own. By the time they retire, 80 percent of these homeowners own their properties outright, making it possible for those who face financial difficulties in the later years of retirement either to sell and invest the proceeds or to take reverse mortgages that enable them to remain in their homes and receive regular incomes for life, provided that they make the issuers of their mortgages the beneficiaries of these properties.

About a third of older adults live alone in their own homes or condominiums. Many of those whose ability to function independently declines substantially with advancing age become members of shared housing arrangements, in which several older people live together or reside with family members in intergenerational settings. Sometimes intergenerational families add on to their homes, building so-called "mother-in-law" apartments that are attached to their own dwellings yet are separate, independent units.

About 25 percent of all older Americans rent. Their rentals are often substandard, badly heated units with structural defects. Rentals subsidized by the federal government are usually better maintained than dwellings offered privately, but too few federally subsidized dwellings exist to meet the actual needs of the elderly.

For the approximately 25 percent of older adults who live alone and require help in such routine activities as dressing, bathing, feeding themselves, or using the toilet, a variety of options exist so that they may remain relatively independent. These include nursing and other custodial services, homemaker services, meals on wheels, and various transportation programs that enable them to go shopping, keep medical appointments, and generally continue the activities that have become established parts of their lives. The cost of such services is usually geared to recipients' incomes and their ability to pay.

Retirement Communities. Retirement communities exist in a variety of forms, ranging from mobile home parks to residential hotels to plush gated communities, in which affluent retirees own homes that are usually equipped to accommodate wheelchairs and otherwise help those with handicaps. Such communities often require that residents pay substantial cash fees before moving in, many of which are nonrefundable. Monthly fees usually include some meals and often medical insurance. The best retirement communities guarantee continuing, lifelong custodial care to residents who become disabled, although such care has become increasingly less available as life expectancy and the costs of custodial care have increased.

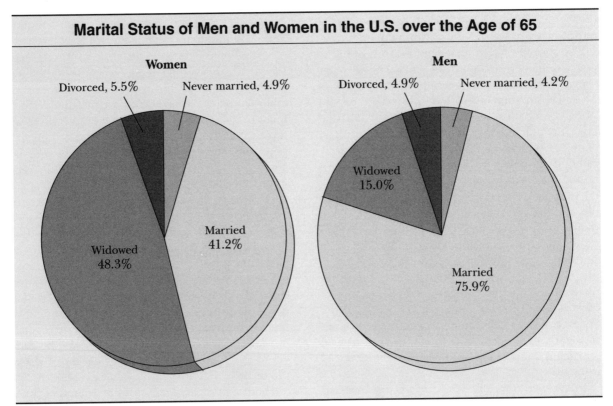

Source: Bureau of the Census (1992)
Note: Percentages are rounded to the nearest 0.1%.

Services such as Mobile Meals help many older persons to cope with their restricted mobility. (James L. Shaffer)

Because of the substantial social interaction in retirement communities, members usually remain active longer than those who have chosen to live on their own in typical neighborhoods. Planned activities encourage participation and help residents maintain their physical and mental resilience. The healthy diets and exercise opportunities that retirement communities offer improve the quality of life for residents and keep them functioning at high levels for considerable periods. The chief disadvantage of retirement communities is that they are segregated by age. No matter how luxurious these communities are, residents often complain that the constant interaction with those whose activities center on leisure rather than productive work offers them little stimulation.

Long-term Care. About 25 percent of all Americans more than eighty-five years of age live in group houses that provide room and board as well as the personal care and supervision that many older people require. Such accommodations are usually equipped to handle twenty-five or fewer residents. In 1990, about six million Americans required long-term care. This number is expected to reach nine million by 2005 and twelve million by 2020. Many of these people are or will be accommodated in group housing. Others live with their families, who place them in adult day-care facilities for the better part of the working week.

Although about 20 percent of all elderly Americans and Canadians will be confined to a nursing home at some point in their later lives, many others require secondary care offered by an intermediate-care facility, such as an adult day-care center. Elderly people not suffering from immediate medical problems requiring intense medical supervision or intervention are well served by intermediate-care facilities, where they receive assistance in grooming, eating, walking, and dressing.

Most Americans delay admission to nursing homes as long as possible. Some do so because of the high cost of nursing care, which can exceed three thousand dollars a month, while others do so because they are aware that a sense of hopelessness overtakes many nursing-home residents who feel that they have reached the end of the road and are merely awaiting death. Most long-term nursing-home patients are white, often childless women with chronic illnesses or mental disabilities such as Alzheimer's disease.

A Special Week for the Aging

Every year the National Institute on Adult Daycare sponsors national Adult Day Care Center Week in the third full week of September. The purpose of this annual event is to encourage people across the United States to recognize the contributions that the adult care programs make to society as a whole. Individual communities are encouraged to stage festivals, open houses, and other community events to call attention to the work of adult day care professionals.

Many elderly people find that their world shrinks drastically with advancing age. Whereas most of them move about freely in their sixties, those who have reached their eighties find it difficult to get around. The aches and pains that accompany old age make movement difficult and painful. The decrease in visual and auditory acuity makes driving inadvisable for large numbers. As a result, most retired people over the age of seventy-five spend 80 percent of their time at home, often alone and idle. Even those most socially inclined eventually have to acknowledge that they do not have the mobility to engage in the sorts of social interactions they once cherished. Their link with the outside world may be exclusively via television, although the Internet and other computer-related programs can bring the outside world into their homes.

Economics of Aging. In earlier Western societies and in many modern Third World cultures the physical and financial care of the elderly was the responsibility of the family. In cultures in which the extended family commonly exists, older members of the family remain in the intergenerational setting and are integrated into the life and economy of the family. In the industrialized world, however, government and private employers have devised means of providing dependable incomes to those who are no longer in the workforce. Typically, a specific retirement age is stipulated, although the disabled or the dependents of deceased wage-earners may qualify for benefits earlier.

The first government pension scheme was devised in Germany by Chancellor Otto von Bismarck in 1880 for purely political reasons. Because few Germans survived to the age of sixty-five, the age at which pensions became available, the initial cost of funding the program was small. By the 1920's, government-supported pension plans were in effect in Great Britain, the Scandinavian countries, Switzerland, the Netherlands, France, and Belgium.

The United States was slow to implement such plans, however, largely because of the nation's commitment to economic and political individualism and its reluctance to embrace intrusive government policies. The Great Depression of the 1930's changed the temper of the nation, however. In 1937 a social security system was instituted under which all employees were taxed 1 percent on their first three thousand dollars of income. In order to qualify for a pension, all employees, except those who had entered the new system immediately prior to retirement, were required to contribute to the program for at least forty quarters. The 1 percent tax continued until the early 1950's, when rates began to increase. Under great financial pressure, the compulsory contribution rates to Social Security by 1992 amounted to 15.3 percent each from employees and employers on all adjusted earnings up to $55,000.

Other pension plans exist for government employees, who draw benefits from the Civil Service Retirement system, for railroad employees, who draw benefits from the Railroad Retirement Program, and for veterans, who may qualify for the Veterans' Pension Program. Most of those who have worked in the United States for ten or more years derive benefits from one or more of these pension programs and may receive separate incomes from private pensions as well.

In 1993, 37 percent of all retirement incomes in the United States were derived from Social Security or other government-funded pension plans, while 18 percent were derived from private pensions. Another 25 percent were incomes from stocks, bonds, real estate, or other assets. An estimated 18 percent came from the earnings provided by post-retirement employment, and 3 percent came from other sources. In 1990 the mean amount drawn from the Social Security Old-Age and Survivors' Insurance Program, which was subject to annual cost-of-living increases, was $6,163 a year. Approximately 92 percent of older Americans received Social Security income. In 1992 the median annual income of families of two with a head of household sixty-five years of age or older was $25,315, while the median income for individuals sixty-five years of age or older was $10,624. Economically, older men have higher incomes than older women, whites have higher incomes than African Americans or Hispanics, and those with the most formal education have the highest retirement incomes. Among older people not living in families, 69 percent had annual incomes of $14,999 or less, while 20 percent of their counterparts who lived in families fell into this category. Of those who lived in families, 16 percent had annual incomes in excess of $50,000.

Typical American retirees suffer a decline in income upon retirement and experience a stagnation or decline in inflation-adjusted income throughout their retirement years, although incomes from Social Security and many private pension plans are indexed for inflation. In 1992 the median income in the United States of those more than sixty-five years of age was $14,548 for men and $8,189 for women, many of whom had worked considerably fewer years than men. Although the inflation-adjusted income of older Americans increased by 10 percent between 1982 and 1990, that increase disappeared after 1990. Most retirement incomes are about one-half that of preretirement incomes. Unless they have private assets, people are economically pinched during their retirement years, despite a decrease in many of their expenses.

Afterword. As the elderly population in industrialized nations expands, society faces many dilemmas relating to their care and the inroads that providing such care makes upon family structures. Fortunately, not many elderly Americans and Canadians will require total financial support from their families, although they may require supplemental support. Most people will need ungrudging spiritual support, but this may well be shortchanged in families working under the time pressures that typify American and Canadian family life. Various government agencies and such organizations as the American Association of Retired Persons (AARP) are seeking workable solutions to the problems of elder care that are bound to present themselves in the coming decades.

—R. Baird Shuman

BIBLIOGRAPHY

Aiken, Lewis R. *Aging: An Introduction to Gerontology.* Thousand Oaks, Calif.: Sage Publications, 1995. An exhaustive study containing the chapters "Economics and Aging" and "Living Arrangements and Activities," both of which have broad implications for the effects of elderly care on intergenerational families.

Beaver, Marion L., and Don A. Miller. *Clinical Social Work Practice with the Elderly: Primary, Secondary, and Tertiary.* Belmont, Calif.: Wadsworth, 1992. Provides a comprehensive overview of social services available to the elderly at all levels of need that is timely, and accurate.

Bengston, Vern L., K. Warner Schaie, and Linda M. Burton, eds. *Adult Intergenerational Relations: Effects of Societal Change.* New York: Springer, 1995. Focuses on how families are affected by having the responsibility of caring for the aged; includes an especially useful and insightful discussion on family finances,

Berger, Raymond M. *Gay and Gray: The Older Homosexual Man.* Urbana: University of Illinois, 1982. Presents case studies of a representative group of elderly homosexuals, some of whom are in or have been in committed relationships and some of whom have not. A landmark book in the field.

Binstock, Robert H., and Linda K. George, eds. *Handbook of Aging and the Social Sciences.* 3d ed. San Diego: Academic Press, 1990. Useful especially for its insights into the social supports available to the elderly and its chapter on families and aging.

Coni, Nicholas. *Aging: The Facts.* New York: Oxford University Press, 1992. Presents the physiological and social consequences of aging, relating this effectively to the pressures felt in families responsible for caring for and, in some cases, providing for the elderly.

Crewes, Douglas E., and Ralph M. Garruto, eds. *Biological Anthropology and Aging: Perspectives on Human Variation over the Life Span.* New York: Oxford University Press, 1994. Presents contrasting views on how various societies deal with the aging process and how they care for their elderly, establishing a valuable historical perspective.

McQuire, Francis A. *Leisure and Aging: Ulyssean Living in Later Life.* Champaign, Ill.: Sagamore, 1996. Emphasizes the healthy aspects of life after retirement, focusing upon the role travel plays in keeping older people viable. An upbeat book offering a how-to approach to making the later years of life fruitful.

Medina, John J. *The Clock of Ages: Why We Age, How We Age, Winding Back the Clock.* New York: Cambridge University Press, 1996. Addresses the physiological and genetic aspects of aging and offers information about impeding the process. A cogent presentation for those interested in taking preventive measures that will retard the aging process.

Nichols, Barbara, and Peter Leonard, eds. *Gender, Aging and the State.* New York: Black Rose Books, 1994. Essentially considers disparities in the treatment of elderly men and women in need of assistance and carefully presents and assesses the role of government in providing assistance. Presents a particularly revealing and cogent discussion from a feminist perspective on the dependency relationship between mothers and daughters.

See also Ageism; Alternative family types; Alzheimer's disease; Elder abuse; Extended families; Family caregiving; Father figures; Living wills; Older Americans Act (OAA); Persons of opposite sex sharing living quarters (POSSLQ); Retirement; Retirement communities; Senior citizen centers; Social Security; Substitute caregivers.

Aid to Families with Dependent Children (AFDC)

RELEVANT ISSUES: Economics and work; Law; Parenting and family relationships

SIGNIFICANCE: Aid to Families with Dependent Children is a government-sponsored public assistance program providing minimum income support to impoverished families, especially women and their children

Originally titled Aid to Dependent Children (ADC), Aid to Families with Dependent Children (AFDC) was established in 1935 as one provision of the Social Security Act, a key piece of legislation during the New Deal era. The purpose of AFDC is to provide cash public assistance to needy families with children. It is a combined federal and state-administered program, with states defining the definition of "need" and the level of payments.

In 1993 approximately 5,050,000 families, or 9,598,000 children and 4,659,000 adults, received AFDC payments. The typical AFDC family included a mother and one child who remained on welfare for less than two years. The average monthly payment per family was $377, with payments varying greatly from state to state. In 1993 New England and some West Coast states granted the highest average benefits of more than $500 per month, while the eastern and western South Central states granted the lowest, with family benefits averaging slightly more than $160 per month. The state with the highest average monthly benefits was Alaska ($748), and the state with the lowest was Mississippi ($120).

States must comply with federal guidelines in order to qualify for financial grants. However, states are free to decide whom they will assist, how much assistance they will grant, and how assistance will be administered. In all states, adult recipients must register for employment and training. Each state also computes a "needs standard," which takes into account the cost of food, shelter, utilities, clothing, health care, and other necessities. If families' needs exceed their income and assets, they may qualify for the program, but the federal government does not require that states provide the full amount of the difference between needs and income if they choose not to do so.

In many states, the standard of need is set below the official poverty level. This means that thousands of poor families are ineligible for benefits. In addition to financial need, for families to be eligible children generally must be under the age of eighteen. Eligible families are usually headed by single mothers, but in some states the AFDC-UP program provides coverage for dual-parent families with unemployed fathers.

History. As a minimum income support system, ADC was modeled after Mother's Aid legislation passed by many states in the early 1900's, which established widow's pensions. These entitlements were designed to help working-class widows keep their children out of orphanages. When ADC was created in 1935 Congress's intention was to cushion poverty and to enable mothers to stay home with their children. Early relief was based on the assumption that only certain categories of people

qualified. Those who did qualify were closely monitored in terms of need, resources, and sexual behavior. Unwed mothers were denied assistance.

The 1930's program was established in the face of great opposition from conservative business and government officials throughout the United States, who argued that government intervention on behalf of the poor would undermine their desire to work. Southern legislators also felt that generous assistance would erode the low-wage structure of employment. They were particularly opposed to ADC and other programs that provided aid for the poor. Fearing that federal officials would be more sympathetic, especially to impoverished African Americans, they fought to ensure local control over the administration of ADC.

Despite fierce opposition, ADC provided cash to assist children who had been left without a parent because of disability, death, or continued absence. Because ADC was administered at the state and local levels, there were vast differences in payment levels. Regional differences in ideologies concerning the poor as well as differences in local economies resulted in unequal entitlements. For example, in 1939 Arkansas provided an average of $8.10 monthly while Massachusetts provided $61.07.

For fifteen years ADC provided funds for dependent children only. It contained "man in the house" rules, which mitigated against benefits when a male resided in the household and discriminated against African American mothers and against unmarried women, who were thought unsuitable. In some states recipients were also expected to work low-wage jobs in return for their benefits. In 1950, when the program was renamed AFDC, Congress passed a provision that included a caretaker grant to help pay for mothers' essential expenses. In 1964 the administration of President Lyndon B. Johnson launched the War on Poverty, increasing federal matching funds so that state and county welfare departments could accept more applicants. Throughout the late 1960's, as pressure from the National Welfare Rights Organization and the Civil Rights movement mounted, the Supreme Court continued to remove barriers to eligibility. Relief was expanded, and reform permitted states to extend aid to families with an unemployed father at home.

Welfare Reform. Despite expansion during the 1960's, politicians continued to fuel anti-welfare

Aid to Families with Dependent Children has been especially important to single parents. (Mary LaSalle)

sentiment. By the 1980's the "privatization" initiatives of the administration of President Ronald Reagan reduced services in the public sector, resulting in a dramatic decrease in the number of poor families receiving aid. During the administration of President Bill Clinton, the Personal Responsibility and Work Opportunity Reconciliation Act of 1996 marked a commitment by the federal government to cut funding for AFDC further. This act was comparable to earlier battles over welfare control that pitted states against the federal government. With this act, states have more individual control over the nation's neediest citizens. With grants from the federal government, states will run their own welfare programs. To qualify for money, all states must comply with certain broad provisions, including a lifetime family benefit limit of five years. After receiving aid, recipients must also find work within two years. Other provisions include cuts in food stamps and aid to immigrants and disabled children.

The Personal Responsibility and Work Opportunity Reconciliation Act replaced AFDC with a program known as Temporary Assistance for Needy Families (TANF). This act represented a clear break with the New Deal policies begun in the 1930's. It was based on the assumption that the poor remain poor because they lack motivation to succeed and that government assistance encourages an unproductive life. It was argued that if aid is denied, poverty will be made more brutal and people will no longer choose to remain on welfare because they will have to work.

During the last two decades of the twentieth century, few people denied that the AFDC system needed to be moved forward and improved. As in earlier times, however, analysts disagreed about how to accomplish this. While some advocated minor changes, others sought to change the system completely or to abolish aid altogether. The 1990's initiatives were criticized for failing to address the root causes of poverty in the United States, for ignoring the work done by welfare mothers in the home, and for failing to acknowledge that half of all single mothers who spend any time on AFDC are also employed during that period.

Some of the major barriers to economic advancement faced by AFDC recipients include a low-wage labor market that leaves poor people permanently on the brink of crisis, difficulties in financing transportation and child care, infrequent access to health care on the job, limited educational and work skills, and, for approximately 8 percent of recipients, severe disabilities.

Effects on Families. Many myths exist surrounding the impact of AFDC on families, including the belief that welfare causes an increase in out-of-wedlock births and fuels high divorce rates, particularly in African American families. Research during the 1980's found no significant relationship between the percentage of children in single-parent households and the level of AFDC benefits. The birthrate among women receiving this aid is lower than that of the rest of the population. Divorce rates also fluctuate independently of family assistance benefits. For example, during the period between 1925 and 1960 divorce increased despite the fact that significant welfare benefits were not yet available.

Research does suggest that AFDC reduces the likelihood that an unmarried pregnant woman will obtain an abortion or marry in haste. Mothers who receive benefits also remarry less rapidly after a divorce. In the past AFDC has also allowed single mothers to establish their own households independently of their parents or kin, who have often been poor themselves. —*Eleanor A. LaPointe*

BIBLIOGRAPHY
Abramovitz, Mimi. *Regulating the Lives of Women: Social Welfare Policy from Colonial Times to the Present.* Boston: South End Press, 1988.
Cozic, Charles P., and Paul A. Winters, eds. *Welfare: Opposing Viewpoints.* San Diego: Greenhaven Press, 1997.
Gordon, Linda. *Pitied but Not Entitled: Single Mothers and the History of Welfare.* New York: Free Press, 1994.
Quadagno, Jill S. *The Color of Welfare: How Racism Undermined the War on Poverty.* New York: Oxford University Press, 1994.
Rank, Mark Robert. *Living on the Edge: The Realities of Welfare in America.* New York: Columbia University Press, 1994.
Sidel, Ruth. *Women and Children Last: The Plight of Poor Women in Affluent America.* New York: Penguin, 1992.
Teghtsoonian, Katherine. "Promises, Promises: 'Choices for Women' in Canadian and Ameri-

can Child Care Policy Debates." *Feminist Studies* 22 (Spring, 1996).

See also Family economics; Family Protection Act; Personal Responsibility and Work Opportunity Reconciliation Act; Poverty; Social Security; Welfare; Work.

Al-Anon

DATE: Founded in 1951, as Al-Anon Family Groups

RELEVANT ISSUES: Health and medicine; Parenting and family relationships

SIGNIFICANCE: An offshoot of Alcoholics Anonymous (AA) and closely allied to the twelve-step self-help approaches of AA, Al-Anon has contributed to ongoing family wellness since its inception in 1951

Created for the well-being of spouses of alcoholics, Al-Anon originally encouraged and safeguarded the sobriety of alcoholic members of families. Over a period of time it has become much more directly a gathering place for the significant others of alcoholics and other drug-dependent persons seeking to get on with their own growth and recover from the primary relational problem called codependency. Codependency, the altered behavior of persons with chemically dependent and troubled relatives, is characterized primarily by persons' excessive focus on others' needs and neglect of themselves. This self-help program provides group sharing and support at the same time that it provides factual information about chemical substances and family relational issues; education on the dynamics of drug, alcohol, and process addictions; and insights encouraging behavior changes.

Al-Anon, like Alcoholics Anonymous (AA), affects the total family constellation in that behavior change in individuals "around the table" influences the health of the larger family system. Just as the members of Alcoholics Anonymous share experience, faith, hope, and data, so also do the members of Al-Anon. The common support, insight, and shared practice of those gathered in meetings around discussion tables accentuates and accelerates behavior change and personal growth. Those with problems find support in others who understand their experience. They derive insight into working through their problems as they participate in a group com-

First published in 1965, Al-Anon Faces Alcoholism *reflects the organization of Al-Anon itself by presenting first-hand accounts of both professionals in the treatment of alcoholism and Al-Anon members.* (Arkent Archive)

mitment to recovery from the upset, pain, and dysfunction of relational codependency. The social engagement provided by Al-Anon is particularly helpful in dealing with the isolation that can come from the secret-keeping and the emotional upset affecting families dealing with alcoholism. Feelings of guilt and embarrassment, as well as difficulty in seeing the effects of alcoholism, find healing as significant others of alcoholics and other drug-dependent persons experience the reality that they are not alone in their concerns.

Participants in Al-Anon do not attend meetings to discuss or complain about the problems and dynamics of the alcoholic persons they love. Rather, they go to learn about themselves, their needs, their responses, and their own ties to affected persons and other family members. They continue to tend to their own personal growth and wellness, becoming more aware of the fact that the addiction of one family member affects all family members. Since the disease of alcoholism has affective, relational, and behavioral components, the total family has a greater opportunity for family health as Al-Anon members tend to their own affective, relational, and behavioral problems. Al-Anon influences family health in a number of ways, including, but not limited to, indirect changes in the family system, growing respect for the differences in family members, continuing support for and encouragement of honest communication, increase in personal flexibility, and development of wider varieties of problem-solving approaches. —*Frances R. Belmonte*

See also Alateen; Alcoholism and drug abuse; Codependency; Couples; Health problems; Mothers Against Drunk Driving (MADD); Recovery programs; Support groups; Wilson, William G.

Alateen

DATE: Founded in 1957
RELEVANT ISSUES: Children and child development; Health and medicine; Parenting and family relationships
SIGNIFICANCE: Alateen is a self-help, peer support group that provides teenage children of alcoholics with a reservoir of experience at a particularly important time in the growing process and in family life

The Alateen program helps teenagers to make cognitive sense of the emotions experienced in relating to alcoholic parents. The sharing, insight, and support received from others of their own age with similar experiences enables teenagers to negotiate more easily the ordinary transitions of the teenage years that become more difficult in the face of alcoholism. As in Al-Anon, the primary issue of codependency is discussed in the Alateen setting, but it is done so specifically from the teenage point of view and from the standpoint of the problems and concerns shared by adolescents.

Alateen provides some preventive effect while allowing teenagers to deal with family relationships. It accomplishes this by helping persons to discover ways to relate honestly and respectfully both to themselves and to others. Thus, Alateen can help establish patterns of healthier family interaction. Whether or not alcoholic parents receive help or are in recovery mode, adolescents have opportunities to benefit from self-help groups such as Alateen. By sharing insights, support, and information, teenagers break the unwritten code of isolation that tends to develop in families dealing with alcohol or other types of drug dependencies. Some have called this code "Don't trust, don't talk, don't feel." Teenagers who share their experiences around Alateen discussion tables learn to see what they see and say what they say so that they can break through the denial that sustains dysfunction in the alcohol- or drug-dependent family. In the company of other teenagers they learn to trust, talk, and feel so that they can come to terms with their experiences and their situation.

Children of alcoholics, who are four times more likely than others to become alcoholics themselves, can receive another form of preventive help in Alateen. Since alcohol is the most widely used drug in the United States across all grade levels, the factual information teenagers are likely to receive in Alateen as well as the ideas on emotional and family dynamics they share in peer groups helps not only in terms of family risk but also in terms of societal exposure to alcohol. Alateen teaches that children are not the cause of their parents' drinking, that they can deal with feelings of secrecy and embarrassment, that they can risk close relationships despite being disappointed by the untrustworthy behavior of alcoholic parents, that a daily schedule and a sense of knowing what to expect can help in dealing with the confusion generated by the inconsistency and mood and behavior changes of alcoholic parents, and that they can ask for help in their peer support groups. —*Frances R. Belmonte*

See also Al-Anon; Alcoholism and drug abuse; Codependency; Family therapy; Health problems; Puberty and adolescence; Recovery programs; Support groups.

Alcoholism and drug abuse

RELEVANT ISSUES: Children and child development; Health and medicine; Parenting and family relationships; Violence

SIGNIFICANCE: Alcohol and drug problems affect 60 percent of American families physically, mentally, emotionally, socially, and financially

Alcohol and drug abuse occur when individuals continue to use substances despite the significant social, work-related, family, emotional, mental, or health problems that arise. Individuals may develop tolerance to such substances, so that they require ever larger amounts to achieve the same effects. They may also experience withdrawal symptoms when they stop using drugs or cut down on their use. Such problems result from using cigarettes, beer, wine, distilled liquor, marijuana, caffeinated beverages, inhalants (such as glue), stimulants (such as cocaine, crack, or amphetamines), hallucinogens, opiates (such as heroin), and prescription drugs (such as Valium). Once drug problems develop, users may have difficulty stopping because they experience relapse or a return to their habitual drug use.

Genetics and Environment. Alcohol and drug abuse develop in many different ways. For some individuals, substance abuse can develop solely from habitual use. Addiction develops as a result of repeated use. These persons develop problems solely because of the drug's addictive effect. Typically, such persons have no living or deceased relatives with a history of substance abuse.

For others, however, substance abuse can develop as a result of the combined effects of habit and genetic background. Such persons usually report having several generations of family members (such as grandfathers, uncles, and brothers) with histories of substance abuse. Evidence suggests that such persons are more gratified by the substances they use than individuals lacking a similar genetic predisposition. For the most part, the genetic predisposition for substance abuse is stronger in men than in women. It also seems to be more pronounced in persons who develop problems earlier in life than in those who develop them later. Evidence has suggested that women with family members who have experienced problems such as depression and substance abuse may have a genetic predisposition toward substance abuse.

It is difficult to determine exactly the effects of growing up with family

U.S. Public Perceptions of Alcohol Abuse as a National Problem

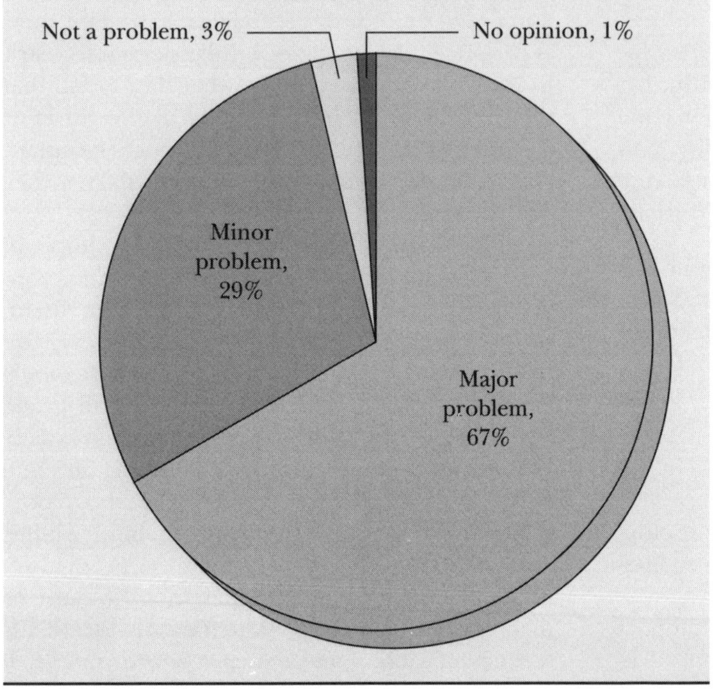

Not a problem, 3%

No opinion, 1%

Minor problem, 29%

Major problem, 67%

Source: CNN/*USA Today*/Gallup Poll
Note: In a 1994 poll Americans were asked how big a national problem alcohol abuse is.

members affected by substance abuse, although it is clear that it significantly affects a person's ability to function. Parents suffering from substance abuse may use parenting techniques that predispose their children to become future substance abusers. Also, they may fail to use parenting techniques that might help to prevent their children from using drugs. Thus, it is difficult to distinguish between the effects of genetics and the effects of living with substance-abusing family members. Parents' attitudes about alcohol and drug use can also affect their children's future. Parental attitudes have effects over and above genetics and parenting practices. If parents generally accept alcohol and drug use, their children will be likely to adopt the same attitude.

Another factor influencing drug and alcohol use is accessibility. Most people are first introduced to drugs or alcohol by family members. Children from families that do not use substances openly or frequently will have less access to them. The less accessible substances are, the less they will be used. Drug use or its advocacy by older siblings affects younger siblings' attitudes toward alcohol and drug use and may directly contribute to the latter's future substance abuse. Thus, while children may be genetically predisposed to use alcohol and drugs, other equally important factors include parenting practices, access to substances, and parental and sibling attitudes toward their use.

Related Problems. Dual diagnosis is another important situation that affects families where drug and alcohol abuse is present. Dual diagnosis means that individuals have two major mental-health problems: a substance-abuse problem and another disorder. In fact, approximately 50 percent of those diagnosed as substance dependent in the United States also have other significant mental disorders. Any single mental-health disorder can profoundly affect a family's functioning. Additional disorders can make matters even worse.

Contrasting Opinions of Parents and Teenagers Regarding Illegal Drugs

62% of parents claim their children are comfortable discussing drugs with them.

45% of teenagers feel the same way.

52% of parents regard drugs as a serious problem in the schools.

34% of teenagers agree.

85% of parents claim to have had serious talks with their children about drugs.

45% of teenagers recall such talks.

Source: USA Today (March 3, 1997)
Note: In 1997 a nationwide survey was made among more than 1,100 randomly selected teenagers and randomly selected parents. This chart summarizes some of their responses on questions relating to illegal drugs.

Problems commonly associated with substance abuse include mood disorders such as bipolar disorder, depression, and anxiety; eating disorders such as bulimia nervosa and anorexia nervosa; thinking and perception disorders such as schizophrenia; trauma disorders such as post-traumatic stress disorder; and sexual disorders. Divorce, sexual abuse, physical and emotional abuse, domestic violence, adultery, juvenile delinquency, crime, and suicide are also often found in families afflicted by substance abuse.

Persons who use drugs or alcohol are at increased risk of contracting many health problems, such as heart, liver, and gastrointestinal disorders. HIV and AIDS may also profoundly affect families in which members have engaged in high-risk behavior, such as unprotected sex or sharing hypodermic needles. Finally, substance abusers may indirectly affect the health of other family members, such as their children, who may suffer from the

Often the main victims of a family member's drinking problem are the other members of the family itself. (James L. Shaffer)

effects of crack cocaine, HIV and AIDS, or fetal alcohol syndrome.

Effects on Families. The physical, emotional, and financial costs of alcohol and drug abuse significantly affect users and their families. Families with members suffering from substance abuse feel isolated socially and emotionally, tense, dependent, unable to express their emotions constructively, out of control, ashamed, and guilty. Moreover, fear and embarrassment may prevent effective problem solving, making it difficult for such families to achieve positive change without outside help.

Persons whose partners are substance abusers may be afflicted by stress. Not uncommonly, they suffer from depression, anxiety, and other stress-related disorders. The threat of divorce, domestic violence, financial insecurity, and lack of safety within the home are problems facing families afflicted by substance abuse. Extended family members may suffer similar problems, as they may feel powerless to help their loved ones. If both adult members of a family are substance abusers, extended family members may be doubly distressed at the helplessness of their relatives and any children the affected couple may have. Unfortunately, extended family members may side with one partner over another in an effort to help and may inadvertently complicate an already difficult situation.

Children in substance-abuse families are in a particularly difficult position. They may come to feel responsible for their families' problems or their inability to solve them. They may suffer from neglect, domestic violence, or emotional, physical, or sexual abuse. They may experience want, as money is spent on alcohol or drugs instead of essentials. Additionally, they may be alone in coping with the everyday tasks of growing up, lacking help, comfort, safety, guidance, fun, and companionship. While they may turn to older siblings, peers, extended family members, teachers, and members of the clergy for help, their families often seek to hide their problems. Seeking help outside the family may be foreign to many, leaving children isolated.

Prevention and Treatment. Primary, secondary, and tertiary prevention are the three basic methods of tackling substance abuse. Primary prevention includes interventions or treatments that affect the whole population. Examples include community efforts to stop drug experimentation by airing advertisements on television that describe the negative effects of drug use (such as smoking cigarettes or using marijuana) and a school system's efforts to increase knowledge about alcohol and drugs, while encouraging discussion about these issues with family members. In both cases, the intended targets of intervention are those who are not yet involved in substance abuse and all members of the community. Primary prevention is typically directed at young people, because most people do not start using "harder" drugs (such as heroin, amphetamines, and cocaine) until they have experimented with more commonly used drugs such as alcohol, tobacco, and marijuana. Since nearly half of all junior-high-school students and nearly 80 percent of those who have reached the age of sixteen have reported experimenting with at least one type of drug—such as alcohol, inhalants, tobacco, or marijuana—early intervention is important.

In contrast, secondary prevention refers to programs for persons at risk of developing significant substance-abuse problems. One form of secondary prevention involves programs for persons convicted of driving under the influence of alcohol or drugs, which seek to prevent offenders from doing so in the future by educating them about the costs and consequences of drunk driving. Another form of secondary prevention involves community centers that provide disadvantaged and endangered teenagers (those suffering from stress, poverty, easy access to drugs and alcohol, and juvenile delinquency) with such services as club activities and midnight basketball. Such programs, by providing alternatives to substance abusers, seek to give young people the types of emotional and social support that impede problem development.

Tertiary intervention refers to treatment services for individuals who already have significant problems with substance abuse and dependence. Typically such treatment is administered because these persons are likely to suffer greater harm if their behavior does not change. Tertiary intervention usually takes the form of detoxification and inpatient or outpatient treatment in hospitals under the care of health providers. Such programs seek to convince substance abusers to abstain from drugs and alcohol, while encouraging them to attend support groups such as Alcoholics Anonymous (AA) and Narcotics Anonymous.

Community support groups may also assist parents, children, and other family members seeking support or information about substance abuse. Children with affected parents can turn to such groups as Alateen or Ala-Tot, while adult children can seek advice from such groups as Adult Children of Alcoholics. Similarly, partners of substance abusers can receive help from such groups as Al-Anon. Groups such as Codependents Anonymous may help persons dealing with other codependency issues. When there is a dual-diagnosis situation, support groups such as the National Alliance for the Mentally Ill (NAMI) may also be an important resource.

Family and Community Involvement. The most important element in combating alcohol and drug abuse in the family is communication. Parents should openly share knowledge, concern, and experience with their children in a thoughtful manner; family members should talk with one another about their problems; public health officials should suggest strategies for action; and individuals should seek out support groups and recovery programs. Communication is valuable to children, who must learn to set limits and distinguish healthy from unhealthy behavior. Although some parents, because of their own experiences, may feel hypocritical and hesitant about speaking to their children, it is important to communicate about substance abuse and related problems. While providing children with accurate information on the benefits and risks involved, such communication also provides opportunities for

Once popular among young people, drinking parties have come increasingly under attack, and even the manufacturers of alcoholic beverages have worked to urge young people to moderate their drinking habits. (James L. Shaffer)

clarifying children's thoughts and values about substance abuse, opening the door to their questions about drugs, alcohol, and experimentation. Communication is critical so that children will feel comfortable about turning to their parents if problems should develop.

—*Nancy A. Piotrowski*

BIBLIOGRAPHY

Black, Claudia. *It Will Never Happen to Me.* Denver: M.A.C. Printing and Publications Division, 1982. Discusses issues facing adults who grow up as children of alcoholics.

Center for Substance Abuse Prevention. *Keeping Youth Drug Free: A Guide for Parents, Grandparents, Elders, Mentors, and Other Caregivers.* Washington, D.C.: National Clearinghouse on Alcohol and Drug Information, U.S. Department of Health and Human Services, 1996. Written for parents with children between nine and thirteen years of age, addresses the reasons why children use drugs and alcohol.

Deutsch, Charles. *Broken Bottles, Broken Dreams: Understanding and Helping the Children of Alcoholics.* New York: Teacher's College Press, 1982. Describes typical problems that arise in families with problem drinkers and approaches to family and individual treatment.

Schuckit, Marc Alan. *Educating Yourself About Alcohol and Drugs: A People's Primer.* New York: Plenum Press, 1995. Summarizes facts on drugs and alcohol as well as information on finding help and treatment.

Stoll, Michael J., and Gary Hill. *Preventing Substance Abuse: Interventions That Work.* New York: Plenum Press, 1996. Summarizes approaches to substance-abuse prevention in the United States and describes programs for many different groups of people.

Wallace, Barbara C. *Adult Children of Dysfunctional Families: Prevention, Intervention, and Treatment for Community Mental Health Promotion.* Westport, Conn.: Praeger, 1996. Compares functional and dysfunctional families in respect to substance abuse, neglect, violence, trauma, and AIDS.

See also Al-Anon; Alateen; Child abuse; Codependency; Domestic violence; Eating disorders; Emotional abuse; Mental health; Mothers Against Drunk Driving (MADD); Recovery programs.

Alimony

RELEVANT ISSUES: Divorce; Law
SIGNIFICANCE: The theory and practice of spousal support have changed in the United States as the cultural and socioeconomic facts of American family life have changed

Alimony, more often referred to as spousal support or maintenance, is payments that a court orders one divorcing spouse to make to the other. It is awarded to the partner who has been economically dependent and whose lifestyle is expected to suffer as a result of divorce. Its purpose is to make divorce as fair as possible to both husband and wife by taking into account the social and economic realities of the marriage. Although any spouse may be awarded alimony, most recipients are women more than forty years of age who no longer live with their children.

Alimony can be temporary or permanent. It can be paid in one lump sum, as part of a property settlement, or in installments. Courts sometimes award temporary alimony payments to allow divorced persons to obtain vocational training so that they can become economically self-sufficient. Alimony may also be granted to spouses who have invested time and energy in enhancing the partner's career—by putting the former spouse through a professional school, for example. Permanent alimony recognizes the reality that some spouses, notably "displaced homemakers," may never recapture their previous standard of living.

Criteria for awarding alimony are whatever a court considers just and reasonable. Unless a court is limited by an enforceable prenuptial agreement, it typically takes into account one partner's ability to pay and the other's foreseeable needs. Estimates of the latter are based on a family's prior standard of living, the couple's property settlement, each spouse's ability to work, their ages, and their health. A court may also take into account the duration of the marriage and the past conduct of each partner. No-fault divorce, whereby courts do not seek to determine which partner is responsible for the marital breakup, became common throughout the United States in the early 1970's. Nevertheless, in awarding property settlements and alimony, courts have continued to consider who the perpetrators and the victims are.

Courts are often asked to punish whoever appears to be the offending party and to compensate the other.

Who Gets Alimony. During the 1990's the portion of divorce settlements in which alimony was awarded ranged from 14 to 16 percent. One reason for this low figure is that most divorces take place relatively early in marriage, when couples are young. Since the primary breadwinner's earnings in such marriages are still relatively low, the partner's earning potential is not much different. Moreover, property settlements have assumed a more pivotal role in divorces, and child-support allotments have become more important to custodial parents. The courts, in maintaining fairness, have also shifted their philosophy about the role of spousal support. In an age in which both spouses typically work outside the home, the courts have shifted to assessing spouses' ability to be self-sufficient rather than their previous standard of living. Finally, when economically dependent spouses are considered to be at fault in a divorce—such as in the case of adultery—they may be forced to forfeit alimony.

Amount and Period of Payments. After a court makes its ruling, neither the amount of alimony it awards nor the time frame is unchangeable. The circumstances for modifying the conditions of alimony vary from state to state, depending on state laws and previous judicial decisions. Generally, courts can modify alimony awards if either divorced party can demonstrate that circumstances—for example, the payer or payee's financial situation—have changed sufficiently. An alimony obligation might not end with a payee's death; it might be paid out of a payee's estate. Although a court often terminates alimony when a recipient remarries, unmarried cohabitation is not treated the same way. The cohabitation must be shown to improve a former spouse's financial position.

It is often difficult to collect alimony from a former spouse who leaves the state in which both resided. States have statutes and precedents addressing such matters. Moreover, in 1992 the National Conference of Commissioners on Uniform State Laws substantially revised the Uniform Reciprocal Enforcement of Support Act. However, by 1997 only half of the states had adopted this model legislation.

Determination of Fairness. Spousal support should be viewed in the cultural and socioeconomic context of divorce. The fact is that divorced women generally suffer economically. On average, former husbands' standard of living rises 42 percent one year after divorce, while that of former wives declines by 73 percent.

Marriage is an investment of time and commitment. Both partners contribute individual competencies, skills, and assets that may differ partly because of gender. Feminists have argued that an equitable alimony award should recognize a woman's sacrifices in favor of "their" marriage and "his" career. Women with some college education tend to lose 7 percent of their earning power for each year they are out of the workplace, while their families become increasingly dependent on the husbands' earning power.

The typical alimony recipients are white women more than forty years of age who live alone. The circumstances and needs of these middle-aged women, who unexpectedly find themselves on their own, must be fully recognized, appreciated, and addressed. Divorce carries serious financial implications for older persons. Most divorcees are not eligible for Aid to Families with Dependent Children and too young for Social Security and other benefits for older persons. Nevertheless, society and its courts have come to view wives as persons who should be or should have the resources to become self-sufficient. Emphasis in alimony awards has shifted away from maintaining economic balance between former spouses and upholding a predivorce standard of living. Many judges no longer think of marriage in terms of the mutual contributions of husband and wife to a joint endeavor. Society has increasingly perceived women as separate from their husbands, expecting them to be economically productive in pursuit of their own businesses and careers. Divorced women are thus expected to become economically independent and have the ability to care for themselves after a sufficient length of time. In reality, however, divorced women's economic decline along with the increase in female-headed, single-parent households, has led to what sociologists and economists describe as the "feminization of poverty."

New Directions in Alimony. The social purposes of alimony have changed. Originally, alimony offered well-to-do husbands the freedom to live apart from their wives without losing control over their former spouses' property and behavior. It also has been used as a bargaining chip by spouses with the greatest or least desire to terminate their marriages. Alimony has often been punitive in nature; often men have been forced to pay it if they are judged to be responsible for the breakup of their marriages and women denied it if they are deemed responsible. Nevertheless, the ideal role of alimony is to compensate spouses for their human investments in relationships and to provide for the postdivorce economic well-being of the parties most in need. To some extent, the advent of no-fault divorce has rendered earlier roles of alimony obsolete. At the same time, the number of "traditional" American families—with breadwinner husbands and homemaker wives—has fallen to about 12 percent of all marriages, while divorce rates have continued to rise and gender-role distinctions have continued to blur. The rules guiding men and women as they marry, raise families, and participate in the workforce have become increasingly unclear.

Alimony may be falling into public disfavor because of the more widely accepted assumption of equality between women and men. However, the assumption of economic equality is not accurate. Alimony is thus a concept that needs to be reviewed and renewed based on the economic and cultural facts of modern American life. Spousal support will continue to be necessary until household work and family caregiving are shared equitably, until employment opportunities and average wages are equal, and until the different needs of an aging population are adequately addressed.

—*Robert E. Lee*

BIBLIOGRAPHY
Ahlberg, Dennis A., and Carol J. DeVita. *New Realities of the American Family.* Washington, D.C.: Population Reference Bureau, 1992.
Emery, Robert E. *Renegotiating Family Relationships: Divorce, Child Custody, and Mediation.* New York: Guilford Press, 1994.
Harwood, Norma. *A Woman's Legal Guide to Separation and Divorce in All Fifty States.* New York: Scribner, 1985.
Hochschild, Arlie. *The Second Shift.* New York: Avon, 1989.
Minton, Michael H., and Jean L. Block. *What Is a Wife Worth?* New York: McGraw-Hill, 1984.
Weitzman, Lenore J. *The Divorce Revolution: The Unexpected Social and Economic Consequences for Women and Children in America.* New York: Free Press, 1985.

See also Aid to Families with Dependent Children (AFDC); Child support; Child Support Enforcement Amendments; Displaced homemakers; Dual-earner families; Family law; Feminist sociology; Feminization of poverty; Gender inequality; No-fault divorce; Prenuptial agreements; Single-parent families; Social Security; Uniform Marital Property Act (UMPA); Uniform Marriage and Divorce Act (UMDA); Wealth.

Allowances

RELEVANT ISSUES: Children and child development; Economics and work; Parenting and family relationships
SIGNIFICANCE: Money management is a lifelong skill that should be acquired as early as possible; allowances can contribute to teaching this skill

Allowances are fixed amounts of money given to children, usually by their parents, on a regular basis. They are normally allotted for children's minor recurring expenditures. For some children, an allowance is only one component of the money they receive, which may also include earnings from part-time jobs, cash gifts, and other funds received from parents or relatives. The size of an allowance and its timing, frequency, conditions, and arrangements are determined by a family's income and wealth, the parents' values and philosophy, and the age, maturity, and peer environment of the child. Because of the diversity of these factors, the meaning, purpose, conditions, and management of allowances have been ambiguous within American society.

Although the majority of American parents view allowances as an important part of children's economic and social experience, some have rejected them, believing that they commercialize family relationships. During the mid-1990's a little more than half of all American families gave their children allowances. Most of the children who did not receive allowances stopped getting them because they had obtained jobs.

Allowances often take the form of cash payments for good behavior. (James L. Shaffer)

Types of Allowance. Three types of allowance reflect different parental philosophies. Educational allowances offer children the opportunity to become self-reliant, competent in managing money, and experienced in financial decision making. Since the focus of this type of allowance is the development of children, how the allowance money is spent is not stipulated. The parents' main objective in awarding such allowances is to encourage their children to draw up spending plans, manage funds, and practice budget balancing. Entitled allowances, the second form of allowance, offer basic support to children, especially in covering their expenditures on necessities and wants. The rationale behind this type of allowance is that children are automatically entitled to a share of the family income. It represents the parents' recognition of their children's right as family members to a part of the joint resources of the family, implying that there should be no strings attached and that allowances should be unconditional. If parents recognize and respect their children's rights, children, in turn, should acknowledge and honor their responsibilities as family members to share in routine household tasks. According to this philosophy, children should help around the house, behave well, or achieve good grades in school not for rewards, but to demonstrate attachment and belonging to their family while conforming to its values and principles.

The third form of allowance involves payments for services, products, or time spent at specific activities. These include payments for performing household chores and rewards for achievement and good behavior. Administration of these allowances is modeled after the paid-employment experience in the labor market. It may simulate a business contract by which specific responsibilities, compensation, and authority relationships are set out in advance. Payment of earned allowances implies that services rendered may be monitored and that the outcome may be evaluated to determine compliance with the terms of the agreement. Failure to conform with the agreement may result in docking or withholding the allowances. Because there is no accountability for the use of earned income in the marketplace, earned allowances are not contingent on how they are spent. Unlike educational and entitled allowances, which focus on learning and self-actualization, earned allowances emphasize conformity and obligation. One study has shown that about half of American parents believe that children should perform household chores in exchange for their allowances. In another, 80 percent of children reported that they had to do household work in order to receive their allowances.

Advice from Experts. Child-rearing experts generally agree that children can learn many financial and moral lessons by receiving regular allowances. Family economists have argued that through the receipt, and use, of fixed and periodic amounts of money, children learn how to make economic decisions within their own constraints. Allowances can, over time, become an effective mechanism to foster children's economic socialization, teaching them to become adult consumers.

Some authorities believe that earned allowances

teach children a valuable lesson by instructing them how to work for pay, while others believe that the notion of earned allowances undermines the collective character of the family. Most experts, however, take a middle road, arguing that instead of making allowances contingent entirely upon doing household chores, greater benefits may come from hiring children to do only special household tasks for which their parents would otherwise hire somebody else, such as shoveling snow and mowing lawns. Such arrangements should be businesslike, and wages and job performance should be fair.

One study found that children who receive unconditional allowances, such as for doing chores, had a better understanding of financial concepts than those who receive conditional and those who receive no allowances. Another study concluded that allowances cannot be classified as good or bad; rather, *how* they are managed determines how values and orientation are instilled in children.

Experts have also emphasized the importance for parents of discussing money matters with children, establishing consistent approaches to teaching them about money, and including them in decision-making processes. Experts have suggested that children can begin to receive allowances as soon as they understand that money is used to buy things. Allowances are usually begun when children reach the age of six to eight years old, unless there are older children in the family, in which case children may receive them when they are four or five years old. Allowances should be given at regular intervals, such as weekly or bimonthly. Moreover, experts recommend that parents should not give their children any money between pay periods and not give them advances, as such practices defeat the purpose of allowances.

Parents and children should agree in advance on the amounts of allowances, paydays, and the conditions, if any. Allowances may be increased annually to reflect general economic inflation and changes in children's needs. Experts recommend that parents not withhold allowances as a disciplinary measure, for children may come to see money as a power tool that could be used at their convenience. For that matter, using allowances as rewards for achievement and good behavior may have the same effect, leading children to believe that money is the only incentive to do things and teaching them to assign monetary values to character and accomplishments. While rewarding achievement is positive, rewards should be detached from children's allowances. Family parties, picnics, and dining out are more appropriate forms of awarding children for their achievements.

Statistics. A national survey on allowances published by *Zillions* magazine in early 1997 found that half of U.S. children aged nine through fourteen received allowances. The median amount was five dollars a week. More than half of those who did not receive regular allowances got occasional handouts. Some 40 percent received automatic

Surveys have shown that more than half of American children aged nine through twelve receive allowances, about three-quarters of which are linked to performance of household chores. (James L. Shaffer)

annual raises, and 75 percent reported that their allowances were tied to chores. The survey also reported that while 70 percent of the children came up short at least once a month, half of them successfully negotiated getting advances. Approximately 40 percent had some of their allowances withheld, and 10 percent were unhappy with the amounts they received. One-third had part-time jobs and earned a median income of ten dollars a week.   —*M. J. Alhabeeb*

BIBLIOGRAPHY
Alhabeeb, M. J. "Teenagers' Money, Discretionary Spending and Saving." *Journal of Financial Counseling and Planning* 7 (1996).
"Allowance: Survey Results." *Zillions* 7 (1997).
Berg, Adriane G. *Your Kids, Your Money.* Englewood Cliffs, N.J.: Prentice-Hall, 1985.
Godfrey, Neale S., and Carolina Edwards. *Money Doesn't Grow on Trees: A Parent's Guide to Raising Financially Responsible Children.* New York: Simon & Schuster, 1994.
Miller, J., and S. Yung. "The Role of Allowances in Adolescent Socialization." *Youth and Society* 22 (1990).
Moretimer, J., K. Dennehy, C. Lee, and M. Finch. "The Prevalence, Distribution, and Consequences of Allowance Arrangements." *Family Relations* 43 (1994).
Weinstein, Grace W. *Children and Money.* New York: New American Library, 1985.

See also Cultural influences; Disciplining children; Family economics; Family values; Moral education.

Allport, Gordon

BORN: November 11, 1897, Montezuma, Ind.
DIED: October 9, 1967, Boston, Mass.
AREAS OF ACHIEVEMENT: Children and child development; Race and ethnicity; Religious beliefs and practices
SIGNIFICANCE: In his work on personality and social ethics, Allport emphasized the unique constellation of traits, values, and sentiments that characterize each individual

According to Gordon W. Allport, traits are neurophysiologically based. Some, but not many, people have cardinal traits—general dispositions that in-

fluence almost every aspect of their behavior. More commonly, people have five to ten central traits, which characterize most of their behavior, and secondary traits, which have a narrower influence than central or cardinal traits.

Allport believed that human motivation and development are discontinuous. Motives learned under one set of circumstances for particular purposes could later become "functionally autonomous," serving new, modern needs or goals. Therefore, Allport saw early childhood experiences as less crucial for later personality than did Freudian psychologists. The self system, or "proprium," which gradually develops from the end of the first year of life through adolescence, was seen as providing the unity and motivating force of personality.

Allport's interest in social values was manifested in his study of prejudice and religious beliefs. He saw personality characteristics, such as susceptibility to conformity and authoritarianism, as the basis of prejudice. He distinguished between intrinsically religious persons, who practice religious devotion as an end in itself, and extrinsically religious persons, who practice religion to acquire social status, comfort, or security. The extrinsically religious are more likely to be prejudiced than the intrinsically religious.   —*Susan E. Beers*

See also Freudian psychology; Religion.

Alsager v. District Court

DATE: Ruling issued on December 19, 1975
RELEVANT ISSUES: Law; Parenting and family relationships
SIGNIFICANCE: This decision of a U.S. district court, upheld in a court of appeals, recognizes that parental rights cannot be terminated except for extremely good reasons

Social workers in Polk Country, Iowa, decided that Charles and Darlene Alsager were not taking good care of their six children. Circumstances included untidy living conditions, a lack of warm clothing in winter, and poor school attendance. After the case was referred to the county district court, the local judge, following the state's relevant statute, decided to terminate the Alsagers' parental rights over five of their children, after which the children were placed in foster homes. The parents challenged the action in the federal courts, where they prevailed.

The U.S. Court of Appeals made two major rulings. First, from the perspective of substantive due process the state had not shown any "high and substantial degree of harm to the children," and thus the state had not established an adequate basis for termination of parental rights. Second, from the perspective of procedural due process, the notice for the hearing had not included factual information necessary for the parents to prepare a defense. Thus, Iowa's parental termination statute was declared unconstitutional, and the case was sent back to the county court for resolution. This federal precedent requires courts to use the "compelling state interest test" to justify any termination of parental rights.   —*Thomas T. Lewis*

See also Child abuse; Child custody; Foster homes; Parenting.

Alternative family types

RELEVANT ISSUES: Divorce; Law; Parenting and family relationships
SIGNIFICANCE: Alternative family types are families in which children are not raised by their biological parents

In the best of all possible worlds, children would be raised by their well-adjusted biological parents. However, this does not always happen. Children's fathers or mothers may die, whereby a surviving parent must assume all the responsibility for raising the children. Many marriages end in divorce. Divorce is traumatic for children and is exacerbated because many people associate an increasing divorce rate with the moral decline of society. This unnecessary criticism often alienates divorced parents from their married friends. Frequently when divorced men and divorced women marry, there are emotional conflicts in their blended families. Successful stepparents accept the fact that their stepchildren identify much more closely with their biological parents who raised them alone for a period of time.

Societies tend to be tolerant of single parents, divorced parents, and stepparents, but other types of families exist that many societies are unwilling to accept. Children may be raised by gay or lesbian parents. Because of homophobia, some judges have assigned custody of children to other family members, such as grandparents, aunts, uncles, or a nonhomosexual biological parent. Other children are raised in communal environments, such as communes, which conservative elements in society view as highly detrimental to children.
—*Edmund J. Campion*

See also Blended families; Communal living; Divorce; Domestic partners; Gay and lesbian families; Institutional families; Single-parent families; Widowhood.

Alzheimer's disease

RELEVANT ISSUES: Aging; Health and medicine
SIGNIFICANCE: Formerly called "senile dementia" and regarded as merely an inevitable result of aging, Alzheimer's disease is actually a disease with observable symptoms and physiological changes that often has devastating effects on sufferers and caregiving families

Since the 1960's and 1970's, diagnostic methods have improved to the point that the loss of physical and mental capacities by aging persons is no longer considered a mysterious and inevitable process. Many cardiovascular problems have yielded to new treatments by drugs or surgery, joint diseases have been improved or cured through the use of arthroscopic surgery or replacement, and whole-organ transplants have become common. Even physical deterioration has been reversed by programs of diet and exercise. The area of deterioration that has not yet responded to medical treatment, however, is the across-the-board loss of mental capacity that leads by gradual steps to personality change, inability to function in a world that comes to be too much for elderly individuals, and finally virtual mindlessness and death. Yet hope has dawned even in this area through the recognition that mental deterioration is often the result of a definable disease: Alzheimer's disease. Although a cure has not yet been discovered, much has been learned about the nature of Alzheimer's disease, and efforts to find a remedy continue.

Incidence and Symptoms. In the 1990's about four million Americans, or roughly 1.5 percent of the U.S. population, were estimated to have Alzheimer's disease. With the increased life expec-

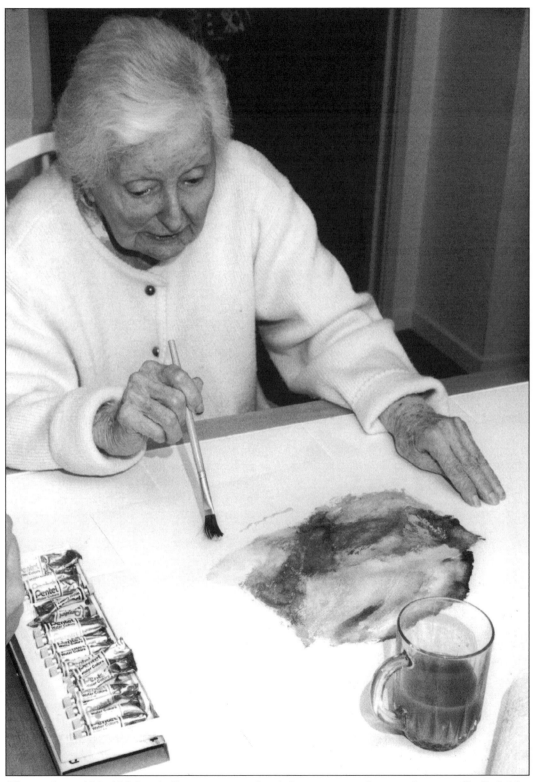

The speed at which Alzheimer's disease conquers its victims may vary; however, it eventually diminishes all of its victims' mental and physical abilities. (Ben Klaffke)

tancy of the U.S. population, this figure was expected to double by 2040 to considerably more than 3 percent.

The behavioral symptoms of Alzheimer's disease are probably familiar to many by hearsay, if not by actual contact: forgetfulness; change or loss of personality traits; and loss of ability to handle housekeeping chores and physical maintenance tasks such as cooking, dressing, grooming, bathing, doing laundry, and performing toilet functions. These problems can be associated with other causes, however, and are not a definitive diagnosis of Alzheimer's disease. The only reliable evidence is obtained by postmortem examinations, which reveal an alarming loss of brain cells, or neurons, ranging as high as 40 percent. Remaining neurons appear clogged with neurofibrillary tangles (protein fibers that are twisted together like yarn within the neuron) and neuritic plaques (cores of a protein called amyloid that are surrounded by debris from broken-down neurons). Certain chemicals, such as acetylcholine, appear to be drastically depleted. These chemicals transmit nerve impulses from one neuron to an-

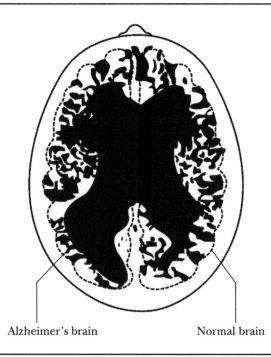

Alzheimer's brain   Normal brain

Alzheimer's disease causes the volume of the brain to shrink substantially.

other, thereby producing the concerted function of areas of the brain that results in thought and action. When the chemicals are in short supply, this function is reduced or absent.

Research for Causes and Cures. Alzheimer's disease research has looked more or less simultaneously for causes and cures, searching for clues in human genetics. In genetic investigation, three defective genes have been found on chromosomes 1, 14, and 21 that are associated with the early-onset form of the disease (appearing in people younger than sixty-five years of age). The discovery of this association does not mean that the ultimate cause of the disease has been found, for other factors, which have yet to be identified, are involved in turning these genes on or off. A gene on chromosome 19 that takes three forms has been implicated in late-onset Alzheimer's disease. Various permutations of the three forms (one from each parent) produce symptoms of Alzheimer's disease of varying degrees of severity and age of onset. Persons who possess these genes do not necessarily contract Alzheimer's disease, and persons without them are not necessarily free of the disease. These preliminary findings, however, are promising. Other findings by epidemiologists who study large populations of individuals with and without Alzheimer's disease suggest such links as diet and socioeconomic class. A possible link between the disease and aluminum ions has not been demonstrated. The depression suffered by many Alzheimer's patients has been investigated, but the cause-and-effect relationship between the disease and depression is not clear. Other suggested causes include immune system deficiencies and infection by prions (protein particles that are believed to cause such infectious diseases of the nervous system as Creutzfeldt-Jakob disease). All of these potential causes must be regarded as speculative.

Proposed cures for the disease are speculative as well. These remedies include dietary supplements, such as lecithin and choline; antioxidants, such as vitamin E and deprenyl; the ergot-derived drug Hydergine; the drug Tacrine, which has been approved by the Food and Drug Administration (FDA) and appears to slow deterioration from the disease but which can produce side effects such as liver damage; and even tissue implants to increase acetylcholine levels in the brain. Many of these

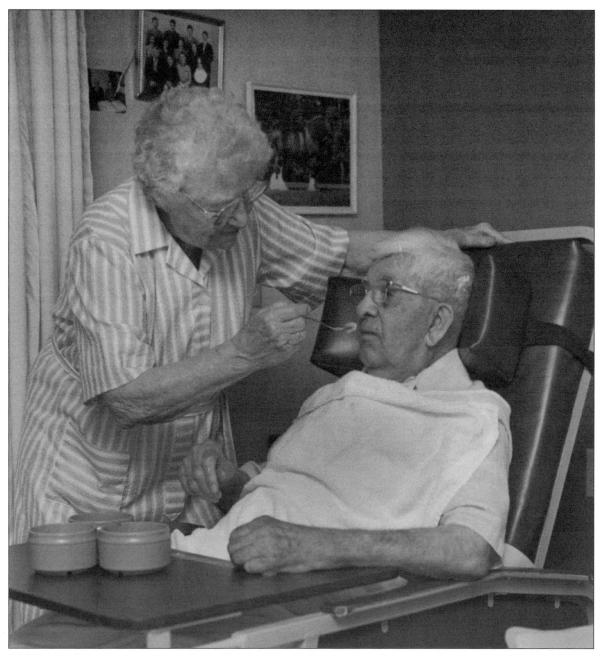

Alzheimer's disease imposes extraordinary burdens on family members who personally care for its victims. (James L. Shaffer)

proposed cures are in the preliminary stages of laboratory testing.

Stages of the Disease. Medical professionals and social workers who deal with Alzheimer's patients have identified three to five stages of increasing severity in the progress of the disease. Initially,

patients become forgetful, groping for words, misplacing objects, losing spontaneity and problem-solving ability, and becoming irritable or anxious. This stage often goes unnoticed or is passed off as a normal consequence of aging. Later stages, however, make the problem clearer. Recent memory of current events becomes erratic, making conversation confusing. Judgment is impaired, and activities such as driving, cooking, and paying bills become unpredictable and irregular.

Later, memory loss and memory fluctuations become a daily or even hourly problem, rendering conversation disjointed at best. Social situations become too complex for patients' deteriorating memory to cope with, and withdrawal is common. Many basic life chores—bathing, dressing, and toilet functions—are retained but may be left unfinished as the conclusion of each task is forgotten. In the next stage, language begins to disappear, and patients begin to look ill. With further loss of memory, patients become unfamiliar with their surroundings and may seem hostile. Sleep disturbance and nighttime wandering are common as are agitation, delusions, and obsessive behavior. Patient mobility deteriorates; this situation, coupled with memory loss of bathroom location and management of clothing, often leads to incontinence. In the final stage, personality gradually disappears. Walking, sitting up, and even eating become impossible, and eventually coma and death follow.

Challenges for Caregivers. The worsening symptoms of Alzheimer's disease suggest some, but not all, of the problems faced by family caregivers, many of whom cannot afford either extra home assistance or institutional care. The physical side of caring for elderly relatives—dressing, bathing, feeding, managing toilet use, transporting on occasional outings—is demanding enough with someone who is physically frail but alert and cooperative. The loss of mental capacity experienced by Alzheimer's patients often compounds such demands to an almost unbearable level. Even in the early stages of forgetfulness, patients' refusal to recognize the existence of a problem can lead to accusations that others are hiding or taking their belongings. Later, these small suspicions can develop into full-blown paranoia, patients' belief that their spouses are engaging in infidelity or that they are even impostors, fear of common activities such as bathing, and nighttime hallucinations that prevent sleep or induce wanderings in the small hours.

Patients must be watched at all times to prevent disasters arising from forgetfulness: leaving unlit burners on a gas stove, burning food, heating empty pots, or leaving potentially dangerous kitchen appliances or power tools running. Problems can develop with the half-forgotten rituals of feeding, chewing, and swallowing. Even when patients are all but bedridden, hostility and suspicion often persist. Added to this is the knowledge that in many cases the former salary of a family member is being sacrificed for an indeterminate period of time. Help and advice are available for caregivers and their patients: The American Association of Retired Persons (AARP), the Alzheimer's Association (headquartered in Chicago), and many state agencies offer assistance.

—*Robert M. Hawthorne, Jr.*

BIBLIOGRAPHY

Cohen, Donna, and Carl Eisdorf. *The Loss of Self: A Family Resource for the Care of Alzheimer's Disease and Related Disorders.* New York: W. W. Norton, 1986.

Dawson, Pam, and Donna L. Wells. *Enhancing the Abilities of Persons with Alzheimer's and Related Dementias: A Nursing Perspective.* New York: Springer, 1993.

Greutzer, Howard. *Alzheimer's: A Caregiver's Guide and Sourcebook.* New York: John Wiley and Sons, 1988.

Harvard Health Letter, ed. *Alzheimer's Disease (Special Report).* Cambridge, Mass.: Harvard Medical Health Publications, 1994.

Khachaturian, Zaven S. "Plundered Memories." *The Sciences* 37 (July/August, 1997).

Zarit, Steven H., Nancy K. Orr, and Judy M. Zarit. *The Hidden Victims of Alzheimer's Disease: Families Under Stress.* New York: New York University Press, 1985.

See also Aging and elderly care; Family caregiving; Family crises; Generational relationships; Health problems; Heredity; Living wills; Nursing and convalescent homes; Sandwich generation; Substitute caregivers.

Amerasian children

RELEVANT ISSUES: Parenting and family relationships; Race and ethnicity

SIGNIFICANCE: With U.S. participation in wars and occupations in Asia, American servicemen have fathered children with women in several Asian countries, posing the issue of immigration rights for Amerasian children and their Asian mothers

The term "Amerasian" was coined by the American novelist Pearl S. Buck to denote the child of a U.S. serviceman and a woman born and raised in East Asia. The Pearl Buck Foundation, set up in 1964 to help such children, continued its work after her death. The existence of Amerasian children has posed knotty questions for judges and policymakers in the areas of immigration and citizenship law. The issues involved are not merely political. Amerasians were sometimes raised out of wedlock, sometimes adopted, and sometimes raised by both natural parents. Studying Amerasian children and youth in both East Asia and the United States permits sociologists and psychologists to assess the relative weights of different handicaps—their status as members of minorities, their foreign-language background, and their fatherlessness—impeding their progress toward healthy and productive adulthood.

Historical Development of Amerasian Populations. After Japan's defeat in World War II, U.S. servicemen occupied Japan. Within six years about 24,000 Amerasian children were born to Japanese women. After Japan regained sovereignty in 1952, several U.S. air bases remained on Japan's home islands, and Okinawa remained under U.S. occupation. Mixed marriages and the births of Amerasian babies continued. The U.S. occupation of South Korea in the late 1940's was followed by the Korean War. After the armistice in 1953, some U.S. soldiers remained. Hence, some South Korean women bore Amerasian babies into the early 1980's. Amerasian children were also born to women from Taiwan, which was protected by the United States Navy against the People's Republic of China after 1950.

After the French left Vietnam in 1954 and Vietnam was split into Communist North Vietnam and anticommunist South Vietnam, the United States decided to defend the latter. About 30,000 Amerasian children were born to South Vietnamese women during U.S. involvement in the Vietnam War from 1964 to 1975. During this time some Amerasians were also born to women in Laos, Cambodia, and Thailand, which was a base for U.S. air raids in Vietnam. When North Vietnam

conquered South Vietnam in April, 1975, normal economic and diplomatic relations with the United States ceased, not to be restored until the mid-1990's. Hence, no Amerasian babies were born in Vietnam after 1976.

In the Philippines, Amerasian children were born soon after the United States acquired the islands in 1898. Although independence was granted in 1946, Amerasian births continued until 1992, when Clark Air Force Base and Subic Bay Naval Base were closed. By 1992 about 50,000 Amerasians lived in the Philippines. In 1993 Filipino prostitutes sued the U.S. government for financial aid in raising their Amerasian children. In November, 1997, Lorelyn Penero Miller, the Filipina daughter of a U.S. serviceman born out of wedlock, challenged the U.S. citizenship law in the U.S. Supreme Court.

Family, Citizenship, and Immigration. Unlike France, which offered citizenship rights to its colonial Eurasians, the U.S. government recognized Amerasians as citizens only if they were born within the bonds of marriage. Amerasians born out of wedlock could be recognized as U.S. citizens only if specific American men recognized them as their children and provided documentary proof of fatherhood.

Out-of-wedlock births resulted from institutional obstacles to marriage as well as from individual irresponsibility. Until 1967 several American states prohibited white-Asian and black-Asian marriages. In 1945 U.S. immigration law still prohibited the entry of Japanese. Although the U.S. Congress twice gave Japanese war brides the opportunity to immigrate to the United States, many couples could not meet the deadlines. From the passage of the McCarran-Walter Act of 1952, which permitted all Asian spouses of U.S. servicemen to immigrate to the United States, until 1965, roughly half of all Korean and Japanese immigrants to the United States were servicemen's wives. Until 1992 many Filipino immigrants were the wives of servicemen. Despite the time-consuming requirement of approval by superior officers, which sometimes came through only after soldiers had been transferred back to the United States, more than 6,000 marriages between South Vietnamese women and U.S. servicemen occurred between 1965 and 1972.

Most Japanese and Korean Amerasians entering the United States were either preteen children of intact interracial families or preteen orphans adopted by American couples. Aside from twenty college-age Korean Amerasians sponsored yearly by Gonzaga University after 1980, relatively few Amerasian teenagers or young adults from Korea or Japan have ever immigrated to the United States.

Vietnamese Amerasians, by contrast, did not immigrate to the United States in large numbers until they were already late adolescents and young adults. Only a few Vietnamese Amerasian children, including many of the 2,000 orphans airlifted out of South Vietnam in April, 1975, left South Vietnam before the Communist triumph. Although a 1982 U.S. law stipulated that Amerasians born between 1950 and 1982 from Vietnam, Thailand, Laos, Cambodia, and Korea (but not Japan) had priority in immigrating to the United States, it did little for Vietnamese Amerasians. Relatives were not allowed to accompany their

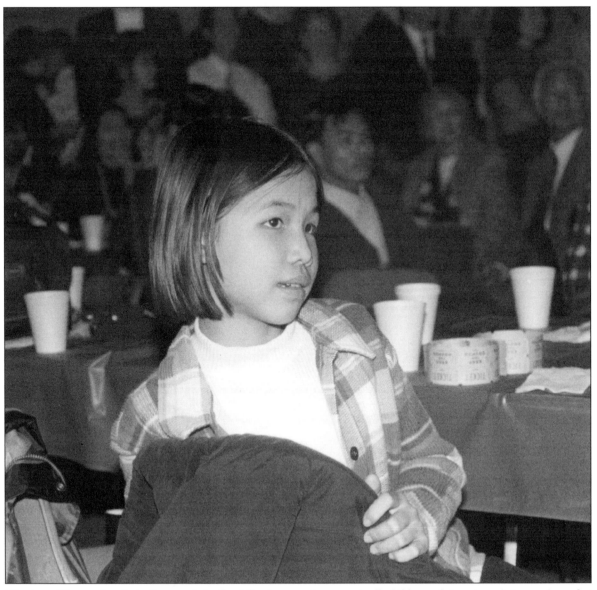

The term "Amerasian," as it was originally defined, encompasses not all children of American-Asian unions, but only those of Asian women and American servicemen. (James L. Shaffer)

children and the United States had no diplomatic relations with Vietnam. Although well-publicized reunions between preteen Amerasian children and their fathers did occur in the United States in October, 1982, children claimed by their American fathers after 1975 were only a tiny percentage of all Vietnamese Amerasians.

From 1982 to 1988 about 4,500 Vietnamese Amerasians and 7,000 accompanying relatives entered the United States as refugees. The Amerasian Homecoming Act (1987) speeded up the exodus by permitting all Vietnamese Amerasians born between January 1, 1962, and January 1, 1977, to immigrate without proving that they had a specific American father and by permitting them to bring their mothers and siblings along. After 1991 Amerasians' spouses and children could come as well. By 1994 about 20,000 Vietnamese Amerasians and 60,000 relatives had settled in the United States.

Adjustments in East Asia and in the United States. Because Amerasians usually had some of the physical features of their white or African American fathers, those raised in East Asian countries were usually discriminated against by their countries' racial majorities. However, being half white was socially acceptable in the Philippines. In Japan, Amerasians raised on U.S. military bases by intact dual-parent families were shielded somewhat from prejudice. Most Amerasians raised in East Asia, however, grew up without fathers, in societies where fatherlessness was stigmatized. Their mothers sometimes abandoned them to the care of relatives or orphanages or even to the streets, while stepfathers mistreated them. In their mothers' countries, Amerasians had difficulty in receiving an education, finding jobs, and marrying spouses. In post-1975 Vietnam they received on average no more than one to two years of schooling.

Fatherlessness was not confined to Amerasians reared in Asia; some Amerasians born in the United States, or taken there by their natural parents at an early age, saw their childhood disrupted by parental divorce. Of all Amerasians in the United States, those adopted by American couples at an early age and those whose natural parents' marriages remained intact throughout their childhood probably had an easier transition to adulthood than others. Thus, Vietnamese Amerasians

airlifted to the United States as small children for adoption in 1975 and those reunited as preteen children with their natural fathers in 1982 faced fewer problems than post-1987 teenage and young adult Vietnamese Amerasian immigrants. The latter were usually accompanied by only one parent or by no parent at all and had to struggle to learn English while seeking to hold down a job.

Amerasian adolescents' search for an acceptable ethnic identity followed a course different in the United States from that in East Asia. In the United States, Amerasians who were half white usually suffered less from majority prejudice than those who remained in East Asia, while half-black Amerasians suffered no more from majority prejudice than African Americans in general. The latter, however, were not always accepted by African Americans. Vietnamese Amerasians rejected in Vietnam were often also rejected by the Vietnamese refugee community in the United States.

—*Paul D. Mageli*

BIBLIOGRAPHY

Bass, Thomas A. *Vietnamerica: The War Comes Home.* New York: Soho Press, 1996.

Conn, Peter J. *Pearl S. Buck: A Cultural Biography.* Cambridge, U.K.: Cambridge University Press, 1996.

Field, Norma. *In the Realm of a Dying Emperor: A Portrait of Japan at Century's End.* New York: Pantheon Books, 1991.

McBee, Susanna. "The Amerasians: Tragic Legacy of Our Far East Wars." *U.S. News and World Report* 96 (May 7, 1984).

Spickard, Paul R. "Madam Butterfly Revisited." In *Mixed Blood: Intermarriage and Ethnic Identity in Twentieth-Century America.* Madison: University of Wisconsin Press, 1989.

Valverde, Kieu-Linh Caroline. "From Dust to Gold: The Vietnamese Amerasian Experience." In *Racially Mixed People in America*, edited by Maria P. P. Root. Newbury Park, Calif.: Sage Publications, 1992.

Westbrook, Peter. *Harnessing Anger: The Way of an American Fencer.* New York: Seven Stories Press, 1997.

Williams, Teresa. "Prism Lives: Identity of Binational Amerasians." In *Racially Mixed People in America*, edited by Maria P. P. Root. Newbury Park, Calif.: Sage Publications, 1992.

See also Adoption issues; Antimiscegenation laws; Children born out of wedlock; Interracial families; Unwed fathers; Vietnamese Americans; War brides.

American Association for Marriage and Family Therapy (AAMFT)

DATE: Founded in 1942
RELEVANT ISSUES: Marriage and dating; Parenting and family relationships
SIGNIFICANCE: This organization is the oldest and largest professional association of marriage and family therapists

The American Association for Marriage and Family Therapy was initially established in 1942 as the American Association of Marriage Counselors (AAMC). The organization changed its name to the American Association of Marriage and Family Counselors (AAMFC) in 1970 and later to the American Association for Marriage and Family Therapy (AAMFT) in 1979. With more than 25,000 members, the organization is the largest professional association of marriage and family therapists in the United States, Canada, and abroad.

The AAMFT was established to advance the marriage and family therapy profession and promote marriage and family well-being in general. It endeavors to encourage and facilitate professional practice, research, and education by offering professional development conferences, publications, and services for marriage and family therapists.

The association's annual conference and summer institutes offer numerous presentations, workshops, and other opportunities for professional development in marriage and family therapy. Numerous additional conferences, institutes, and workshops are organized by the various regional, provincial, and state divisions of the AAMFT.

The organization produces numerous publications and other products for marriage and family therapists. The *Journal of Marital and Family Therapy*, a professional journal containing peer-reviewed articles on research, theory, and practice, is published quarterly. *Family Therapy News*, a newspaper designed to keep therapists informed of current issues and events, is published bimonthly. *Practice Strategies Newsletter*, a newsletter for practitioners, is published monthly. Numerous other publications, books, pamphlets, and training videos are listed in the *AAMFT Catalog*, available from the association.

The AAMFT offers various services designed to facilitate or support the professional practice of its members. Professional liability insurance and legal consultation programs are available. A standardized format for advertising in the telephone company yellow pages is provided.

To foster the profession and protect the public, the AAMFT sets standards for graduate education, supervision, professional ethics, and clinical practice. The AAMFT reviews and accredits graduate and postgraduate training programs in marriage and family therapy. On the individual professional level, the AAMFT evaluates credentials and awards Clinical Membership and/or Approved Supervisor Designation to professionals whose qualifications meet the association's standards. Members are expected to adhere to the association's Code of Ethics and may be expelled or disciplined for infractions of the code. The AAMFT has also taken a leadership role in encouraging state legislatures to recognize appropriate standards in licensing or certifying marriage and family therapists. As a result, marriage and family therapists are licensed or certified in most states. —*John W. Engel*

See also Divorce mediation; Dysfunctional families; Family counseling; Family therapy; Genetic counseling; Grief counseling; Marriage counseling; Mental health.

Americans with Disabilities Act (ADA)

DATE: Enacted on July 26, 1990
RELEVANT ISSUES: Health and medicine; Law
SIGNIFICANCE: This act empowered disabled persons to obtain equal rights

Starting in 1973 Congress passed various laws that required the removal of architectural barriers so that persons with disabilities could gain access to buildings, the provision of translation services for the deaf, accommodation to the mobility needs of blind persons, arrangements for disabled per-

These hearing-impaired children are among the 43 million persons who stand to benefit from laws such as the Americans with Disabilities Act. (AP/Wide World Photos)

sons to ride on various forms of public transportation, and designated parking spaces for the handicapped.

These laws did not cover disabled persons' employment problems. Moreover, caregivers of disabled persons were often subjected to discrimination. Accordingly, lobbying groups for the disabled pressured legislators for broader coverage. On July 26, 1990, Congress responded by passing the Americans with Disabilities Act, known as ADA, to fill the gaps in the earlier legislation. An estimated 43 million people were affected.

The term "disability" is defined in the 1990 law as a substantial limitation of one or more major life activities, but the statute also covers persons believed to have a disability and those closely associated with disabled persons, such as partners of persons with acquired immunodeficiency syndrome (AIDS). Another major provision in the law is the requirement of "reasonable accommodation," which means that agencies and private firms must do whatever they can reasonably afford so that disabled persons will have equal opportunity to enjoy the benefits of public programs and private-sector facilities. As a result, the disabled can contribute more to society and are less of a burden to their families.   —*Michael Haas*

See also Acquired immunodeficiency syndrome (AIDS); Aging and elderly care; Disabilities; Family caregiving; Health problems; Pediatric AIDS; Substitute caregivers.

Ancestor worship

RELEVANT ISSUES: Kinship and genealogy; Religious beliefs and practices

SIGNIFICANCE: Although it does not assume the same importance in modern North America as in Asia and Africa, ancestor worship is often found in cultures organized around lineage systems; it reinforces traditional family hierarchies, unifies both families and communities, and serves to promote traditional social norms

Ancestor worship is the expression of reverence for the spirits of one's ancestors, who are regarded as powerful supernatural beings. As practiced in North America, Asia, Africa, and elsewhere, ancestor worship rests on assumptions that ancestors survive death; that it is possible to communicate

with them; that if the living perform appropriate rites for their ancestors, the latter will benefit them, but if the living do not, the ancestors may bring them misfortune. Sometimes it is unclear whether a culture that believes in ancestral spirits actually worships them, as it may only attempt to commune with them as respected elders.

Ancestor Worship in North America. Immigrants to the United States and Canada from some parts of Africa and Asia sometimes continue their traditional ancestral rites. Native American peoples as well have such customs. The traditional religion of the Zuñi, a Pueblo tribe living in western New Mexico, involves ancestor worship.

As it has been for a thousand years, Zuñi life is organized around matrilineal households, clans, and religious societies. The kachina society is one of the most important of these societies. Kachinas are ancestral spirits, or the masked, costumed dancers who impersonate them. The Zuñi pray to their collective ancestors rather than to individual ancestors.

Before meals, the Zuñi offer pinches of their food to the ancestral spirits and say a traditional prayer to them for water, seeds, and longevity. On special days devoted to their ancestors, the Zuñi throw large amounts of food in nearby rivers, believing it will reach the kachinas living in villages at the bottoms of sacred lakes.

The Zuñi ritual calendar includes religious ceremonies nearly every week of the year. Whatever the ceremony, ancestors from the kachina village are believed to be present in spirit, represented by kachina society dancers. When kachina dancers don their masks, they are supposed to become ancestral spirits. Aiming to please the ancestral spirits, the kachina society dances to help the corn grow, to bring rain, to make women fertile, and to create cosmic harmony.

All fourteen-year-old males are initiated into the kachina society, as membership is supposed to be necessary for afterlife in the kachina village. Although women are seldom members of the kachina society, they may join their husbands in the kachina village if they get along together well.

A child's parents determine which part of the kachina society he will join. Some offices within religious societies are restricted to certain clans. For instance, the leader of the kachina society itself is always from the antelope clan. Families that are hereditary keepers of the masks of kachina priests have, as a result, a relatively high standing in the community.

The extensive Zuñi ritual calendar provides many opportunities for family gatherings, at which children observe the rich ceremonial traditions of their community. For instance, when a family builds a new house, kachina dancers join the housewarming celebration at year's end to bless the new home. Although ancestral spirits are generally regarded as beneficent, there is one annual ceremony at which bogeyman kachina dancers search for naughty children supposedly to carry them away or eat them. This ceremony aims to help parents raise well-behaved children. At other ceremonies, kachina priests sketch ideal character traits for the Zuñi, such as kindness and inoffensiveness, to help promote harmony in community and family life.

Ancestor Worship in China. Ancestor worship has had pronounced influence in Asia. Chinese artifacts going back to at least 1000 B.C.E reveal that ancient Chinese kings practiced ancestor worship. By 200 C.E. the practice was widespread among the Chinese masses. Well into the twentieth century, ancestor worship was an integral part of traditional Chinese family life among all classes of society.

In traditional Chinese society, when the head of a family died, it was incumbent on his eldest son to conduct rites aimed at giving his father safe passage to the shadowy spirit realm. After announcing his death to the guardian divinity of the spirit world, the son would spread replica paper money before his father's coffin on the way to the cemetery to discourage evil spirits from interfering with his father's passage. Most important, the son provided an ancestral tablet in which his father's spirit could reside.

Usually, the carved wooden tablet was not more than eighteen inches high and four inches wide and was enshrined in the home in a special niche or room. Periodically, family members performed sacrificial rites in front of the tablet to honor the deceased. Particularly pious families might burn incense and candles every morning before the tablet to attract the spirit or provide it with sustenance. More elaborate rites were performed on the ancestor's birthdays and death days; the first and fifteenth day of each month; and autumn,

spring, and New Year festival days. Offerings were also made to the ancestors when their descendants notified them of important events in the life of the family, such as births or promotions.

In these more elaborate rites, the senior male in the family offered a feast of food and drink to the ancestral spirit. He prostrated himself before the ancestral tablet, praised the ancestor, and petitioned him to bless his living descendants. The feast was left before the tablet for the spirit to enjoy its essence, and then the living relatives ate and drank. Traditionally, a family performed rites before ancestral tablets going back three to five generations.

Ancestor worship permeated traditional Chinese family life. Besides the many rites performed at home, there were autumn and spring ancestral feasts at clan halls, among clans wealthy enough to have them. Once or twice a year the family had a picnic-like sacrificial meal in the family graveyard. Moreover, ancestor worship was a crucial part of marriage ceremonies; marriages were not regarded as legally valid unless the bride had worshiped the groom's ancestors. The common belief was that the dead were an ongoing part of the family and that they, as a matter of propriety, should be cared for and revered by the living.

Filial piety (*hsiao*) was a major ideal undergirding ancestor worship in China. In Chinese, the word for *hsiao* combines the symbols for *old* and *son*. In traditional Chinese society a son's primary duty was to serve his parents with propriety in life and in death. The ideal of filial piety was expressed in explicit rules of propriety; for example, sons were required to go to their parents at daybreak and gently ask whether they needed anything, such as a basin for washing. Not living with one's parents or grandparents was considered unfilial and was punishable by law. The child's marriage was arranged to serve the parents, not satisfy the child. The bride and her husband both owed obedience to his parents. Having a male child was a filial duty, because the eldest son was next in line to continue the ancestral rites. In the absence of a male child, a son from a concubine or a close relative, if possible, would be adopted to ensure that the ancestral rites would be continued.

Ancestor worship helped maintain the traditional Chinese family hierarchy. In general, the rites promoted deference to parental authority,

In many societies visiting family graves is an expression of ancestor worship. (Skjold Photographs)

particularly the authority of senior males. In many families the order of kowtowing and praying before the ancestral tablets reinforced the family structure, with the head male going first, being followed by others in order of seniority. Even those Chinese intellectuals who doubted the reality of the ancestral spirits saw that the rites promoted harmonious family relations, since the respect and affection shown to the deceased parent in performing the rites provided a model for how a son should treat a living father.

Ancestral rites thus helped stabilize the traditional Chinese family system. During the mortuary rites, the collective family weeping at the mourning altar served to unify the family at a time of loss. For most Chinese, the sacrificial rites signified that the family bond was so strong that even death could not break it. Ancestral ceremonies at clan temples promoted group cohesion as well. Speeches glorifying ancestors, their philosophies of life, and their accomplishments were designed to inspire group loyalty and unity.

By supporting traditional ways, ancestor worship helped support traditional political structures in China for centuries. By the 1960's, however, mainland China's Communist Party government dubbed ancestor worship a superstition, discouraging its practice with some success, especially in urban centers.

Ancestor Worship in Japan. In contrast to China, nineteenth and twentieth century Japanese governments encouraged ancestor worship, seeing it as a unifying political force. Government promotion of ancestor worship was based on early Shinto writings, such as the *Koji-ki* (*Records of Ancient Matters*) from 712 C.E. and the *Nihon shoki* (*Chronicles of Japan*) from 720 C.E., writings originally put forward to legitimize imperial rule that accounted for the origins of the imperial line, the gods, and the Japanese people. According to these texts, Amaterasu, the sun goddess, sent her grandson, Ninigi, to rule Japan. His great grandson, Jimmu, became the first emperor. Along with Ninigi, Amaterasu sent gods that she and her brother, the moon god, had created. These gods became the founders of other Japanese lineages. Since most, if not all, Japanese people descended from gods, in worshiping the gods the people worshiped their own ancestors.

From the late nineteenth century until the end of World War II, Japanese schoolchildren were taught to believe that common ancestry tied all Japanese people to the emperor. They were taught to believe that by supporting the emperor they were showing respect for their ancestors. Taking for granted their ties to the emperor and the gods, many Japanese came to regard the nation as one divine household with the emperor as its father. As filial piety was a deeply rooted Japanese value, they also believed that the emperor, as father, was owed devotion, loyalty, and obedience. Thus ancestor worship became a basis for patriotism in twentieth century Japan.

Shinto-inspired ancestor worship declined significantly when, at the end of World War II, the emperor publicly denied his own divinity. Yet, at the end of World War II Buddhist-inspired worship of deceased family members remained, as before, an important part of Japanese religious life. Between the years 600 and 1700 Buddhism had become closely associated with funeral and ancestral rites in Japan.

When a person dies, Buddhist monks chant scriptures to transform the soul of the dead into an enlightened one. A lacquered memorial tablet is made for the deceased and added to the Buddhist ancestral altar (*butsudan*) in the home. Family members, especially older ones, pray before the tablet, asking for blessings and offering the ancestral spirit rice and water for spiritual sustenance.

The cremated remains of the departed one are placed in a container and interred in a family grave, often in the cemetery of a Buddhist temple. Traditionally, Japanese mark anniversaries of their ancestors' deaths at set intervals of thirty-three or fifty years. Graves symbolize the families' continuity, and families tend to visit them at set times, such as during autumn and spring equinoxes and the summer festival of the dead.

Families come to clean the graves and make offerings to their ancestors. If a family has not suffered a recent loss, these visits can be enjoyable family outings. During the summer festival of the dead the souls of the dead are supposed to return to visit their relatives. For many Japanese, this becomes a time for festive family reunions.

Ancestor Worship in Africa. Ancestor worship is an important tradition in some parts of Africa. A representative example can be found in the traditional religion of the Yoruba tribe of southwestern Nigeria. Traditional Yoruba religion includes a supreme deity (Olorun), lesser deities (orishas), nature spirits, and ancestral spirits. The Yoruba use the word *bo* to refer to the worshiping of divinities and the making of offerings to ancestors. Both divinities and ancestors are regarded as powerful beings that must be revered. At the New Yam festival, the people offer their ancestors palm wine and kola nuts, because they believe that good harvests depend on lesser deities, their ancestors, and the people working together.

The male head of the traditional Yoruba family is responsible for ensuring that the family ancestors are shown due respect. If he learns of serious misbehavior in his family, he punishes the wrongdoer and conducts rites at the family shrine in the home to assuage his ancestors. Before his children marry, he performs sacrifices to his ancestors, asking them to bless the marriage.

In some cases, however, the mediators between the living and the dead are masqueraders (*egungun*), instead of family heads. Members of all-male secret societies, these masqueraders don masks that are supposed to make them channels for communication between the living and the dead. At funerals, masqueraders may try to console the living relatives with messages from the dead. At important family and community events, such as rites of passage and fertility festivals, the masqueraders may try to regulate social behavior by performing dances ridiculing immoral behavior and praising moral behavior.

Generally, only persons who have lived long, good lives and whose descendants revere them can become ancestor spirits. After a man dies and is buried, his family performs a ceremony called "bringing the spirit of the deceased into the house," at which time it sets up a shrine to him in the family home, reaffirming its ties to him and its desire that he continue to watch over them. Having returned home, the ever-watchful ancestor, with the power to reward or punish, serves as a guardian of the family's traditional morality.

From a traditional Yoruba outlook, the family is

made up of the dead, the yet-to-be-born, and the living. A traditional Yoruba person regards the birth of a child as the reincarnation of an ancestral spirit. —*Gregory P. Rich*

BIBLIOGRAPHY

Benedict, Ruth. *Patterns of Culture*. Boston: Houghton Mifflin, 1934. Includes a long chapter analyzing Zuñi culture, particularly its family system and religious societies.

Earhart, H. Byron, ed. *Religious Traditions of the World*. San Francisco, Calif.: Harper, 1993. Collection of short introductory books on world religions, including those in China, Japan, Africa, and native America.

Newell, William H., ed. *Ancestors*. Paris: Mouton, 1976. Collection of essays focusing on ancestor worship in Japan, Africa, and Taiwan.

Ray, Benjamin C. *African Religions*. Englewood Cliffs, N.J.: Prentice-Hall, 1976. Surveys numerous African cultures on such topics as belief in an afterlife and the relationship between ancestors and ethics.

Smith, Robert J. *Ancestor Worship in Contemporary Japan*. Stanford, Calif.: Stanford University Press, 1974. This book's opening chapter details how modern Japanese governments have used ancestor worship to serve their political goals.

Thompson, Laurence G. *Chinese Religion*. 4th ed. Belmont, Calif.: Wadsworth, 1989. Contains an excellent discussion of filial piety.

See also Amerasian children; Clans; Death; Familism; Filial responsibility; Funerals; Japanese Americans; Lineage; Religion.

Annulment

RELEVANT ISSUES: Divorce; Law

SIGNIFICANCE: Annulment in its civil or religious form is a method of terminating a marriage, meaning that a valid marriage never existed and that both parties have been returned to a premarital state

Divorce is the legal termination of a valid marriage. A civil annulment means that no valid marriage ever existed from a legal perspective, and a religious annulment means that a marriage is declared invalid for theological reasons while the couple may remain legally married. Laws for granting annulments differ from state to state. Marriages may be legally annulled when persons are underage, already married, impotent, insane, or blood relatives involved in an incestuous relationship. Marriages may also be annulled in cases of fraud, force, or coercion. Children of an annulled marriage may be declared illegitimate by the courts. Property brought into such marriages is returned to original owners, and neither party is required to financially support the other.

The Roman Catholic Church views marriage as a Sacrament that can be dissolved only by death. The church does not recognize divorce or civil annulment. Roman Catholics must obtain a religious annulment through the Church in order to marry again and have the subsequent marriage recognized by the Church. Roman Catholics must obtain a civil divorce prior to obtaining a religious annulment. Grounds for Church annulment include abduction, incestuous marriage, nonconsummation of marriage, impotence, intent by a spouse not to have children, marriage entered under coercion, and lack of love.

A dramatic rise in annulments occurred when "grave lack of discretion of judgment" was added to the list of reasons for granting annulments in 1983. This was interpreted to mean that one or both parties' ability to fulfill the basic obligations of marriage were interfered with for various reasons, such as personality or psychological problems or premarital pregnancy. Controversy regarding the granting of Church annulments was accentuated when Joseph P. Kennedy II, eldest son of Robert Kennedy, asked the Roman Catholic Church for an annulment of his marriage to Sheila Rauch Kennedy after thirteen years of marriage and the birth of two sons. In her book *Shattered Faith* Sheila Rauch Kennedy describes her opposition to a Church annulment.

—*Marie Saracino*

See also Divorce; Family law; Marriage laws; Roman Catholics.

Antimiscegenation laws

RELEVANT ISSUES: Law; Marriage and dating; Race and ethnicity

SIGNIFICANCE: Antimiscegenation laws are legislative measures that were designed to prevent, limit, inhibit, or penalize sexual relationships between individuals of different races

The mixing of races through sexual liaisons to the point of contracting into legal marriage was a matter of official concern from the earliest days of the British colonization of the New World. It is difficult, however, to determine exactly when this concern became an obsession that was transferred into legal terms. As early as 1609, Anglican preachers warned would-be Virginia settlers against consorting with the "heathen that were uncircumcised." These injunctions seem to have been very loosely observed in regard to intimate relations among European Americans and Native Americans and, after 1619, Africans.

A chronic shortage of white women, combined with the unique frontier conditions of the colonial settlements, contributed to interracial association. In more than a few instances in early seventeenth century America, particularly in areas where labor shortages posed a problem, white masters encouraged their white female servants to mate with black male servants in order to assure a larger number of mulatto (mixed-blood) servants. Legitimate and illegitimate unions between the races apparently received little public censure until the 1660's, when slavery began to take on the status of an established institution, replacing indentured servitude as the primary source of plantation labor. It was not until 1691 that the first antimiscegenation acts were passed by the Virginia assem-

A story about a light-skinned African American who "passes" for white, Pinky *(1949) was banned in some communities because of its implied miscegenation theme.* (Museum of Modern Art, Film Stills Archive)

bly. These statutes were thorough, providing for punishment in all cases involving marital or extramarital association between white individuals and those of any other racial background.

During the 1870's notions of white supremacy and racial purity replaced institutionalized slavery as the driving motivation behind new antimiscegenation measures. In some states sexual intercourse between individuals of different racial groups was prohibited, but most laws followed the model of Virginia's Racial Integrity Act, which only forbade unions between white people and members of other races. Interracial couples who attempted to circumvent local statutes by marrying in other states or jurisdictions were subject to prosecution when they returned to their home states. Antimiscegenation statutes tended to place maximum strain on interracial couples and encouraged the breakup of mixed-race families. In many cases, couples were compelled to leave their home states to avoid legal penalties and social ostracism, forcing them to confront additional problems associated with physical dislocation. Denying the legality of such marriages raised the issue of illegitimacy, calling into question the valid transfer of property through inheritance to children of interracial couples.

The Supreme Court case of *Pace v. Alabama* (1883) represented an early challenge to antimiscegenation statutes. In its ruling the Court upheld the validity of the antimiscegenation law, asserting that it did not violate the equal protection clause of the Fourteenth Amendment as long as both parties were penalized equally. In 1967 the Supreme Court issued a decision in the case of *Loving v. Virginia*. The Court struck down state antimiscegenation laws as violating the principle of due process under the Fourteenth Amendment, since the sole purpose of such laws was the perpetuation of racial discrimination.

—*Raymond Pierre Hylton*

See also Eugenics; Interracial families; *Loving v. Virginia*; Marriage laws; Slavery; *Zablocki v. Redhail*.

Apgar, Virginia

BORN: June 7, 1909, Westfield, N.J.
DIED: August 7, 1974, New York, N.Y.
AREA OF ACHIEVEMENT: Health and medicine

SIGNIFICANCE: Virginia Apgar developed an internationally recognized test for assessing the general health and condition of newborn babies

Virginia Apgar was graduated from Mount Holyoke College in Massachusetts in 1929 and earned a medical degree from New York's Columbia University College of Physicians and Surgeons in 1933. She was the first woman appointed to a full professorship at that medical school, holding the position of professor of anesthesiology from 1949 to 1959. She also held a position as attending anesthesiologist at Columbia Presbyterian Medical Center and numerous other posts during her career. Apgar estimated that during her career in pediatric medicine she assisted in the delivery of more than twenty thousand babies.

In 1952 Apgar developed the evaluation procedure that carries her name. The Apgar score is an assessment of the heart rate, respiration, muscle tone, reflex, and skin color of newborn babies. The evaluation is made in the delivery room twice following delivery, the first time only sixty seconds after birth and the second at five minutes. The evaluations aid doctors and nurses in identifying babies who may need help in sustaining their lives. By identifying babies at high risk, the Apgar scoring procedure has resulted in saving the lives of numerous infants. Apgar also devoted her career to the prevention and treatment of birth defects, serving as vice president and director of basic research for the March of Dimes from 1959 to 1974.

—*Richard Adler*

See also Birth defects.

Arranged marriages

RELEVANT ISSUES: Marriage and dating; Race and ethnicity
SIGNIFICANCE: Arranged marriages are those in which parents of a man and woman make arrangements for their children to marry, usually based on religion, culture, finances, and class

Arranged marriages have declined in popularity, but they still occur frequently in Muslim countries, such as Saudi Arabia, Kuwait, and Pakistan. Wealthy families often arrange marriages to preserve their property. Most parents in Middle Eastern countries hope that their children will accept

Many arranged marriages among Asian Americans produce happy and successful families. (Ben Klaffke)

arranged marriages but usually do not force arranged marriages upon them. In India more than 90 percent of marriages are arranged. The divorce rate in India is approximately 2 percent, compared with 50 percent in the United States, where partners, not parents, choose their own brides and grooms. Indians explain their low divorce rate by claiming that couples are committed to marriage as an institution and to the family. For four thousand years Chinese society allowed parents to choose their children's mates, and gifts to brides' parents were similar to wife purchase. In modern times, however, industrialization and education have led to a widespread revolt against these practices.

Arranged marriages are a contract between families. The man's parents investigate the girl's family background before beginning negotiations. They want to make sure that the girl's family is of the same class, in a comparable financial situation, has a good reputation among class elders, and has no hereditary diseases. The purpose of arranged marriages is to match people from the same religious, economic, and educational background so that couples do not differ substantially in their fundamental values.

The man's family meets the prospective bride before the man does. They try to determine her willingness to conform with their family's living style. The future bride is expected to obey her mother-in-law and meet her expectations. Usually a meeting is arranged between the man and the woman. If the couple is willing to marry, the parents select the dates for engagement and marriage. In some families, the children do not dare disagree with their parents, but in others they have a right of refusal.

By its very nature of mate selection, arranged marriages lead to inbreeding. They further class differences in society. Arranged marriages tend to promote a patriarchal power structure. Wives bear the responsibility of caring for the children and the home while husbands provide for and protect the family.

In arranged marriages persons do not experience traditional Western-style courtships. Intimacy begins after marriage, at which time couples' bonds hopefully increase with the arrival of children. Men's role as heads of the family and women's role as caring wives and mothers is sup-posed to ward off chances of power struggles or marital rifts. Women must be skilled in cooking, sewing, and home management, while men must be able to earn a living. If couples disagree on issues, their parents invariably tell them to compromise. In arranged marriages it is out of the question to blame difficulties on a wrong choice of mates.   —*Marian Wynne Haber*

See also Courting rituals; Cultural influences; East Indians and Pakistanis; Hinduism; Mail-order brides; Middle Easterners; Patriarchs; Weddings.

Art and iconography

RELEVANT ISSUE: Art and the media
SIGNIFICANCE: As the definition of family has changed over the centuries, so has its iconography, or how the family has been portrayed in the visual arts

While the twentieth century has idealized the family as a nuclear group of father, mother, and the children they nurture, this construct has not always been the accepted definition of family in the past and is undergoing change. In earlier epochs the concept of family was important only insofar as it related to a political context or exemplified ideal religious, ethical, or moral concerns. This began to change in the early twentieth century as new family problems became part of the vocabulary of visualizing the family.

Mother and Child. The mother and child image, as separate from other representations of the family, has recurred in many cultures and many eras. In Christian art, images of Mary and the child Jesus are among the most easily recognized representations of family. Raphael, painting in Renaissance Italy, became famous for his sweet-faced, tender Madonnas. A mother goddess and her child appeared in Mesopotamian art in about 2000 B.C.E. and in Mayan art around present-day Mexico City at the beginning of the European Christian era. Similar examples have been found in such varied places as Egypt (Isis and Horus), Oceania, and Africa. Such widespread use of the mother-child image attests its power to project multiple levels of symbolism. In contrast, the twentieth century ideal of the nuclear family does not often correspond to the family images appearing in early Western art or in other indigenous cultures.

Perhaps the single most popular theme among Renaissance painters was that of the Madonna and child. (Blumenthal's Olean)

Prehistoric Era. Anthropologists tend to agree that human subjects in the art of the Paleolithic period represent fertility symbols. When the mother and child image appears, it is part of this imagery. Other examples of fertility figures are adult males and females with extremely enlarged primary and secondary sexual characteristics. Stone Age dwellers understood the need for procreation to perpetuate humanity, and they saw the paintings on the walls of their caves and the small carvings they made as necessary to ensure a high birthrate. The nuclear family group is absent from their art, but a basic iconography of the family had begun.

Mesopotamia and Egypt. During the Mesopotamian period, the artistic representations of family were limited to the religious symbolism of a mother goddess and her child. The goddess is remote; she commands respect and does not encourage thoughts of intimacy between herself and her child.

During the Egyptian period, imagery of the nuclear family crept in briefly. During the Late Period (about 1400 B.C.E.) scenes appeared in low relief tomb carvings of the Pharaoh Akhenaton and his wife Nefertiti showing the couple holding and kissing their children. This form of iconography is called a "conversation piece," because it depicts discussion and familiar interaction among groups of people, in this case among family members. Such an intimate scene of family feeling was highly unusual for the time, when rulers were shown as distant, powerful, and unemotional. It was also uncharacteristic because it portrayed the adults not as anonymous facial types but as they actually looked, even if such depictions were not true portraits. The purpose of such tomb representations was to contain the soul and protect and sustain it in the afterlife.

The Greco-Roman World. There are occasional artworks from both the Greek and Roman eras, usually funerary monuments or vase paintings, that portray scenes of family life. Narrative scenes are commonly found, as on a vase from the fifth century B.C.E. that depicts a drunken husband returning from a party and hammering on the door of his house while his wife, with one hand holding a lamp and the other up to her mouth, apprehensively approaches the door. Affectionate interactions between family members, grandparents included, can also be found.

By the first century C.E., ancestor worship and the concept of the self as part of a lineage had become so important in the Roman world that realistic portrait busts of male ancestors were created. Painted portraits of married couples also existed in this period.

Nefertiti, the queen of Egyptian pharaoh Akhenaton. (Library of Congress)

The Medieval World. By the Middle Ages, the portrayal of the family as a dynastic unit was used to proclaim legal land titles. Inheritance of earthly goods and titles, necessary to support the continuation of royal lines and the aristocratic class, were rendered symbolically in paintings and sculpture by the manner of dress. Fathers, as family heads, figured most prominently in family groups and symbolized their entire families. Fathers were displayed alone or with their sons to signify that they were the heads of their families and that they or their sons were responsible for carrying on family lines. When entire families were portrayed, the women often appeared smaller than the men to indicate that they were less important.

Family life as a subject for artworks was far less important than religious devotion, which dominated art. In the fifteenth century *Cleves Book of Hours* the Christian communion service was alluded to in the form of baking bread in a kitchen setting. In this way ordinary family life was linked to the much more important aims of religion. Such scenes of home life were infrequently used and confined to relatively insignificant objects, such as painted prayer books depicting the seasons or the months of the year and carved capitals in churches.

The Madonna and Child appear often and in prominent places. Their appearance was connected with religious and cultural symbolism, not with daily life as people lived it. Except in nativity scenes, the Holy Family did not often appear together. When Joseph was portrayed, he was relegated to the background, while the theme of the Madonna and Child appeared everywhere. In the early medieval period, in the tenth and eleventh centuries, depictions of the Madonna and Child had a monumental, distant, and austere presence. The seated mother became a throne upon which the miniature adult was displayed, as seen in the *Imad Madonna* (c. 1060). Much later, in the thirteenth and fourteenth centuries, the Madonna stood in a graceful swaying pose, appearing elegantly fashionable. She was both an earthly queen and the queen of heaven who, when she held her infant, seemed baby-like in appearance. An example of this is the *Vierge Dorée* sculpture at Chartres Cathedral (1240-1260). Neither in early nor in high medieval art was Mary meant to appear as an ordinary mother, although she intentionally evoked earthly motherhood. In keeping with theological interpretation, she was the throne of God or the queen of heaven.

The Renaissance World. With the advent of the Renaissance and its emphasis on exploring the world and earthly life as well as religious subjects, portrayals of the family group became more realistic in appearance, more familiar in treatment, and more common. While the variety of family subjects did not broaden greatly, the ways in which the family was portrayed grew significantly. Portraiture, as in the Roman period, became more important and was often tied to the recording of family generations and dynastic lines. With the great increase in the merchant class, family business activities were recorded in portraiture.

Religious subjects were often tied to depictions of family and everyday life. Paintings of the birth of Mary were set in contemporary Renaissance bedrooms, in which visitors to the nativity scene were often members of the families who commissioned such paintings. Here religious settings were really excuses for group portraits of family women. An example of this form is Filippo Lippi's *Madonna and Child with the Birth of the Virgin* (c. 1452), in which a group of women appear as the background to the Madonna and Child attending Anne at the birth of Mary. The infant Jesus, held by Mary, is portrayed as a completely realistic baby. The miniature adult of the medieval era was gone and the tender affection of mother and child evident. Leonardo da Vinci pictorialized the lineage of Jesus in a new way in his *Madonna and Child with St. Anne* (c. 1508-1513), an affectionate treatment of what appear to be ordinary people with one difference: An adult Mary is seated on her mother Anne's lap with Jesus playing at their feet with a lamb. Mary reaches out to him to complete three generations of family ties. Since Roman Catholic doctrine held that Mary and Jesus were products of virgin births, it was appropriate to exclude their fathers. In Michelangelo's *Doni Madonna* (c. 1503), however, the figure of Joseph plays an important role as he stands behind a seated Mary to help the infant balance on her shoulder, thus creating a group in tender and physically close interaction. By viewing such portrayals of the Holy Family, one can understand that the family was highly regarded during the Renaissance.

Donor figures connected real people with religious scenes. The husbands and wives who commissioned religious scenes would often be shown on the far left and right kneeling in prayer as they faced the scene. In Hugo van der Goes's *Portinari Altarpiece* (c. 1474-1476), Tommaso Portinari and his sons kneel at the left watching the Nativity scene while Portinari's wife, Maria Baroncelli, and daughter kneel at the right. Sandro Botticelli's *Adoration of the Magi* of the early 1470's goes a step further by placing portraits of the Medici family close to the Holy Family. Joseph stands well behind Mary, who holds the infant Jesus. The Magi appear along with a large group of people. The faces of two of the Magi are members of the Medici family while another Medici male appears in the crowd. The artist himself prominently appears among the crowd.

Marriage scenes presented couples surrounded by symbols relating to marriage. For example, in Jan van Eyck's *Wedding Portrait of Giovanni Arnolfini and Giovanna Cenami* (1434) a dog which represents fidelity stands at the couple's feet and a pair of wooden clogs lies on the floor, symbolizing the holy ground where they have performed the sacrament of the Roman Catholic Church.

A high point of family celebration is found in Andrea Mantegna's *Room of the Newlyweds* in the Ducal Palace in Mantua (1474). The walls of the room are frescoed with portraits of the Gonzaga family, who are gathered to welcome home a son, a cardinal in the Church. The figures are larger than life-size and appear to be gathering together outside the palace—a magnificent example of the continuation of medieval dynastic ideas into the Renaissance and a grand display of family accomplishment and status. Such artworks reveal the importance of the public image of family during the Renaissance.

The Seventeenth and Eighteenth Centuries. With the Dutch art of the seventeenth century, the Baroque period, scenes of family life became common. The United Provinces, or Holland, had a limited aristocratic tradition, and displays of status, while they had their place, were not as important in portraits as elsewhere. Subjects covered the entire range of home activities: playtime, meals, prayers, housekeeping, celebrations, work. Such domestic activities were depicted in accurate settings: in the street, the home, the workplace, and public places. In *The Feast of St. Nicholas* (c. 1665-1668) by

Jan Steen, a family is shown celebrating the pre-Christmas festival. The children have received gifts if they have been good and a birch rod if they have not. Three generations of family members are present amid a welter of toys and holiday foods spread throughout a room containing furniture and windows. Steen's *The Baker Arent Oostward and His Wife* (1658) is a portrait of a couple at work. These artworks contain an ethical or moral message. In *The Feast of St. Nicholas*, children are being taught that a good Christian behaves in a certain way; in *The Baker Arent Oostward and His Wife*, good Christians take pride in work well done, which keeps them out of trouble and leads to success in life.

As in the Roman Catholic art of the Middle Ages and Renaissance, depictions of the Madonna and Child also appeared in Dutch Protestant art. Gabriel Metsu's *The Sick Child* (c. 1660) shows a mother holding her young child, whose lassitude suggests that the child may not live. This symbolizes the shortness of life on earth and the Christian teaching that one must prepare for the life hereafter in heaven.

The seventeenth century in Holland was a great age of portrait painting. The portrait was first and foremost a record of people's existence and their place in the family. To fulfill this function, portraits of married couples and family groups were common. In such portraits, people interacted with one another; parents, especially mothers, played with their children and babies.

Family group portraits in other countries were often used to project a much more stately image. The Flemish painter Anthony Van Dyck, painting in England, produced a huge canvas titled *The Fourth Earl of Pembroke and His Family* (1633-1634). This ambitious work covered most of one wall in the largest room of the family's country mansion. The portrait contains ten standing figures: the parents, children, and children's spouses. A dynastic statement that set stately figures in a magnificent columned terrace outside their country home, its purpose of conveying public image was all-important.

The strong ethical strain in seventeenth century Dutch art continued in eighteenth century family portraits. Religious overtones were gone, often to be replaced by a strong narrative thread. In William Hogarth's satirical series of six works entitled *Marriage à la Mode* (1744), which he painted to

The second in William Hogarth's series of satirical Marriage a la Mode *paintings, this picture is titled "Shortly After Marriage."* (Archive Photos)

expound upon the evil of arranged marriages, a wealthy, titled Englishman marries his son to the daughter of a wealthy tradesman. From their first meeting on, the husband and wife progress through a series of disasters as they live their own lives and die sad deaths. Jean-Siméon Chardin painted family scenes sounding a quieter and happier key in which fathers were usually not present. Mothers or nurses taught young children lessons for future conduct, as in *Grace at Table* (1740), which conveyed the idea that the family exists to socialize children.

By the last quarter of the eighteenth century, the definition of the nuclear family had solidified into the three-generation standard of grandparents, parents, and children, which could be de-

picted in powerful ways. The French Revolutionary period bent that image in a political direction. *The Oath of the Horatii* (1785) by Jacques Louis David compared historical themes of the Roman period with contemporary times. A father exacts the pledge from his sons that they will stretch family loyalties for the well-being of the state. Here conflicting family loyalties applied to the theme of civil war in France, as Frenchman was pitted against Frenchman.

The Nineteenth Century. The Victorian era, which began around the middle of the nineteenth century, celebrated home and family as a haven from the outside world. Ethical and moral standards were as emphatically a part of that setting as they were in Hogarth's paintings. A painting of

Queen Victoria, Prince Albert, and their first baby shows the happy family in an ideal setting. Edwin Landseer's *Windsor Castle in Modern Times* (1841-1845) displays the ruler of England as any family of the time would like to have lived—happily in a homey castle. Dogs tumble gayly about, producing an attractive disorder, while the prince displays the birds he has just hunted with the dogs' help. Mother and child admire his efforts. She may be the wealthy ruler of England, but he is the head of the family, a lesson for all who wish for domestic bliss.

The despair of life could also be found in presentations of contemporary issues. *The Irish Famine* (c. 1850) by George Frederic Watts employed a desolate scene, emptied of everything but a horizon line, to paint the suffering of the three impoverished generations who form a tight group in the midst of nothing.

By the 1860's the visual arts began to disassociate from the historical past by creating new approaches to their subjects. The didactic approach was dropped as subjects were presented without comment. Mary Cassatt's paintings of the women's world of home and family reflected this attitude. *Mother About to Wash Her Sleepy Child* (1880) is a Madonna and Child without the religious, ethical, and moral overtones. Cassatt presented a straightforward picture of the mother-child bond without sentimentality.

Portraits of children had been painted in the seventeenth century, but it was not until the nineteenth century that they became common. *The Daughters of Edward D. Boit* (1882) by John Singer Sargent is an informal arrangement in which four children wear pinafores instead of dressier garments and two of the girls stand partly shaded in an interior doorway. Sargent's intention was to produce the informal stop-action effect of photography, which had been invented in this period and which made it possible to capture on film the kinds of subjects which had heretofore been painted and sculpted. While the public image of stately behavior remained the preferred way of portraying families, informal compositions also became common. Henry Peach Robinson's *Fading Away* (1858), a staged composition depicting the familiar plight of a person's slow death from tuberculosis, has a family gathered together around the reclining figure of a dying daughter. The father deals with his grief by turning his back to look out the window. Such sentimental and popular subjects projected the kind of family unity that the period favored.

The Twentieth Century. It remained for the twentieth century to present the erosion of family values and the changes in the nuclear family that accelerated in this period, as families were often reduced to mothers and their children. Formal portraiture became the domain of photography. *The Family of Saltimbanques* (1905) by Pablo Picasso is an early example of the alienation theme that became so common in the twentieth century. Alienation within a family of circus performers, the emotional separation of people living in close physical proximity, prevents the individuals from looking at one another. Even as they face one another, stand beside one another, and hold one another's hands, they wistfully look away. The young girl is seated in the corner, the bottom of her body dematerialized as her thoughts move away from the group. A quieter depiction of this theme was painted by Alex Colville in *Family and Rainstorm* (1955). Two children climb into a car followed by their mother. A swim ended by a storm is emblematic of family tensions. Artworks of the 1980's and 1990's reflected the growing awareness of incest, addiction, violence, and the disruptions to normal development which follow. In *Bad Boy* (1981) Eric Fischl, a painter of suburban life who often deals with middle-class taboos, portrayed an adolescent standing with his back to the viewer looking at his sleeping nude mother while he fishes in her purse to steal money. Viewers must confront two taboos at once, whether they want to or not.

Artists still produce works presenting a happier view of family life, but they are fewer and farther between. During World War II Norman Rockwell painted his *Four Freedoms* series as a patriotic response to President Franklin D. Roosevelt's "Four Freedoms" speech, which rallied the American people to the war effort. "Freedom from Want" made Thanksgiving Day its subject. A family excitedly presses around a table while the grandparents bring a turkey to it. There are no problems here. The great American family holiday makes everyone happy and that happiness, it is implied, must not be endangered by losing a war.

Modern depictions of family life sometimes offer what persons want to believe about families; often they expose the disturbing conditions in which many people live. Twentieth century art presents images of change that family life faces everywhere.   —*Ann Stewart Balakier*

BIBLIOGRAPHY

The literature on the iconography of the family is very slim; information on this subject must be gained for the most part from general works on art history.

Franits, Wayne E. *Paragons of Virtue: Women and Domesticity in Seventeenth-Century Dutch Art.* New York: Cambridge University Press, 1993. A general art and cultural study of the roles of women in the United Provinces of the seventeenth century.

Garrett, Elisabeth Donaghy. *At Home: The American Family 1750-1870.* New York: Harry N. Abrams, 1990. Family settings researched through paintings and drawings. A cultural history of family, not just a history of interior decoration.

Hoffman, Katherine. *Concepts of Identity: Historical and Contemporary Images and Portraits of Self and Family.* New York: HarperCollins, 1996. A rare book-length treatment of the iconography of the family in the visual arts, presented in the form of cultural history and dealing mainly with the twentieth century. Not strictly a visual arts discussion, it also contains film and literary examples.

Hughes, Diane. "Representing the Family: Portraits and Purposes in Early Modern Italy." In *Art and History: Images and Their Meaning*, edited by Robert I. Rotberg and Theodore Rabb. New York: Cambridge University Press, 1988. A discussion of how fifteenth century Italian family representations perpetuated ideals rather than actuality.

Langer, Cassandra. *Mother and Child in Art.* New York: Crescent Books, 1992. Mainly a picture book of artworks organized according to simple themes. A few of the examples are non-Western.

Lovell, Margaretta. "Reading Eighteenth-Century American Family Portraits: Social Images and Self-Images." *Winterthur Portfolio* 5 (1987). A discussion of the proper decorum for formal portraits of groups including all ages.

Pacey, Philip. *Family Art.* Oxford: Polity Press, 1989. Family art is art created within a family about itself. It can be visual, written or the creation of ceremonies.

Rybczynski, Witold. *Home: A Short History of an Idea.* New York: Penguin Books, 1986. Another cultural history based on interior decoration that reveals much about family life. This one deals with both Europe and North America.

Steichen, Edward. *The Family of Man.* New York: Museum of Modern Art, 1955. Exhibition catalog for the definitive photography show on this subject, and it is still the best. All aspects of family are covered from first love through home building to building a family. All ages, all cultures, and all definitions of family are here.

See also Cassatt, Mary; Childhood history; Entertainment; Family: concept and history; Film depictions of families; Literature and families; Rockwell, Norman; Television depictions of families.

Attachment theory

RELEVANT ISSUES: Children and child development; Parenting and family relationships

SIGNIFICANCE: Attachment refers to the emotional connection that forms in the first year of life between infants and parents or primary caregivers, a connection that has a great impact on infants' emotional development, specifically how they will form future affectionate relationships

According to attachment theory, pioneered by John Bowlby in the 1960's, infants develop a sense of self based on their interactions with their parents (or primary caregivers). The attachment relationship begins before birth, because expectant mothers' feelings about their babies influence attachment. At birth, infant behaviors such as crying, smiling, and vocalizing encourage parents' response to their infants. Over time, if parents are warm and responsive to infants' physical and psychological needs, infants develop the idea that they are worthy of love. On the other hand, if parents are unresponsive and rejecting or unavailable, infants may develop the internal belief that they are unworthy of love. When this happens, the ability to form positive, loving relationships is impaired. Events such as abuse, neglect, and early separation and loss can adversely affect attachment and may lead to negative behavioral patterns.

In 1964 attachment theorist Mary Ainsworth developed an experiment known as the Ainsworth Strange Situation, the purpose of which was to assess the quality of the attachment relationship. Infants (usually at twelve or eighteen months of age) are observed with their parents in an unfamiliar playroom during a series of separations and reunions. Observers watch to see how the babies react when their parents leave and then return. Ainsworth identified three types of attachment in children. Securely attached children show distress when the parents leave, seek and accept comfort

According to the proponents of attachment theory, the first year of a child's life is critical to development of a sense of self. (James L. Shaffer)

from them during the reunion, and then continue to play. Children with insecure/ambivalent attachments show extreme distress at the separation from their parents and, when the parents return, alternate between clinging to them and resisting physical closeness. Children with insecure/avoidant attachments show less distress during separation from their parents and avoid and actively resist any physical contact with them during the reunion.

Reactive attachment disorder (RAD) refers to the inability of persons to form normal, affectionate relationships with others. Insecurely attached children, particularly children with insecure/avoidant attachments, are at risk of this disorder. RAD children, described as violent, unpredictable, self-abusive, and unfeeling, have experienced early trauma, such as multiple foster care placements and placements in orphanages.

Attachment theory has influenced family life in a number of ways. The 1996 death of toddler David Polreis, an adopted child who was being treated for symptoms of RAD and whose mother was charged with his death, brought to the forefront the growing recognition of attachment disorder. Attachment disorder was seen as accounting for self-abusive behaviors and potentially abusive behaviors by frustrated parents unable to deal with the severe behaviors of their unattached children.

Custody battles portrayed in the media have also emphasized the need to consider the impact of attachment on emotional development. The 1993 two-year custody battle over Baby Jessica, waged by her birth parents and her adoptive parents, resulted in Jessica's separation from her adoptive parents, with whom she had formed attachment relationships after having lived with them since her birth. —*Holly E. Brophy-Herb*

See also Bonding and attachment; Stranger anxiety.

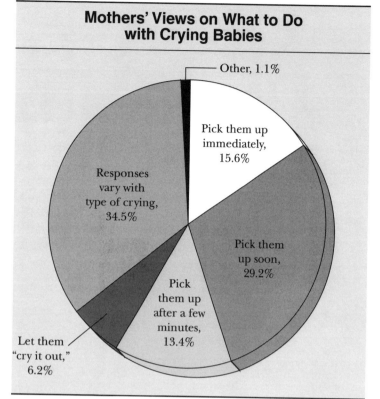

Mothers' Views on What to Do with Crying Babies

Other, 1.1%
Pick them up immediately, 15.6%
Responses vary with type of crying, 34.5%
Pick them up soon, 29.2%
Pick them up after a few minutes, 13.4%
Let them "cry it out," 6.2%

Source: Moms Online website (1998)

Note: Moms Online conducted an informal survey among visitors to its website, asking mothers what to do with crying infants. This chart summarizes their responses.

Attention-deficit hyperactivity disorder (ADHD)

RELEVANT ISSUES: Children and child development; Education; Health and medicine

SIGNIFICANCE: A disorder that involves inattention, impulsivity, and hyperactivity, attention-deficit hyperactivity disorder affects children's development and often afflicts persons when they reach adolescence and adulthood

Attention-deficit hyperactivity disorder (ADHD) is one of the most prevalent childhood disorders reported by schools and mental health clinics. Formerly known as attention-deficit disorder (ADD), it is one of the most researched conditions in the United States both because of concern about the status of ADHD as a disorder distinct from others and because of its impact on children's development and on their families, classrooms, and com-

One of the reasons that attention-deficit hyperactivity disorder has been closely studied is the devastating effect that it can have in disrupting classrooms. (James L. Shaffer)

munities. Difficulties of ADHD often follow children into adolescence and adulthood. These persons are at risk of experiencing future adjustment, education, and employment problems and require appropriate prevention, intervention, and related services to obviate such problems later in life.

Although persons with ADHD vary in the type and severity of their symptoms, the core features of the disorder are inattention, impulsivity, and hyperactivity. Originally, ADHD was thought to be a form of "minimal brain dysfunction" (MBD). Although many studies have indicated possible neurological differences between individuals diagnosed as having ADHD and those without ADHD, ADHD is no longer recognized as a form of MBD. In fact, the general MBD category has been rejected, because modern classification and diagnostic systems emphasize observable criteria for disor-

ders. Along with these changes in classification, investigators identified behaviors related to ADHD: hyperactivity, restlessness, impulsivity, aggression, distractibility, and short attention span. These symptoms formed the three behavioral constructs inattention, impulsivity, and hyperactivity described by the American Psychiatric Association. In 1994 the American Psychiatric Association began using the term Attention-Deficit/Hyperactivity Disorder (AD/HD) and described three different subtypes: combined type, predominantly inattentive type, and predominantly hyperactive-impulsive type.

There is disagreement among researchers as to the cause of ADHD. A number of biological, genetic, and environmental factors have been implicated in the development of ADHD in children. Speculation has included environmental factors, genetic inheritance, prenatal influences, brain structural differences, neurological injury during birth complication, vitamin deficiencies, and food additives, to name but a few. Most authorities agree that there are most likely multiple causes for a family of ADHD-type disorders.

Several types of medications are useful in treating ADHD. These medications are no longer limited to psychostimulants such as methylphenidate (Ritalin), dextroamphetamine (Dexedrine), and pemoline (Cylert), which have been shown to have dramatically positive effects on attention, overactivity, visual motor skills, and even aggression in 70 percent or more of ADHD children.

Some parenting styles work better than others. Parenting styles typically cluster under four classifications: authoritative, authoritarian, permissive, and uninvolved. The authoritative style is generally the most effective one. Authoritative parents provide a loving, supportive home environment; hold high expectations and standards for their children's behavior; enforce household rules consistently; explain why some behaviors are acceptable and others not; and include children in family decision making. Although the authoritative style is the preferred parenting style, the use of authoritarian, permissive, and uninvolved styles is not necessarily the cause of negative behaviors in some ADHD children.

Attention deficit hyperactivity disorder is frustrating for all involved. In the 1990's, however, further research shed light on the nature of the disorder. The key to the disorder is first identifying and diagnosing the problem; often this is done by a teacher in a school setting, with corroboration by qualified persons. The next step is to meet the needs of individual children with a program that is carefully planned, coordinated, and implemented to assure their best development and access to an appropriate education. Finally, parents must choose to understand and desire to learn more about ADHD and the ways in which they can help their children manage this disorder.

—Bruno J. D'Alonzo

See also Behavior disorders; Disabilities; Educating children; Education for All Handicapped Children Act (EHA); Genetic disorders; Health of children; Health problems; Learning disorders; Mental health.

Au pairs

RELEVANT ISSUES: Children and child development; Demographics; Economics and work; Parenting and family relationships

SIGNIFICANCE: Au pairs help satisfy working parents' need to find care for their children at a reasonable cost

There is a pressing need for the growing number of parents who work outside the home to find household help. For the wealthy, this service may be provided by children's nurses or nannies, but a less costly alternative are au pairs, usually young foreign visitors who are treated as family members. Au pairs perform light domestic duties, including child care, cleaning, cooking, and laundering, in exchange for room and board, a weekly stipend, and the opportunity to learn the language of the families with whom they stay.

Prior to 1986 it was a fairly common practice to hire illegal immigrants as au pairs, but the Immigration Reform and Control Act of 1986 increased the penalties that can be imposed on the employers of such workers. Au pairs play an important role in the growth and development of children under their care and in helping to foster and maintain family unity. *—Alvin K. Benson*

See also Baby-sitters; Child care; Day care; Nannies; Work.

Baby-boom generation

RELEVANT ISSUES: Aging; Demographics; Economics and work; Parenting and family relationships; Sociology

SIGNIFICANCE: As the largest birth cohort in North American history, the baby-boom generation has had a substantial impact on the processes and structures that characterize and have led to change in family life

Baby boomers, generally defined as persons born from 1946 to 1964, grew up in families that were larger than those of their parents. This boom in the birth rate was fueled by delayed parenting, which was brought on by Great Depression economics and World War II and was promoted by an economic boom that made people more comfortable having multiple dependents.

Postwar Suburbanization. The large numbers of children in families in the postwar era both affected and reflected the suburbanization of society in the 1950's and 1960's. Family life during this era was reflected in such popular television shows as *Ozzie and Harriet* and *Leave It to Beaver*. In both of these shows, as in most American households of the time, mothers were exclusively housewives and did not have to be economically productive. While nonworking motherhood had long been the social ideal, baby boomers were the only American generation that was able to afford the luxury of having one parent who could devote all her time and energy to housekeeping and caring for the children. However, the ideal of the single-earner household began to break down as the boom continued, and this ideal has not characterized the families that the baby boomers themselves have created.

During the early 1960's, baby boomers began to experience what some have called a sea-change in American family life. As more wives and mothers moved into the paid workforce, largely spurred by economic need, they began working earlier in their lives and in the lives of their children. This gave them more power in their lives, families, and society and came to reflect the growing ideology associated with the "women's movement." With the increasing participation of women in the workforce and increasing rates of marital dissolution, more persons born toward the end of the baby-boom generation grew up in dual-earner or single-parent households than had been the case in earlier generations. These influences intensified as baby boomers reached maturity and began to form their own families.

Baby Boomers and Marriage. While the average age at which persons first married declined throughout most of the twentieth century and reached a low point in the early 1960's, it began to inch up almost as soon as the earliest baby boomers reached marriage age. With this development, the average age at which men first married was comparable to that at the beginning of the twentieth century, and the average age at which women first married was even higher. These increases have been attributed to a number of influences. Baby boomers seemed to be more hesitant about marriage because their families had experienced high rates of divorce while they were growing up. The economy had begun to worsen, making it incumbent on those entering the job market to have completed higher levels of education than their parents, so that they could find desirable and profitable occupations. Finally, alternatives to marriage, such as cohabitation, had become more prevalent and increasingly acceptable in the late twentieth century. Such alternatives were not viewed as permanent but rather as advanced forms of courtship or as "trial marriages." U.S. Census Bureau statistics indicate that perhaps one in twenty American households were cohabitational during the 1990's.

When baby boomers—especially those who were born at the beginning of the boom—did marry, they seemed less committed than preceding generations to the traditional family as idealized in the marriage vow "until death do us part." Divorce rates in the United States and Canada continued to climb until about 1980, at which time

Changing U.S. Birth Rates, 1910-1996

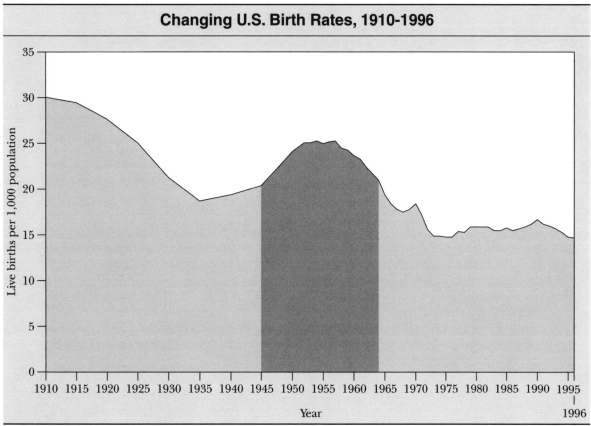

Source: *The Time Almanac 1998.* New York: Information Please, 1997.
Note: Baby-boom years are shaded dark gray.

they stabilized. Later baby boomers seem to have experienced somewhat fewer instances of divorce than their older siblings.

The fact that baby boomers have been late to initiate marriages and more inclined to end them than earlier generations does not signify that they are entirely disenchanted with marriage as an institution. They have a high rate of remarriage. Indeed, a slight majority of all American marriages in the 1980's and 1990's have been remarriages for at least one spouse.

Baby Boomers and Parenting. The marital patterns of baby boomers have undoubtedly affected and reflected their parenting characteristics. Baby boomers—especially those who were born during the early phase—have approached parenthood as they have approached marriage—belatedly and with what appears to be a lower level of commitment. Their rates of reproduction have been low enough to prompt some observers to refer to

them as the "birth dearth" and the "baby bust." Indeed, significant numbers of female baby boomers have gone through their fertile years without ever having children, although their rates of reproduction are not as low as those that characterized women's reproductive rates during the Great Depression of the 1930's. However, when female baby boomers finally did begin to bear children, the large size of the baby-boom generation offset the low rate of per capita births so that a significant increase in the U.S. birth rate resulted. This has been referred to as a "boomlet" or, more appropriately, as an "echo boom." There are indications that the actual rate of reproduction and the timing of first births among late baby boomers are more comparable to that of preceding generations than to that of their older baby-boom siblings.

For a variety of reasons, baby boomers have tended to be rather nontraditional in their parent-

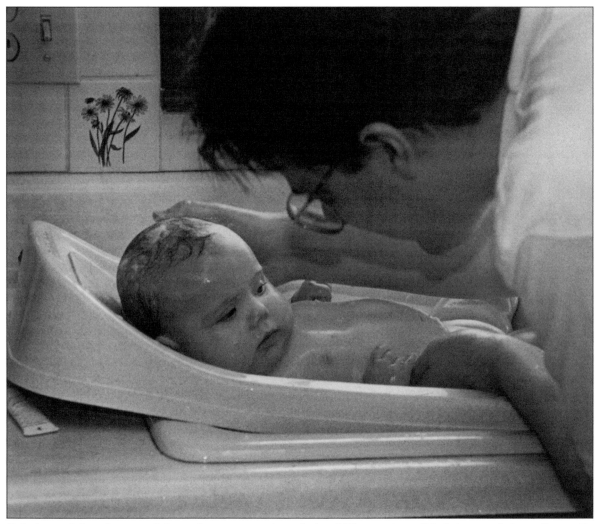

Baby-boom fathers have tended to take a more active role in child care than did their own fathers. (James L. Shaffer)

ing styles. The increased rates of dual-earner families and divorce among baby boomers have resulted in their children spending less time with their parents than was the case in previous generations. Thus, more children of baby boomers spend time in day care or have come to be known as latchkey children because of their lack of supervised care after school. More children of baby boomers have been functionally fatherless or have spent time in blended families than was the case earlier in the twentieth century. However, in late twentieth century North America African Americans have experienced historically higher rates of fatherlessness and blended families than whites.

While baby-boom fathers among intact families have been more active in the care of their children than were their fathers—largely because of women's changing roles in the family—they have not picked up the slack in parenting created by the dual-earner family. Moreover, they tend to involve themselves in low-demand child care (for example, playing with or watching their kids) rather than the high-demand functions of feeding and bathing children, which have continued to be the domain of baby-boom wives and mothers.

Baby Boomers and the Extended Family. With increasing life expectancy in the twentieth century adult baby boomers are more likely than previous generations to have living parents and perhaps even living grandparents. Since families have traditionally borne much of the responsibility of caring for elderly family members—and baby boomers appear to be unexceptional in this regard—many baby-boom parents find themselves squeezed between the demands of their elderly parents, on one hand, and their dependent children, on the other. Those in this position have sometimes been referred to as the "sandwich generation."

For those adult baby boomers who experienced the divorce and remarriage of their parents, relations in later life may be more tenuous than for those from intact families. Estrangement from absent fathers and aged stepparents—especially after the death of a natural parent—may prove more challenging than the relationships that characterized later life earlier in the twentieth century.

—*Scott Magnuson-Martinson*

BIBLIOGRAPHY

Coontz, Stephanie. *The Way We Never Were: American Families and the Nostalgia Trap.* New York: Basic Books, 1992.

Gerber, Jerry, Janet Wolff, Walter Klores, and Gene Brown. *Lifetrends: The Future of Baby Boomers and Other Aging Americans.* New York: Macmillan, 1989.

Light, Paul C. *Baby Boomers.* New York: W. W. Norton, 1988.

Michaels, Joanne. *Living Contradictions: The Women of the Baby Boom Generation Come of Age.* New York: Simon & Schuster, 1982.

Owran, Doug. *Born at the Right Time: A History of the Baby-Boom Generation.* Toronto: University of Toronto Press, 1996.

Russell, Cheryl. *The Master Trend: How the Baby Boom Generation Is Remaking America.* New York: Plenum, 1993.

Zill, Nicholas, and Christine Winquist Nord. *Running in Place: How American Families Are Faring in a Changing Economy and Individualistic Society.* Washington, D.C.: Child Trends, 1994.

See also Baby boomers; Blended families; Child support; Cohabitation; Day care; Divorce; Echo effect; Equalitarian families; Family demographics; Generation X; Latchkey children; Marriage squeeze; Single-parent families; Women's roles.

Baby boomers

RELEVANT ISSUES: Aging; Demographics; Parenting and family relationships

SIGNIFICANCE: Baby boomers, people born between 1946 and 1964, represent a huge bulge in the population and have thus affected nearly every social institution in the United States

The close of World War II marked a dramatic increase in both marriages and childbirth in the United States. This increase continued for nearly twenty years, producing a generation that came to be known as the "baby boomers." The large numbers of people born during this period forced wide-scale social change as they moved through each stage of their development.

In the early 1950's the first of the baby boomers started school. Throughout that decade, the number of school-age children skyrocketed, resulting in overcrowded classrooms, inadequate buildings, and teacher shortages. Because most boomers chose to remain in school until graduation, they became the best-educated generation in American history. In addition, the increasing mobility of American families throughout the 1950's and 1960's meant that many boomers were raised in nuclear families without the benefit of multigenerational family members close at hand.

The young adulthood of the baby boomers coincided with U.S. involvement in the Vietnam War. The soldiers who fought the war were nearly all members of the baby-boom generation. Many other baby boomers chose to avoid the draft through educational deferments, putting additional pressure on crowded universities.

Many baby boomers put off marriage and childbirth until much later in their lives than did their parents. Baby boomers were the first generation to have access to reliable birth control as well as legal abortion. In addition, divorce became increasingly common, meaning that many children of baby boomers have been raised in single-parent or blended families.

As the baby boomers moved into middle age, there was an upturn in the sales of cosmetics, nutritional supplements, vitamins, and hair coloring. In addition, because the most powerful jobs in society are held by persons in their fifties, the baby boomers have represented a potent force in the economy not only as consumers but also as producers. For baby boomers, midlife has also brought family challenges. Their parents have increasingly needed their help while their children have often returned home after college or divorces. Consequently, baby boomers have often found themselves sandwiched between two generations needing their financial support.

In the late 1990's, companies such as Merrill Lynch reported that baby boomers as a group had saved much less toward their retirement than they should have. Indeed, the stock market boom of the late 1990's has been attributed to baby boomers' belated attempts to put money away for their old age. During the closing years of the twentieth century, baby boomers neared retirement. It has

Traders working the floor of the New York Stock Exchange in March, 1998, when the market was moving toward record highs, thanks, in part, to heavy retirement investing by baby boomers. (AP/Wide World Photos)

been predicted that Social Security, health care, nursing homes, and retirement benefits will come under pressure as the baby boomers enter old age in the twenty-first century.

—*Diane Andrews Henningfeld*

See also Baby-boom generation; Echo effect; Generation X; Generational relationships; Marriage squeeze; Sandwich generation; Social Security.

Baby-sitters

RELEVANT ISSUES: Children and child development; Parenting and family relationships

SIGNIFICANCE: By providing care for children when their parents are away, baby-sitters can profoundly affect the development of children

The term "baby-sitter" is used for any persons caring for children in the absence of the children's parents. As an increasing number of women work full-time or head single-parent households, finding qualified, responsible baby-sitters has become an important issue for families. The first documented use of the word "baby-sitter" was in an American magazine article in 1947. Of course, it is likely that the term was popularly used in North America for some time before it first appeared in print.

Historical Background and Modern Usage. Although many people believe that in the past mothers assumed complete responsibility for their children twenty-four hours a day, this is erroneous. During the eighteenth and nineteenth centuries, for example, wealthy women employed wet nurses to care for their babies and governesses to supervise and educate their older children. Children from wealthy families generally spent more time with servants employed to care for them than they did with their parents. In addition, poor women often depended on a network of family and friends to care for their children while they worked outside the home.

The term "baby-sitter" encompasses a wide variety of caregivers. Perhaps the most common usage applies to teenagers, usually girls, who care for children on an occasional basis. Parents generally pay these baby-sitters an hourly rate far below the legal minimum wage. Teenage baby-sitters may care for children in the evening so that parents can go out or after school until parents return from work. Generally, however, teenagers are not used as full-time caregivers. Often, baby-sitting is one of the first paying jobs a young person (often a girl, but increasingly boys as well) might have. Responsibilities of occasional baby-sitters often include playing with the children, preparing simple meals, putting the children to bed, and putting away toys.

Sometimes, relatives such as aunts or grandmothers may provide regular baby-sitting for children. Usually this kind of baby-sitting takes place in the relatives' homes. In families in which both parents work or in single-parent households, such family networking can provide a needed service. Frequently, relatives provide child care without payment, an arrangement that can cause resentment and problems within families. However, under the best of circumstances, the children are cared for by a loving family.

At the other end of the spectrum are full-time, professional baby-sitters. Again, nearly all full-time baby-sitters are women; recent surveys suggest that more than 96 percent of all child care workers are women. Full-time baby-sitters may watch children in their own homes or in the children's parents' homes. Wealthier families may employ live-in nannies to care for their children on a full-time basis. In one kind of arrangement, parents may employ young foreign women to join their household for a year. In exchange for caring for the children, these young women, often called "au pairs," receive room, board, and a small stipend. Live-in baby-sitters are often responsible for more than child care. They are often expected to help with the housework, cook meals, and transport the children to school or other activities.

According to the *National Child Care Survey, 1990*, about 20 percent of the children of working mothers are cared for by relatives, live-in help, or other types of baby-sitters. Thus, while most families who need child care turn to organized day-care centers, a significant number rely on a variety of baby-sitting situations.

Issues. There are a number of issues concerning baby-sitters that affect family life directly. For example, finding qualified and reliable full-time baby-sitters can be a daunting task. Parents often have to decide whether they wish to opt for baby-sitters who charge low rates but whose skills are

Although television has increasingly taken over baby-sitting roles, many baby-sitters still take their job seriously. (James L. Shaffer)

limited or whether they want more educated, skilled caregivers who charge considerably more. For many families, child care is the third largest family expense, coming just after housing and food costs. Consequently, families often opt for the least expensive option.

Although such a large portion of family income must be dedicated to child care, most baby-sitters are very poorly paid; indeed, child-care workers are generally at the very bottom of the wage-earning scale in North America, often not earning enough to pull themselves out of poverty. Furthermore, baby-sitters are often paid in cash, their employers not reporting their wages to the federal government. As a result, while baby-sitters often do not report their incomes to the government or pay taxes on their earnings, they are also not protected by minimum wage laws nor do they contribute to Social Security. Baby-sitters are only rarely provided with any kind of health care insurance. Therefore, educated, career-minded women who want to work outside their own homes rarely find baby-sitting an attractive, long-term option. Thus, the women who are available for baby-sitting may be poorly educated or unable to hold other kinds of jobs. Certainly, there are exceptions to this. For example, sometimes young mothers with children offer to care for friends' children for little pay as a way to stay home with their own children and still generate some income. Such an arrangement can be mutually beneficial to both parties.

While live-in arrangements, such as that provided by au pairs, might seem to be the best solution for families who want quality, low-cost care for their children, such arrangements are not without problems. Often, there is a discrepancy between the expectations of au pairs and North American families. Young foreign women come to North America expecting a safe cultural experience similar to that of exchange students. When this expectation confronts the expectations of parents who want au pairs simply as a means of obtaining low-cost child care, conflicts naturally arise. Furthermore, even in the best of circumstances, such young women often find themselves isolated, homesick, and unable to make friends in North America because of their duties and the expectations of their employers. Sometimes such frustration can have tragic results. In a 1997 criminal case, a young English au pair, Louise Woodward, was convicted of causing the death of an infant in her charge. The testimony in the case revealed a profound difference of opinion between the young woman and her employers as to what her duties and privileges should have been.

Fearing that their children will be abused by their baby-sitters, some parents install hidden cameras so that they can videotape interactions between their baby-sitters and their children. That such devices are marketed to parents for this express purpose speaks to the degree to which parents worry about abuse. Ironically, a final problem that families face concerns beloved baby-sitters.

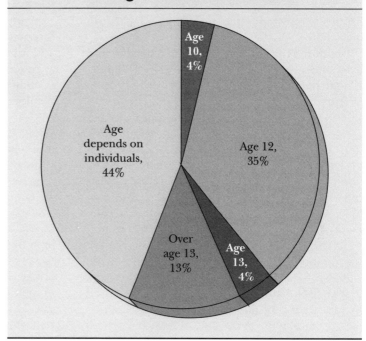

Parents' Opinions on Leaving Children Home Alone

Age 10, 4%

Age depends on individuals, 44%

Age 12, 35%

Over age 13, 13%

Age 13, 4%

Source: Parentsroom website (1998)

Note: In early 1998 Parentsroom conducted an informal poll among visitors to its website, asking them at what age children should be allowed to stay at home alone. This chart summarizes responses.

Children often suffer emotional stress and trauma when baby-sitters who have provided excellent care start new jobs. The low salaries paid to most private baby-sitters often make their departures inevitable.

Resources for Parents. Parents who need to hire baby-sitters, whether for an evening or full-time, should have baby-sitters recommended to them by friends and family. They should interview baby-sitters and observe their interactions with the children before leaving them alone together. In addition, parents should leave a clear set of written instructions for baby-sitters as to parents' expectations, rules, and emergency procedures. Parents can evaluate the performance of their baby-sitters by listening carefully to their children's comments, by arriving home a bit early to observe, and by talking to neighbors or family who might have the opportunity to observe baby-sitters and the children together. Finally, parents should expect to treat their baby-sitters fairly, notifying them well in advance if they do not need their services and paying them in full at the time of service. Families and baby-sitters may benefit from reading one of the many published guides for baby-sitters. By so doing, it is more likely that parental, child, and baby-sitter expectations will mesh and that the experience will be a positive one for all involved.

—*Diane Andrews Henningfeld*

BIBLIOGRAPHY
Brown, Robin, ed. *Children in Crisis.* The Reference Shelf. Vol 66. New York: H. W. Wilson, 1994.
Heins, Marilyn, M.D., and Anne M. Seiden, M.D. *Child Care/Parent Care.* New York: Doubleday, 1987.
Hofferth, Sandra L., et al. *National Child Care Survey, 1990.* Washington, D.C.: Urban Institute Press, 1991.
Litvin, Jay, and Lee Salk, M.D. *Super Sitters: Parent's Resource Guide.* Mequon, Wis.: Super Sitters, Inc., 1988.
Peters, Joan K. *When Mothers Work.* Reading, Mass.: Addison Wesley, 1997.
Wrigley, Julia. *Other People's Children.* New York: Basic Books, 1995.

See also Au pairs; Child abuse; Child care; Child Care and Development Block Grant Act; Nannies; Substitute caregivers.

Baby talk

RELEVANT ISSUES: Children and child development; Parenting and family relationships
SIGNIFICANCE: Baby talk is the common term for an important child development concept, "parentese," which plays an important role in children's language, cognitive, and emotional development

When talking with infants and very young children, many adults naturally adapt their speech by cooing and talking in short, melodic phrases and sentences. This modification is parentese, and it is an important and beneficial strategy to use with young children. Parentese is characterized by higher pitch, melodic sounds, short utterance length, simple, repetitive wording, and increased use of facial expressions and gestures.

The special intonation patterns and wording unique to parentese are heard in a variety of languages including English, Arabic, Mandarin Chinese, and Japanese. Both mothers and fathers use parentese. While the characteristics of parentese are the same around the world, there are differences in the sounds of parentese. American babies hear combinations of sounds such as "br" (as in brush) and "sh" (as in shoe), but they do not hear sound combinations common to other languages such as "db," "gd," or "ng."

At one time, parentese was not thought to influence children's development, although parents knew that babies responded with smiles and laughter when they used parentese. Research about infant brain development, however, confirms that infants' brains are biologically programmed to respond to rising and falling pitches, such as the higher pitch and sing-song tones common to parentese. Parentese is composed of short, sing-song utterances, such as "hel-lo ba-by!" Newborn infants' brains are genetically programmed to process about 1.2 seconds of information, the length of most parentese utterances. As infants grow into toddlers and young children, they are able to process longer bits of information so that parents and caregivers begin to use more complex language. Even when adults begin to use longer sentences and phrases with children, parentese is still an appropriate language strategy.

The slow, repetitive nature of parentese allows

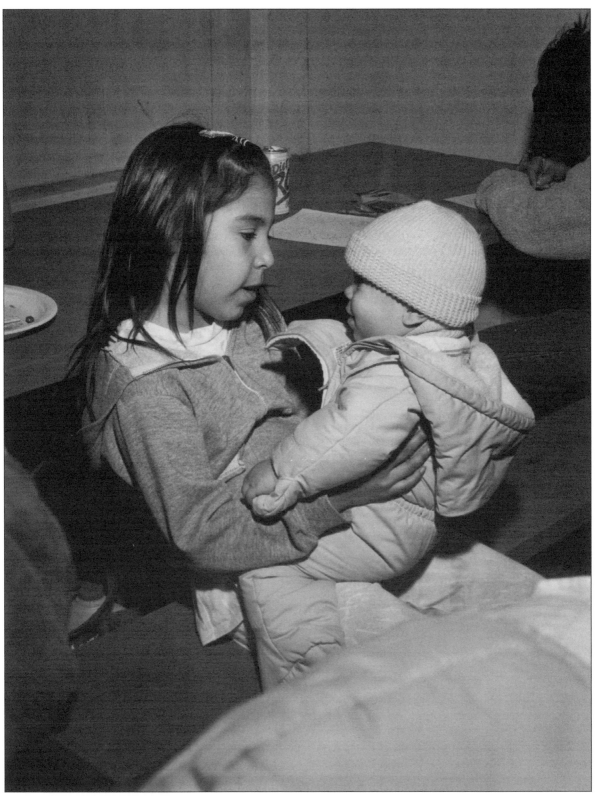

Older siblings can play an important role in helping babies learn to talk. (James L. Shaffer)

infants and toddlers to hear specific vowel sounds and the grouping of sounds. This helps with later word pronunciation. Short utterances give infants and toddlers the opportunity to grasp grammar more easily than long, complicated sentences. The use of parentese during toddlerhood helps children to match a word with the object it represents. Particularly in early toddlerhood, when children learn to speak simple words, parentese involves the use of invented words, such as "wa wa" for water. For example, because toddlers might be unable to pronounce "bottle," "ba" may be temporarily used.

Not only is parentese important to language and cognitive development, it also plays an important role in the emotional relationship between children and parents. The early, sensitive, and mutually satisfying conversations between adults and infants and toddlers help children feel loved, cherished, and powerful. These feelings are important to the development of secure attachment.

—Holly E. Brophy-Herb

See also Attachment theory; Parenting.

Baptismal rites

RELEVANT ISSUES: Parenting and family relationships; Religious beliefs and practices

SIGNIFICANCE: Baptism is a Christian ceremony or rite in which water is applied to individuals to symbolize their commitment to Christian faith

There have been different teachings from earliest times about modes of baptism. Entire immersion under water and sprinkling of water are the two most common methods. Some groups practice in-

Infant baptism is one of the first rites of passage through which some Christian children go. (James L. Shaffer)

fant baptism, in which parents have their babies baptized as a sign of their commitment and intention to raise them in the Christian faith. Others practice believers' baptism and teach that only those old enough to understand their own actions can be baptized.

Baptism was introduced in the New Testament by John, the cousin of Jesus. He preached to the people of their need to repent of sin and be baptized, and Jesus came to be baptized by John at the beginning of his public ministry. In the last recorded words of Christ to his disciples, he told them to go into the world and make disciples and baptize them in the name of the Father, the Son, and the Holy Spirit (Matt. 28:19). Throughout the history of the church, baptism has been one of the major Sacraments practiced in one form or another.

It is believed that most baptisms in early Church history were carried out by immersion. Ancient drawings and sculptures portray persons bowing forward while being baptized, but as time went on it became more common for individuals to bend backwards into the water. New Testament writings describe the baptismal rite as like the death and resurrection of Christ.

In the second and third centuries, the practice of baptizing infants increased. At the Synod of Carthage (251 C.E.) the bishops unanimously agreed that all infants should be baptized. The practice of sprinkling instead of immersion became prevalent at this time. It was understood that through baptism children's parents and godparents (close friends of the family) dedicated children to God. Persons took sacred vows that they would live exemplary lives, teaching and guiding children until they reached an age at which they could choose faith for themselves. Church members were called on to be a supportive Christian community for children. Some believe that the rite of infant baptism is the Christian counterpart to the Jewish rite of circumcision, because both symbolize identification of infants with the culture and faith of their families.

Those who practice infant baptism base their understanding on the biblical account of Jesus taking children in his arms and blessing them (Matt. 19:13-14) and the accounts in Acts 16 in which "entire households" believed and were baptized. In contrast other groups practice infant

dedication and reserve baptism for a later time when children mature and desire to receive the Sacrament of believers' baptism.

Some churches hold strongly to one form of baptism and some to another, while others allow individual choice. A few do not practice any of the Sacraments, teaching that outward forms and rites are not necessary for true faith.

—*Katherine H. Houp*

See also Compadrazgo; Godparents; Latinos; Religion; Roman Catholics.

Bar Mitzvahs and Bas Mitzvahs

RELEVANT ISSUES: Children and child development; Religious beliefs and practices

SIGNIFICANCE: Bar Mitzvahs and Bas Mitzvahs, important rites of passage in the Jewish religion, mark children's entry into adulthood

Bar Mitzvah literally means "son of the commandment" and Bas Mitzvah "daughter of the commandment." At the onset of puberty, identified in Judaism as the age of thirteen for boys and twelve for girls, Jewish youths become Bar or Bas Mitzvahed and take on adult responsibilities for fulfilling all of God's commandments. This includes assuming the responsibility for performing ethical duties, such as visiting the sick, as well as ritual duties, such as observing fast days. Within many Jewish families, Bar and Bas Mitzvah time marks the taking on of traditional religious gender roles, which require women and girls to make Jewish homes and men and boys to meet publicly with other men for prayer and study. Bar and Bas Mitzvahs indicate religious maturity only, as Jewish youth are still required to continue their schooling, obey their parents, and follow their nations' laws concerning adolescent privileges and prohibitions.

Jewish teenagers are responsible for fulfilling adult religious and ethical duties whether or not they participate in special Bar or Bas Mitzvah ceremonies. Although Judaism is thousands of years old, formal synagogue ceremonies were introduced for Bar Mitzvah boys in the 1600's and for Bas Mitzvah girls in the 1900's. Typically, girls in the traditional Orthodox movement still do not celebrate Bas Mitzvahs in the synagogue, as traditional religious duties for women center on the

Within traditional Jewish culture, the Bar Mitzvah is a rite of passage by which boys pass into manhood. (James L. Shaffer)

home. Occasionally adult converts to Judaism, graduates of religious education programs, or new female members of gender-egalitarian congregations choose to have Bar and Bas Mitzvah ceremonies. At synagogue ceremonies, individuals celebrating their Bar or Bas Mitzvahs participate in honoring the Torah (the Five Books of Moses) and in leading the congregation in prayer. Jewish law, however, offers no official rules about how to celebrate this important rite of passage, and many

Jews who came of age during wartime or as new immigrants did not have the opportunity to participate in formal Bar and Bas Mitzvah ceremonies.

Twentieth century custom established Bar and Bas Mitzvahs as an important family event. For as much as a year before Bar or Bas Mitzvah ceremonies and celebrations, much of a nuclear family's attention and financial resources are directed toward preparing them. Youths complete intensive courses of religious education in preparation for these ceremonies, while parents plan large parties. The conflicting emotions of stress and pride color the family's year. Such ceremonies and celebrations are considered by Jewish families to be as important as weddings, and extended family members often travel long distances in order to attend them, join in the celebration, and bring gifts to the new Jewish adults.   —*Laura Duhan Kaplan*

See also Holidays; Jews; Religion; Rites of passage.

Battered child syndrome

RELEVANT ISSUES: Parenting and family relationships; Violence

SIGNIFICANCE: Battered child syndrome is a phrase used to describe children who have been repeatedly abused physically and who have sustained serious injuries

Battered child syndrome is an accepted medical diagnosis used to describe the condition of physically abused children. The term refers to children with a multitude of physical injuries caused by repeated abuse. This diagnosis is reserved for the most extreme physical injury cases. The concept of battered child syndrome was coined in 1962 by C. Henry Kempe, a pediatrician at the University of Colorado. He used the term to describe the injuries he observed in children who had been battered by their caretakers. The injuries included lacerations, bites, skin and muscle bruises, brain injury, fractures, dislocations, internal organ trauma, burns, and scalds.

The effects of extensive physical battering associated with battered child syndrome can be significant to victims and family life. In most instances, battered children are removed from their homes because of concern for their immediate safety. Generally they are reunited with their families after the parents have undergone extensive treatment and the home is determined to be safe for the children's return. These children are at greater risk of developing emotional disorders and behavior problems than nonbattered children. They may experience delays in language, physical growth, and mental development. If physical abuse victims and their families receive treatment, however, the prognosis for positive change and

healing is quite good. Proper intervention with and treatment of offending parents significantly decreases the likelihood of continued abuse.

—*Edwin James Heimer*

See also Behavior disorders; Child abuse; Child Abuse Prevention and Treatment Act (CAPTA); Cycle of violence theory; Dysfunctional families; Emotional abuse; Postpartum depression.

Bedtime reading

RELEVANT ISSUES: Children and child development; Education; Parenting and family relationships

SIGNIFICANCE: Intimate and highly individualized bedtime story reading rituals enrich family relationships, influence children's development, and strengthen connections between home and school

Reading and telling stories aloud, reciting nursery rhymes, and playing simple word and story games at bedtime have long been cherished traditions in many families. During the second half of the twentieth century, educators and family specialists became aware of the role such rituals play in enriching family relationships and enhancing children's development. As the implications of the simple but pleasurable activity of reading to children at bedtime became evident, interactions and strategies used by parents and children were studied in detail and applied to other reading and learning situations at home and school.

Reading Rituals and Family Relationships. The pace and demands of modern life have reduced the amount of time parents and children spend together. Bedtime rituals are routines ensuring that parents and children spend time together each day. The feeling of physical and emotional closeness that develops at such times strengthens bonds between children and parents, opens lines of communication, and promotes family emotional health. Young children need consistency, which nightly reading and storytelling rituals provide, along with a sense of security and the chance to interact with a parent on a one-to-one basis. Children also benefit psychologically, as nighttime separation fears are replaced by feelings of safety, calmness, and control over a recurring situation. Parents benefit emotionally and psychologically as they relax, let go of the day's stresses, and immerse themselves in the story-sharing routine. The bedtime reading and sharing tradition is a warm and relaxing experience that ends the day on a positive note.

The ritual's continuity extends beyond the time set aside for reading. Studies and surveys have shown that beloved books are read over and over again and are revisited with pleasure and affection years later when children are much older or have become parents themselves. Children grow up and share their favorite stories with their own offspring. Thus, a routine involving a particular book becomes a family tradition and part of a family's heritage.

Reading Rituals and Child Development. In the sixteenth century, Martin Luther emphasized the relationships among family life, reading, and personal salvation. Early nineteenth century educators, such as Johann Heinrich Pestalozzi and Frie-

Many authorities on child rearing believe that it is never too early to begin familiarizing children with books. (James L. Shaffer)

drich Wilhelm Froebel, also stressed the role of parents, especially mothers, in teaching their children by reading to them and playing with them. However, it was not until the latter half of the twentieth century that educators and others interested in children's learning and development began to appreciate the impact of family reading rituals on child development and school success.

During the 1950's and 1960's educators in the United States, Canada, Great Britain, New Zealand, Australia, and other countries prepared their citizens to compete in an increasingly complex world by examining factors contributing to the school success of children. A strong link was found between children's home environment and their school performance. In 1964 the Plowden Commission in Britain emphasized the role of parents and home in helping children succeed. The commission's findings were instrumental in triggering detailed scrutiny of the home environment's impact on development, especially when parents read regularly to children from birth onward.

In the 1960's, 1970's, and 1980's interest in various aspects of children's literacy and language development increased. Gradually, the value of print-rich home environments and print-related home activities was documented. It became clear that children who participated with their families in bedtime reading rituals, whose parents read to them regularly before they entered school, had a greater chance of succeeding than those who did not experience such routines. Children involved in family reading sessions developed a rich and varied vocabulary, had good listening and communications skills, and were able to recall and retell stories more easily than those who did not. They developed an understanding of how stories are structured and could create their own tales, ask and respond to questions, and predict outcomes. Their language development was closely linked to cognitive development as they labeled, hypothesized, and interpreted during the reading ritual

Encouraging Children to Read

Childrearing authority Sylvia Rimm has outlined tips for teaching children reading habits that will last throughout their lives:

- Families should start reading together, silently or aloud, when children are in their infancy.

- Children should be allowed to stay up briefly past their regular bedtimes to read to themselves in bed.

- Children permitted to stay up to read in bed should be permitted to read whatever they want—even comic books, magazines, easy-reading books, or materials they have previously read.

- Parents should set examples by letting their children see them with books and other material they enjoy reading.

- Children should be taken regularly to public libraries and encouraged to visit libraries on their own when they are old enough.

- Parents should visit bookstores with their children and allow them to select books for purchase themselves.

- Parents should monitor the time their children watch television and play video games.

Source: Family.com website (1998).

and examined problems and searched for alternative solutions. These skills are acquired as children and parents interact, share ideas, discuss, and question during nonthreatening, relaxed reading sessions together.

As children listen to their parents read, they become attuned to the uses of intonation and voice manipulation to express meaning. As they watch their parents read, they learn the essentials of what is known as "bookhandling": how books are held, where to begin and end a book, the direction in which to read the print, and how and when to turn the page. These technical skills give children a sense of control and are milestones on the road to reading.

Children who experience family reading environments in which fantasy and imaginative play are shared with parents and siblings learn to stretch their imaginations as they visit people, places, and times outside their daily lives. They begin to see other points of view; this, along with the role-playing that often accompanies storytelling, helps them to grow out of egocentricity—a developmental characteristic of all young children. Conversely, studies of family reading sessions have shown that parents help children associate stories and texts with their own everyday lives, giving meaning to the different and unfamiliar while creating closer, more personal meanings that the family shares for years to come. In this way, cognitive and emotional development are linked by family reading rituals.

Other types of development are also influenced by families reading together. Affective development occurs through physical and emotional closeness. Social and personality development is stimulated by social interaction, questioning, responding, communicating, turn-taking, and appreciation of differing opinions and points of view. Finally, aesthetic development occurs as parents and children look at illustrations together, delight in them, laugh at them, and learn to recognize the work of individual illustrators.

Family Literacy. The influence of family reading on children's development and school achievement inspired educators to encourage all parents to read with their children at home. It became apparent that urging was not enough, however, especially in families considered economically, socially, culturally, or academically at risk. Parents in such families might be willing to read to their children but lack sufficient reading or language skills or the self-confidence to make reading a family ritual. Family literacy—the development of skills and strategies that stimulate literacy among adults as well as children—became an increasing concern in the 1980's and 1990's. In the United States, government and agency funding was provided for programs such as Even Start, Families Reading Together, and the Toyota Families for Learning Program. Applying the knowledge of how successful family reading routines and rituals have worked, these programs focused not only on improving parents' literacy level and skills, but also on parent-child relationships and interactions.

Family literacy programs acknowledge that literacy rituals in certain social classes and cultural groups may consist of nonreading events, such as oral storytelling or singing at bedtime. Some elements are common to most bedtime traditions: sharing and verbal interactions; physical and emotional closeness; a sense of security, consistency, and belonging. Other features, however, are dif-

Special Times for Reading

Not all Americans know it, but St. Valentine's Day, February 14, also marks Read to Your Child Day. The motto of this annual event is "Show your kids you love them: Read to them." A similar annual event, sponsored by Scholastic, Inc., is National Family Reading Week, held during the last week of April.

ferent. Reading rituals help develop print-related skills and knowledge along with other language skills. Oral storytelling and singing routines exclude books. The experience they provide is more direct; meaning must be derived from the teller's or singer's tone, pitch of voice, and expression, without the additional aid of text or pictures.

All types of family bedtime rituals that involve closeness and sharing are valuable, especially for the emotional health of families and the strengthening of family relationships. However, mainstream schooling in the United States, Canada, Great Britain, and other developed countries tends to emphasize reading rituals, thus putting some minorities and social classes at a disadvantage. Family literacy programs stress the importance of maintaining oral and other activities as parts of family traditions, encourage families to read together, and teach skills and strategies to make these reading sessions more meaningful.

—*Nillofur Zobairi*

BIBLIOGRAPHY

Butler, Dorothy, and Marie Clay. *Reading Begins at Home: Preparing Children for Reading Before They Go to School.* London: Heinemann, 1979.

Copperman, Paul. *Taking Books to Heart: How to Develop a Love of Reading in Your Child.* Reading, Mass.: Addison-Wesley, 1986.

Heath, Shirley B. "What No Bedtime Story Means: Narrative Skills at Home and School." *Language in Society* 11 (1982): 49-76.

Matthias, Margaret, and Beverly Gulley, eds. *Celebrating Family Literacy Through Intergenerational Programming.* Wheaton, Md.: Association for Childhood Education International, 1995.

Taylor, Denny. *Family Literacy: Young Children Learning to Read and Write.* Exeter, N.H.: Heinemann Educational Books, 1983.

See also Bonding and attachment; Children's literature; Children's magazines; Educating children; Literature and families; Myths and storytelling; Parenting.

Behavior disorders

RELEVANT ISSUES: Education; Health and medicine; Parenting and family relationships

SIGNIFICANCE: Epidemiological surveys show that 14 to 20 percent of children and adolescents have some form of behavior disorder; behavior disorders have a negative impact on the children, as well as on their families and society

Behavior disorders are clusters of abnormal or inappropriate behaviors exhibited by individuals. These maladaptive patterns of behavior may occur

To young children the difference between proper and improper behavior is only what they are told by adults. (James L. Shaffer)

because of stress, negative experiences, dysfunctional environments, heredity, or a combination of these factors. While most of these disorders begin in childhood or adolescence, many persist over time or recur throughout a person's lifetime.

Developmental Perspectives. Since behavior disorders usually begin in childhood and affect children's psychological growth, it is helpful to put them in a developmental perspective. First, some behavior disorders can be viewed as deviations from what is appropriate for certain ages (for example, a ten-year-old child who cannot sit still and pay attention in class). Behavior disorders may also be exaggerations of normal developmental

Many behavior problems of children are not revealed until they enter school, where they are constantly pressured to follow group behavior. (James L. Shaffer)

trends (for example, the rebelliousness of adolescence may increase to antisocial behavior). Behaviors that interfere with normal development and age-appropriate experiences may also constitute a behavior disorder (for example, children exhibiting separation anxiety may refuse to leave their mothers to play with peers).

In determining if a behavior disorder is present, both the severity of the behavior and its frequency must be considered. For example, feelings of sadness are common, but if they become severe enough to cause persons to lose interest in usual activities and contemplate suicide, then a disorder is present. Similarly, some fears in childhood are normal, but frequent, intense fears may indicate a behavior disorder.

Types of Behavior Disorders. There are a number of clusters of maladaptive behaviors that are considered to be disorders. The most common behavior disorders that are usually first diagnosed in childhood or adolescence are attention-deficit hyperactivity disorder; disruptive behavior disorders, including oppositional defiant disorder and conduct disorder (a type of antisocial behavior disorder); pervasive developmental disorders, such as autism; feeding and eating disorders, including anorexia nervosa and bulimia nervosa; and separation anxiety. Other behavior disorders may begin in childhood, adolescence, or adulthood. These include mood disorders, especially depression and the related behavior, suicide; anxiety disorders, such as phobias and obsessive-compulsive disorder; substance abuse; and schizophrenia. Some individuals with developmental disorders such as mental retardation or learning disabilities may also display a behavior disorder. In fact, it is common for children with one behavior disorder to have another. One disorder may cause another, or the factors causing one disorder may cause another.

Causes of Behavior Disorders. The study of the causes of behavior disorders has primarily focused on genetics and environmental factors; more recent research has examined how these may work together to produce behavior disorders. Family studies have been conducted to determine the role of heredity. In these studies the extended family is investigated to see how many relatives of persons with behavior disorders have the same or similar disorders.

Another strategy has been to compare sets of identical and nonidentical twins. If one twin has a behavior disorder, will the other twin have it also? If this is more often true for identical twins, who have exactly the same genes, than for nonidentical twins, then the disorder is believed to be caused by heredity. Because nonidentical twins share only 50 percent of their genes, if the disorder is caused by heredity it is less likely that two nonidentical twins will have the disorder.

Yet another way to determine the role of heredity in behavior disorders has been to study persons who were adopted by nonrelatives early in life, as well as their biological and adoptive families. If a behavior disorder is present in adoptees and their biological families it is believed to be caused by hereditary influences. However, if it is present in adoptees and their adoptive families, the disorder is believed to be due to environmental factors, as such children share the environment, but not the genes, with their adoptive families.

Behavior disorders that have been found to be at least partially caused by heredity include attention-deficit hyperactivity disorder, obsessive-compulsive disorder, depression, schizophrenia, and alcoholism. Some behavior disorders are believed to be caused by environmental factors. These factors may include experiences at any time in the developmental process, including disease or injury before or during birth. Environmental factors can include psychologically traumatic experiences, stress, and dysfunctional family environments.

Environmental Factors. The family is believed to be the most crucial environmental factor in behavior disorders. While some dysfunctional families may be the primary cause of a behavior disorder, it is more likely that the family environment is just one of a number of causal factors. The family environment may also serve to maintain a disorder caused by factors outside the family. One of the most useful models of family influences on behavior disorders is the learning-based approach. This model conceptualizes an individual's behavior, whether normal or disordered, as a result of learning within the family environment. Although behaviors may first be learned in childhood, they often continue into adulthood.

There are several ways behaviors are learned: through observation of role models, through reward or punishment, or through association of a behavior with a specific event. Maladaptive behaviors, including aggression and fears, may be learned by observing and then imitating others in the family. Alternatively, parents, siblings, or other family members may unknowingly reward maladaptive behaviors or punish appropriate behaviors. For example, children exhibiting fears may receive extra attention and privileges to soothe them. This could function as a reward that strengthens fearful behavior. In fact, this has been proposed as an explanation of how school phobia, or school refusal, develops. Children may also develop behavior disorders through learned associations. For example, abused children who are frequently locked in closets may develop a fear of all small places, known as claustrophobia. In this case, it is not the feared situation itself (small places) that has caused the fear, but the abusive family environment. Such children learn to associate closets with the fear they have felt as a result of abuse.

These learning processes need not occur separately. It is common, for example, for children to imitate parents or older siblings and then be reinforced. The apparent transmission of antisocial behavior across generations is an example of this. Children may observe aggressive behaviors in other family members and imitate them. The family may overtly reward such aggressive behavior, which they interpret as being an appropriate way to assert one's rights. Children's behavior may also be reinforced inadvertently because it leads to tangible rewards. For example, children who hurt others in order to take their toys receive awards for such aggression in the form of the toys they have acquired.

Beyond direct learning of maladaptive behaviors, families also influence their members through parents' family management. These are parenting behaviors such as disciplinary practices, supervision, and the emotional quality of the home environment. For example, parents who provide little supervision and lack control of their children are more likely to have aggressive children who display antisocial behavior.

The impact of various family environments on behavior disorders has been studied. These environments all involve circumstances that disrupt family management practices, thereby indirectly causing behavior disorders. Factors such as poverty, substance abuse, marital discord, and mental illness all disrupt family management. These stressors can lead to inappropriate or ineffective discipline, poor or nonexistent supervision, and negative emotional environments.

With most behavior disorders, there is not a single identifiable cause. Multiple factors, including heredity, environment, learning, and family practices are most likely involved. The disorders develop after a lengthy period of time in a multistep process. The interaction of hereditary predisposition and environmental stressors is believed to be the best explanation of why behavior disorders occur.

Effects of Behavior Disorders on Individuals and Families. Behavior disorders have varying negative impact on children's ability to achieve their full educational potential. Children in the United States with behavior disorders may be eligible for special educational services under the Education for All Handicapped Children Act (EHA) (1975) or the Americans with Disabilities Act (1990). Some children with severe or multiple behavior disorders are educated in separate classrooms for children with special needs; there they have teachers with training in management of behavioral problems. Other children, especially those with less severe disorders, are educated either full- or part-time in regular classrooms.

In addition to lower educational achievement, persons with behavior disorders may be less successful in their careers and employment than persons without behavior disorders. Some adults may be limited in their employment options because of lower educational achievement, while those adults who have chronic or recurrent behavior disorders may be bypassed for promotions or terminated from their jobs because of inappropriate behavior. For example, 50 percent of children with attention-deficit hyperactivity disorder experience continuing emotional, relationship, or work problems as adults.

The educational and employment problems of persons with behavior disorders have a serious impact on family life. Parents may have to provide extra help to their children with behavior disorders, perform additional daily activities, and cope with difficult behavior at home. Moreover, child care may be less available. They also have the added burden of fighting so that their children receive appropriate educational and ancillary services. As these children grow, their parents may find that they require more time and effort than other children of the same age. Parents expect children to be less dependent as they grow; youth and adults with behavior disorders, however, may require continued high levels of support from their parents.

Siblings may feel neglected because of the special needs of their behavior-disordered brothers and sisters, or they may be embarrassed by their inappropriate behaviors. Coping with a family member with a behavior disorder puts stress on the entire family. Remembering that some behavior disorders are actually caused or maintained by family dysfunction, it is imperative that the whole family participate in mental-health services such as family counseling and family therapy to treat the behavior disorder and to prevent it in the future.

Treatment. Behavior disorders in children have historically been treated with some form of psychological therapy. A single treatment method or a combination of treatments may be used. Psychotherapy for behavior disorders can be provided in a number of modalities: Children may receive individual treatment, family therapy, or group therapy. Parent training may be provided as the main form of treatment or as an auxiliary to child therapy. The theoretical approach used by mental-health professionals also varies. Some treatments based on psychological theories include behavioral treatment, which is based on learning theory; psychoanalysis, which is based on psychoanalytic theory; or client-centered therapy, which is based on nondirective theory. Many mental health professionals are eclectic and choose treatments based on the nature of the children's disorders, their age or developmental level, and whether the family is willing to participate in therapy.

Although a biological basis for many behavior disorders has been hypothesized, there are no medications to cure behavior disorders, although medications are used to manage their symptoms. Stimulants are the most frequently used of all medications for treating behavior disorders in children. Stimulants are most commonly prescribed for attention-deficit hyperactivity disorder; 75 percent of children diagnosed with this disorder improve with stimulant medication. Other medications used to treat behavior disorders include antidepressants, antianxiety, and antipsychotic medications. However, because medications may have different effects on children's growing bodies than they do on adults and because of potential side effects, children with behavior disorders are less likely than adults to be treated with medications.

Many behavior disorders begin in childhood and persist through adulthood. Some disorders with a strong biological basis, such as autism or attention-deficit hyperactivity disorder, are chronic even when treated, because no cure for these disorders has been found. Some behavior disorders can be managed with appropriate treatment, even if they cannot be cured. Other behavior disorders may be cured with appropriate and early treatment. Without treatment, these disorders may continue, or they may have negative long-term effects on individuals because they disrupt normal development. For many behavior disorders, not enough is known about the complex interaction of causes to predict what the long-term outcome will be. The negative consequences of behavior disorders on individuals, families, and society make it imperative that their causes be better understood and that the knowledge acquired be used to develop more effective treatments. The ultimate goal is to find ways to prevent behavior disorders.   —*Deborah Harris O'Brien*

BIBLIOGRAPHY

Cytryn, Leon, and Donald McKnew. *Growing Up Sad: Childhood Depression and Its Treatment.* New York: W. W. Norton, 1996. Includes explanations of the symptoms, causes, and treatment of childhood depression and the relationship between depression in children and adults.

Hart, Charles A. *A Parent's Guide to Autism.* New York: Pocket Books, 1993. Discusses the symptoms and types of autism, possible causes of autism, treatment choices and educational issues facing families living with autism.

Husain, Syed Arshad, and Javad H. Kashani. *Anxiety Disorders in Children and Adolescents.* Washington, D.C.: American Psychiatric Press, 1992. Examines the relationship between childhood and adult anxiety disorders and explains the subtypes of anxiety disorders and the main treatments for these disorders.

Kazdin, Alan E. *Conduct Disorders in Childhood and Adolescence*. Thousand Oaks, Calif.: Sage Publications, 1995. Focuses on types of antisocial behaviors that begin in childhood or adolescence, and pays special attention to risk and protective factors, treatment, prevention, and the course of disorders over the life span.

_____. "Developmental Psychopathology: Current Research, Issues, and Directions." *American Psychologist* 44 (1989). Highlights recent advances in diagnosis, assessment, and treatment of behavior disorders with a specific discussion of how these disorders emerge, evolve, and attenuate during the course of development.

Quinn, Patricia O., ed. *ADD and the College Student: A Guide for High School and College Students with Attention Deficit Disorder*. New York: Magination Press, 1994. Written for adolescents and young adults, this guide addresses practical strategies for coping with their disorders at home, school, and in peer groups.

Rutter, Michael, ed. *Psychosocial Disturbances in Young People: Challenges for Prevention*. New York: Cambridge University Press, 1995. Overview of several behavior disorders that focuses on these disorders' individual, family, and societal causes and how they can be prevented.

Wicks-Nelson, Rita, and Allen C. Israel. *Behavior Disorders of Childhood*. Englewood Cliffs, N.J.: Prentice-Hall, 1996. Examines the major behavior disorders first manifested in childhood and provides a comprehensive explanation of assessment, diagnosis, and treatment of these disorders.

See also Attention-deficit hyperactivity disorder (ADHD); Child abuse; Childhood fears and anxieties; Eating disorders; Family counseling; Family therapy; Heredity; Juvenile delinquency; Learning disorders; Mental health; Toilet training.

Bernard, Jessie Shirley

BORN: June 8, 1903, Minneapolis, Minn.
DIED: Oct. 6, 1996, Washington, D.C.
AREAS OF ACHIEVEMENT: Marriage and dating; Parenting and family relationships; Sociology
SIGNIFICANCE: Bernard's sociological studies of the role of women in marriage and the family provided support for the feminist movement of the late twentieth century

After earning her bachelor's and master's degrees from the University of Minnesota, Jessie Shirley Bernard earned her Ph.D. from Washington University in St. Louis, Missouri, in 1935. She was a faculty member at Pennsylvania State University from 1947 to 1964. After retiring from her position at Penn State, Bernard worked as scholar in residence for the U.S. Commission on Civil Rights in Washington, D.C.

Bernard's first book, *American Family Behavior* (1942), used impersonal social and demographic statistics to suggest that the American family was less than perfect in the socialization, protection, and affection it offered its members. Her full conversion to a feminist approach did not occur until the 1960's. In 1968, Bernard was commissioned to write a book summarizing the literature on marriage. Exposed to consciousness-raising sessions led by younger scholars, Bernard was led to rethink her position. In five books and a dozen scholarly articles published during the following two decades, she challenged the image of marriage as a state where males sacrificed their freedom to provide shelter and protection for women.

Bernard's heavily documented books, *The Future of Marriage* (1972) and *The Future of Motherhood* (1974), as well as articles collected in *Women, Wives, Mothers: Values and Options* (1975), argued that every marriage was essentially two marriages, offering different expectations and experiences to males and females. Marriage was often good for men but hazardous for women's mental and physical health. *The Female World* (1981) examined the way women lived in Western societies, and *Female World from a Global Perspective* (1987) extended Bernard's analysis worldwide.   —*Milton Berman*

See also Dysfunctional families; Gender inequality; Women's roles.

Bethune, Mary McLeod

BORN: July 10, 1878, Mayesville, S.C.
DIED: May 18, 1955, Daytona Beach, Fla.
AREAS OF ACHIEVEMENT: Education; Race and ethnicity
SIGNIFICANCE: Mary Jane McLeod Bethune was a prominent African American civic leader whose life was devoted to the education of African Americans

Mary McLeod Bethune was born fifteen years after the enactment of the Emancipation Proclamation and was the first of her family to be born a free American. Her early years were deeply spiritual and religious. As a young girl she was primed to believe in herself and her ability to lead. The strong spiritual and religious roots of her family life were the foundation of her belief in neighborliness, kindness, and humanitarianism. The concept of self-reliance within her family nurtured and strengthened her lifelong qualities of concern for others, independence, persistence, and perseverance.

Bethune's life is a study of dedicated involvement with African Americans, civil rights, politics, and women's issues. She gained stature nationally and internationally through her strong civic commitment and advocacy role. In 1911 she opened a hospital to serve African Americans who were refused treatment at their local hospital. She was the founder of the Bethune-Cookman College in Daytona Beach, Florida, and the National Council of Negro Women. She also served as president of the Association for the Study of Negro Life and History. As director of the National Youth Administration from 1936 to 1944, she was the first African American woman to head a federal agency.

Her whole life centered on advancing her race and improving the lot of working-class people regardless of race. In her later career, she was concerned about world peace and brotherhood, ideals that stemmed from her early family upbringing. Indeed, the traits of her family were highly symbolic of the life she led. She believed in the importance of teaching children what she called the head, hand, and heart of life: Heads think, hands work, and hearts have faith.

—*Barbara G. Blackwell*

See also African Americans; Educating children; Slavery; Volunteerism.

Mary McLeod Bethune. (Associated Publishers)

Big Brothers and Big Sisters of America (BBBSA)

DATE: Founded in 1904
RELEVANT ISSUES: Children and child development; Parenting and family relationships
SIGNIFICANCE: The Big Brothers and Big Sisters organizations provide role models and mentoring programs to children from single-parent families

Big Brothers, Inc., was founded in 1904 in New York City. The group organized to provide young, fatherless boys with father figures who would spend time with them and help guide them. Over the years, similar organizations were founded in large cities throughout America. A central organi-

A Big Brothers/Big Sisters office in North Carolina. (James L. Shaffer)

zation, Big Brothers of America, was established in 1946 to supervise the numerous Big Brother groups operating across the country. In 1977 Big Brothers of America merged with the Big Sisters Organization to form the combined Big Brothers and Big Sisters of America headquartered in Philadelphia, Pennsylvania. Local chapters are in charge of matching children to adult mentors. Many also offer additional services such as sexual-abuse and drug prevention programs.

Big Brothers and Big Sisters of America is geared to providing services to children between the ages of seven and seventeen who live in single-parent families. Such children are referred to Big Brothers and Big Sisters by parents, guardians, schools, and other social organizations. These children are without mothers or fathers through death, divorce, or abandonment and are in need of strong parental role models. Big Brothers and Big Sisters strive to match these children with adult companions.

Adult companions are volunteers who work to provide positive guidance, friendship, and advice to children on a continuing basis. Volunteers must be eighteen years of age or older and are all screened by Big Brother and Big Sister caseworkers. Couples are also encouraged to volunteer together for individual children. Caseworkers match children with adult volunteers, and it is hoped that long-term relationships will result. Volunteers are expected to meet with the children a few times a month and spend time together. They are encouraged to participate in activities with the children, such as films, fishing, and ball games, that might spark new interests in them.

Big Brother and Big Sister caseworkers assist in

assessing the needs of the children referred to them. The children need to show a willingness to cultivate relationships. Caseworkers also interview and screen potential adult volunteers and match them with suitable children. Caseworkers then maintain contact with the children and their families to make sure that the relationship is beneficial to the children.

The ultimate goal of Big Brothers and Sisters is not only to introduce children to new activities and interests, but also for the "Little Brothers" and "Little Sisters" to develop positive self-images. The friendship and championship between adults and children can help the latter learn to establish and maintain meaningful relationships later in life. It is also hoped that mentors can help the children make decisions regarding their future education and careers. —*Leslie Stricker*

See also Community programs for children; Father-son relationships; Fatherlessness; Single-parent families; Support groups; Volunteerism.

Bigamy

RELEVANT ISSUES: Law; Marriage and dating
SIGNIFICANCE: Although a preferred form of marriage in most of the world, bigamy is practiced by only a small percentage of the population

Bigamy is being married to more than one spouse. Bigamy can be divided into four categories: polygyny, in which one husband has two or more wives; polyandry, in which one wife has two or more husbands; group marriage, in which several husbands have several wives in common; and polygamy, which refers generally to polygyny, polyandry, or group marriage.

Polygyny is the preferred form of plural marriage in most of the world's societies. Nevertheless, the majority of marriages in such countries are monogamous because of two factors. First, the number of men eligible for marriage commonly equals the number of women eligible for marriage. Thus, if one man marries more than one wife, a second man has no woman to marry. Additionally, the cost of having more than one wife is expensive. Therefore, only the most powerful and wealthy men in those societies can afford to have more than one wife.

In the United States, polygyny has been prac-ticed by members of the Church of Jesus Christ of Latter-day Saints (Mormons). In the 1870's Congress passed legislation that prohibited anyone from being married to more than one spouse at a time. Although each state within the United States governs and controls marriage laws, this federal law prohibited states from allowing the practice of bigamy. Nevertheless, there are some communities of Mormons in the United States that continue to practice polygyny in defiance of federal law. —*Lisa Mize*

See also Marriage; Marriage laws; Monogamy; Mormon polygamy; Polyandry; Polygyny; Serial monogamy.

Bilateral descent

RELEVANT ISSUES: Kinship and genealogy; Marriage and dating
SIGNIFICANCE: Bilateral descent is a form of kinship system that affiliates people more or less equally with the relatives of both their fathers and mothers

Bilateral descent defines kinship more broadly, at least in theory, than does patrilineal or matrilineal descent. In practice, however, families that follow bilateral descent distinguish closer from more distant relatives. In American society this distinction dictates who might be invited to weddings or be expected to attend funerals. The line is not always clear-cut, but few Americans keep up with relatives more distant than second cousins and might limit most invitations to first cousins. Reunions, on the other hand, cluster around a family name and do not usually attract people with other names except in those families in which mothers bore the family name before marriage. As lines of descent may also influence a society's definition of incest, bilateral descent excludes potential sex partners on both sides of one's family, although perhaps not as distantly as in unilineal societies.

Since lines of descent often have to do with the passing on of property or other wealth, bilateral descent typically includes both sons and daughters of nuclear families. This means that more children share in the distribution of property. In cases in which a substantial part of families' wealth is concentrated in one item (for example, a house, a small business, or a farm), it may be impractical to divide or share it or for one heir to buy out the other(s), thus forcing them to sell the property.

—*Paul L. Redditt*

See also Clans; Consanguinal families; Extended families; Lineage; Matrilineal descent; Patrilineal descent.

Birth control

Relevant issues: Health and medicine; Marriage and dating; Religious beliefs and practices
Significance: Improved technology, different conditions of life, and changing behavioral norms regarding sex and family life have altered the ethical, religious, and legal parameters of contraception

In most cultures nature or society has intervened in some way to control humans' biological potential to reproduce. In families and societies, however, numerous children were often viewed as prestigious and in fact necessary for the support of older parents and more generally for the survival of a particular society or the human race. Eventually, in an increasingly industrial, mobile, and urban society with improved hygiene and medical technology, the larger number of surviving children came to be perceived as a handicap in nineteenth century Western Europe and, less acutely and generally, in the developing world of the late twentieth century. Accordingly, concepts of resource sustainability and carrying capacity entered into the demographic equation. Thus, a higher infant survival rate, improved contraceptive technology, and changing social attitudes toward sex and procreation—for example, the view that conception is no longer necessarily women's destiny—came to alter government policies.

Modern Developments. In Western Europe, North America, and most other advanced industrialized societies these and other factors reduced the fertility rate to approximately the replacement, or zero-growth, level of 2.1 infants per female reproductive lifetime. Thus, in these regions, which contain about a fifth of the world's population, natural demographic growth has nearly ceased. Yet, the population explosion widely predicted for the developing world of the twenty-first century may be more difficult to overcome.

International governmental and nongovern-mental agencies have publicized the idea that family planning can now be promoted and practiced in ways that are sensitive to the cultures and religions of almost all societies. These institutions have promoted family planning on the grounds that it can save the lives of many women who die every year from pregnancy and childbirth-related causes and also prevent many disabilities that are the common consequence of high-risk and often unwanted births. Family planning, they have said, can also prevent numerous illegal abortions, many of them performed under dangerous conditions that claim additional lives. Even more vocally, they have asserted that family planning can drastically improve the quality of women's and children's lives by helping women to time and space births desirably. In short, these agencies have emphasized that family planning can bring more benefits to more individuals at less cost than any single available technology. They have also insisted that one of the most effective ways of improving overall quality of life involves reducing the number of unplanned pregnancies that result in unwanted and "high-risk" children.

Birth Control Methods. Individuals and societies have relied on numerous contraceptive techniques, some dating back to time immemorial. These include behavioral methods such as total abstinence or periodic abstinence as in the rhythm method, intercourse without penetration or with withdrawal, or prolonged breast-feeding. Another group of birth control techniques are barrier methods, such as male or female condoms, diaphragms, cervical caps, sponges, and suppositories. A third group are chemical methods, such as injected Depo-Provera, spermicides and foams (used with or without mechanical devices), vaginal rings, intrauterine devices (IUDs), subdermal Norplant capsules, and "morning after" pills. Additionally, there are surgical procedures such as male sterilization (vasectomies), female sterilization (tubal ligation), and—by stretching the meaning of the term "contraception"—abortions. Generally speaking, because it is easier to control the female reproductive system than the male, contraceptive methods have focused mostly on women.

Despite thousands of years of contraceptive methods, there is no ideal or fail-safe form of birth control. Accordingly, alternatives that make repro-

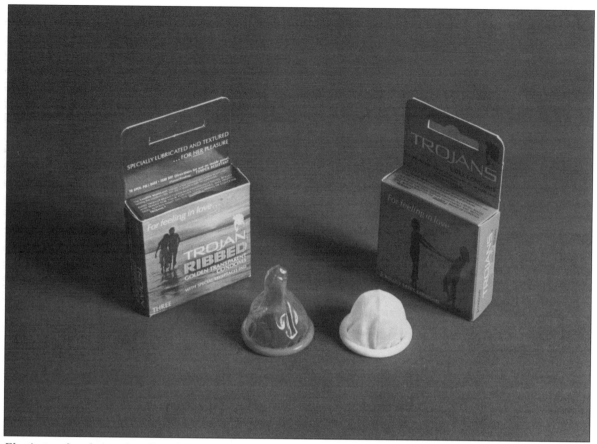

Elastic pouches designed to fit tightly over the male sex organ, condoms prevent conception by blocking the passage of semen from men to women during sexual intercourse. (James L. Shaffer)

duction more difficult or costly—disincentives—may be necessary if families and societies wish to curb population growth significantly. Often because of the expense of parenting, Europe, North America, Japan, and a few other countries have provided examples of successful voluntary restraints. China has demonstrated the effectiveness of controls by government fiat. Besides economic factors, cultural and religious ones also impact on partners' decisions on whether or not to use contraceptives or to choose particular methods. In male-dominated societies, as is the case in much of the developing Third World, such decisions are often one-sided—a situation that feminist groups have striven to change.

Canadian women, married and unmarried, practice contraception mainly by means of sterilization and the birth control pill. Indeed, Canada has the highest sterilization rate in the world,

about a third higher than in the United States and much above that in Europe. Some persons have expressed regret at their usually irreversible decision to undergo sterilization. Delayed marriages, divorce, and the wide use of contraceptives have reduced Canadian birth levels since 1972 to below the replacement rate.

Family-Planning Strategies. The term "birth control" was coined by Margaret Sanger, the leading American exponent of the birth control movement. While birth control refers to limiting reproduction, the broader term "family planning," or "planned parenthood," designates strategies used by families or government policies to regulate childbearing. The latter thus refers to the avoidance of conception or the spacing of childbirths and the various means used to accomplish these objectives. New methods of contraception and new means of overcoming infertility—such as arti-

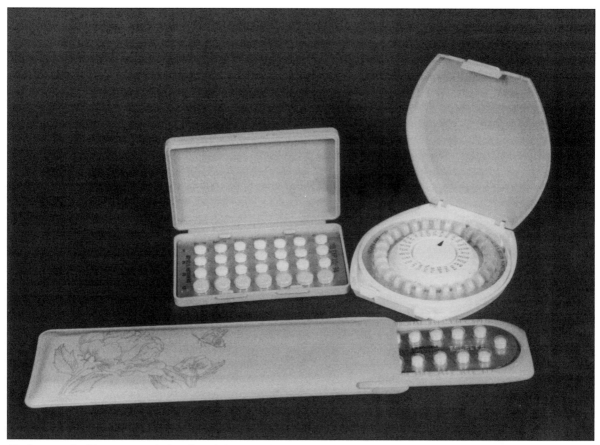

Birth control pill cases are designed to help users keep track of the days on which they take the pills. (James L. Shaffer)

ficial insemination, in vitro fertilization, cloning and other forms of genetic engineering, and surrogate parenting—have aroused social and religious controversy nearly as strident as has the question of abortion as a form of regulating births. The abortion controversy has centered on abortion's morality and legality and on whether public funds should be used to pay for the procedure. The shadow of acquired immunodeficiency syndrome (AIDS) and other sexually transmitted diseases has also had an impact on the use of barrier as opposed to nonbarrier contraceptive methods.

Changing Perceptions of Family Planning. Historically, one of the major roles of individuals and the family has been to reproduce and perpetuate the human species. In the first half of the twentieth century relatively few married couples were childless in the advanced Western countries such as the United States and Canada. Thereafter, the number of families with few or no offspring increased, especially as more and more women entered the job market and greater numbers of them became professionals. Many career women have decided to delay pregnancies or forgo having children entirely.

The change in American society's perception of family, lifestyle, and children is in part a function of the shift from an agricultural, rural nation to an industrial-urban and subsequently a post-industrial service-based one. As space in urban homes shrank, so did family size. Other technological advances, such as labor-saving home appliances, helped free women so that they could engage in market-oriented and leisure activities. In short, DINKs (dual income, no kids) have become commonplace. Especially in feminist circles, there has been a growing perception that children are only one part of a full and satisfying life.

Ethical Issues. The most traditional view of sex—still widely held on moral or religious grounds—is that its primary purpose is reproduction and that its only ethical context is marriage and the family. This view may have had physical and economic underpinnings, given that children in the United States were seen—and in much of the developing world are still seen—as assets contributing to parents' physical and economic security when they become old or incapacitated.

A certain ambivalence has entered the entire issue of population control, however. One reason for this is that feminist groups have tended to focus on the education and empowerment of women, reproductive health and rights, and the prevention of AIDS rather than on demographic objectives that they dismiss as potentially coercive. While feminists' goals may be commendable, they are of a longer-term nature. Assuming that better educated women in full possession of their reproductive—that is, their fundamental—rights would opt for fewer children, they would still have to be supplied with effective family planning programs and contraceptive delivery systems. In the meantime, the 1994 International Conference on Population and Development in Cairo, Egypt, skirted the issue that high fertility in many developing countries is a major problem and that demand for smaller families must be generated.

With the threat that the total world population will increase from approximately six billion at the close of the twentieth century to approximately eight to ten billion a few decades later, there is great interest and significant funding for the further development and wider distribution of contraceptive technology. Yet, some Western innovations may be too advanced for developing societies and thus inappropriate. Such devices—or contraception in general—may intrude on these societies' views of family, culture, or religion. Also relevant is the fact that contraceptives of the nonbarrier variety leave users exposed to sexually transmitted diseases. The implanted subdermal Norplant may additionally condemn its users to extended periods of infertility pending removal of the capsules from women's arms. This can only be performed by expert medical personnel—by definition in short supply in developing countries in which the population "problem" is viewed as most acute.

Religious Issues. Religion has had an impact on birth control methods and family planning. Thus, the rhythm method, based on the fact that women are infertile at certain times of their menstrual cycle, is the only method acceptable to the Roman Catholic Church, because it is considered "natural." Accordingly, the Roman Catholic Church prescribes celibacy and late marriages as alternatives.

Other mainstream religions have tended to alter their attitudes toward contraception in keeping with high population growth, improved technology, and social evolution. In North America, for example, many Protestant denominations have come to favor birth control. By the 1930's, conferences of the United States Council of Churches and the Canadian United Church, among others, expressed guarded approval of contraception. Given the explosive population growth rates in the developing world, most Western churches eventually came to accept family planning as a moral duty to safeguard the well-being of parents and children, to improve marital relations, and to check population growth.

Legal Issues. After the birth control movement got under way in the United States, most American states enacted "little Comstock" laws prohibiting the dissemination of birth control information or the sale of contraceptives. The prototype federal Comstock Law of 1873 had additionally banned the distribution of contraceptive information or devices by mail. In New York City, Margaret Sanger was jailed in 1916 for her activities, but her message was generally well received.

After many twists and turns, in 1965 the United States Supreme Court took up the challenge to Connecticut's "little Comstock" law prohibiting the dissemination of information and sale of birth control devices to married couples. The majority of the Court formulated a constitutional "penumbra" doctrine covering the newly discovered right of privacy which, it opined, was implied in the U.S. Bill of Rights. The principle was extended to unmarried adults in Massachusetts in *Eisenstadt v. Baird* in 1972 and to first-semester abortions in the landmark *Roe v. Wade* case the following year.

Considerable ambivalence remained involving teenagers and contraception, as evidenced in common law, which, with only minor exceptions, required that teenagers receive parental consent

Some conservative Christians regard procreation as the only justification for sexual intercourse and oppose all practices designed to prevent conception. (Dick Hemingway)

for medical or surgical treatments "to preserve family relationships." In fact, the very question of who was a minor became unclear as several states, following ratification of the U.S. Twenty-Sixth Amendment in 1971 granting eighteen-year-olds the right to vote, were in the process of lowering the majority age to eighteen. After *Roe v. Wade* the U.S. Congress and the U.S. Supreme Court came to accept the idea that teenagers, like their elders, were experiencing a sexual revolution.

In the 1976 case *Planned Parenthood of Central Missouri v. Danforth* the Court, arguing the right to privacy which by now covered both abortion and contraception, struck down laws mandating parental consent for minors' abortions. The following year, in *Carey v. Population Services International,* the Court held that even unmarried minors (in this case, children under the age of sixteen in New York State) could not arbitrarily be denied the sale of over-the-counter contraceptives. By about 1980 the Supreme Court required states to pay for contraceptives for those who could not afford them—including teenagers—or to facilitate girls' abortions even in the face of their parents' disapproval.

Years earlier "the pill" had already become the most widely used contraceptive in the United States, a factor as important as legal measures in facilitating the sexual revolution. The U.S. Food and Drug Administration continues to have the authority to approve new birth control drugs, devices, and other technology before they become available to the general public.

By the late twentieth century, a few governments around the world encouraged birth control policies. In the United States, however, there was a temporary reversal of direction during the so-called Reagan Revolution of the 1980's (and to a lesser extent following the Republican "Contract with America" of the 1990's). Because of its emphasis on family values and its antiabortion stance, the administration of Ronald Reagan supported the view at the 1984 World Population Conference that "development is the best contraceptive." In Canada there was a corresponding movement. Like family-values advocates in the United States, the Canadian movement was also often viewed as a backlash against the gains made by feminism for women in the family, society, and under the law.

—*Peter B. Heller*

BIBLIOGRAPHY

Fathalla, Mahmoud F., et al., eds. *Family Planning.* Vol. 2. Park Ridge, N.J.: Parthenon Publishing Group, 1990. Authoritative, illustrated manual on human reproduction sponsored by the World Health Organization (WHO).

Feldblum, Paul, and Carol Joanis. *Modern Barrier Methods: Effective Contraception and Disease Prevention.* Research Triangle Park, N.C.: Family Health International, 1994. Illustrated presentation focusing on the advantages of barrier contraceptives as being female-controlled, providing significant protection against sexually transmitted diseases and, unlike chemical contraceptives, having the fewest side effects.

Heller, Peter B. "Ethical Considerations in the International Distribution of New Contraceptive Technology: The Case of Norplant and RU 486." In *The Internationalization of American Business: Ethical Issues and Cases,* edited by John R. Wilcox. New York: McGraw-Hill, 1992. Considers the technological appropriateness and ethics of new Western birth control techniques for Third World societies and cultures.

Jones, Elise F., et al. *Pregnancy, Contraception, and Family Planning Services in Industrialized Countries.* New Haven, Conn.: Yale University Press, 1989. Comparative study of the relationships between fertility, pregnancy, contraceptive use, and family-planning public policies and programs especially in the United States, Canada, Britain, and the Netherlands.

Luker, Kristin. *Dubious Conceptions: The Politics of Teenage Pregnancy.* Cambridge, Mass.: Harvard University Press, 1996. Includes considerable material on contraception and family planning for minors.

McLaren, Angus. *A History of Contraception: From Antiquity to the Present Day.* Oxford: Basil Blackwell, 1991. Summarizes the history of reproductive technologies over the millennia and points to their liberalizing and their coercive potentials.

Sachdev, Paul. *Sex, Abortion, and Unmarried Women.* Westport, Conn.: Greenwood Press, 1993. Highlights an in-depth study of the sex lives, contraceptive practices, and abortions of seventy young unmarried Canadian women.

Zeidenstein, Sondra, and Kirsten Moore, eds. *Learning About Sexuality: A Practical Beginning.*

New York: The Population Council, 1996. Series of essays by various contributors evaluating the progress made in contraception and women's reproductive health programs.

See also Abortion; Childlessness; Eugenics; Family size; Family values; Planned Parenthood Federation of America (PPFA); Reproductive technologies; Roman Catholics; Sanger, Margaret; Sex education; Sterilization; Zero Population Growth movement.

Birth defects

RELEVANT ISSUES: Children and child development; Demographics; Health and medicine; Kinship and genealogy; Marriage and dating; Race and ethnicity

SIGNIFICANCE: Most birth defects occur in all races and both sexes and affect millions of families who have looked forward to the birth of healthy children

Birth defects are abnormal conditions that range from minor to severe and may result in debilitating disease, physical or mental disabilities, or even early death. Most birth defects occur in all races and both sexes. Some defects, however, are more prevalent among certain nationalities and ethnic groups. For example, the highest incidence of spina bifida (open spine) is among the people of the British Isles, especially in Northern Ireland. A few defects strike only males, and at least one condition affects only females. While science does not yet know the causes of most birth defects, ways to prevent or correct some of them are available.

One in every twenty-eight children born has one or more of the more than 3,000 birth defects. The March of Dimes estimates that 7 percent of all Americans have some form of a significant birth defect, including genetically determined degenerative diseases that appear in later life. The Centers for Disease Control (CDC) estimate that 2 percent to 3 percent of American infants are born with serious or disabling malformations each year. Nearly one-third of the children in hospital wards are there because of birth defects. Birth defects are the leading cause of infant death.

Classifying Birth Defects. Birth defects are variously classified. Some malformations are present at birth, such as heart abnormalities or spina bi-

fida. Others are metabolic defects or diseases of body chemistry, such as cystic fibrosis, which affects the glands and digestive system. Still others are blood disorders such as sickle-cell anemia and hemophilia. Others are chromosomal abnormalities such as Down syndrome, which causes mental retardation. Perinatal damage can be caused by drugs or other chemicals and maternal disorders such as diabetes or high blood pressure.

The causes of birth defects are many. For example, there are genetic influences that parents probably cannot control, such as hemophilia or Down syndrome. Environmental factors, which parents can control, are another cause; these include nutrition, cigarette smoking, alcohol consumption, drug abuse, or infections such as German measles and sexually-transmitted diseases. Also playing a role are interrelated heredity and

Down syndrome is characterized not only by impaired mental ability but also by a complex of physical traits that may include short stature, stubby fingers and toes, protruding tongue, a single transverse palm crease, slanting of the eyes, small nose and ears, abnormal finger orientation, congenital heart defects, and other defects that vary from individual to individual.

environmental factors, including radiation, lead, and methyl mercury.

The weapons of war have also apparently played a role as causes of birth defects. For instance, during the Vietnam War the U.S. government sprayed millions of gallons of Agent Orange, a combination of defoliants and the contaminant dioxin, as part of a scorched-earth offensive strategy. Veterans have persistently claimed that their own health has been affected and that their children have been born with birth defects. Studies have shown that women who served in the Persian Gulf War have a higher percentage of children with birth defects than other female military personnel.

Few birth defects can be attributed to a single cause. At times, the interaction of genes from one or both parents plus environmental factors may contribute to birth defects. Malformations of the mouth such as cleft palate, congenital heart defects, and water on the brain or hydrocephalus are examples of multifactor defects.

Prevention and Treatment of Birth Defects. Prevention is the best solution to the problem of birth defects. The detection and diagnosis of birth defects are often achieved through genetic counseling performed before pregnancy to learn the risk of inherited disease or an abnormal pregnancy outcome. Blood tests, ultrasound, amniocentesis, and chorionic villus sampling are also used to detect birth defects. Counseling, dietary modification, and various forms of physical therapies can be employed in the prevention and treatment of birth defects. An array of chemical agents, drugs, types of surgery, and radiation treatments are available. Indeed, human gene therapies are being developed to help with these cases. Despite extensive medical treatments, patients are frequently left suffering and in need of additional or improved therapy. Physicians are able to treat the symptoms of a disease, but not its source.

Sadly, there are times when nothing that parents or medicine can do will prevent a birth defect. Birth defects can—and do—happen. Sometimes getting early, regular prenatal care, eating well, avoiding cigarettes, alcoholic beverages, and drugs are not enough. Sometimes the only way to avoid genetic birth defects in a child already conceived may be to prevent the birth by terminating the pregnancy. For some parents, abortion may be unacceptable for religious or moral reasons. For

Amniocentesis

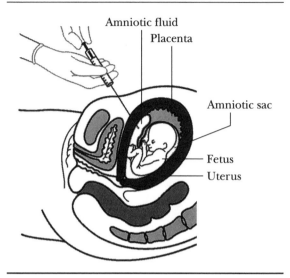

Removal and analysis of fluid from the amniotic sac that surrounds a fetus during gestation can be used to rule out or confirm the presence of serious birth defects or genetic diseases.

others, the severity of the defect may determine whether to abort the pregnancy.

Children with most birth defects can be treated medically or surgically, or they can at least be helped to cope more effectively with their disabilities through technology and physical therapy. Few birth defects can be completely corrected. Many significant birth defects, however, can be treated so that their harmful effects are slowed, stopped, or even reversed. The idea is to enable affected youngsters to reach their potential and to live lives that are as satisfying as possible. Medical and scientific research is underway to increase our understanding of what goes wrong before, during, and after pregnancy so that all children can fulfill their greatest potential.

Birth Defects and Society. Children with birth defects have been treated differently at different times and places. Sometimes, they have been considered "monsters" and put to death. This was often the case with obvious birth defects in ancient Sparta or with dwarfs in Adolf Hitler's Germany. The ancient Greeks interpreted the birth of deformed children as punishment inflicted upon their parents by the gods.

Modern technological advances, such as ultrasound, enable physicians to detect birth defects during early stages of pregnancy. (American Institute of Ultrasound in Medicine)

Legends and myths may have their origin in tales about children with birth defects. Cyclopean people with one eye in the middle of their foreheads, tribes with heads and eyes in their chests, beings with wings, and people with tails may be examples of stories of birth defects. In ancient Greece, people thought that the features of children could be improved before they were born if their mothers looked at beautiful statues.

Birth defects have been seen as divinely sent

omens of disaster or portents of doom. Disabled children have also been worshiped as if they were themselves divine, although rarely without overtones of fear and revulsion. Severely malformed fetuses have been aborted as in the case of thalidomide babies in the 1960's. By the time the drug, which physicians prescribed to women in early pregnancy to overcome the unpleasantness of morning sickness, was taken off the market, 10,000 to 12,000 babies worldwide were born with missing or malformed limbs, facial deformities, and defective organs. About half died as infants. Fetuses are sometimes allowed to die through the removal of life-support systems. Helen Keller, the blind and deaf advocate for the disabled, favored letting deformed infants die.

Attitudes toward infanticide, mercy killing, not treating defective newborns, and the right to die have changed over time. Since the 1870's, the introduction of morphine, anesthetics, and other potent painkillers helped physicians develop a sense of professional duty that accepts some risk to life in proportion to the amount of suffering relieved. As medicine has gained new power to cure pain, it has made the remaining incurable pain seem even less tolerable, both for sufferers and those who empathize with them. The treatment of impaired infants or the withholding of treatment so that death occurs is still a widely controversial and debated topic.

Birth defects may be organic in origin but their impact on the lives of their victims is social. In some societies even the severely disabled are well accepted and can achieve a high degree of normalcy. In others, they are considered outcasts. Attitudes toward persons with disabilities may change over time and differ from society to society. For example, among Middle Eastern Muslims the term "saint" is applied to mentally retarded persons, who are given benevolent and protective treatment. Before the nineteenth century disabling conditions were not seen as social problems and were handled by the family in the home. Segregated asylums for the mentally and physically disabled were built during the 1800's.

The location of treatment shifted from the institution to special classes and then to mainstream classes in the schools. The growth of intelligence testing following World War I and the rise of the special-education movement in the twentieth cen-

tury caused this change. From the 1970's on, federal law has mandated that no federally funded program may discriminate against persons because they are disabled. In addition, all disabled children must receive a free, appropriate education to meet their individual needs. Each student must have a written, individualized education plan constructed jointly by parents and school personnel.

Birth Defects and Families. Birth defects can have a profound effect on the daily lives of millions of people and their families. The birth of an afflicted child is a crushing blow to parents. Many parents have little or no personal experience with disabled children. They are likely to hold the same stereotyped and stigmatizing attitudes toward the disabled as others in their community, family, circle of friends, or cultural group.

Parents must not only grieve for children with birth defects but must also deal with the often overwhelming feelings of depression, loss, anger, guilt, and despair. Parents must also learn to care for and treat such children which will require extra time, money, and emotional resources. They must also decide, in especially severe cases, whether to bring their babies home or to place them in institutional or foster care. Despite the challenges, many children born with defects live full, active, and rewarding lives.

The physically and mentally disabled are often judged in a way that results in degradation or stigmatization. Parents of congenitally disabled children often encounter negative attitudes. Their everyday interactions with family, friends, neighbors, and strangers are likely to be more stressful and complicated than those of parents whose children have no defects. Many people are likely to stigmatize children who are different through hostility, avoidance, or, at best, "fictional acceptance." As a result, families may engage in "impression management" to hide their children's "differentness." Some parents try to "pass" their disabled children off as normal under stressful, complicated, or awkward circumstances. Eventually, most parents abandon such attempts. Many, however, develop relationships with other families who share their stigmatized status to maintain their self-esteem and to gain support. Families sometimes join support groups to learn more about their children's birth defects and how to manage them.

Research has shown that most parents of children with birth defects learn to love their children in spite of their disabilities. Parents of disabled children probably do not differ all that much from other parents, because most parents do not see themselves as having perfect children. They have or develop an attitude of realistic acceptance toward themselves and their children. Such parents can help their children develop a realistic acceptance of themselves.

Marriages do not usually appear to be adversely affected in the long run by children born with birth defects. Although such children undoubtedly place a strain on marriages, many couples seem able to adjust, and some even feel that their marriages are stronger as a result.

Siblings, in the vast majority of cases, are apparently able to adjust well to having a brother or sister with a birth defect. Having such a sibling is in many ways more difficult than having a normal brother or sister. Such children are more likely to encounter stigmatization in the community and may have more responsibilities at home such as baby-sitting. Severely disabled children create many challenges for their families. Although the emotional impact cannot be denied, most of the problems involve practical difficulties in caring for a child with unusual, long-term needs. These practical problems may continue long after parents have successfully come to terms with their guilt and sorrow.

Good extended family, social, and community support can enable families with children suffering from relatively severe birth defects to maintain a practically normal lifestyle. In many cases, researchers have found that the family life of those with disabled children is not significantly different from that of families whose children are not disabled.

—Fred Buchstein

BIBLIOGRAPHY

Darling, Rosalyn Benjamin, and Jon Darling. *Children Who Are Different: Meeting the Challenges of Birth Defects in Society*. St. Louis: C. V. Mosby, 1982. Provides an in-depth discussion of the social aspects of children with birth defects, their family experiences, and practical advice for professionals who help them.

Donley, Carol, and Sheryl Buckley, eds. *The Tyranny of the Normal: An Anthology*. Kent, Ohio: Kent State University Press, 1996. Collection of nonfiction essays and fiction about people with deformities that focuses on what it means to be abnormal from the point of view of health care professionals, writers, and people living with such conditions.

Fishbein, Morris, M.D., ed. *Birth Defects*. Philadelphia: J. B. Lippincott, 1963. Provides an overview of the nature of birth defects, including a history of how such defects have affected individuals, families, and society.

Garland, Robert. *The Eye of the Beholder: Deformity and Disability in the Graeco-Roman World*. Ithaca, N.Y.: Cornell University Press, 1995. Explores the meaning of having an imperfect body in a world that expected bodily and mental perfection.

Gliedman, John, and William Roth. *The Unexpected Minority: Handicapped Children in America*. New York: Harcourt Brace Jovanovich, 1980. Explain what it means to be disabled so that friends, family members, and others will better appreciate the challenges.

Gravelle, Karen. *Understanding Birth Defects*. New York: Franklin Watts, 1990. Covers what birth defects are, how to prevent them, what to do for children who have them, and their impact on children and families.

Pernick, Martin S. *The Black Stork: Eugenics and the Death of "Defective" Babies in American Medicine and Motion Pictures Since 1915*. New York: Oxford University Press, 1996. Narrative about physicians and filmmakers and the euthanasia of children with severe birth defects, especially in the early twentieth century.

Reuben, Carolyn. *The Healthy Baby Book: A Parent's Guide to Preventing Birth Defects and Other Long-Term Medical Problems Before, During, and After Pregnancy*. New York: Jeremy P. Tarcher/Perigee, 1992. Straightforward how-to guide that offers advice to parents.

Thomson, Rosemarie Garland. *Freakery: Cultural Spectacles of the Extraordinary Body*. New York: New York University Press, 1996. Anthology that explores how people with birth defects have been treated in the marketplace by promoters such as P. T. Barnum.

Wilson, Dudley. *Signs and Portents: Monstrous Birth from the Middle Ages to the Enlightenment*. London: Routledge, 1993. History about changing attitudes and knowledge of birth defects.

See also Abortion; Acquired immunodeficiency syndrome (AIDS); Alcoholism and drug abuse; Childbirth; Death; Euthanasia; Genetic disorders; Health of children; Health problems; Heredity; Infanticide; Pediatric AIDS; Pregnancy; Sudden infant death syndrome (SIDS).

Birth order

RELEVANT ISSUES: Children and child development; Parenting and family relationships

SIGNIFICANCE: The order of siblings' births in families influences both how they interact with other family members and the personal characteristics they develop

Birth order has been of great interest in both ancient and modern times. Early in Western history, the firstborn was considered heir to the fa-ther's estate. Order of birth was part of the formula to determine who would become monarch in royal families. In the late nineteenth and twentieth centuries, psychiatrists used birth order as a key to understanding children's personality characteristics. Family therapists have seen birth order as a key to understanding how each child in the family can experience the same family differently.

"Birth order" means the actual numerical order in which a person is born into a family. Related terms include "sibling position," "systemic position," and "place in the family constellation." In contrast to birth order, other terms concern the roles that evolve for family members because of the interplay between family needs at the moments of their births and their individual needs.

Three major models of birth order have evolved. Alfred Adler postulated differences between only, oldest, middle, and youngest children.

Children become aware of their own birth-order positions from an early age. (James L. Shaffer)

Walter Toman was interested in how marriage and dating partners carry patterns of their relationships with their siblings into mate selection and marriage. The systemic model proposed by Margaret H. Hoopes and James M. Harper identified specific characteristics of birth order for first, second, third, and fourth children.

Only Children. Folklore about only children painted them as spoiled and pampered. However, modern research has shown that "only children" compare favorably with others. They are most like first children. This is not surprising, since all first children are only children for some part of their lives.

The major differences between only children and other types of siblings occur in the areas of achievement, language use, and need for affiliation. Like first children, only children are disproportionately represented in higher levels of education and tend to enjoy higher occupational and educational achievement than other sibling groups. Only and first children have larger vocabularies than children in other sibling positions and tend to rely on verbal skills for coping. One explanation for this tendency is that older children have more interaction time with adults, and the adult world is largely one of verbal expression. Only children appear to spend more time in solitary activities and do not feel a need to seek out social contacts as much as other children. Nevertheless, only children seem to develop good social skills and interpersonal relationships.

Because of the problems single-parent families face, there is some concern that the emotional health of only children may be more at risk in single-parent than in dual-parent families. However, children with siblings in single-parent families tend to be less at risk than only children. Only children in single-parent families are especially affected by the lack of social support of siblings. Because a single parent has only one child to talk to, the demand on the child to support the parent is greater than when there are additional children.

First and Oldest Children. First children in healthy families learn to be achievers. They are exposed to all the hopes and fears not only of their parents but also of extended family members. The first smile, first word, first step, first tooth, and first day of school are watched by parents, grandparents, and other relatives. If expectations are too high, first children may give up and become rebellious and underachieving. However, most first children learn to achieve results that are important to their families. Firstborn children are disproportionately represented in professional occupations and in politics.

Firstborn children's sense of security depends largely on meeting others' expectations. They have trouble admitting that they are wrong and feel threatened when they are not "right." Consequently, they often insist that their perceptions are correct, despite all evidence to the contrary. Having assumed the role of trying to be "good enough" for their parents, firstborn children base their evaluations of themselves on what they achieve and what others think of their achievements—in other words, on what they do, rather than on who they are.

In their worldview, firstborns focus on the most observable, explicit details. An important part of explicit detail is language. They are verbal and use language to their advantage in conflict with others. When threatened, firstborn children often resort to arguments over what is meant by a specific word, or they may report in detail what has been said. They often gather information in excess and want to know details about everything. They may not be good at setting limits for themselves. For example, firstborn students may feel they have to exhaust every reference in the library before they can start writing a paper. When family members appear to have secrets or withhold details, firstborn children tend to pester them for information.

Second Children. Parents anticipating the birth of a second child often wonder whether they have enough love, resources, and space to meet the needs of an additional child. With the birth of a second child, parents tend to be more concerned with creating a "place," both physically and psychologically, than they are with the birth of a first child. This is a time of introspection for the family. Parents are more focused on internal organization and resources. They must cope with the increased complexity of more family members.

Second children learn that having a place is important. Moreover, family introspection conditions them to pay attention to underlying feelings and desires. When second children feel their physical or emotional "place" is threatened, they

Behavior Characteristics of Four Sibling Positions

	First/Only Child	Second Child	Third Child	Fourth Child
What helps them feel secure	Being right	Having physical and emotional place	Being given choices	Having harmony in family
What threatens them/ How others can help	Disapproval/ Approving their efforts and intent	Losing sense of place/ Accepting them as persons with separate identities	Having choices removed/ Offering appreciation and choices	Disruptive pain in family/ Assuring them it is not their fault
How they respond when threatened	Becoming immovable; compartmentalizing; insisting they are right	Becoming rebellious; seeing things as black and white; becoming either very emotional or very rational	Appearing apathetic; not committing to single choices; turning inward	Appearing irresponsible; cutting out important information; acting helpless
How they make sense out of the world	Gathering facts and details; wanting to know everything	Visualizing and creating images; looking for unspoken rules	Seeing connections among things	Looking for purpose; connecting information to larger pictures
Problems their ways of making sense can create	Rigid thinking	Making unsubstantiated assumptions	Ignoring details and focusing only on connections	Ignoring information when it becomes overwhelming

appear uncooperative. If they feel that their parents do not provide an emotional place, they will pester them, not necessarily about a place but about inconsequential things.

Because of the interplay between the family's inward focus and the child's need to belong, second children view their world as full of unspoken information. They pay attention to others' underlying moods, their nonverbal behavior, and their tone of voice more than to the content of words. They are often aware of how others feel even when they do not express emotion. They are sensitive to incongruencies between outward behavior and underlying feelings in family members and in the family as a whole. They often try to get other family members to acknowledge their feelings. When others do not admit what they are feeling, second children can become confused and have difficulty making sense out of what they themselves feel. They sometimes make the mistake of

assuming that others' feelings are their own. Second children can be highly emotional one minute and flip to the other extreme of being highly intellectual or rational the next.

In interpersonal relationships, second children often act like extensions of other persons. They are especially sensitive to the parent whose role is most related to stability and emotions in the family. For example, second children might become so sensitive to their mothers that they lose their sense of separateness. They might make sure that the mothering functions are carried out and that their mothers are doing what good mothers should do.

Third Children. When a third child is born, the family becomes much more complex. Because of the number of people in the family, third children are more exposed at birth to other two-person relationships in the family than are older siblings. They often find themselves with both their parents, or with one parent and another sibling, or with two siblings. As a consequence, they focus on how two people relate, what their rules are, and how things work between them. They learn that they have the power to harmonize or disrupt these relationships depending on how they relate to each of the two other people. Other family members often experience the behavior of third borns as "in and out." They can seem involved, caring, and attentive one moment and emotionally far away the next. This in-and-out quality is often confusing to others. When there is conflict, third children often withdraw, consider things in their minds, and then conclude that everything has been resolved. Others then often become confused as to how things have been resolved.

Choices are important to all siblings, but especially to third children. If they feel that others will take their choices away, they will fight. They sometimes appear to others to be indecisive, but that is because when they choose something, they are aware of giving up other available choices. They weigh such opportunity costs more than children in other positions.

Third children are interested in how things relate or are connected to each other. Ideas have meaning when they can be synthesized and related to other ideas. In terms of understanding people, third children understand individuals by watching how they relate to others.

Fourth Children. When the family grows with the birth of a fourth child, relationships become more complex than when any of the older siblings were born into the family. The main issue for the family is how to maintain harmony and stability. Fourth children internalize this issue and become guardians of harmony. When anything is disruptive to the family, fourth children take notice. They may even feel responsible for the entire emotional tone of the family. They often assume far too much responsibility by performing too many activities at once or by taking blame that is not theirs.

In terms of viewing the world, fourth children want to know how pieces of information are connected to the whole. Growing up watching entire families function, they first see the whole and then try to understand how individual family members fit in. If new information does not jibe with the big picture, it is often discarded or distorted.

A Special Day for Middle Children

The Mid-Kid Company of Sebring, Florida, has designated the second Saturday of August to be Middle Children's Day. Its purpose is to celebrate those whose upbringing is limited because they always seem to be either "too young" or "too old."

Fourth children tend to be outgoing in healthy families. They work to draw people together and can be pleasant and playful. They reassure other family members that things will be all right.

Middle and Youngest Children. The category "middle children" includes second, third, fourth, and more children if they fall between the oldest and the youngest child. Middle children always share their parents' attention with other children. Thus, they learn to be cooperative, but they also compare themselves with their older siblings and behave as if they are trying to "catch up" with them. Middle children are described as "squeezed" in between the oldest and the youngest. Parents pay attention to first children because they are first, and they pay attention to the youngest children when they know they mark the end of child-rearing, but middle children often do not get as much adult attention.

Youngest children have older siblings to imitate. They often feel special because both their parents and their siblings treat them in a unique way. After all, they are the last. They learn to expect special treatment. When they do not get it, they can become demanding and angry. Youngest children are often charming and learn to get what they want from others by being "cute."

Other Issues. Variations in family structure affect these birth-order characteristics. With twins, families ascribe a role to each child based on which was born first. Most twins know precisely how many minutes apart they were born. When a child dies, parents remember the role that child played, so that the next child in line rarely assumes the birth-order characteristics of the deceased sibling. Spacing children apart can also make a difference. The larger the span between the births of two siblings, the more likely it is that the younger sibling has some characteristics of an only child. In remarriage, when two sets of children are combined in a stepfamily, the children assume the same birth-order role they had in their original family. This situation can create competition, for example, between two firstborn children.

Birth order is a concept that is helpful to parents in understanding how their children view the world and in teaching them how to respond differently to each child. The concept is also helpful to family therapists in understanding families and each sibling in the family.   —*James M. Harper*

BIBLIOGRAPHY

Ernst, Cecile. *Birth Order: Its Influence on Personality.* New York: Guilford Press, 1983. Discussion of personality characteristics of only, oldest, second, middle, and youngest children.

Frie, Lucille K. *The Birth Order Factor: How Your Personality Is Influenced by Your Place in the Family.* New York: Pocket Books, 1976. Identifies characteristics associated with oldest, middle, and youngest children.

Hoopes, Margaret H., and James M. Harper. *Birth Order Roles and Sibling Patterns in Individual and Family Therapy.* Rockville, Md.: Aspen, 1987. Discusses how families create birth-order effects and examines characteristics of first, second, third, and fourth children, implications for parenting, mate selection, and remarriage.

Leman, Kevin. *The Birth Order Book: Why You Are the Way You Are.* New York: Dell, 1987. Examines descriptions of oldest, second, and youngest children.

Marinello, Bonnie. *All in the Family: Possible Effects of Birth Order.* New York: Brunner/Mazel, 1990. Identifies characteristics of first, second, only, middle, and youngest children.

Sulloway, Frank J. *Born to Rebel: Birth Order, Family Dynamics, and Creative Lives.* New York: Vintage Books, 1997. Asks the question why some children, when they become adults, become farsighted individuals who initiate radical revolutions, answering that individual differences arise within the family.

Toman, Walter. *Family Constellation: Its Effects on Personality and Social Behavior.* New York: Springer, 1976. Focuses on position of birth and gender of the child and the kinds of persons chosen as marital partners and friends.

Wilson, Bradford. *First Child, Second Child: Your Birth Order Profile.* New York: Bantam, 1985. De-scribes patterns of behavior exhibited by first and second-born children.

See also Child rearing; Family counseling; Family size; Family therapy; Multiple births; Only children; Siblings; Stepfamilies.

Blended families

RELEVANT ISSUES: Children and child development; Demographics; Parenting and family relationships

SIGNIFICANCE: Encompassing a variety of family types, the blended family is formed when members of previously broken families merge and create a new family system

The most common type of blended family is the stepfamily. In a stepfamily, one or both partners in a remarriage have one or more children from a previous marriage. Historically, stepfamilies were established after a spouse died and the surviving partner remarried. By the mid-twentieth century, however, most stepfamilies were formed following divorce. It is estimated that some 40 to 60 percent of all marriages are second or subsequent marriages, with under 10 percent of all remarriages involving someone who lost a spouse through death. More than 80 percent of remarriages include children from a prior marriage, and about 45 percent of children will live in a stepfamily at some point in their lifetimes. By the twenty-first century, the stepfamily is expected to outnumber all other types of families in the United States.

Other types of blended families include the adoptive family and the foster family. An adoptive family is formed when an individual or a couple becomes the legal parent or parents of another person's child or children. A foster family, on the other hand, is one that provides substitute care for one or more children who cannot be cared for in their own homes. Often children are placed in a foster family by a governmental agency when the children's own parents are either unable or unwilling to provide for their care. Traditionally, one of the main differences between adoptive families and foster families has been the ongoing involvement of natural parents with their children living in foster care. Yet, in recent times many adoptive families have encouraged natural parents to remain involved with their children, while many children in foster families have no contact with their natural parents. Moreover, foster parents are often encouraged to adopt the children placed in their homes. U.S. Census Bureau statistics suggest that slightly more than 1 percent of children under the age of eighteen live in adoptive families, while less than 1 percent of children live in foster families. At any given time, about one million children live with at least one adoptive parent, while about 200,000 live in foster families.

Misunderstandings About Blended Families. Blended families have long suffered from the adage that "if it is different, there must be something wrong with it." The traditional nuclear family, consisting of two biological parents and their natural children, remains the standard by which other family types are judged. Blended families are viewed as dysfunctional simply due to their blended heritage, and labels such as "step," "adoptive," or "foster" convey a negative stereotype.

When remarriage suddenly joins two three-member families, each person must suddenly deal with five other people instead of only two. (R. Kent Rasmussen)

Typically, society does not know how to respond to blended families, and few guidelines are offered for how family members should relate to one another. Consequently, blended family members may feel different, inadequate, or deficient.

Given the standard of the traditional nuclear family, it is generally assumed that blended families should be the same as nuclear families. Thus, one expectation for newly formed blended families is that they transform into a nuclear family. Unfortunately, such an expectation is unrealistic and can lead to disillusionment. The factors involved in forming blended families are very different from those involved in forming a traditional nuclear family. Blended families are created after the breakdown of nuclear families. Children bring experiences with natural parents, while adults may bring experiences from prior marriages. In the traditional nuclear family, children are born gradually into the family unit and remain with their natural parents. Blended families, on the other hand, are formed instantly through the decisions of adults. Based on their previous family cultures, children and adults often bring very different expectations of family life to their blended families.

The rapid consolidation of adults and children into a one-family unit has led to the belief that blended family members should instantly adjust to one another. The assumption of instant adjustment implies that love, trust, and cooperation should develop spontaneously. Yet, adjusting to life in a blended family takes time and effort on the part of all involved. There will be many challenges and frustrations. New rules and roles for all family members must be developed. Feelings of fear, failure, and anger are common. Satisfying relationships among members of a blended family evolve only gradually, and emotional bonds take time to develop. Successful adjustment to life in blended families requires a realistic view of the issues and concerns that are likely to arise.

Sources of Stress. There is little doubt that blended families experience a number of stressors uncommon to the traditional nuclear family. Statistics suggest that 60 percent of stepfamilies end in divorce, 50 percent of adoptive families seek mental health services, and a disproportionate number of foster children experience multiple family placements. Conflict and jealousy among family members are common, and children are at risk of experiencing depression, anxiety, troublesome behaviors, and school problems.

Lack of societal support combined with unrealistic expectations serve as significant sources of stress for blended families. In denying blended families the status of being "real families," chances for success are undermined. It is not uncommon for relationships to decay in a nonsupportive environment. Ridicule can lead to a sense of shame, and family members may deny that they belong to blended families. If family members sense that they do not fit in, they may assume that they are bound to fail. The lack of societal guidelines for how members of blended families should relate can lead to confusion and strife as adults and children alike attempt to forge their own rules and roles. Moreover, unrealistic expectations can send family members down many unproductive paths.

Another significant source of stress arises from the fact that blended families are born of loss. Entrance into blended families can serve as a clear reminder to children that their original families are no more. Familiar surroundings and friends are often left behind, and daily routines change. Parents may be healing from divorce or the realization that they are unable to bear biological children. Foster families may experience frequent losses as children come and go based on changing placement decisions. Prior losses can make trust in new relationships difficult. When adjustment to the loss of a previous family has not been completed, adjustment to life in a blended family can be especially stressful.

Stress in blended families also arises due to ongoing ties to prior families. Children may be reluctant to bond to their new parents for fear of being disloyal to their biological parents. Discipline problems may arise as children counter parental authority with "you're not my real parent." Parents, on the other hand, may be reluctant to enforce limits when they feel a child is not their own. Parents may also struggle with balancing their time, resources, and affections between prior and new children. Conflict may arise when parents hold different expectations about how discipline should be handled and resources allocated. Further complications may arise when relationships have to be maintained with persons outside the immediate family. Biological parents, stepparents,

Yours, Mine, and Ours

The 1968 film *Yours, Mine and Ours* starred Henry Fonda and Lucille Ball as a couple whose marriage brings together a houseful of children with different combinations of parents. Parenting Without Pressure recalls the film's title by making January National Yours, Mine and Ours Month to call attention to the special needs of blended families.

siblings, former in-laws, former spouses, and agency workers may be involved in the blended family. Children may feel uncertain about whom they belong to, while parents question their responsibility to persons outside the household.

Keys to Success in Blended Families. Even though they face significant stressors, most blended family members view their circumstances positively. Adaptation to blended family living offers multiple opportunities for personal growth and the development of fulfilling personal relationships. In order to be successful, blended families need accurate information about the unique challenges they are likely to encounter. They also require support from friends, extended family, and larger social institutions. It is important for blended families to relinquish expectations of mirroring the nuclear family and allow all family members the opportunity to grieve for past losses. Good communication and conflict-resolution skills are important to building successful relationships, as are mutual respect and appreciation for individual differences. While it is important for blended families to achieve a unified identity, it is also important that positive relationships be maintained with family members living outside the household. Affectionate relationships within the blended family take time to develop. Blended families can expect the adjustment process to take between two and five years. The path to success requires mutual cooperation and decision making and a commitment to succeed.

—*Jamie Sinclair-Andersen*

BIBLIOGRAPHY
Chilman, Catherine S., Elam W. Nunnally, and Fred M. Cox, eds. *Variant Family Forms: Families in Trouble Series.* Vol. 5. Newbury Park, Calif.: Sage Publications, 1988.
Cohen, Joyce S., and Anne Westhues. *Well-Functioning Families for Adoptive and Foster Children: A Handbook for Child Welfare Workers.* Toronto, Canada: University of Toronto Press, 1990.
Furukawa, Stacy. "The Diverse Living Arrangements of Children: Summer 1991." *Current Population Reports*, Series P70, No. 38. Washington, D.C.: U.S. Bureau of the Census, 1994.
Humphrey, Michael, and Heather Humphrey. *Families with a Difference: Varieties of Surrogate Parenthood.* New York: Routledge, 1988.
Newman, Margaret. *Stepfamily Realities: How to Overcome Difficulties and Have a Happy Family.* Oakland, Calif.: New Harbinger Publications, 1994.
Samuels, Shirley, C. *Ideal Adoption: A Comprehensive Guide to Forming an Adoptive Family.* New York: Plenum Press, 1990.

See also Adoption issues; Adoption processes; Alternative family types; Baby-boom generation; Divorce; Dysfunctional families; Foster homes; Remarriage; Serial monogamy; Stepfamilies.

Bonding and attachment

RELEVANT ISSUES: Children and child development; Parenting and family relationships

SIGNIFICANCE: Bonding sets the stage for attachment, the first social relationship, which has far-reaching influence on social and personality development

Bonding refers to the mother "falling in love" with her infant. Made popular by Marshall Klaus and John Kennell in the late 1970's, it was shown that women had more positive interactions with their infants during the first year if they had immediate, close physical contact after birth and continued extra contact in the days and weeks following birth compared to women with the usual amount of contact. In some instances, the effect continued for months and even years. Consequently, Klaus and Kennell suggested that the time period that occurs shortly after birth is critical, serving as the foundation for later attachment between mothers and their children. Many hospitals now make a point of placing newborn children on mothers' stomachs immediately after birth to facilitate bonding. Attachment can occur without bonding, but the bonding experience does seem to be a rewarding one for many mothers. For infants deemed "at risk," this experience can be especially important.

Concept of Attachment. An attachment is a special relationship. It is a close emotional tie persons form between themselves and other persons and for which both infants and adults appear to be biologically primed. This emotional tie endures over time. When people are attached to one another, they try to be near one another and interact often. Similar to other social relationships, attachment relationships develop as the result of social interaction. However, attachment differs from all other social relationships.

Attachment describes specific relationships that deal with safety and security. For children these relationships typically begin with their mothers. Although individuals are often attached to more than one person, it is unlikely that they will have a large number of attachment relationships. Attachment is specific and discriminating in nature and it implies an intense emotional investment. Once the primary attachment has been formed, usually during the second half of the first year, others follow. In fact, after 18 months few infants have just one attachment figure. Specifically, children may form attachments with special playmates, a teacher or relative, and even a household pet. These relationships are all similar in that the attachment object is seen as special and continued contact is desired.

Measuring the Attachment Relationship. Nearly all infants develop special attachments to their caregivers. However, some infants are more securely attached than others. Generally, when distressed infants seek out and are readily comforted by their caregivers and they use their caregivers as a "secure base" from which to venture off and explore their environment, such infants are said to be securely attached. When playing, secure infants may look back at their mothers from time to time and return to them briefly just to "touch base" and share. In contrast, insecure attachments are often recognizable by infants' anger, fear, or even indifference toward their caregivers. Less confident, such infants may be reluctant to let go of their mothers, or they may play aimlessly with no effort to maintain contact with their caregivers.

The Strange Situation is the classic procedure for measuring attachment. This procedure allows researchers to observe and measure infants' interactions with their caregivers under increasingly stressful situations. This is typically done with infants between one and two years of age in a room equipped with toys. The interaction is closely observed during a series of eight, three-minute episodes which gradually increase the level of stress experienced by the infants. The episodes involve infants and mothers, infants with their mothers and a stranger, infants alone with a stranger, and infants alone. How infants behave in the strange environment with their mothers, when a stranger enters the room, when they are left with the stranger, and when their mothers return allows researchers to classify infant attachment patterns.

Nearly 70 percent of all infants tested in the Strange Situation show secure attachment patterns. They explore the room and toys, usually stop playing and protest when their mothers leave the room, and smile or actively greet them when they return. These infants are more cooperative, self-directed, and less aggressive than infants who lack secure attachment patterns. The secure attachment is based on a history of mother-child interactions in which mothers are responsive to their infants' needs, are sensitive to infants' signals, and openly show warmth and love toward their infants.

For some infants one of three patterns of insecure attachment may be demonstrated. Approximately 10 percent of babies tested in the Strange Situation are classified as anxious-resistant. The anxious-resistant pattern is seen when infants fearfully cling to their mothers even before separation and therefore do not explore or play. They cry very loudly each time their mothers leave and they refuse to be comforted when they return. In general, these children tend to be more easily frustrated than children who show secure attachment. Mothers in this situation typically show insensitivity toward their infants, interfere with or ignore them, and moderately reject them.

Approximately 20 percent of infants tested are classified as anxious-avoidant. In the Strange Situation, these infants typically interact very little with their mothers. They are apparently indifferent to their mothers' presence or absence, showing no signs of distress when they leave. When they re-

Attachments formed between mothers and their children usually last through, and often well beyond, childhood. (Mary LaSalle)

turn, the infants avoid contact with them, sometimes turning their backs on them. In other arenas, these children tend to be more noncompliant and aggressive than securely attached children. Their mothers tend to dislike physical contact, show more rejecting behaviors, and express their feelings inconsistently. A relatively new category of behavior, disoriented-disorganized, describes infants who do not adequately fit into the above three categories. The first three categories illustrate consistent patterns of behavior, but disoriented-disorganized infants show no steady behavioral patterns. This is typically the result of inconsistent and troubling mother-infant interactions. The infants inconsistently mix their behaviors, sometimes seeking to be near their mothers, while avoiding them at other times. These children may "freeze" in the middle of an action or walk toward their mothers backward.

Attachment and Contextual Influences. Attachment relationships form as the result of mother-infant interactions within a social and cultural arena. The quality of the marital relationship and the amount and quality of fathers' involvement with their children can also affect attachment. Furthermore, if family circumstances change drastically—for example, if parents change their jobs, become unemployed, or fall severely ill—and the familiar pattern of interaction within the family is altered, the attachment relationship is likely to be altered as well.

Cultural expectations and traditions may also influence attachment. For example, when Strange Situation results are compared cross-culturally, Israeli and Japanese children show more anxious-resistant patterns of attachment than Americans, and some Western European infants show greater anxious-avoidant behaviors. However, it seems that most infants throughout the world are reassured by their mothers' presence and go to them for comfort when they feel distressed. Although infants are strongly disposed to forming attachments with their caregivers, neither children nor caregivers cause attachment. Other influences influencing attachment include availability of social supports, stress, and even parents' developmental history.

Significance of Attachment. Children learn how to interact with others by interacting with their parents. They create an internal "working model" of themselves and others based primarily on these parent-child interactions. A model that depicts the parents as responsive and loving and the children as being worthy of that love allows the children to expect more positive interactions with others. However, children who feel worthless and whose model includes nonresponsive and distant parents may well distrust their peers and expect negative or nonresponsive interactions with others.

Although insecurely attached infants may become fearful or hesitant—and even destructive—of future intimate relationships as adults, attachment quality also has an immediate impact on infants. Insecure infants do not actively explore their environment or interact effectively with adults, activities that are directly related to cognitive development and the actual formation of pathways in the brain. Children may not become all they can become without these experiences. Experiences in the first three years of life are thus of immeasurable importance. —*James G. Hanson*

BIBLIOGRAPHY
Ainsworth, Mary D. S. "The Development of Infant-Mother Attachment." In *Review of Child Development Research*, edited by B. M. Caldwell and Henry N. Ricciuti. Chicago: University of Chicago Press, 1973.
Bowlby, John. *Attachment and Loss.* Vol. 1 in *Attachment*. 2d ed. New York: Basic Books, 1982.
Karen, Robert. *Becoming Attached: Unfolding the Mystery of the Infant-Mother Bond and Its Impact on Later Life.* New York: Warner Books, 1994.
Klaus, Marshall H., and John H. Kennell. *Maternal Infant Bonding.* St. Louis: Mosby, 1976.
West, Malcolm L., and Adrienne E. Sheldon-Keller. *Patterns of Relating: An Adult Attachment Perspective.* New York: Guilford Press, 1994.

See also Adoption issues; Attachment theory; Child rearing; Favoritism; Freudian psychology; Love; Mother-daughter relationships; Separation anxiety; Social capital.

Bradshaw, John

BORN: June 29, 1933, Houston, Tex.
AREAS OF ACHIEVEMENT: Health and medicine; Parenting and family relationships
SIGNIFICANCE: A public television personality and author, John Elliot Bradshaw was responsible

for popularizing the concept of the "dysfunctional family"

Himself a product of a dysfunctional family, John Elliot Bradshaw dropped out of college due to alcohol problems, eventually joining Alcoholics Anonymous (AA) in 1965. He then pursued a successful career as a speaker and consultant on alcohol-related issues. Having earlier trained as a Roman Catholic priest, he found that his theological training gave him insight into the complexity of the psychological conditions of troubled people.

In 1969 Bradshaw began a private counseling practice. Yet, it was his local television work in Houston, Texas, that led the Public Broadcasting Service to hire him to do a miniseries, *Eight Stages of Man* (broadcast from 1982 to 1984). This series was followed by the far more successful *Bradshaw on the Family* (first broadcast in 1986). In 1990 Bradshaw published *Homecoming: Reclaiming and Championing Your Inner Child*. This book popularized the idea of an "inner child," who incorporates the failings and often abusiveness of its parents. The inner child needs to be coaxed out of its shell and then healed of its "codependent" lingering attachment to its family trauma in order for a fully integrated, adult personality to emerge. Bradshaw was primarily responsible for the fact that the term "dysfunctional family" entered the public lexicon. This term was used to cover situations ranging from incest to negligence to narcissistic insensitivity.

Detractors, especially on the political Left, have criticized Bradshaw for blaming all problems on persons' parents, thus lessening social responsibility. Nevertheless, millions of people throughout the world have found comfort and inspiration in his teachings. —*Margaret Boe Birns*

See also Alcoholism and drug abuse; Codependency; Dysfunctional families; Family counseling.

Brazelton, T. Berry

BORN: May 10, 1918, Waco, Tex.
AREA OF ACHIEVEMENT: Children and child development
SIGNIFICANCE: Brazelton, known worldwide for his dedication to good parenting, developed the widely used Neonatal Behavioral Assessment Scale and authored *What Every Child Knows* and other popular "how-to" child-care books

T(homas) Berry Brazelton's interest in children began when, in his teens, he baby-sat as many as eleven children at once at his family's reunions. His ease with children led him into a career in general pediatrics. Brazelton received his M.D. in 1943 from New York City's Columbia College of Physicians and Surgeons. A final residency in child psychiatry at Putnam's Children's Center in Roxbury, Massachusetts, completed his medical education. He entered private practice in 1950 in Cambridge, Massachusetts, and joined the Harvard University medical faculty in 1951. Dissatisfied with the direction of his research, Brazelton shifted his focus from children's diseases to a study of infant behavior and methods of parenting. He developed the Neonatal Behavioral Assessment Scale (NBAS) as a tool to help speed adoption procedures. Known simply as "the Brazelton," this thirty-minute diagnostic test measures infants' response to sensory stimuli and enables doctors to quickly pinpoint potential developmental problems. "Normal" children can thus be placed without the delays caused by the lengthy testing methods that accompanied adoptions prior to the NBAS.

With colleague Edward Tronick, Brazelton cofounded the Child Development Unit at Children's Hospital Medical Center in Boston in 1972. This facility offers students and other medical professionals an opportunity to research child development and prepare themselves to involve parents in the treatment of their children.

The author of more than twenty-five books, Brazelton has published such popular "how-to" books on pediatrics and child development as *Infants and Mothers: Individual Differences in Development* (1969), *What Every Baby Knows* (1987), *Touchpoints* (1992), and *Going to the Doctor* (1996). His narrative-style books describe real-life situations faced by every parent. Liberally sprinkled with Brazelton's commentaries, examples, and suggestions for better parenting, his books do not tell readers how to recognize such illnesses as chicken pox but explain what behavior can be expected of two-year-olds.

In addition to writing books, Brazelton has hosted the show *What Every Baby Knows* on the Lifetime cable television channel. *Family Circle* and *Redbook* both carry a monthly article by Brazelton, and he authors a syndicated weekly newspaper column. A series of videotapes that follow the day-to-day lives of actual parents and their young children as they cope with various problems adds to Brazelton's list of accomplishments. As a member of the National Commission on Children, Brazelton helped pass the 1993 legislation requiring large companies to allow employees an extended leave of absence following the birth of a child or a family emergency.

Brazelton has long been considered a successor to Benjamin Spock, whose books deal with the recognition and treatment of childhood diseases. Unlike Spock, Brazelton has concentrated on the psychological well-being of children. Brazelton's chief goal has been to help parents effectively interact with their children.   —*Barbara C. Stanley*

See also Child care; Child rearing; Health of children; Maternity leave; Spock, Benjamin; Toilet training.

Breast-feeding

RELEVANT ISSUES: Children and child development; Health and medicine

SIGNIFICANCE: Breast-feeding is considered the best method for infant feeding because of the many benefits it provides to both babies and their mothers

Breast-feeding clearly provides the best food for infants. Breast milk contains all nutrients essential for normal growth and development of human infants. In addition, breast milk provides health benefits to babies. Compared to formula-fed infants, infants fed breast milk are less likely to suffer from ear infections, colds, influenza, pneumonia, diarrhea, vomiting, allergies, and other common childhood illnesses. Breast-feeding is also beneficial to mothers, helping them to lose weight after delivery and reducing their risk of developing breast cancer later in life. In addition, breast-feeding is less expensive, more convenient, and better for the environment than formula feeding.

Obstacles to Breast-feeding. Because of the many advantages associated with breast-feeding, health professionals in both the United States and Canada strongly support breast-feeding as the best method for feeding infants. In spite of this, only about 60 percent of American and Canadian infants are breast-fed for any length of time. This is far below the goal of 75 percent set by Healthy People 2000, a health promotion and disease prevention program sponsored by the United States Department of Health and Human Services.

Women's decision to breast-feed is influenced by several factors. In general, older, well-educated women are most likely to breast-feed. Because women tend to rely on past experience, those who have breast-fed a previous child are more likely to breast-feed a future child. Attitudes and beliefs also play a role in the decision-making process. Often-cited reasons for not breast-feeding include embarrassment, inconvenience, fear that breast milk will not provide enough nourishment, and indifference or discouragement on the part of infants' fathers. To combat these barriers, women need access to accurate breast-feeding information and an environment supportive of their decision to breast-feed. To encourage breast-feeding, promotion and educational programs should be aimed not only at women but also at the society in which they live.

Physiology and Breast-feeding. Breast-feeding is a complex physiological and psychological process. The breasts mature and become prepared for breast-feeding during pregnancy under the influence of the hormones estrogen and progesterone. Two pituitary hormones, prolactin and oxytocin, which are released in response to suckling, control breast-feeding. Prolactin is responsible for the production of milk. Once produced, the milk is stored within the breast tissue. Oxytocin releases the milk from storage sites, allowing it to travel to the nipples. The release of oxytocin (and subsequently milk) can be blocked by several mental and physical stress factors, including anger, frustration, embarrassment, and fatigue. Clearly, a calm supportive environment is of great value in assisting women to breast-feed successfully.

Contrary to popular opinion, breast milk is not normally produced immediately following delivery. Instead, very small amounts of colostrum, often called "first milk," is initially made. This thin yellowish liquid is rich in immune system components, providing infants with early protection against viral and bacterial illnesses. Although little colostrum is produced, most healthy infants need no other nourishment until mature breast milk production begins two to five days after birth. In fact, supplementing colostrum with formulas or

Nutritionists, health professionals, and mothers agree that there is no satisfactory substitute for mother's milk. (James L. Shaffer)

other liquids can have a negative impact on the breast-feeding process. Oral supplements discourage infant suckling at the breast; this reduces prolactin levels and, in turn, milk production. In addition, in the early weeks of life infants are particularly vulnerable to "nipple confusion" between the firm artificial teat, which is suckled at the tip of the nipple, and the soft pliable breast, which is suckled with the nipple drawn far back into the mouth. Once underway, breast-feeding follows the principle of supply and demand—increased suckling by infants increases milk production.

Initial Problems. Difficulties may arise during the early weeks of breast-feeding. Engorgement, described as breast fullness due to additional blood flow and swelling of the breast tissue, may be experienced by some mothers when mature milk production begins. Although engorgement usually subsides within days, the fullness can be reduced by suckling babies often and by applying warm or cold compresses to the breasts. Breast-feeding is not normally painful; however, nipple soreness may occur as a result of incorrect positioning of babies at the breast. Whether mothers sit up or lie down, babies' entire bodies should face and be close to mothers' bodies. While almost every woman is capable of producing sufficient milk for one (and often two) infants, mothers may be concerned that they are not producing enough milk for their babies. Frequent suckling of the infant and limited use of pacifiers and bottles generally assure an adequate supply of milk. Although difficulties may arise, most of them can be overcome with appropriate support and information.

Breast-feeding Tips. Breast-feeding support and information come in a variety of forms. Family and friends are invaluable sources of emotional support and encouragement. La Leche League, an international breast-feeding organization, offers local support group meetings, at which women can share their experiences and ask questions in

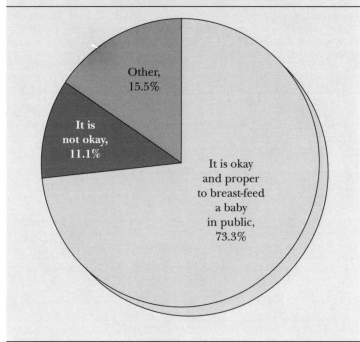

Public Opinion on Breast-feeding in Public in 1998

Other, 15.5%

It is not okay, 11.1%

It is okay and proper to breast-feed a baby in public, 73.3%

Source: Parentsroom website (1998)

Note: In early 1998 Parentsroom conducted an informal poll on its website. It asked visitors to the site—most of whom are presumably sympathetic to parenting problems—whether it is "okay and proper" publicly to breast-feed a baby. This chart summarizes responses. Percentages are rounded to the nearest 0.1%.

an informal setting. Health professionals with extensive training in the area of lactation, such as certified lactation consultants, can be located through local hospitals, obstetrical practices, pediatric clinics, and health departments. These consultants offer a wide range of services, from group classes for expectant parents to individualized counseling for breast-feeding mothers. In addition, reading and audiovisual materials on breast-feeding can provide women with general information and offer solutions to breast-feeding difficulties. These items can be found in most bookstores and public libraries. Whatever the source, support and information are essential, providing women the encouragement and knowledge needed for breast-feeding success.

Working Women and Breast-feeding. Because maternity leaves in the United States are typically brief, many women breast-feed while employed

Expressing milk from a mother's breasts into bottles permits the father to play a more direct role in early child care without denying the child the benefits of mother's milk. (James L. Shaffer)

outside the home. While some women work flexible hours or work part-time to accommodate breast-feeding, others make child-care arrangements that allow them to breast-feed their babies during meal breaks. Another option is to express breast milk. While milk can be expressed from the breast by hand, some women use manual or electric breast pumps for expression. These pumps can be purchased or rented from drugstores, hospitals, and lactation consultants. The expressed breast milk can be stored and given to infants by child-care providers. In infants less than six weeks old, the milk may be given by cup or syringe to avoid nipple confusion. In older infants, who usually can transition easily between breasts and artificial teats, the milk may be offered from a bottle. Although breast-feeding conducted outside the home may require additional time, many working women find breast-feeding and the special mother-infant bond it provides well worth the extra effort.

Weaning. There are several ways to answer the question about when children should be weaned from the breast. The average length of breast-feeding worldwide is 4.2 years. The World Health Organization (WHO) recommends that every child be breast-fed for at least two years. The American Academy of Pediatrics advocates breast milk for at least the first year of life, with gradual introduction of solid foods beginning at four to six months of age. In contrast to these guidelines, only 20 percent of American and Canadian infants are breast-fed at five to six months of age.

Ideally, weaning takes place slowly when moth-ers and children are both ready. Unplanned or premature weaning, however, is very common. Reasons for early weaning include mothers' belief that they are not producing enough milk, sore nipples, babies' refusal of the breast, and maternal feelings of anxiety or embarrassment. These difficulties, while serious, can all be overcome with support and information from breast-feeding professionals.

Even under the best of circumstances, women may have mixed emotions about weaning—pleased by the growth and independence the child has gained, yet saddened by the loss of the emotional closeness provided by breast-feeding. When weaning occurs prematurely, women may experience seemingly contradictory feelings of relief that the responsibilities of breast-feeding are over and guilt because they failed to breast-feed as planned. Because maternal emotions play such a large role in the weaning process, all women, whether weaning gradually or abruptly, need support during this time of transition.　　　　　　　—*Jo Carol Chezem*

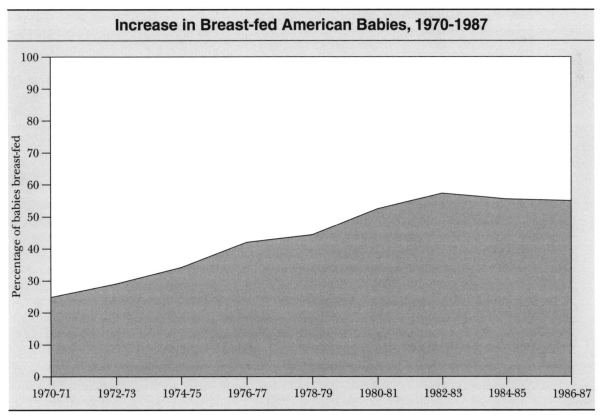

Increase in Breast-fed American Babies, 1970-1987

Source: The Time Almanac 1998. New York: Information Please, 1997.

BIBLIOGRAPHY

Baumslag, Naomi, and Dia Michels. *Milk, Money, and Madness: The Culture and Politics of Breastfeeding.* Westport, Conn.: Bergin and Garvey, 1995.

Huggins, Kathleen. *The Nursing Mother's Companion.* Boston, Mass.: Harvard Common Press, 1995.

_____, et al. *The Nursing Mother's Guide to Weaning.* Boston, Mass: Harvard Common Press, 1994.

La Leche League International. *The Womanly Art of Breastfeeding.* Schaumburg, Ill.: Author, 1995.

Pryor, Gale. *Nursing Mother, Working Mother: The Essential Guide for Breastfeeding and Staying Close to Your Baby After You Return to Work.* Boston, Mass.: Harvard Common Press, 1997.

See also Child care; Health of children; Maternity leave; Postpartum depression; Pregnancy.

Bride-price

RELEVANT ISSUES: Economics and work; Marriage and dating; Parenting and family relationships

SIGNIFICANCE: Bride-price and bride service involve goods presented by grooms' kin to brides' kin or work that grooms perform for their brides' families to legitimize a marriage

In traditional societies with descent groups, people enter marriage with the help of their extended descent groups. Patrilineal descent-group members often are required to contribute to bridewealth, a customary gift before, at, or after marriage from husbands and their kin to wives and their kin. Another term sometimes used interchangeably with the term "bridewealth," the term "bride-price," is technically inaccurate. People following this custom do not regard the exchange as a sale or a commercial relationship between a man and an object that can be bought and sold. Bridewealth compensates brides' groups for the loss of brides' companionship and labor. More important, it makes the children born to women full members of their husbands' descent groups. Bridewealth must be distinguished from dowry, which is a presentation of goods by brides' kin to the families of grooms. Dowry is sometimes interpreted as compensatory payment from brides' families for giving an economic liability to the groom's family, who take on that liability. Dowry correlates with low female status in societies in which women are perceived as burdens, rather than as assets, to their families.

The essence of marriage is that it is a publicly accepted relationship involving the transfer of certain rights and obligations between participating parties. Whatever the exact nature of the exchange of goods or services in marriage, the transfer of rights in a marriage is a public affair, generally surrounded by ritual and ceremony. These ceremonies are a way of bearing witness to the lawfulness of the transaction. They distinguish marriage from other kinds of unions that resemble it. For example, cohabitation, a practice in modern North American society, may have some of the same emotional functions for two individuals as marriage, but it does not involve obligatory economic exchanges or establish relationships between individuals and their partners' kin.

Among the Kwakiutl and Salish Indians of the Pacific Northwest, bridewealth and bride service were frequently used by males to convert wealth and labor into prestige by "marrying up" into families of higher social status. Anthropologists also note that the payment of bridewealth and the performance of bride service also legitimize and provide legal sanction for other cultural practices. Husbands gain domestic and sexual rights over their wives and wives can hold their husbands accountable for violations of conjugal rights. Thus, these practices serve to stabilize marriages. Such payments actually enhance, rather than diminish, the status of women by enabling both husbands and wives to acquire reciprocal rights to each other. —*Robert D. Bryant*

See also Arranged marriages; Cohabitation; Dowry; Family: concept and history; Kinship systems; Mail-order brides; Marriage; Patrilineal descent; Wealth; Weddings.

Bruner, Jerome

BORN: October 1, 1915, New York, N.Y.

AREA OF ACHIEVEMENT: Children and child development

SIGNIFICANCE: A psychologist noted for his work in cognitive studies, Bruner developed theories about child development that contributed to government funding of day-care centers

Overcoming near-blindness in infancy and the loss of his beloved father in 1927, Jerome Seymour Bruner developed an interest in psychology during his undergraduate years at Duke University. At Harvard University, where he obtained an M.A. in 1939 and taught, he investigated perception and sensation. One of his most significant achievements was a theory of perception according to which "errors" of perception were variations of psychological interest and that perception was influenced by values. This theory contradicted the so-called law of central tendency, which holds that guesses about size or magnitude err toward the middle. In the early 1950's Bruner applied new research techniques to an investigation of cognitive processes in general, which led to a revival of "mentalistic" concepts and implications for social psychology, learning theory, and other related fields. He opened the Center for Cognitive Studies at Harvard in 1960, attracting such luminaries as Noam Chomsky, Barbel Inhelder, and Roman Jakobson. He was also instrumental in educational reform—particularly for the science curriculum—downplaying mastery of facts and techniques and promoting a flexible, progressive approach.

One of his most famous ideas was the multistage theory of cognitive development in children. Influenced by Jean Piaget and Lev Semyonovich Vygotsky, Bruner articulated three modes of representation (the enactive, the iconic, and the symbolic) without making any value judgment regarding the superiority of one over another.

Bruner's research contributed to the establishment of government funded day-care centers and early childhood education programs. Tired of Harvard politics, he accepted an appointment at Oxford University in England, where, inspired by Oxford's language theorists, he examined children's transition from "prelinguistic to linguistic" communication by recording on videotape the interaction of mothers and children as they ate, played, and read together. Bruner discovered that it is through these "formats" that language is introduced to the child.   —*Keith Garebian*

See also Allport, Gordon; Attention-deficit hyperactivity disorder (ADHD); Behavior disorders; Brazelton, T. Berry; Cultural influences; Educating children; Family values; Skinner, B. F.

Bundling

RELEVANT ISSUES: Marriage and dating; Religious beliefs and practices; Sociology

SIGNIFICANCE: Bundling afforded unmarried couples an opportunity to spend intimate time together without defying the sexual mores of their society or religion

Eighteenth century sexual mores imposed strict restrictions on the behavior of unmarried couples. Bundling afforded an opportunity for men and women to spend intimate time together in an environment in which they could not engage in sexual contact. When bundling, a man and woman were tightly wrapped or sewn into a bedroll. Then they were allowed to sleep in the same bed or cuddle under a blanket together. Variations included separating the couple with a board, binding the woman's legs, dressing the woman in many layers of petticoats, or providing parent chaperones.

The practice of bundling evolved in Western societies that prohibited sexual intercourse prior to marriage. It was prevalent among the middle classes, among whom engagement before marriage was often a prerequisite. Bundling originated in rural communities in northern Europe, especially in the British Isles, Scandinavia, and the Netherlands. English and Dutch settlers imported it to America, where it was practiced primarily in the New England colonies. Bundling's popularity peaked during the years before the Revolutionary War. Urbanization and an emphasis on adopting the mainstream culture led to the decline of bundling.   —*H.C. Aubrey*

See also Courting rituals; Engagement; Family: concept and history; Mennonites and Amish; Sexuality and sexual taboos.

Cassatt, Mary

BORN: May 22, 1844, Allegheny City, Penn.
DIED: June 14, 1926, Château de Beaufresne, France
AREA OF ACHIEVEMENT: Painting
SIGNIFICANCE: Considered one of America's greatest artists, Mary Cassatt was associated with the innovative Impressionist school of painting in the late nineteenth century

Born into a socially prominent, well-to-do family, Mary Cassatt was determined to become an artist, despite social disapproval. While Cassatt's family did not encourage her aspirations, it was nevertheless instrumental in her development as an artist. She visited Europe to broaden her cultural horizons and spent four years at the Pennsylvania Academy of the Fine Arts, where she learned her craft. Returning to Paris in 1866, Cassatt continued her development, making trips to study the great art collections of Italy and Spain. Maintaining contact with her family, which often visited her in Paris, Cassatt emerged as a notable artist at a time when French painters, including Edgar Degas, were launching an artistic movement known as Impressionism. Degas invited Cassatt to exhibit with the Impressionists in 1877. That same year, Cassatt's parents and her sister Lydia took up permanent residence in Paris. The home they provided enabled Mary Cassatt to work uninterrupted.

Most of Cassatt's paintings were portraits of mothers and children. Her mother, her sister Lydia, and her brothers' children often sat as models. Cassatt, who never married, helped support her family, caring for her sister and overseeing the development of her brothers' children. Her output diminished considerably after the death of her parents and ceased entirely after 1915, when cataracts interfered with her vision. She continued to be active in the art world, however, organizing an exhibition of her work and that of Degas to benefit the cause of woman suffrage. She died in her French country home in 1926.   —*Nis Petersen*

See also Art and iconography; Rockwell, Norman.

Child abandonment

RELEVANT ISSUES: Children and child development; Parenting and family relationships
SIGNIFICANCE: The phenomenon of abandoned infants and children has been documented in European history and in recent accounts of mother abandonment and infant homicide

Black's Law Dictionary defines child abandonment as the desertion or willful forsaking or forgoing of legal and moral parental duties. Abandonment is the voluntary relinquishing of control over children by their natural parents or guardians, whether by leaving them somewhere, selling them, or legally consigning authority to some other person or institution.

Accounts of child abandonment range from desperate unwed mothers, plagued by the economic struggles of life and unable to maintain their offspring, to married women with reasons that are considered best under the circumstances. The quest for the ideal image of family life is countered by women's perceptions of reality that contradict this ideal. For some, the model family has never been a reality and is not their dream. The emotional well-being of the mother, as well as economic status, affects the life views and capacities of the abandoned child. The life with which children struggle if they survive abandonment or the loss of parents because of unkind conditions forces them to rely on their wits, the kindness of others, or state policies pertaining to the protection of children.

History of Child Abandonment. The care and protection of children have evolved through centuries of changing family behavior. Children have been loved and cared for, but they have also been treated as chattel to be abandoned or killed when they have been of no economic use. Child abandonment and maltreatment were committed by parents of every social class in a wide variety of circumstances throughout Europe, from Hellenistic antiquity to the end of the Middle Ages. It probably reached its peak from 2500 B.C.E. to the eleventh century C.E.

From ancient to modern times the law has feared to tread on families' bond of blood. Fathers' rights included the freedom to sell or use their assets as they saw fit. Human property could be abandoned at the edge of marketplaces. Some accounts report that infants were left on hillsides.

Child abandonment reflects women's and sometimes both parents' desire to get rid of children for various reasons. In *The Kindness of Strangers* (1988), John Boswell expands the definition: Parents abandon children in desperation, when they are unable to support them because of poverty or disaster; in shame, when they are unwilling to keep them because of the children's physical condition or ancestry or when they are "illegitimate" or the product of incestuous relations; in self-interest or in the interests of another child, whereby inheritance or domestic resources would be compromised by parents' having to feed another mouth; in hope, whereby parents believe that someone of greater means or higher standing may find the children and raise them; in resigna-

tion, whereby children are of unwelcome gender; and in callousness, if parents simply cannot be bothered with parenthood.

In early Christian Europe children were left at church doors. Subsequent efforts led to the establishment of hospitals to house and raise discarded children. An infanticide law enacted in Massachusetts in 1624 was geared toward prosecuting mothers of abandoned children born out of wedlock. Modern American laws provide penalties against child abuse and infanticide. However, European society as a whole did not levy strong sanctions against the cruel treatment of children. Concern developed when the legal question was raised as to whether children could take action against their parents for support in respect to estates, income, and inheritance. If abandoned children could prove their relationship to their parents, they had grounds to sue for support from their share of their fathers' estates.

Children's literature has many examples of children's lives and suffering. *Hansel and Gretel* is the

The popular 1990 film Home Alone *found humor in accidental child abandonment by having a large family inadvertently leave one child (Macaulay Culkin) behind in the confusion of going to Europe.* (Museum of Modern Art, Film Stills Archive)

classic tale of abandoned children. *Cinderella* and *Snow White* both present views of abused children and their fantasies or attempts to escape to a better life.

Economics and Family Life. Several types of families developed among immigrants to the United States. There were families and unmarried individuals. There were various conditions of wealth and poverty and different degrees of freedom and bondage. Many women came as indentured servants. The nuclear family was only one of several different family systems. Social class and regional differences influenced the perceptions and roles of children and parental conduct.

Middle-class values romanticized the role of mothers, and moralists underscored a mother's importance to the nation's stability. It was expected that a mother could nurture children to create sober, self-controlled citizens. Marriage transformed primary economic unions into relations that focused on companionship and child development. However, the realm of life inhabited by poor women is often stormier than that portrayed in social ideals. Poverty was often the most compelling reason for mothers to abandon their offspring. The rise of the market society left poor women subject to economic changes. Women were forced to work outside the home if they could find work. This change gave poor women few choices about the care of their children. They sometimes chose to abandon their infants and children. According to *The World Almanac, 1997,* the national poverty rate in 1995 was 13.8 percent. Children were overrepresented among the poor, with a poverty rate of 20.8 percent.

Homelessness and Children. The plight of poverty is further illustrated by the homeless population. Single parents represent a major part of the low-income population. Families with inadequate income or lost employment may lose their housing. Homes may be lost as the result of fire or eviction. Limited resources may not allow for repairing damages or obtaining replacement shelter. Subsequent transitions may result in families breaking up and moving, inadequate supervision of children, and decreased school attendance. Families may be plagued by other emotional burdens that eventually account for cases of child abandonment.

Conditions that result from unstable homes or families experiencing crises are often conditions from which children run away. Emotional and economic circumstances may become so intolerable that older children seek attention from other sources. Some join gangs or other groups. Many run away. Some parents search for them, while some do not. In one case, a teenage girl's mother remarried and the new husband did not want the woman's daughter. After the mother reluctantly acceded to her new husband's desires, the teenage girl was abandoned. She ran away.

Another form of abandonment results from psychological and emotional neglect. Although family members may live together, parents may not nurture or supervise their children, so that neglected children become emotionally disturbed. Such neglect, although outside the scope of actual physical abandonment, may be a precursor to it.

International Perspective and North America. Child abandonment as a social problem exists all over the world. There are examples of abandoned children in Rwanda, Romania, Japan, Argentina, Brazil, Russia, Bosnia, China, Canada, and Great Britain. Most accounts of child abandonment in these countries, carried in professional journals, deal with abandoned infants and children as a result of national conflicts, wars, disasters, national policies on family size, illegal immigration, and disease. As legal questions have been raised, moral issues related to these situations of abandonment have surfaced. Countries have had to deal with the legality of denying foster care, health care, and other services to the abandoned children of illegal immigrants.

Homeless children in all countries often face special problems. Lacking homes, they are forced to wander the streets. Not only do they fear being brutalized by others who take advantage of unprotected youngsters, but their very living situations may also be dangerous. While abandoned houses are available to some, others may find security under bridges, in abandoned mines, in caves, or in old factories. Often these locations are environmentally hazardous.

While the concept of child abandonment may seem fairly clear to many, some cultures do not accept it. In Native American culture, if biological parents are unable to care for infants or children, they are taken in by someone in their extended family. African American and Latino families have also traditionally accepted children of biological relatives or from the community at large through informal rather than formal adoption procedures. However, as families become isolated and separated from family support systems, extended families may not be available to provide a home for children whose parents are unable to care for them.

Child Protection Policies. In the United States cruelty toward children was formally addressed in the 1874 court case *People v. Connolly*, which dealt with eleven-year-old Mary Ellen, whose mother had beaten and abused her. A wealthy woman took Mary Ellen's situation to the president of the Association for the Prevention of Cruelty to Animals. It was argued that children were certainly comparable to animals and that they should receive comparable support. Mrs. Connolly was charged with assault and battery and was sentenced to one year of hard labor in a penitentiary. The judge removed the child from the mother's home and placed her in foster care. Since then, legislation has been enacted to protect children and their families. The effectiveness of these programs is continuously under scrutiny.

Federal and state governments and private agencies have responded to the issue of child abandonment by developing various services to identify and protect children who in many cases have been abandoned because of inadequate resources. Social welfare policies have ranged from financial assistance for mothers to help them take care of their children to foster care and group homes that take in children without parents.

Aid to Families with Dependent Children, Title IV-A of the Social Security Act, has been the means-tested program that provides cash benefits to needy children and their parents or caretakers. The proposed assistance program, Temporary Assistance for Needy Families is supposed to help needy families with minor children by providing them with job preparation and employment opportunities and to reduce the rate of out-of-wedlock births.

The child welfare system essentially exists to provide protection, but not all persons who seek out such services abuse or neglect their children. More often, families run out of money and cannot get needed services. Although many services in the community are available to children and their families, getting to them is sometimes difficult. Traditional and innovative programs include in-school services, family preservation, home-health assistance, and community building. Community building is perceived to be an important strategy for helping families develop their strengths to support the financial and emotional needs of their children.

In addition to government initiatives, there are also private local, state, national, and international resources to aid parents in preventing conditions that force them to abandon their children. There are also resources that abandoned children can seek out for themselves. Organizations such as the United Nations Children's Fund (UNICEF) and the Red Cross sometimes offer services to refugee children or children abandoned in disaster areas. A well-known retreat for homeless or abandoned children and runaways is Covenant House. Rather than accept child abandonment as the recourse of poor or unwed mothers, the modern emphasis is on helping mothers and their families to identify resources and take advantage of opportunities to help them raise and nurture their children.   —*Gwenelle S. O'Neal*

BIBLIOGRAPHY

Baca Zinn, M., and S. Eitzen. *Diversity in Families.* New York: HarperCollins, 1994. Provides an important social analysis of the history of families in the United States, identifies the myth of the ideal family, and reports on issues pertaining to the impact of economic structure, ethnicity, and gender on family forms, transitions, and adaptations.

Boswell, John. *The Kindness of Strangers.* New York: Pantheon Books, 1988. Describes the abandonment of children in Western Europe from late antiquity, provides a thorough historical examination of child abandonment, and expresses the view that these children have been at the mercy of strangers.

Close, James. *No One to Call Me Home: America's New Orphans.* Chicago: Mission of Our Lady of Mercy, 1990. Provides hard life stories of children without homes.

Golden, Renny. *Disposable Children.* Belmont, Calif.: Wadsworth, 1997. Asserts that the problem with the child-protection system is its emphasis on child removal.

Hiner, N. R., and J. M. Hawes, eds. *Growing Up in America: Children in Historical Perspective.* Chicago: University of Illinois Press, 1985. Compilation of historical analyses of childhood in America.

Lazzarino, A., and E. K. Hayes. *Find a Safe Place: A True Life Drama of Adventure and Survival.* New York: McGraw-Hill, 1984. Novel set in the 1960's that describes four boys who are relegated to a reformatory because they are parentless and homeless. Based on actual case histories of thousands of neglected children who had not committed crimes but were placed in the criminal justice system because there was no other place for them.

Ransel, David L. *Mothers of Misery: Child Abandonment in Russia.* Princeton, N.J.: Princeton University Press, 1988. Institutional history of foundling homes in Russia during the late eighteenth and nineteenth centuries that depicts how infants were fostered out to villages and how the system turned into an economic enterprise linking the village to the capital.

Ritter, Bruce. *Covenant House: Lifeline to the Street.* New York: Doubleday, 1987. Estimates that whereas Covenant House has provided aid to more than one hundred thousand children, only about one-third of them succeed in establishing reasonable lives. Most die young, go to jail, become emotionally disabled, or end up as alcohol or drug users.

Walter, V. A. "Hansel and Gretel as Abandoned Children." *Children's Literature in Education* 23 (December, 1992). Describes this children's story in the context of child abandonment.

See also Abandonment of the family; Big Brothers and Big Sisters of America (BBBSA); Child abuse; Children born out of wedlock; Children's literature; Family crises; Guardianship; Homeless families; Infanticide; Latchkey children; Orphans; Paternity suits; Poverty.

Child abduction

Relevant issues: Divorce; Law; Parenting and family relationships; Violence

Significance: The crime of child abduction presents severe challenges to families and society; locating and returning abducted children safely is a complex process that has become more sophisticated and effective

Child abduction has been defined as purposeful removal or concealment of a person under the age of eighteen from the custodial parent or legal guardian without authorization. Sometimes acts of abduction violate laws against kidnapping, the transportation or confinement of a person without consent, or custodial parents' or legal guardians' rights of consent. Because laws are worded and interpreted differently in various states, similar cases may be handled differently.

Missing Persons. Child-abduction cases reported to the police or prosecutors are considered missing-person cases. Police investigations attempt to classify cases according to the apparent cause of disappearance. In 1994 it was estimated that 358,700 young people were abducted in the United States. Most cases involved parental abductions, in which children were usually taken away by a parent undergoing divorce. A smaller number of cases involved abductions by strangers, in which nonfamily members abducted young people. Most missing-person cases have not involved child abductions, but persons classified as runaways— young persons who choose to leave home, sometimes because of child abuse, neglect, or domestic violence. An estimated 450,700 young people in the United States ran away from home in 1994. Other missing children are classified as lost or injured; many are preschoolers who are reported missing but who nearly always return home in less than twenty-four hours. The last category of missing children are called thrownaways, children told to leave home or abandoned by their families. It is estimated that 127,100 young people were thrownaways in 1994.

Public interest in missing children and child abduction as a social problem began in 1932, when the two-year-old son of aviator Charles A. Lindbergh was kidnapped from his home and murdered. Media attention to the investigation and resulting trial focused public concern on the issue, leading Congress to pass the Federal Kidnapping Act (called the Lindbergh Law) that same year, which made kidnapping a federal offense punishable by severe penalties. Since then, public policy to reduce and prevent child abductions and kidnapping has gradually changed. Although abductions are more likely to be reported to the police, many problems remain in enforcing laws and returning abducted young people. Many victims still experience negative effects from being abducted, and family members still face major obstacles in locating and returning their abducted children.

Family Abductions. Half of all children in the United States experience the breakup of their parents' marriage. Conflicts between divorcing parents sometimes result in one parent abducting their children, denying the other parent custody or visitation rights established by a court order. An estimated 354,100 children were abducted by a parent or family member in 1994. Abductors are motivated by the fear that courts will award child custody to the other parents; the fear that the legal custodial parents may not take good care of the children; the fear, based on a past history of violence, that more violence will occur, jeopardizing the safety of the children; the desire to cause psychological pain to the estranged spouses; or the desire to pressure spouses into foregoing divorce. Family abductions rarely involve child sexual abuse.

Nearly half of all children abducted by family members have been taken to other states, and some abductors have moved frequently to avoid capture. Research has shown that even children who are treated well by their abductors suffer negative effects. Nightmares, fears, resentment toward their legal custodial parents, and close identification with their abducting parents make it difficult for abducted children to readjust after being returned to their custodial parents. Such children have lost all contact with friends and activities back home. Some of them have been neglected or kept out of school. Cases become complex when attempts to return located children result in court suits in their new states of residence, often leading to lengthy, costly legal proceedings. In such cases, children are sometimes sent to live with strangers or placed in detention centers.

Abductions by Strangers. The most feared situations involve abductions by strangers or nonfamily members through coercion, trickery, or force. An estimated 3,200 to 4,600 abductions by strangers took place in the United States in 1994. Nonfamily abductions include typical kidnappings for ransom; political kidnappings; permanent abductions; kidnappings of children for profit that sometimes involve organized crime, such as baby selling, illegal adoptions, slavery, prostitution,

child pornography; or kidnappings to sexually abuse or even murder children. Research has suggested that in the late twentieth century between 52 and 158 young people were abducted and murdered each year in the United States, but it was often unclear whether some of them were runaways or thrownaways. Teenage females between the ages of fourteen and seventeen have been most at risk of being murdered by abductors. It has been estimated that some two hundred to three hundred young people have been abducted by persons wishing to keep them permanently. With the use of improved security measures in many hospitals, the number of hospital kidnappings of babies in the United States has declined sharply. Young people are seldom abducted by strangers for sexual or terrorist reasons. Research has indicated that persons seeking children for sexual reasons prefer to befriend rather than abduct their intended victims, gaining their trust and cooperation. Most child molesters have been family members or acquaintances, not strangers.

Responses to Abduction. At one time families of abducted children could often not obtain immediate help from the police, forcing them to hire private investigators and attorneys to travel, locate, and return their children. A more coordinated approach to locating and returning missing and abducted children has evolved, but serious obstacles remain. Changes in law and public policy have produced a network of clearinghouses with databases, cooperative agreements, and resources which link information on every missing-person case in the United States, Canada, and the United Kingdom. This network aids families of victims, police, and prosecutors and discourages child abduction.

Research on child abuse stimulated public interest in the problems of missing children, leading Congress to pass the Missing Children's Assistance Act of 1984. This law created the National Center for Missing and Exploited Children (NCMEC) to serve as the national clearinghouse for information, expertise, and investigation of missing or abused young people. One of its best-known resources is its twenty-four-hour hotline, which receives information about missing young people and transmits it to appropriate authorities. Operated and funded by both government and private sources, NCMEC collects information on all miss-

Among children abducted by strangers, teenage girls are most at risk of being murdered. (Dick Hemingway)

ing young people and assists with cases in which North American children have been abducted to other countries or where children from other countries have been brought to North America.

To resolve disputes arising when civil courts in different states consider child-abduction or kidnapping cases, all states passed the Uniform Child Custody Jurisdiction Act between 1969 and 1983. Although this act required that courts determine whether orders involving particular children had been issued by courts in other states before issuing new orders, in practice they often neglected to do so. Sometimes parents in different states have both been granted legal custody of their children. To solve such disputes, Congress passed the Parental Kidnapping Prevention Act in 1980, which gave the Federal Bureau of Investigation (FBI) the authority to issue arrest warrants for parents who kidnapped their children and the power to investigate cases in which children were abducted across state or national borders. The FBI formed a team called the Child Abduction and Serial Killer Unit

(CASKU) to work on selected cases in cooperation with the National Center for Missing and Exploited Children.

A major change took place in the investigation of abductions when Congress passed the National Child Search Assistance Act in 1990. This act requires that the police take reports of missing children immediately and send descriptions of the victims to the National Crime Information Center (NCIC) for placement on their database. Not all police departments have complied with this provision, citing their lack of training and their limited capacity to take reports and investigate abductions quickly. A team of volunteer retired police officers, called the Morgan P. Hardiman Task Force on Missing and Exploited Children has been formed to assist local departments with investigations of missing-children cases.

State Action and International Cooperation. States have also made progress in enacting laws and formulating public policy aimed at reducing child abductions. Most states have clearinghouses that collect information on missing persons and share it with neighboring states and Canadian provinces. Thus, local police quickly receive information about missing persons and suspected abductors. Another change involves improving conditions for young people who must testify in court regarding abductions or kidnappings. Most states have passed laws to protect the rights of children and lessen the trauma of testifying in court. Some states allow children to testify on videotape or closed-circuit television so that they must not appear in courtrooms filled with adults.

International child abductions may be increasing, presenting major challenges to families seeking the return of their children. Although the United Nations agency INTERPOL collects information on criminals who cross national borders and shares it with police agencies, resources which may be devoted to child abductions are limited. In 1988 Canada and the United States signed an international law called the Hague Convention on the Civil Aspects of International Child Abduction, an agreement by more than 40 nations to share information on abducted children and assist one another in returning them promptly to their native countries. The joint efforts of the Hague agreement and the National Center for Missing and Exploited Children have produced some positive results, but the problem remains that court orders issued in one nation usually need not be honored in courts of another, and different nations' laws and procedures may lead to different court decisions. In 1993 the International Parental Kidnapping Crime Act was passed, which makes it easier to arrest parental abductors who flee to other countries and to apply kidnapping laws to a broader array of cases.

At a more fundamental level, the problems of child abduction and missing children are highly impacted by the quality of family relationships. The prevalence of divorce, domestic violence, child abuse, runaways, thrownaways, and parental abductions reflect a need for greater social support for family life and an ethic of peacemaking within the home. —*Shela R. Van Ness*

BIBLIOGRAPHY

Allen-Hagen, Barbara. *Preliminary Estimates Developed on Stranger Abduction Homicides of Children.* Washington, D.C.: U.S. Department of Justice, Office of Juvenile Justice and Delinquency Prevention, 1989. Presents research on child homicides by strangers.

Girdner, Linda K., and Patricia M. Hoff. *Obstacles to the Recovery and Return of Parentally Abducted Children: Research Summary.* Washington, D.C.: U.S. Department of Justice, Office of Juvenile Justice and Delinquency Prevention, 1994. Identifies continuing weaknesses in the procedures and mechanisms for locating and returning abducted children and presents recommended changes in law and public policy to overcome problems.

Hotaling, Gerald, and David Finkelhor. *The Sexual Exploitation of Missing Children: A Research Review.* Washington, D.C.: U.S. Department of Justice, Office of Juvenile Justice and Delinquency Prevention, 1988. Discusses the findings of numerous studies on missing young people with reference to family backgrounds, prostitution, and pornography.

Kappeler, Victor, Mark Blumberg, and Gary Potter. *The Mythology of Crime and Criminal Justice.* 2d ed. Prospect Heights, Ill.: Waveland, 1996. Discusses the difficulty of defining child abduction and measuring the frequency of cases, while cautioning that public panic over abductions has overestimated the size of the problem.

"Missing Children": Found Facts. Washington, D.C.: U.S. Department of Justice, Office of Juvenile Justice and Delinquency Prevention, 1990. Presents results from research on the prevalence of cases of missing and abducted children in the United States and defines key terms.

A Report to the Nation: Missing and Exploited Children. Arlington, Va.: National Center for Missing and Exploited Children, 1997. Reviews states' progress in enacting legislation favored by the Center and summarizes ways in which computer databases and the computer "aging" of long-term missing children have led to the location and return of many missing young people.

Takas, Marianne. *Using Agency Records to Find Missing Children: A Guide for Law Enforcement, Program Summary.* Washington, D.C.: U.S. Department of Justice, Office of Juvenile Justice and Delinquency Prevention, 1996. Training text for police officers on how to better locate missing children by accessing records of schools, health care professionals, shelters, social welfare agencies, and clearinghouses on missing persons.

A Voice for America's Children: 1994-1995 Annual Report. Arlington, Va.: National Center for Missing and Exploited Children, 1995. Summarizes activities and accomplishments of the Center in collecting and disseminating information and expertise on cases of missing children.

See also Child safety; Divorce; Domestic violence; Family crises; Juvenile delinquency; Missing Children's Assistance Act; National Center for Missing and Exploited Children (NCMEC); Parental Kidnapping Prevention Act (PKPA).

Child abuse

RELEVANT ISSUES: Children and child development; Parenting and family relationships; Violence

SIGNIFICANCE: Child abuse is a major social problem with diverse behavioral consequences, including crime and deviancy

Child abuse is a complex term that defies a precise, timeless definition. What one generation may regard as acceptable, even desirable child discipline may be regarded by another as unacceptable and abusive. The variable nature of what constitutes child abuse is the result of factors such as knowledge accumulation concerning the effects of childhood discipline and punishment, changing attitudes and values caused by changing political and economic conditions, and different religious traditions. To a considerable extent, the complexity of the term child abuse reflects the complexity of modern social life, especially in societies with diverse populations such as the United States, where people have different ethnic backgrounds.

Traditional child-rearing practices in Western societies generally are heavily influenced by biblical teachings. The Old Testament contains a variety of statements that sanction the physical punishment of children. For example, one finds the following: "The man who fails to use the stick hates his son; The man who is free with his correction loves him" (Prov. 13:24). From such teachings is derived the saying, "Spare the rod and spoil the child," a prevailing justification for physically disciplining and punishing children.

In Western society, it was not until the nineteenth century and the growth of large cities in the wake of advancing industrialization that people began to perceive and seriously question the difference between justifiable child discipline and abusive treatment. The gap between rich and poor and the concentration of poor people in city slums and tenements gave rise to child-reform movements.

Child Reforms. The first formal organization concerned with combating child abuse was the Society for the Prevention of Cruelty to Children, created in New York City in 1874. It was led by private individuals rather than government officials. The same situation was true in England with the formation of the Liverpool Society for the Prevention of Cruelty to Children in 1883 and the London National Society for the Prevention of Cruelty to Children in 1889. Leaders of the two groups modeled their organizations after the example of New York. France chose a more formal route. In 1889 it enacted a law prohibiting parents from practices that threatened the safety, health, or morality of children.

In the United States, the initial governmental structure formed to treat child abuse was the Children's Bureau, created in 1912. The Congressional act behind the bureau's creation mandated the dissemination of child-development information and research on issues involving child development. Interestingly, historians are generally agreed that interest in the problem of child abuse waned between 1912 and the late 1950's. Renewed interest in the subject was not evident until the 1960's. The spur was the publication of "The Battered-Child Syndrome" by C. Henry Kempe and several colleagues in 1962.

Kempe was concerned with calling attention to physical child abuse by parents and family members because he correctly viewed it as a serious problem that was being ignored by professionals with the authority to do something about it. Thus, he strived to alert his fellow pediatricians to the symptoms of child abuse and what they should do to stem its repetition. To dramatize the importance of the problem, Kempe chose to refer to it as the "battered-child syndrome," which he and his co-authors defined as "a clinical condition in young children who have received serious physical abuse, generally from a parent or foster parent." They detailed the physical signs of abuse such as severe bruising, broken bones, and brain damage and indicated that although the battered-child syndrome is not age-specific, it mainly occurred in children under the age of three. Kempe and his colleagues hastened to add, however, that little research evidence was available on the subject, because physicians were either unaccustomed to recognizing the true source of child injuries or loathe to confront parents and others who might be responsible for its occurrence.

Since the publication of the Kempe article, students of the subject have found that physically abused children are generally under the age of five but often older. The term "battered-child syndrome" is now seldom used. However, Kempe is credited with having sparked the great interest in and concern for child abuse that characterized the late twentieth century. He and his colleagues are also recognized for generating interest in requiring professionals who work with children to report instances of abuse that come to their attention.

Child Abuse Reporting. There is no precise annual information on the extent of child abuse in the United States. The best general information available comes from those who report instances that come to their attention to the National Center on Child Abuse and Neglect (NCCAN). The NCCAN is a creation of the United States Child Abuse Prevention and Treatment Act. In addition to providing for the creation of a national center, the act made money available to states for the investigation and prevention of child abuse. By the close of the twentieth century, all fifty states had enacted laws requiring that virtually all professional child-care workers report known and suspected cases of child maltreatment to their local social service agencies.

In all states, those required by law to report include physicians, nurses, emergency hospital room personnel, coroners and medical examiners, dentists, mental health professionals, social

During the 1990's, efforts to prevent child abuse developed into high-profile national campaigns. (James L. Shaffer)

workers, teachers and school officials, day-care workers, and law enforcement personnel. In addition, pharmacists, foster parents, clergy, attorneys, day-care licensing inspectors, film or photo processors, substance-abuse counselors, family mediators, staff volunteers in child abuse information and referral programs, and religious healers may also be required by law to report. Such individuals are required to report instances of known and suspected cases of a broad spectrum of child maltreatment possibilities. Failure to report is a crime and subject to financial penalties ranging from $100 to $1,000 and imprisonment from five days to a year in jail.

Varieties and Incidence of Child Abuse. A publication of the Office of Juvenile Justice and Delinquency Prevention, a unit of the United States Office of Justice Programs, identified the following types of child maltreatment: physical abuse, including physical acts such as kicking, biting, punching, throwing, burning, and poisoning that caused or could have caused physical injury to a child; sexual abuse, or the involvement of children in sexual activity to provide sexual gratification or financial benefit to the perpetrators, including contacts for sexual purposes, prostitution, pornography, or other sexually exploitative activities; emotional abuse, which is defined as acts (includ-

Numbers of Children Who Were Subjects of Child Abuse Reports in U.S. States in 1995

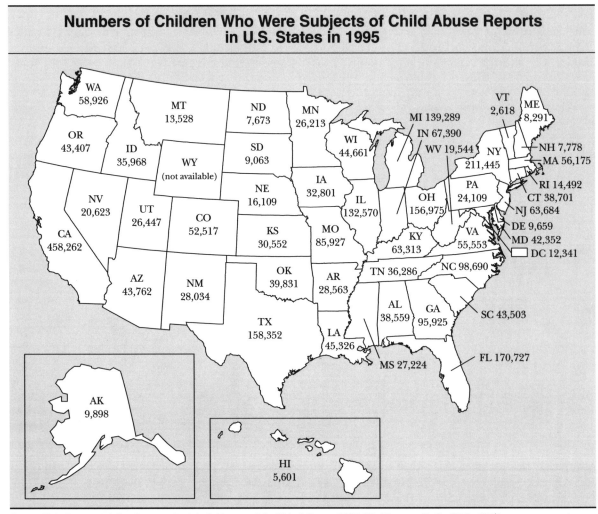

Source: U.S. Bureau of the Census, *Statistical Abstract of the United States: 1997.* Washington, D.C.: GPO, 1997.

Note: A total of 2,959,237 children were subjects of child abuse reports throughout the United States in 1995. This figure represented about 4.3 percent of all children under age eighteen.

Types of Maltreatment in Substantiated Cases of Child Abuse in the United States in 1995

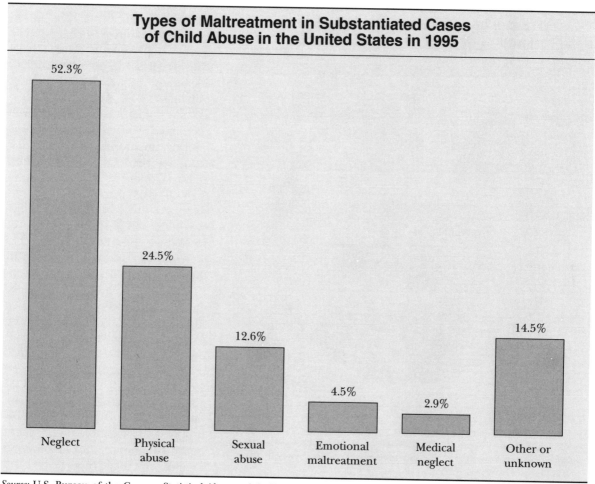

Source: U.S. Bureau of the Census, *Statistical Abstract of the United States: 1997.* Washington, D.C.: GPO, 1997.
Note: These figures are taken from 1,000,502 substantiated cases of abuse (roughly a third of all reported cases). Percentages add up to more than 100 percent because some cases were subjects of more than one form of abuse.

ing verbal or emotional assault) or omissions that caused or could have caused conduct, cognitive, affective, or other mental disorders; physical neglect, which includes abandonment, expulsion from the home, delay or failure to seek remedial health care, inadequate supervision, disregard for hazards in the home, or inadequate food, clothing, or shelter; emotional neglect, which includes inadequate nurturance or affection, permitting maladaptive behavior, and other inattention to emotional or developmental needs; and educational neglect, which includes permitting children to be chronically truant or other inattention to children's educational needs.

The evidence on the extent of child abuse in the United States has been inconsistent. It does, how-ever, indicate that it is extensive. *Physical Violence in American Families* (1990) by Richard J. Gelles and Murray A. Straus is a major source of information on family violence and child abuse. Based on surveys conducted in 1975 and 1985, Gelles and Straus compiled findings from interviews with parents in 8,145 families. The authors differentiate between two types of physical abuse: "very severe" and "severe" violence. By "very severe" they meant instances where surveyed parents admitted doing things to their children such as burning, scalding, choking, slapping, hitting, and kicking, but without the use of objects such as paddles or frying pans. The second type of abuse includes the use of such objects and is therefore viewed by the authors as the better indicator of physical child abuse. On the

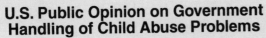

U.S. Public Opinion on Government Handling of Child Abuse Problems

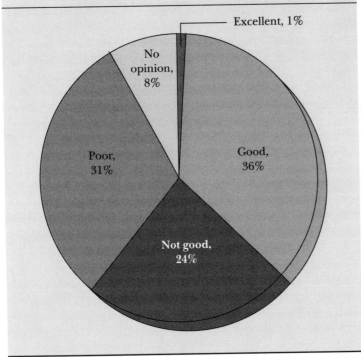

- Excellent, 1%
- No opinion, 8%
- Poor, 31%
- Good, 36%
- Not good, 24%

Source: CNN/*USA Today*/Gallup Poll

Note: In 1994 a cross-section of Americans were asked to rate the way their state governments—including the courts and social workers—dealt with child abuse problems. This chart summarizes respondants' evaluations of the states in this matter.

cluded evidence from official and nonofficial sources such as public health departments. The official data revealed a figure of more than 1.4 million children abused or at risk of being abused. Abuse was defined as "any maltreatment that caused prolonged or worsened some actual injury or impairment of at least moderate severity." Of the 1.4 million children, more than 900,000 were the victims of "demonstrable harm," such as bruises and wounds. The figures indicated an incidence rate of 15 abused children per 1,000 children under the age of eighteen in the entire United States population.

There are a number of reasons for the difference between the evidence supplied by studies such as those conducted by Gelles and Straus and the NCCAN. Of central importance is the difference between reported and unreported instances of child abuse. Most likely, the national samples studied by Gelles and Straus supplied information not brought to the attention of anyone required to make an official report.

The evidence supplied to the NCCAN indicates that the incidence of abuse varies by age and gender but not by race or ethnic background. Females were found to be abused more often than males, and frequency of abuse increased with age regardless of victims' gender. Fatalities were more frequent in younger than in older children.

A finding common to both the Gelles and Straus surveys and NCCAN evidence is a higher incidence of child abuse among poorer families. Straus and Gelles found the highest rates of child abuse in families earning less than $20,000 per year. The NCCAN study found that families with incomes of less than $15,000 evidenced an abuse rate four times higher than families with higher incomes. The neglect rate was found to be eight times higher in low-income families than in higher-income families.

Cycle of Violence. Of great concern to those wishing to identify the causes of abuse and stem

basis of their 1985 survey, they found that 11 out of every 100 children were the victims of instances of child abuse. They said that if this rate were to be applied to the estimated 63 million children in the United States in 1985, it would indicate about 6.9 million children abused per year.

Reports to the National Center on Child Abuse and Neglect are based on information supplied by professionals to social service agencies on the variety of child abuse forms. To date, between 50 and 60 percent of reports have been found to be false. The problem is related to the fact that the required standard of proof varies from state to state. In some states the standard of proof is a social worker's judgment. Other states require what is referred to as "credible evidence," a "preponderance of evidence," or some data to verify a claim. Thus, to obtain the most accurate information possible, the NCCAN sponsored a study that in-

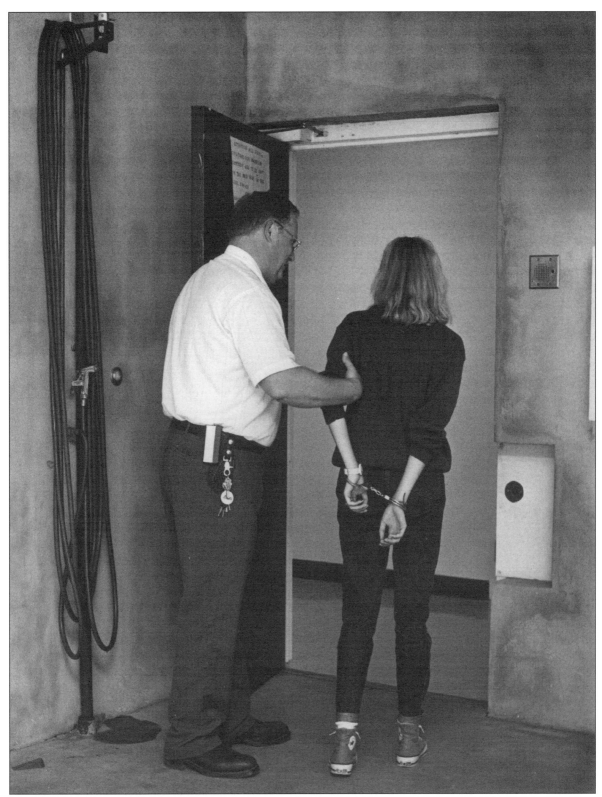

A high proportion of adults arrested for child abuse were abused as children themselves. (James L. Shaffer)

the problem is whether or not child abuse is perpetrated by adults who were themselves victims of child abuse. Of no less concern is whether or not abused children are disproportionately likely to become criminals, particularly violent offenders.

While data on the subject are sparse, what is available supports the hypothesis that abusing parents were themselves abused as children. Unfortunately, Gelles and Straus did not precisely examine this subject. They did find a relationship between the amount of physical punishment experienced by parents and the use of abusive physical punishment toward their own children. Those who have been convicted of violent offenses against children are much more likely than those who victimize adults to have been physically or sexually abused as children.

Solid evidence is available on the relationship between being abused and becoming a criminal. Studies sponsored by the National Institute of Justice in 1992 and 1996 followed 1,575 male and female arrestees from childhood to adulthood. The sample included males and females who were victims of physical and sexual abuse or neglect from 1967 to 1971 in a Midwestern county. A control group of matched individuals who were not abused was devised for comparison.

While pointing out that most members of both groups had neither a juvenile nor an adult criminal record, those abused or neglected as children were much more likely to have been arrested as juveniles or adults and for violent crimes. Evidence has shown that victims of childhood neglect were also more apt to become violent criminal offenders than those who were not; victims of childhood sexual abuse were no more likely to become sex offenders than those victimized by other types of physical abuse or neglect; sexually abused children had a greater likelihood of later arrest for prostitution than other maltreated victims; and youngsters who were not physically abused but who were exposed to family violence had higher rates of violent behavior than those not exposed to family violence. —*Calvin J. Larson*

BIBLIOGRAPHY

Bender, David, and Bruno Leone, eds. *Child Abuse: Opposing Viewpoints.* San Diego, Calif.: Greenhaven Press, 1994. Opposing viewpoints on basic child abuse questions such as "Is Child Abuse a Serious Problem?," "What Causes Child Abuse?," and "How Can Child Abuse Be Reduced?"

Besharov, Douglas J. *Recognizing Child Abuse.* New York: Free Press, 1990. Details the nature and extent of the problem of child abuse and what can and should be done about it, while placing the problem in historical perspective by examining available information.

Coleman, Antoinette A. *Child Abuse Reporting.* New York: Garland, 1995. Focusing on Baltimore, the book contains a concise history of efforts to require the reporting of child abuse cases.

Gelles, Richard J., and Murray A. Straus. *Intimate Violence.* New York: Simon & Schuster, 1988. Major work by pioneers in the study of family violence and the culmination of fifteen years of research and writing that focuses primarily on child and wife abuse and is based primarily on more than 6,000 interviews.

Greven, Philip. *Spare the Child.* New York: Alfred A. Knopf, 1991. Detailed historical analysis of the religious roots of child punishment and the psychological effects of physical abuse.

Moorhead, Caroline, ed. *Betrayal: A Report on Violence Toward Children in Today's World.* New York: Doubleday, 1990. Collection of articles on the status of abused and neglected children in Africa, Europe, India, the Middle East, the Philippines, South America, and the United States.

See also Abandonment of the family; Child abandonment; Child Abuse Prevention and Treatment Act (CAPTA); Child molestation; Child rearing; Children's Defense Fund (CDF); Emotional abuse; Family Violence Prevention and Services Act; Incest; Infanticide; National Center for Missing and Exploited Children (NCMEC); Parents Anonymous (PA); Straus, Murray.

Child Abuse Prevention and Treatment Act (CAPTA)

DATE: Proposed as PL 93-247 and passed by Congress on January 31, 1974

RELEVANT ISSUES: Children and child development; Law; Parenting and family relationships; Violence

SIGNIFICANCE: This act brought child maltreatment to national attention and mandated that states report cases of child abuse and neglect

Sponsored by Senator Walter Mondale, the Child Abuse Prevention and Treatment Act provided small grants to states for research and demonstration projects to prevent and treat child abuse and neglect. States were required to mandate the reporting of known or suspected cases of child abuse and neglect, provide immunity for reporting, provide guardian ad litem representation for children, ensure confidentiality of records, provide public education on abuse and neglect, develop tracking, and investigate systems. The act created the National Center on Child Abuse and Neglect, which established regulatory standards for prevention and treatment programs, including twenty-four-hour response services. This act led to the Adoption Assistance and Child Welfare Act of 1980, which mandated that the special needs of children with disabilities, sibling groups, and older-aged children be met. The impact of the Child Abuse Prevention and Treatment Act of 1974 produced services to preserve, strengthen, and reunite families. Its passage resulted in states establishing reporting and tracking systems and coordinated information systems that are essential to permanency and placement procedures.

—*Karen V. Harper*

See also Child abuse; Child molestation; Children's Defense Fund (CDF); Family Violence Prevention and Services Act; Foster homes; Infanticide.

Child and dependent care tax credit

DATE: Enacted on October 4, 1976, as part of the Tax Reform Act of 1976
RELEVANT ISSUES: Economics and work; Law
SIGNIFICANCE: The child and dependent care tax credit is an entitlement program in the U.S. Internal Revenue Code that gives taxpayers an income tax credit for household and dependent care expenses incurred while they are gainfully employed

Prior to the 1976 act, taxpayers could only deduct their dependent care expenses. Congress recognized that the deduction was overly complex and benefited only higher income taxpayers. The 1976 act substituted a tax credit that is normally more advantageous than a deduction. If taxpayers are in the 20 percent tax bracket and have $100 of dependent care expenses, a tax deduction amounts to only $20, while a tax credit amounts to $100. The tax credit is fully refundable, so that even taxpayers with little or no tax liability receive a refund from the government. Taxpayers with zero tax liability who spend $100 on dependent care still receive a refund from the government for $100. This is unlike other tax credits and deductions, which do not reduce tax liability below zero.

The child and dependent care tax credit applies to employment-related expenses incurred by taxpayers to enable them to be gainfully employed. The expenses can only be for household services or the care of qualifying dependents. Baby-sitting in the home, day care outside the home, some housecleaning services, and similar expenses may qualify persons for the credit. Taxpayers must either be working, looking for work, or self-employed.

There are three kinds of qualifying dependents. The first are dependents under the age of thirteen. Such dependents are usually taxpayers' children or stepchildren. The second are physically or mentally incapacitated dependents. Such dependents may be taxpayers' children over the age of thirteen or elderly parents. The third are taxpayers' mentally or physically incapacitated spouses.

Special rules apply to taxpayers who are divorced or living separately. There are also rules determining who gets the credit if dependents live in two or more households during the year.

The amount of the credit is limited. Taxpayers receive only 30 percent of all dependent care expenses. If taxpayers' income exceeds $10,000, the credit percentage gradually decreases to 20 percent. There is also an absolute dollar amount on the credit. For one qualifying dependent, the credit cannot be greater than $2,400. For two or more dependents, the credit cannot exceed $4,800. Finally, if taxpayers are married, the credit cannot exceed the earned income of the lower-paid spouse.

The credit has helped to relieve the tax burden on some families and has made it possible for both parents, rather than just one, to work outside the home. However, the credit is not ideal. The dollar limits can be unrealistic when compared to the

The child and dependent care tax credit enables many parents to continue working full-time by reducing child-care costs. (James L. Shaffer)

actual costs of care. Limiting the credit to persons whose children are thirteen years of age or younger fails to take into account the needs of teenagers. Limiting the credit to the income of lower-paid spouses can cause some people to remain at home. —*David E. Paas*

See also Child care; Earned income tax credit; Family economics; Tax laws.

Child care

RELEVANT ISSUES: Children and child development; Parenting and family relationships

SIGNIFICANCE: An important and demanding responsibility, child care has taken different forms at different times and in different cultures and requires that parents, families, and communities work together

Child care is one of the most difficult challenges that families and communities must face. Infants are completely dependent on their caregivers. As children grow, their ability to explore the world increases, but their need for adult care and attention does not decrease. Each developmental stage has unique needs that must be met if the child is to grow into an independent adult. Human children require more complex and demanding care than the young of any other species. The job of caring for a child from birth to adulthood is a too large for any one person. That may be why child care has always been shared among parents, families, and community members in every culture throughout human history. The quality of child care can affect a child's social, emotional, physical,

The costs of providing adequate care for young children are high because of the need for close and constant adult supervision. (James L. Shaffer)

and intellectual well-being. The importance of child care for the future, as well as the difficulty of providing high-quality care, is reflected in the amount of time and attention people have given to research, theory, and political debate about the best way to care for children.

Child-Care Needs at Different Ages. Newborn infants need feeding, cleaning, cuddling, and interaction around the clock. Most newborns spend nine to fourteen hours sleeping and one to three hours crying every day, and most awaken two or more times at night. Toward the middle of their first year, infants learn to scoot, roll, and crawl around. Once an infant is mobile, constant supervision is required because the child can easily be injured by falling, choking on small objects, or encountering other hazards. Infants need a great deal of social interaction, talking, and touching to develop their senses, emotional attachments, language, and intelligence.

Toddlers, children between the ages of twelve and thirty-six months, learn to walk, speak, eat adult food, and use the toilet. The need for constant supervision increases during this time, because children learn to walk, run, and climb. The highest number of fatal and injurious accidents during childhood occur during the toddler stage. The skills that toddlers learn may seem basic, but they are in fact quite complex. For example, toddlers go from one-word utterances at twelve months to a vocabulary of several hundred words by the age of three. Learning so much so fast can be frustrating for both toddlers and their caregivers, and temper tantrums sometimes occur at this age. Toddlers need constant supervision, safe places to explore, and sensitive caregivers.

Preschoolers, children between the ages of three and five, need supervision and protection. They learn the rules of social interaction, concepts such as space, time, and quantity, and the meaning of abstract symbols (pictures, shapes, numbers, and letters). They need challenges, opportunities to play, and time to interact with adults and peers.

School-age children are in many ways easier to care for than are toddlers or preschoolers. They spend much of the day outside the home; they are more independent and less demanding. They still need supervision, although many children of working parents must come home from school alone. School-age children need time with adults

to learn about adult life and problem solving. Adolescents require less supervision, but they also need time with adults. This age group has the second highest accident rate during childhood and the highest murder and suicide rate. They need safe places to socialize with peers and opportunities to make major decisions that affect them.

Historical and Cultural Differences. Although the sharing of child care is common to all people, actual child-care arrangements and methods differ according to cultural values and traditions. In hunter-gatherer societies, which are most like the earliest human cultures, children spend a great deal of time with parents and extended family members. Children are not segregated by age but spend all their time with adult family members and older children as they eat, work, and sleep. Infants are breast-fed for up to three years, and young infants are carried in others' arms or in slings nearly all the time. These child-care practices help children to stay safe and well-nourished in the hunter-gatherer environment, in which the food supply is not constant. They also allow women to recover from childbirth by distributing the burden of caregiving among adults.

Traditional agricultural societies share many child-care practices with hunter-gatherer cultures. In such societies most child care and education is informal, provided by children's parents with the help of grandparents, aunts, uncles, and older siblings. Because both men and women work in and out of the home each day, young children learn to accompany parents while they work. Fathers participate in educating and caring for children, although mothers provide most of the infant care. Older children are expected to help with the work of the family. Children are a valued resource for agricultural families, because they increase the number of people available to work on the land, care for aging family members, and continue family traditions. Large families and early marriages are highly prized in traditional cultures.

Sharing child care among family members is common to all traditional societies, but actual child-rearing practices and expectations are varied. For example, in traditional Chinese families infants are carried close to their mothers around the clock, sleep and eat on their own schedule, and receive tremendous attention from all family members for up to three years before they are

Child-care needs vary with the ages of the children; as children grow older, the amount of direct supervision diminishes. (Mary LaSalle)

expected to sleep on their own, eat adult foods, and use the toilet independently. In contrast, children in traditional European families are often expected to eat according to a schedule, learn not to cry excessively, and to use the toilet early.

Child Care in Urban Cultures. The urban areas of the world, including most of North America and Europe, have changed from traditional agri-cultural societies to industrial and technical socie-ties, in which formal education and economic pro-ductivity are highly valued. With these changes in the larger culture, child-care arrangements and practices have also changed. Throughout Euro-pean and North American history, there has been a cultural conflict between those who prefer pro-fessional child care and those who believe that young children should be in the exclusive care of their mothers. The first people to break with traditional extended-family child care and experience this conflict were wealthy families. Poor and working-class families stayed with traditional child-care arrangements out of necessity.

In the sixteenth and seventeenth centuries wealthy families either gave their infants to wet nurses—servant women who breast-fed their own children and also nursed others—or they fed their babies a mixture of water and flour. Infant mortality was very high at the time, with nearly half of all children dying before the age of five. According to some social critics of the time, servants cared for the children of the wealthy because husbands wanted wives to attend to their needs and not children's, while others believed that servant women were healthier, less nervous, and thus better able to care for young children. However, by the 1790's maternal care and breast-feeding were common once again, partly because rationalist philosophers such as John Locke and Jean-Jacques Rousseau advocated natural child-rearing methods.

Similarly, during the Industrial Revolution in the early 1800's, when middle-class men began to spend more time away from home in order to earn money, women were encouraged to fill the gap made by their husbands' absence from home and become the sole caregivers and moral educators of their children. Motherhood was seen as a sacred duty and privilege. Following this period, in the late 1800's women's independence and the family's social standing were valued. Middle-class families hired nannies, and children were excluded from many of their parents' activities. There was a great deal of interest in more efficient ways to keep children occupied, well-behaved, and out of trouble. By the early 1920's formal schooling, in which both poor and wealthy children were educated outside the home beginning at the age of six, was the norm. This change allowed parents to spend more time supporting the family and caring for their property and social status, activities that were crucial for their survival.

The Industrial Revolution brought changes to the child-care practices of poor and working-class families as well. Parents and family members had to work outside the home, leaving many younger children on their own. Infant and child mortality increased among the poor, leading in the 1830's to the founding of the first Infant Schools in the United States—day-care institutions that were run by charities. Some poor families paid "baby farms," institutions that accepted children for a small fee and put them up for adoption. The continuing child-care crisis in the 1920's also stimulated the first "mother's pensions," small payments that allowed poor women to stay home and care for their children. These pensions led to the development of Aid to Families with Dependent Children (welfare) in the mid-1930's.

By the early part of the 1900's every type of child care that has persisted in the United States and Canada throughout the twentieth century had begun, and the political tension between maternal care in the home and professional care was firmly established. Because of the economic need for people to work outside the home, the lack of women in the workplace, and the increasing mobility of nuclear families, fathers and extended families—once important members of the child-care team—were no longer mentioned in the debates about child care. Throughout the twentieth century, mothers entered workplaces outside the home by necessity or choice, as during World War II and in the 1970's and 1980's. Each time women have worked outside the home, the debate pitting maternal care against professional care has intensified.

Child-Care Services and Issues. The options for child care increased from 1970 through the 1990's in response to increased demand. In 1995, 70 percent of women with children under the age of five worked outside the home. Although many women with children worked outside the home during the Industrial Revolution, the 1880's, and World War II, the large numbers of middle-class families requiring and demanding high-quality, affordable child care was the unique characteristic of the period from the 1970's to the 1990's that fueled the expansion of child-care options. These included mothers at home, fathers at home, both parents working part-time or on flexible schedules, full day-care centers, day-care homes, part-time preschools, paid care in parent's homes, care by relatives or friends, and—for some—inadequate care or no care at all.

Nearly all families have used a combination of these care arrangements. For example, parents who stayed at home full-time to care for their children often used part-day preschools, paid baby-sitters, and relatives to care for their children. Working parents with school-age children relied on neighbors for after-school care in exchange for providing overnight child care when neighbors were out of town. Single parents formed networks of relatives, friends, and paid caregivers to meet their children's needs. In the 1990's the majority of families with young children in the United States and Canada used informal and home-based child care rather than licensed, center-based care. Many families preferred center-based care but relied on informal care, because center care was not available or flexible enough. For example, although in 1990 one in five workers in the United States worked odd hours or traveled frequently to work, there were only twelve licensed centers in the whole nation that provided twenty-four-hour care.

The cost of child care was another problem facing families and communities. Parent-subsidized care cost 12 to 20 percent of family income by the late 1990's. Working parents who could not afford to pay for child care received government subsidies, although the amount of such subsidies decreased in both the United States and Canada during the 1990's, even as demand was growing. Middle-class parents in the United States received tax credits for a portion of their child-care costs beginning in the 1980's. Federally-funded educational programs for the children of poor parents and children with disabilities have served some—but not all—of the children who have qualified for them.

Concern about the effects of non-maternal care and the low quality of many child-care settings was most intense during the 1970's and 1980's, when some child-development experts and public figures advised women to stay home full-time rather than expose their children to the risks of out-of-home care. This concern and controversy gave rise to studies of the effects of nonmaternal

child care, including a nationwide study of infant day care sponsored by the National Institute of Child Health and Human Development in the United States in the 1990's. This study involved more than 1,200 children in every type of care arrangement, including full-time maternal care. The study concluded that the majority of differences between children (32 percent) arose from family factors such as parents' education and the quality of parent-child interaction. Fewer differences (1 percent) were the result of the effects of nonmaternal child care. Children were not negatively affected by high-quality care. Children in care several hours per week during early infancy or in low-quality care were most likely to be negatively affected by day care. Indicators of high-quality care include a low number of children per adult, a safe and healthy environment, the availability of interesting and appropriate activities for children, and the opportunity for children to interact with

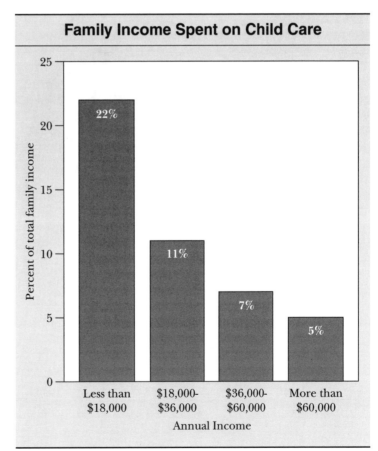

Source: Bureau of the Census (1991)

Like any other commercial enterprise, professional child-care services can benefit from economies of scale. (Diane C. Lyell)

adults who are affectionate and who talk to them. The study also found that many types of informal care that families relied on out of necessity were high in quality, despite the financial and scheduling hardships involved. It seems that in the 1990's, as throughout human history, families adapted and recruited support in order to provide for the care of their children. —*Kathleen M. Zanolli*

BIBLIOGRAPHY

The American Academy of Pediatrics and the American Public Health Association. *Caring for Our Children.* Washington, D.C.: Author, 1996. Presents a set of 981 national health and safety standards for day care that are clear and easy to understand.

Berezin, Judith. *The Complete Guide to Choosing Child Care.* New York: Random House, 1990. Describes all the paid child-care options available, including family day-care homes, in-home care, center-based care, and after-school care, and includes a list of agencies that provide referrals for child care.

Davidson, Christine. *Staying Home Instead: Alternatives to the Two-Paycheck Family.* New York: Macmillan, 1992. Describes many choices other than full-time work outside the home for both parents, including part-time work, job sharing, flexible schedules, and home-based businesses, and addresses the problems of parents who do not have as much time with their children as they would like.

Golant, Mitch, and Susan Golant. *Finding Time for Fathering.* New York: Columbine, 1992. Describes ways that fathers can spend more time with their children, including helping with household chores, involving children in work, and playing with children.

Hardyment, Christina. *Dream Babies: Three Centuries of Good Advice on Child Rearing.* New York: Harper & Row, 1988. Contains child-care advice from philosophers, clergy, doctors, nurses, mothers, social reformers, and psychologists from 1700 to the 1980's and explores insightfully the recurrent issues of paid versus maternal care, harsh discipline versus permissiveness, and natural versus scientific child rearing.

Zigler, Edward, and Mary Lang. *Child Care Choices.* New York: Macmillan, 1991. Describes the child-care system in the United States, the quality, affordability, and availability of child care, and government and social support for child care.

See also Aid to Families with Dependent Children (AFDC); Au pairs; Child rearing; Day care; Family-friendly programs; Family Protection Act; Nannies; Tax laws.

Child Care and Development Block Grant Act

DATE: First introduced in 1987; compromise bill passed in 1990 and signed by President George Bush

RELEVANT ISSUES: Children and child development; Law; Parenting and family relationships

SIGNIFICANCE: The purpose of this act was to improve child-care options for low-income families

Many factors influenced the Child Care and Development Block Grant Act of 1990. One of the most important factors was that by 1990 more than 50 percent of U.S. mothers of infants worked outside the home. Another was that during the 1980's criminal charges were filed against child-care workers in various parts of the United States, alleging that they were guilty of child abuse and neglect. The Child Care and Development Block Grant Act attempted to provide child-care assistance for those working mothers while establishing programs and guidelines to train and monitor child-care workers.

This act was an effort on the part of the federal government to provide support to states to improve child-care options for low-income workers. The act provides funds to low-income families to assist them in paying for child care, to increase the number of community child-care centers in the United States, and to pay professionals to train licensed caregivers and to allow such caregivers to attend training classes. Through a series of modest block grants, states receive money so that they can license and monitor child-care facilities. In general, the act has made more child-care options available to working mothers and has contributed to the public scrutiny of those who work in child-care facilities. —*Annita Marie Ward*

See also Child Abuse Prevention and Treatment Act (CAPTA); Child care; Day care; Single-parent families; Substitute caregivers; Work.

Child custody

RELEVANT ISSUES: Children and child development; Divorce; Parenting and family relationships

SIGNIFICANCE: The welfare of children and the nature of parenting relationships have been dramatically affected by the growing divorce rate

Significant social changes in Western cultures during the late twentieth century—a tripling of unwed mothers and more than a doubling of the divorce rate—have necessitated careful examination of child-parent relationships. One of the most hotly debated aspects of these relationships has been the custody of children. Custody arrangements have significant repercussions for child welfare, the rights of individual parents, and the welfare of society in general.

History of Child Custody. U.S. history has seen four distinct phases of child-custody arrangements. Before the mid-nineteenth century, concepts of child custody were rooted in English common law, which considered children to be personal property. Because married women under common law could not own either real or personal property, children of divorced parents were usually awarded to their fathers.

The pendulum began to swing the other way after a landmark 1842 case known as *Mercein v. People*. This New York state supreme court decision ruled that by "law of nature the father has no paramount right to the custody of his child." A "tender years doctrine" was established, according to which infants, young children, and female children were awarded to their mothers unless the latter were deemed unfit. By the twentieth century, this doctrine had evolved into a "special bond doctrine," which established mothers' custodial rights. Custodial arrangements had come full circle: from fathers' property to mothers' prerogative.

Before the advent of no-fault divorce laws during the 1970's, physical custody of children was usually awarded to mothers, and fathers typically saw their children only on weekends. (James L. Shaffer)

A major shift in the 1970's led to changes in custodial awards. In 1970, California enacted the first no-fault divorce law. Previously, all American divorces had been contested: One partner had to sue the other on proper legal grounds, such as for cruelty. This adversarial situation often led to "good parent versus bad parent" charges, with strong implications for child custody. For fathers to be awarded custody of their children, they had to prove to the courts that their wives were bad parents.

No-fault divorce laws, which were adopted by all other states by the 1980's, had a two-fold impact on children: The number of divorces skyrocketed, greatly increasing the number of custody cases, and a more egalitarian climate for child-custody arrangements was created. California again led the way by introducing the concept of legal joint custody in 1980. By the 1990's the special-bond approach to child custody began to give way to a policy that promoted the best interests of children. Joint custody greatly increased as custody laws were stripped of presumptions about which gender was better qualified to parent children.

Landmark Legal Decisions. From the 1840's until the late 1960's the U.S. judicial system overwhelmingly favored mothers over fathers in custody decisions. Beginning in the 1960's, several key legislative and judicial decisions changed the face of custodial arrangements. The Family Law Act of 1969, while retaining aspects of the "tender years" doctrine, began to base custody decisions on the best interests of the children. The Uniform Child Custody Jurisdiction Act (proposed in 1968 and accepted throughout the United States by 1984) established state-to-state and international recognition of custody decisions. One of the primary purposes of this act was to ensure that court proceedings serve the best interests of children. In 1973 a New York court ruled in *Watts v. Watts* that the "tender years" principle was based on social stereotypes and should therefore be discarded. In *Orr v. Orr* (1979) the U.S. Supreme Court ruled that state laws requiring fathers, but not mothers, to pay child support were unconstitutional. The Uniform Marriage and Divorce Act (1979) firmly established the priority of children's best interests over mothers' rights. This act determined that many considerations, such as children's wishes, home adjustment, and child-parent relations,

must be considered by the court in determining custodial arrangements.

State laws have varied greatly in the degree to which these decisions have affected custodial arrangements. For example, in 1997 judges in South Carolina and Tennessee were still permitted to award custody solely on the basis of the "tender years doctrine," while such judicial prerogative was prohibited in California, Florida, and several other states. Gender considerations have continued to be a factor in custody awards, but they have been the exception rather than the rule. Many other factors, including household stability, parental competence, and personality characteristics, have become more important in making custody determinations. This shift has complicated the process of determining custody, thereby increasing the need for fair and objective custody evaluation procedures.

Custody Evaluation Procedures. American and Canadian courts have increasingly relied on standardized evaluations in awarding custody. One of the most widely recognized evaluation procedures, developed by Barry Bricklin, is a fourfold approach involving interviews, observations, psychological testing, and review of relevant records and documents. Interviews are conducted with parents, children, and others. Observers chronicle children's interactions with their mothers, fathers, and significant others. Several psychological tests developed by Bricklin are administered to parents and children. The Perception of Relationships Test and the Bricklin Perceptual Scales assess children's perceptions of their parents. The Parent Awareness Skills Survey and the Parent Perception of Child Profile measure parents' effectiveness in raising their children. Finally, evaluators conduct careful reviews of school, medical, and legal documents. After this information is compiled, it is used to match the strengths of parents to the needs of children in determining the best custodial fit. While courts do not have to heed these recommendations, the fact that a wealth of information is used to make unbiased decisions carries great weight in judges' decisions.

Custodial Arrangements. There are two basic types of custodial arrangements, with many variations. In sole-custody awards, one parent is granted legal and physical custody while the other pays child support. Children reside in the custodial parent's home (typically the mother's) with a fixed visitation schedule set up for the noncustodial parent. Except under unusual circumstances (such as a history of parental abuse), the noncustodial parent has legally protected access to the children after divorce.

Joint custody grants both parents equal rights in raising their children, entitling them to make medical, educational, and legal decisions involving their children. Although joint custody is often awarded, children's actual living arrangements are similar to those in sole custody. In some instances, physical custody is shared, so that children move back and forth between their mothers' and fathers' homes.

A combination of both sole and joint custody is known as "split custody." Split custody awards both parents primary custody of different offspring. Although gender is not the only determining factor in cases of split custody, children are commonly awarded to their same-sex parent. The success of split custody, as with other custodial arrangements, can vary greatly with the ages of the children and the changing dynamics of child-parent and parent-parent relationships.

Economic Impact. Research in the United States and Canada has demonstrated that single-parent families, usually headed by mothers, are disproportionately subject to financial strains. Studies published in 1996 reported that single-mother families were several times more likely than dual-parent families to live below the poverty line. While children conceived out of wedlock and children whose fathers had died were included in the families studied, the statistical findings demonstrated that divorced mothers awarded custody of their children were likely to experience great financial suffering. However, researchers make contradictory claims about the post-divorce ratio of female-to-male earnings. While some say that the standard of living of women fell about 30 percent and that of men rose by about 10 percent, others indicate that divorced men's income dropped by about 6 percent.

Many combined factors have caused custodial parents' economic situation to decline. Divorced couples have usually established separate households supported by a single income. If one parent has not been working or has worked primarily part time, the economic impact has been felt more strongly than if both parents have worked full time, particularly as child-care needs have increased. Child support is supposed to cushion the economic blow, but according to a 1996 study, divorced mothers received only about 60 percent of the court-awarded child-support money they were due. In the 1990's federal and state legislation was enacted to increase the likelihood that custodial parents would receive their child-support payments. A 1996 study reported that the likelihood of meeting child-support obligations depended on the types of custodial arrangement. More than 90 percent of fathers with joint custody met their child-support responsibilities. At the same time, only 79 percent of noncustodial fathers with visitation rights and only 44.5 percent of fathers with neither visitation nor joint custody rights were current on their child support payments.

Effects on Children. Divorce can benefit children by removing them from conflicted marriages and strife-ridden families. While most children emerge from divorce as psychologically healthy adults, some leading authorities have found that most children do suffer some adverse effects when their parents divorce.

Research conducted between the 1970's and 1990's claimed that after divorce, children reported increased stress, anger, sadness, disobedience, problems in heterosexual relationships, and other behavioral problems. The likelihood and severity of these problems were greatly affected by various factors, particularly the nature of the custodial parent situation.

Joint physical custody has been the subject of numerous research studies, many of which have found that children can suffer added stress in the back-and-forth shifting between two residences. A 1993 study found that joint physical custody was particularly hard on young children. In addition to the stress of the divorce itself, the lack of a secure home base placed further strains on young children's coping resources.

Custodial parents' living situations have also greatly affected the psychological welfare of their children. A 1995 study reported that boys living with mothers who did not remarry were more likely to experience problems from kindergarten through adolescence than boys with married mothers. Female children began to exhibit problems only with the onset of adolescence, when they experienced interpersonal problems, particularly in heterosexual relationships. A 1997 study reported that children of divorced parents tended to fare best when they were psychologically close to the custodial parents of the same sex. Additionally, the more mature and well-adjusted the parents, the better they raised their children. Single parents have usually faced extra responsibilities which, when placed on top of the psychological and social upheaval created by divorce, have depressed them and weakened their ties to their children. Research has shown that depressed parents have displayed more hostility toward and in the presence of their children than nondepressed parents and have put less effort into effective child-rearing strategies. Overall, children's adjustment to divorce is heavily dependent upon the strengths and weaknesses of their custodial parents.

Social Implications. While the last half of the twentieth century has witnessed a growing acceptance of divorce in Western societies, acceptance of noncustodial mothers has lagged behind. A 1983 study found that mothers who did not have custody of their children often faced greater societal criticism than noncustodial fathers. It is often considered "natural" for fathers not to have custody of their children, but mothers are often thought to be unfit if they do not live with their children. Thus, while custody evaluation by the courts became much more gender-neutral in the late twentieth century, gender has continued to play a major role in social attitudes and judgments.

A major concern of many observers has been fathers' waning involvement in the lives of their children. The number of children living with only their mothers in the United States grew from approximately 8 million in 1960 to around 23 million by 1995. In the 1990's nearly 60 percent of American children lived in homes in which their fathers were absent for extended periods. Only about 17 percent of the children in such homes saw their fathers more than once a week, and about 40 percent of them did not see their fathers in the previous year. The 400 percent rise in out-of-wedlock births and the 250 percent rise in divorce from 1960 to 1995 were major reasons for the increase in single-mother families.

The "great divorce experiment" of the twentieth century has forced society to reevaluate the importance of mothering and fathering. Perhaps it is not so ironic that as Americans and Canadians had fewer children and spent less time with them during the late twentieth century, the legislative and judicial systems increasingly stressed the best interests of children over the rights of their parents in divorce proceedings.

—*Kathleen A. Chara and Paul J. Chara, Jr.*

BIBLIOGRAPHY

Arendell, Terry. *Fathers and Divorce.* Thousand Oaks, Calif.: Sage Publications, 1995. Comprehensive study of the impact of divorce on fathers, particularly in regard to custodial arrangements.

Bricklin, Barry. *The Custody Evaluation Handbook: Research-Based Solutions and Applications.* New York: Brunner/Mazel, 1995. Description of the numerous tests and tools needed for an objective and effective custody evaluation.

Guttmann, Joseph. *Divorce in Psychosocial Perspective: Theory and Research.* Hillsdale, N.J.: Lawrence Erlbaum, 1993. Comprehensive cross-cultural examination of the complexities of divorce, with excellent coverage of the impact of custodial arrangements.

Lyster, Mimi E. *Child Custody: Building Arrangements That Work.* Berkeley, Calif.: Nolo Press, 1995. Self-help legal handbook written by a professional child-custody mediator addressing the most common custody issues.

Mason, Mary Ann. *From Father's Property to Children's Rights: The History of Child Custody in the United States.* New York: Columbia University Press, 1994. Examines how social changes in American society have affected child custody.

Myers, Susan, and Joan Lakin. *Who Will Take the Children? Divorcing Mothers—and Fathers.* New York: Bobbs-Merrill, 1983. Two psychotherapists who are also noncustodial mothers explore the myths, realities, and implications of father-granted custody.

See also Child support; Child Support Enforcement Amendments; Divorce; Family law; Fatherlessness; Guardianship; No-fault divorce; Parental Kidnapping Prevention Act (PKPA); Uniform Child Custody Jurisdiction Act (UCCJA); Uniform

Marriage and Divorce Act (UMDA); Visitation rights.

Child molestation

RELEVANT ISSUES: Children and child development; Parenting and family relationships; Violence

SIGNIFICANCE: Child molestation causes significant harm to many children, yet families can do much to prevent it or minimize its long-term effects

Child molestation, or child sexual abuse, is sexual assault on or the sexual exploitation of minors. It includes exposing children to pornography or sexual talk, inappropriate kissing, fondling of breasts or genitals, and oral, anal, or vaginal sex with children. It also includes using children for child pornography or for prostitution. Victims range from infants to adolescents. Estimates from the 1990's indicate that one in four girls and one in five boys will be molested by the time they reach the age of eighteen.

Social Aspects. Child molestation has been documented in many cultures throughout history, and it occurs in all races, socioeconomic classes, and ethnic groups. A view of women and children as objects and possessions often is implicated as a historical backdrop to the societal problem of child molestation. Some people have indicted the media for their role in promoting the idea of women as objects and in confusing the distinction between girls and women as sexual objects. Television situation comedies often include sexual innuendos in programs aimed at younger children, and films have portrayed comic situations in which children are molested or where molestation appears to be taking place.

Child pornography is a problem in itself. It also has been noted that some adult pornography contains references to sex with children. Clothing for young children often is seductive or revealing, and it sometimes is advertised by children in seductive poses.

In recent history, some have viewed children as sexual beings and have attempted to promote the acceptability of sex between adults and children. Alfred Kinsey's *Sexuality and the Human Male* (1948), for example, contains charts for children as young as five months old through adolescence documenting their orgasmic activity while being stimulated repeatedly by adults. This biological capacity to climax has been interpreted as indicating that sex is beneficial to children. The Rene Guyon Society and the North American Man-Boy Love Association attempt to legitimize sex between adults and children by use of the term "intergenerational sex" rather than molestation. These attempts to treat children as adults ignores the fact that brain development is not complete until at least late adolescence, and children simply do not have the cognitive capacity of adults. Because of these considerations and the inherently less powerful position of children, many people argue that a consensual sexual relationship between an adult and a child is not possible. Children submit to molestation out of fear of hurting the feelings of the perpetrator, a need for affection, fear of repercussions to themselves or loved ones, fear of punishment, or a sense of obedience, or because they have been led to believe that this is normal. They are victimized by use of bribes, threats, or force, and molesters often carefully play on children's trust by manipulating their feelings.

Sexual addiction, while not always expressed in child molestation, sometimes plays a role in pedophilia, or sexual attraction to children. Most sex addicts have been molested as children, often by a family member or family friend, creating an underlying belief that any close relationship must involve sex. In addition, the early interruption of the adult's own development may have left him (most child molesters are male) on some levels a child, and on other levels a hurt or angry person. As with any addiction, an attempt to dull pain is sought through mood alteration, and in the case of child molestation it is often the intensity of risk that provides the chemical basis for this.

Another important factor in child molestation is society's ignorance of sexual abuse as a problem. Many adults prefer to believe that such acts against children are rare, and many cling to the image of the stranger as perpetrator. In fact, most perpetrators are the father or stepfather of the victim, a close relative, or a friend of the family. Baby-sitters, teachers, youth workers, clergy, and others find their way into situations that provide access to children. The typical pedophile is male (97 percent) and has hundreds of victims.

In 1990 Eileen Franklin-Lipsker, a twenty-nine-year-old California woman, claiming to have recalled a long-suppressed childhood memory, charged her father with having molested and killed a childhood friend twenty-one years earlier. (AP/Wide World Photos)

Legal Aspects. Child molestation is illegal in the United States and in Canada. Medical, educational, and mental health professionals have a legal obligation to report suspected cases of molestation. Persons not mandated to report usually can report anonymously to family protective services or to law enforcement agencies.

Many of the laws related to child molestation are relatively recent. It was not until 1974 that public law PL 93-247, the Child Abuse Prevention and Treatment Act, passed in the United States. This law requires all states to establish definitions, policies, procedures, and laws regarding abuse and neglect.

A lag often occurs between the passage of a law and the efficient implementation of it, and chang-

ing the societal mentality in regard to child abuse also takes time. Laws requiring the notification of neighbors when a convicted sex offender is released (Megan's Laws), recently passed throughout the United States, already are being contested in court on the basis of concern for the privacy of sex offenders. Proponents view these laws as a step toward the protection of children from potential perpetrators.

Repercussions to the Child. Usually a perpetrator is careful not to cause physical harm to a child, as a means of avoiding discovery. Children as young as three months old, however, have been treated for sexually transmitted disease as a result of molestation. Vaginal or bladder infections or pain may occur, and molested children may experience discomfort walking or sitting. Pregnancy may result for adolescents.

The effects of molestation are primarily psychological. Children are dependent on adults for survival needs, for affection, and for an understanding of relationships and of the world. Molestation interferes with the children's view of adults as those who protect and provide for their well-being. The resolution of proper developmental tasks is interrupted when issues of sexuality are introduced prematurely.

Sexual acts may seem frightening to young children. Children who have been molested may suffer from fears, nightmares, or depression. Imaginative play may be sexualized and include use of objects or mimic adult sexual behavior normally beyond the realm of a child's imagination. Depression, poor self-esteem, and poor peer relationships are common in molested children, as is clingy, passive behavior. Older children and adolescents may experience eating disorders, be excessively modest (avoid undressing during physical education), or be sexually provocative, promiscuous, or involved in prostitution. They also may act out sexually on younger or smaller children. Suicidal tendencies and self-mutilation are not uncommon. Unless a disclosure occurs, however, it may be difficult to detect a molestation because much of the child's behavior will appear normal to his or her development.

It is common for children to block memories of molestation and for memories to surface in adulthood. Although memories may remain suppressed, the psychological trauma may continue to manifest itself through low self-esteem, depression, difficulty trusting or forming lasting relationships, sexual difficulties, a sense of shame, and a deep hatred of one's body.

Prevention. Prevention begins with open and trusting relationships with children. Children need to know they can tell a parent anything without fear of punishment, ridicule, or overreaction. Awareness of the child's environment also is important. Parents must carefully evaluate any person with whom a child spends time.

An important part of prevention is personal safety teaching. This teaching should be ongoing and begin with simple concepts such as correct names for all body parts. Teaching the child which body parts are private and that no one should touch these except to keep them clean or healthy has been found to be effective as a self-protection skill. Family touching rules ("stop" and "no" are to be respected immediately in tickling and wrestling play) help children define personal boundaries. Role playing helps children identify risky situations and respond assertively. Children should know not to keep secrets about touching and that it is never too late to tell.

How adults respond to disclosure will be important to how molested children view themselves and may determine how much a child tells. Children will conceal facts to protect the adult who reacts emotionally. It is important for the adult to whom a child discloses molestation not to show shock or disgust, but to remain calm and focused on the child. Children need assurance that they were right to tell. It is never the child's fault, even if the child experienced pleasure or seemed to participate willingly. Minimizing an assault or refusing to believe the child creates powerlessness: Children rarely make up stories with explicit sexual content, and their stories should be treated as credible.

Early reporting generally stops the abuse and minimizes long-term harm. Children are empowered as they find support in resolving the situation. The ability to overcome trauma is fostered by acknowledging a molestation as a painful event while refusing to view the child as damaged. It is best to show compassion along with high expectations while seeking resources to help the child in the healing process. —*Sally Ashbach*

BIBLIOGRAPHY

Bass, Ellen, and Laura Davis. *The Courage to Heal: A Guide for Women Survivors of Child Sexual Abuse.* New York: Harper & Row, 1988.

Bass, Ellen, and Louise Thornton. *I Never Told Anyone: Writings by Women Survivors of Child Sexual Abuse.* New York: Harper & Row, 1983.

Carnes, Patrick. *Out of the Shadows: Understanding Sexual Addiction.* Center City, Minn.: Hazelden Educational Materials, 1992.

Lew, Mike. *Victims No Longer: Men Recovering from Incest and Other Sexual Child Abuse.* New York: Nevroumont, 1988.

Rush, Florence. *The Best Kept Secret: Sexual Abuse of Children.* Englewood Cliffs, N.J.: Prentice-Hall, 1980.

Wurtele, Sandy K. "Another Look at Child-Focused Sexual Abuse Prevention Programs." In *Prevention Update*. Seattle, Wash.: Committee for Children, 1996.

See also Child abuse; Child Abuse Prevention and Treatment Act (CAPTA); Emotional abuse; Incest; Megan's Law; National Center for Missing and Exploited Children (NCMEC); Sexuality and sexual taboos.

Child prodigies

RELEVANT ISSUES: Children and child development; Education; Parenting and family relationships

SIGNIFICANCE: Studies on how child prodigies develop superior talents provide added insights into the development of human potential

Since antiquity, child prodigies have fascinated, awed, and frightened. For example, the mythic Hercules strangled two snakes. In his cradle, Merlin, the legendary Arthurian magician, spoke at birth and soon thereafter defended his mother's chastity at a public trial. Two-year-old Christian Heinecken (1721-1725) knew all the historical events of the Bible, and six-year-old Wolfgang Amadeus Mozart (1756-1791) toured Europe, playing the piano, violin, and organ. Prodigies of the late twentieth century include Wang Yani, a three-year-old painter recognized for her mastery of watercolor, and Pierino Gamba, a ten-year-old who conducted the Liverpool Philharmonic Orchestra.

Distinguishing Characteristics. The word "prodigy," a Latinate term, originally meant "a prophetic sign," signifying uncanny powers of children with adult-like abilities who were regarded as "unnatural" or freakish. Contemporary usage narrowed the term to individuals with a phenomenal talent or skill, demonstrated early in life. The term prodigy is often used interchangeably with genius or giftedness, but their meanings differ. Prodigies, usually children, achieve renown for a specialized task or tasks, while geniuses often start out as child prodigies and then produce a large body of work of lasting significance. The gifted, on the other hand, have the potential for achieving—often revealed through intelligence or artistic tests—while prodigies actually do achieve.

Autobiographies, biographies, and case studies of child prodigies reveal few consistent attributes other than that such people "stand out among peers." Child prodigies are assumed to have superior intelligence or reasoning powers beyond "high IQ's." They exhibit superior talents, often possess high degrees of self-confidence and self-awareness, and appear to be driven in exercising their talents. External forces, such as a challenging environment and the presence of luck at critical junctures, enhance prodigies' chances for success.

Memorizers, Writers, Musical Prodigies. Studies of child prodigies have dealt primarily with their special abilities; their extreme inborn capacities; and their motivation, practice, and development of special techniques, such as mental imaging, word association, and memory devices. Examples of notable memorizers include Johannes Huber who, after a single hearing, could recall a series of 150 figures, either forward or backward; W. J. M. Elottie, known as "Datas," who specialized in historical dates on demand; and the physicist André Ampère, who recalled at will any passage from a twenty-volume encyclopedia. Mental calculator Maurice Dogbert played the violin from music he scanned for the first time while extracting the cube root of four dissimilar numbers, each in the hundred millions. Studies of chess prodigies, such as Bobby Fischer, reveal skills similar to those used by both memorizers and calculators—the power of concentration, the memorization of all moves made on the chess board, and the ability to see patterns of anticipated moves in the mind's eye.

Studies of musical prodigies reveal that they often come from musical families who surround their prodigies with music and like-minded friends and provide them with numerous opportunities to practice their specialized talents at very early ages. For example, Yehudi Menuhin played the violin at age three, becoming the foremost violin virtuoso at thirty-two. "Blind Tom," an African American minstrel, played piano at age four, creating original pieces at five.

Some fields, such as physics and the natural sciences, produce few child prodigies. Only a few artistic prodigies have won renown, such as Michelangelo, Henri de Toulouse-Lautrec, and Pablo Picasso, for the very young do not seem able to produce creative works comparable to those of

Despite being blind, this California girl plays the piano with extraordinary skill. (McCrea Adams)

strong desire to satisfy inner drives. Prodigies are also often believed to be physically weak or sickly. The mother of the British historian, author, and statesman Thomas Macaulay, for example, feared that his brilliance would lead to an early death. To the contrary, he lived a long, fruitful life.

Child prodigies are thought to suffer from "early ripe, early rot," burning out and ending in despair. The foremost example of this was William James Sidis (1898-1944), hailed as "the world's greatest child prodigy." Sidis' father, Boris, a prominent psychologist and psychiatrist, publicized the "superior" educational methods he used in producing his brilliant son, who read and wrote at age two, spoke six languages at age six, passed the Harvard Medical School anatomy examination at eight, entered Harvard at eleven, and graduated at sixteen. As the son approached adulthood, however, he suffered a nervous breakdown and experienced a series of devastating failures, including disownment by his father. The media hounded Sidis until he disappeared into obscurity and destitution.

Sidis' sad, unfulfilled life was quite atypical, according to Norbert Weiner, one of five child prodigies, including Sidis, who entered Harvard University in 1909. Weiner pointed out that in contrast to the failed Sidis, one child prodigy became a notable diplomat, one a famous composer, and Weiner himself a prominent mathematician. The same may be said of "The Quiz Kids," extraordinary children who appeared on a radio and television game show and knowledge contest during the 1940's and 1950's. A follow-up of "The Quiz Kids" as adults showed that although a few suffered burnout, on the whole they had successful careers and fulfilled lives.

highly artistic adults. Also rare are writing prodigies, such as the Brontë sisters (Anne, Charlotte, and Emily). In recent years, studies of prodigies have broadened, including child performers such as Noël Coward, Shirley Temple, and Judy Garland, and athletic prodigies such as tennis player Boris Becker, decathlon winner Bob Matthias, boxer Mike Tyson, and golfer Eldrich "Tiger" Woods.

Myths and Realities. According to myth, the extraordinary talents of child prodigies come in spontaneous flashes, arriving full blown without conscious effort. This is seldom true, for a great deal of groundwork happens beforehand. Prodigies' talents may grow faster than those of average individuals, but the same processes of inner maturation take place, usually through prodigies'

Personal Problems of Prodigies. An estimated 25 percent of child prodigies have psychosocial difficulties as compared to 12 percent of average children. During their early years, child prodigies usually keep company with adults, who sometimes deny them necessary give-and-take experiences with other children. In their teenage years, some prodigies have trouble finding friends with similar interests. School bores them, and their classmates—out of envy—may resort to ridicule, bullying, and persecution. Alienated, some prodigies become lost in a fantasy world, or they rebel, throwing away their talents and chafing against the restrictions of adults. During the transition from child prodigy to adult, some individuals experience a "midlife crisis" as they attempt to transform their childlike expertise into more adultlike behavior. Support from family, friends, and spouses can often facilitate a successful transition.

Developing the Talents of Prodigies. Theories and methods abound on how child prodigies develop their supertalents so early. The oldest theory, reincarnation, holds that children's early talents were originally developed in a previous life and that they have been reenergized in a new life. Another theory, forced education, restricts prodigies to certain regimens. For example, James Mill (1773-1836) deliberately isolated his son John Stuart Mill from the contaminating influence of other children and force-fed him a daily diet of the classics, history, and mathematics. This regimen resulted in the son's mental breakdown at age twenty. With the opposite theory, laissez-faire, parents who are wary of damaging unusual talents allow youngsters to do as they please and choose their activities freely as long as no harm befalls them. An alternative is that of eugenics, the so-called science of producing the finest offspring either through selective breeding (such as through allowing only the most intelligent individuals to marry and reproduce) or through genetic manipulation. In California, for example, women underwent artificial insemination using sperm from Nobel Prize winners, hoping to produce child prodigies.

Finally, there are advocates who believe that child prodigies' core of extraordinary talents can only be developed successfully if parents, families, teachers, and mentors provide guidance and support. They recommend that parents assess children's strengths, offering them suitable play opportunities, enjoyable experiences, and ample resources. They should always spark children's curiosity by making available a wide range of potential pathways and opportunities. Having high expectations, parents should not exert undue pressure on children to perform remarkably, since prodigies may believe that they have value only when they have outstanding success. Child prodigies should be placed in accelerated educational programs that take into account not only intellectual development but also social and emotional development. Teachers and mentors should be selected for their knowledge in prescribed fields, their sensitivity to prodigies' needs, and their ability to monitor prodigies' transition to adulthood. Supporters should also teach prodigies how to handle cruel detractors, avoid harmful publicity, and make prodigies' extraordinary talents seem as normal and inconspicuous as possible.

—*Richard Whitworth*

BIBLIOGRAPHY

Feldman, David H. *Nature's Gambit: Child Prodigies and the Development of Human Potential.* New York: Basic Books, 1986.

Gardner, Howard. *Extraordinary Minds: Portraits of Exceptional Individuals and an Examination of Our Extraordinariness.* New York: Basic Books, 1997.

Radford, John. *Child Prodigies and Exceptional Early Achievers.* New York: Free Press, 1990.

Simonton, Dean K. *Greatness: Who Makes History and Why.* New York: Guilford Press, 1994.

Wallace, Amy. *The Prodigy.* New York: E. P. Dutton, 1986.

See also Eugenics; Heredity; Schools.

Child Protection and Toy Safety Act

DATE: Enacted on November 6, 1969
RELEVANT ISSUES: Children and child development; Law
SIGNIFICANCE: This act defines substances as hazardous if they pose the unreasonable risk of injury or illness, bans certain products if they are deemed dangerous, and requires special labeling for others that may cause harm or injury

The Child Protection and Toy Safety Act is the title of an amendment to the Federal Hazardous Substances Act of 1969. Under the authority of the Consumer Product Safety Commission, this act defines substances as hazardous if they present an unreasonable risk of personal injury or illness during any normal or reasonably anticipated use or abuse. Hazardous substances for children include toys or products that may present mechanical, electrical, or thermal hazards.

Mechanical hazards are found in easily broken or disassembled toys. Such toys may have sharp edges that cut, sharp points that puncture, or small parts that could be swallowed or lodged in the respiratory tract. Other mechanical hazards include exposed moving parts capable of causing amputations, crushing, fractures, or bruises to parts of the body, including fingers and toes.

Electric shock hazards may be found in electrically powered toys or toys that could conduct electricity, such as kites, which may become entangled in electrical power lines. Thermal hazards may be present from heated parts, substances, or toy surfaces.

Toys or products that present unreasonable risk of personal injury are banned from sale. However, certain inherently hazardous toys, such as chemistry sets, may be sold if product labeling gives adequate directions and warnings for safe use. Even with government and industry monitoring of toy safety, parents and caregivers have an important role to play in child protection. Adequate adult supervision ensures that children learn safe play habits and the responsible use of toys.

—*Cherilyn Nelson*

See also Child Abuse Prevention and Treatment Act (CAPTA); Child safety.

An official of the U.S. Public Interest Research Group conducting a press conference in Washington, D.C., in 1995 to raise public awareness of hazardous toys on the market. (AP/Wide World Photos)

Child rearing

RELEVANT ISSUES: Children and child development; Parenting and family relationships

SIGNIFICANCE: Developing children experience a variety of different milestones as they mature, requiring that parents and other family members constantly adjust to meet their children's needs

At its broadest definition, childhood demarcates the period of the life span from birth to adulthood. During this time, development occurs within a family context. As children mature, they are influenced by the child-rearing practices that their families have adopted. The types of family environments can vary greatly from child to child, and as a consequence children can develop in any number of directions based on their unique experiences. Despite family style diversity, there is not one "family formula" for raising healthy, competent children. Progressing from infancy through adolescence, children emerge from this period as unique and independent persons, who were greatly influenced by the nature of their home environments.

Historical Perspectives of Child Development. Throughout much of recorded history, theories and perspectives of child development have been largely influenced by advancements and trends in biology and philosophy. Dating from premodern times (approximately 500 C.E.) until the twelfth century, the treatment of children constituted what most modern, civilized nations would later define as child abuse and neglect. In medieval Europe, children were generally viewed as possessions or pieces of property. Parents were free to treat their children in any way they saw fit. Most children were expected to grow up quickly, taking on adult responsibilities and behaviors as early as the age of six years old. These types of behaviors included dressing like adults, working long hours, and even marrying. Children in the European Middle Ages were considered inherently evil and had no rights under any laws. The role of parents was to stifle by any means necessary their children's supposed natural tendency to be evil, even if their methods resulted in death. Moreover, it was not until the twelfth century in Christian Europe that infanticide was defined as murder.

Prior to this, parents were not held accountable for the deaths of their children, no matter what the circumstances.

It was not until the seventeenth century that more modern concepts of childhood came into being. Children were viewed as distinctly different from adults and were allowed more freedom to engage in "child-like" behavior. The general philosophy of the time was that children were innocent souls who should be protected by their parents from the evil ways of the world.

For much of the seventeenth and eighteenth centuries parents turned to philosophers for advice on the proper methods of raising their children. Of particular influence were the enlightenment philosophers John Locke (1632-1704) and Jean-Jacques Rousseau (1712-1778), who maintained that children were not inherently evil. Locke contended that children could develop in any number of directions depending upon their experiences. Moreover, it was parents' responsibility to help children develop good habits.

In industrialized countries, the end of the nineteenth century saw dramatic changes in perspectives of child development. By this time most countries had some form of child-labor laws, and the overall notion was that although children were economically worthless to the workings of society and the family, they were emotionally priceless to their parents. The nineteenth century also saw the rising influence of science as the primary source of advice on the proper methods of raising children. A number of noted biologists began to carefully observe the growth and development of their own children, resulting in a variety of detailed biographies of infant and child development. The most influential biography of this type was written by Charles Darwin (1809-1882), who meticulously documented his son's daily physical development. In addition, many other scientists began to specialize in particular areas of child development, resulting in dramatic advancements in our understanding of how children develop cognitively and socially.

By the twentieth century, society's views regarding child rearing stemmed almost exclusively from scientific research. The perception was that competent, healthy adults can arise only from reasonably normal and healthy childhoods. The notion that parents had to be perfect was minimized, and

British naturalist Charles Darwin, best known for his theory of evolution, kept a daily record of his son's physical development. (National Archives)

a wider perspective of child rearing began to take shape, one that encompassed the importance of the community as well as the family in raising healthy children.

Family Styles and Child Development. The family represents the primary and most influential environmental factor in children's lives. The types of families into which children are born can dramatically affect their later lives. Families have profound early influence on children's beliefs, including their religious and political beliefs and their opinions that in many cases last a lifetime. Families also expose children to certain expectations. Children may be expected by their families to achieve specific goals in life, such as certain levels of education, particular careers, and marriage.

Extended families are those in which many relatives and several generations live with or close by children. The children may be cared for by a variety of people in addition to their parents, including grandparents, aunts and uncles, older siblings, and even cousins. This type of family was much more common in North America and Western Europe before the rise of industrialization. With increasing industrialization people became more economically and physically mobile, usually moving away from their birthplaces or family units to start families of their own. Extended families in late twentieth century North America have been observed in poorer areas of large cities and on Native American reservations in the United States.

Communal families are those in which children are raised in a social system that reinforces conformity and cooperation and discourages individualism and deviance from group standards. Communal families are more common in countries that follow socialist doctrines. However, they also exist, to a lesser degree, in the United States and Canada. Children raised in communal families are treated as segments of society, not as the property of individual parents. Parents in communal families usually give up their rights to raise their own children, granting the community the right to raise all of its children together. All members of the community, regardless of whether or not they have actually produced children, have a part in raising all the children. In the United States and Canada, the communal family has never been considered part of mainstream society, largely because of these countries' widespread cultural diversity.

The nuclear family has traditionally been that form of family in which married men and women—as a separate unit apart from relatives, neighbors, and friends—raise their unmarried

In many families televisions play an important role in occupying the attention of children and thus serve as surrogate caregivers. (Cindy Beres)

children. Many people in Western societies have considered the nuclear family to be the customary or "normal" family form. The traditional ideal of the nuclear family considered husbands and fathers to be the financial and controlling heads of households, while wives and mothers were responsible for housekeeping and child rearing. The nuclear family in this traditional form has been eroding in the United States and Canada. Beginning in the 1970's, rising divorce rates and greater numbers of unmarried mothers have resulted in many children being raised in single-parent families. Consequently, more of the responsibility of child rearing has been placed on vast networks of social institutions, such as day-care centers, school systems, and even television.

Nontraditional families are those in which children are raised in environments that are vastly different from the traditional nuclear family. Examples of nontraditional families include those in which children are raised by their grandparents, those headed by gay and lesbian parents, and those with unwed teenagers. Grandparents typically become the legal or primary guardians of their grandchildren when their own unwed children have unplanned and unwanted pregnancies. Unwed children are usually teenage daughters who do not possess the emotional maturity or financial stability to raise their own children. In some cases grandparents are awarded custody of their grandchildren when the natural parents are legally declared unfit to raise them.

With the continued social acceptance of gay men and lesbians in the United States and Canada, it has become possible for homosexual parents to obtain legal guardianship of adopted or biological children. Their decision to rear children involves their desire to create a family atmosphere in which their own goals of parenthood can be achieved without sacrificing their gay or lesbian relationships.

Not all unwed teenage mothers opt to grant legal guardianship of their children to their parents. Some teenage mothers decide to raise their children themselves. If mothers are financially and physically separated from their parents, their decision to raise their children often means that they will drop out of school, obtain a minimum-wage job or some form of public assistance, and try to obtain child support from the biological

fathers. In such cases, the future is not very bright for the mothers and children. On the other hand, if mothers continue to live with their parents while raising their children, they face a brighter future. Largely because they enjoy greater financial freedom, teenage mothers who decide to live with their parents tend to continue their education. They also tend to have more help in caring for their children. Often the parents of teenage mothers provide free day care for their grandchildren, enabling mothers to pursue other interests without the cares facing other unwed teenagers.

Prenatal Development and Family Adjustment. Prenatal development begins with fertilization and progresses until childbirth. Although they are as yet unborn, the maternal and family adjustments made during pregnancy set the stage for children's lives. Adjusting to parenthood is a major task for adults, especially when they are involved in first-time pregnancies. In order to assimilate their children, new parents must modify their lives economically, socially, and emotionally. Parents who have planned pregnancies often meticulously plan their children's future by attending parenting classes, setting up trust funds, and exploring day-care options.

For expectant parents who already have children, adjustments made during prenatal development encompass the existing siblings. Compared to the physical and emotional changes the mother undergoes, the experiences of the rest of the family may appear to be minor. However, fathers and siblings undergo major transitions prior to the birth of new children. Many fathers reorient their goals to accommodate new children in addition to experiencing many of the stresses and joys of their partners' pregnancies. Siblings must make adjustments to their roles in the family by learning such new skills as sharing and patience. The more families or parents are prepared during pregnancy, the better able they will be to accommodate their newborn children into their lives.

Parental Bonding and the Development of Relationships. The environment immediately after childbirth is chaotic for newborn children. Within minutes infants begin the process of bonding, a unique form of attachment, with their parents. Infants' close physical contact with their parents in the form of stroking, cuddling, and breast-feeding enable them to begin to recognize the unique smells, sounds, and textures of their parents. Some psychologists believe that early parent-infant interactions may help to establish stronger attachments in later years. Fathers and other caregivers who actively establish early contact and care of their infant children are usually more sensitive to their children's changing developmental needs throughout their lives. Early infant contact has been found to be especially important in establishing strong attachments with high-risk and teenage mothers who have little or no experience with caring for newborn children. In most cases, parents and family members who participate in early infant bonding report less anxiety and greater confidence in child rearing. Although early parent-infant bonding helps to form strong attachments, parents who are denied this early contact are not prohibited from forming strong and healthy attachments later. At any age, children are more than capable of forming deep and lasting attachments with their caregivers and family members.

Infancy marks the period of development during the first two years of life. During this time children experience profound changes in physical and cognitive maturation. Physically, infants progress from lying on their stomachs when they are one month old to walking well by themselves around the time of their first birthdays. Cognitive changes are less visually obvious, but just as profound. During infancy, children's brains grow rap-

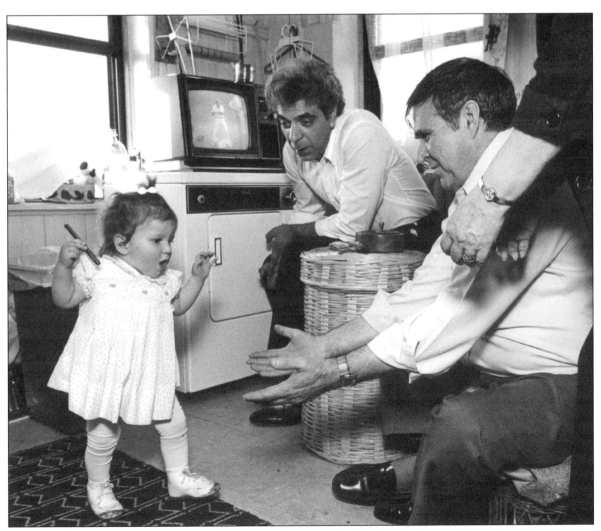

Children generally learn to walk by themselves around their first birthdays. (Hazel Hankin)

idly and become increasingly specialized. This specialization enables infants to acquire a number of intellectual skills, including imitation, babbling, memory, object permanence, and the use of familiar objects.

From a social perspective, during their first two years children begin to establish and cultivate their first relationships. Many children develop within a social context that permits multiple early attachments. In addition to bonding with their mothers and fathers, children can establish very strong attachments to siblings, grandparents, aunts and uncles, and even baby-sitters or day-care teachers. It is usually the case that no one person in children's lives provides all of the emotional support they need. With multiple attachments infants have the opportunity to choose and discriminate between relationships depending on what they need in specific situations.

An overwhelming amount of research has focused on the relationship between infants and their mothers. However, fathers, siblings, and grandparents each provide infants with unique perspectives on their social environment. As primary caregivers, fathers tend to relate to their children in much the same way as mothers. Mothers tend to engage in subtle and gradual play with their infants. However, fathers who share caregiving responsibilities interact very differently with their children than mothers. Fathers often play with their infants more physically, spontaneously, and excitingly. Siblings offer their own style of interaction. Older siblings provide infants with an important social model. Children learn how to share, help, and empathize by watching their older siblings. Although much has been made of the negative aspects of sibling relationships, the positive aspects, such as a lifelong friendship, far outweigh the negative in terms of social impact. Grandparents who are not involved with primary caregiving tend to relate to infants in a more relaxed and playful manner. Grandparents are also able to offer children an overall perspective about how the children fit in the family's history and about family traditions.

Early Childhood and Cognitive Development. The period defined as early childhood covers development from the age of three to about five years old. While children continue to progress in all developmental domains, including physical growth and social attachments, a major aspect of the children's experience during early childhood concerns their cognitive development. Cognition, which in its most simplistic sense refers to mental processes, includes thinking, reasoning, imagining, and language. Children's cognitive development serves as a bridge to encourage and refine other aspects of life, such as social and personality development.

The task of acquiring language is one of the most complex and vital areas of development. In fact, the ability to communicate using language is one of the things that makes human beings uniquely human. As children learn a specific language, they absorb aspects of their social environment that they were previously denied. As they begin to understand and communicate, children gain a greater degree of independence and control over their lives.

Superficially, it appears that children acquire language without learning it. It is known, for example, that parents do not actively sit down with their children and teach them to talk. The noted linguist Noam Chomsky contends that many of the processes needed for language acquisition are genetic. In other words, human beings are "prewired" to acquire language, just as they are "prewired" to acquire arms instead of legs. Although parents do not teach their children language, this is not to say that they do not influence language acquisition. The very nature of children's linguistic environment dictates what language they will learn, and for most children up to the age of three or four years old the primary linguistic environment consists of their parents. For example, hearing children born to deaf parents who communicate with some form of sign language will acquire sign language, not speech, as their first language. In addition, when parents communicate with their children they provide them with information about the culture in which they live. Simply through linguistic communication, parents demonstrate to their children the concepts that their society finds important. Parents also provide their children with a situation in which errors in language usage can be corrected. Such "correcting" need not be explicit; children often correct their language errors simply by observing and mimicking their parents.

Older siblings also contribute to younger sib-

Parents can play an important role in the cognitive development of their children by assisting them in their play activities. (James L. Shaffer)

lings' linguistic environment. In some instances this influence has a positive effect on younger siblings. Children with at least one older sibling can reach certain linguistic milestones faster than only children. For example, four-year-olds may acquire a vocabulary that is consistent with that of their seven-year-old siblings. Older siblings can also have a negative linguistic impact on their younger siblings. If older siblings speak on behalf of their younger brothers and sisters, the younger children may experience delays in language acquisition.

Another unique area of cognitive development in early childhood involves play. Play has often been referred to as "the work of childhood," and it provides a way for children to experience the world. Play promotes creativity, physical activity, and social interaction. It is intrinsically motivating and becomes more creative and complex as children develop. Parents play a specific role in children's play behavior. Many adults engage in some form of what psychologists refer to as play-tutoring. Play-tutoring takes place when adults actively participate in or modify children's play behavior. Sometimes parents may correct their children's illogical or inappropriate play scenarios. When adults participate in games, children often become less distracted, playing becomes more detailed and meaningful, and children learn how to engage in sustained activities. Direct adult involvement also demonstrates to children that their activities are worthwhile. During a developmental stage when parental approval is so important to children, play-tutoring provides parents with a unique opportunity to teach and influence their children's development.

Middle Childhood and Starting School. The period defined as middle childhood covers development from the age of six to approximately twelve years of age. Middle childhood is marked by a sequential process of physical growth and change that follows a similar path for all children. There is, however, great variation in rates of development. Children in the same age groups mature physically at different tempos. It is also normal for development rates across domains to vary between children. For example, children may be advanced for their age in terms of cognition while being less than advanced in terms of motor development.

During middle childhood children are profoundly affected by their school experiences. Parents play a large role in their children's school success in a number of ways. Parents of successful children tend to have a realistic grasp of their children's abilities, while encouraging them to set high standards. Parents of successful children also tend to use discipline strategies to keep their children goal-oriented in school. Most important, parents of successful children tend to communicate with their children on a daily basis. Through talking, parents establish trust with their children and usually become a welcome part of their children's life away from home. Interestingly, it is immaterial whether children come from single-parent families, belong to minority groups, or live in poverty—they can still be successful in school. What matters is that children have caring and supportive families who believe in the importance of a good education.

Adolescence and Becoming an Adult. In Western cultures, adolescence is the period of transition between childhood and adulthood. It can stretch over the better part of a decade and often has an ambiguous end. During adolescence individuals experience unique biological changes including the onset of puberty. Parents' reactions to their developing adolescents are often as unusual as those experienced by maturing children. As children cope with great physical changes, greater independence, and profound anxiety, parents and other family members find themselves trying to adjust to accommodate their teenagers' growing independence, while coping with their frequent emotional conflicts.

Adolescents are very much influenced by their families. Teenagers' identity within the family structure often involves a dual struggle. On one hand, adolescents find themselves in the position in which they experience many of the emotional, physical, and social concerns of adults. On the other, young adolescents often still live at home and continue to require of their families much of the same emotional, physical, and social support they craved as children. Family rules and general parenting philosophies influence teenagers to the extent that family environments that nurture as well as discipline tend to produce teenagers who are well adjusted and better able to cope with their growing independence.

During late adolescence families are influenced more by their adolescents than adolescents are by their families. As teenagers prepare to leave home, families must adjust and renegotiate roles, especially in terms of how they will cope with absent members. In most cases, families function best during the separation process when they are flexible and adaptable. Allowing teenagers to express their freedom (within certain limits) while keeping the avenues of communication open helps to reduce frictions and to preserve lifelong family cohesion.

—*Evelyn M. Buday*

BIBLIOGRAPHY

Belsky, Jay, Richard M. Lerner, and Graham B. Spanier. *The Child in the Family*. Reading, Mass.: Addison-Wesley, 1984. Covers many of the issues and problems surrounding child rearing in a family context, with attention to how to resolve family conflicts.

Franck, Irene M., and David M. Brownstone. *Parenting from A to Z*. New York: HarperCollins, 1996. Previously published in 1991 as *The Parents' Desk Reference*, this updated work serves as a practical guide that covers many of the basic aspects of child development.

Gemelli, Ralph J., ed. *Normal Child and Adolescent Development*. Washington, D.C.: American Psychiatric Press, 1996. Covers and summarizes research pertaining to normal child development, with an emphasis on psychological issues.

Graber, Julia A., and Judith Semon Dubas. *Leaving Home: Understanding the Transition to Adulthood*. San Francisco, Calif.: Jossey-Bass, 1996. Provides an in-depth look at issues related to adolescence, with an emphasis on older teenagers and the special circumstances that arise between parents and children when the latter leave home.

Kay, Kenneth. *The Mental and Social Life of Babies: How Parents Create Persons*. Chicago: University of Chicago Press, 1982. Provides a detailed look at how parents influence the cognitive, social, and personality development of their children.

Santrock, John W. *Child Development*. Madison, Wis.: Brown and Benchmark, 1996. A comprehensive textbook covering a variety of domains in child development, from the prenatal through adolescent periods.

Schor, Edward L. *Caring for Your School-Age Child: Ages 5 to 12*. New York: Bantam Books, 1995. An easy-to-read guide covering discipline, personal and social development, and the maintenance of good heath habits among school-age children.

Singer, Elly. *Childcare and the Psychology of Development*. New York: Routledge, 1992. Covers most issues relating to the psychological aspects of child development, with an emphasis on the history of child care and child development.

Slade, Arietta, and Dennie Wolf. *Children at Play: Clinical and Developmental Approaches to Meaning and Representation*. New York: Oxford University Press, 1994. An extremely detailed discussion of the research related to children's play behavior.

See also Child care; Childhood history; Family advice columns; Parenting; Puberty and adolescence; Schools; Social capital; Time-out; Toilet training.

Child safety

RELEVANT ISSUES: Education; Health and medicine; Parenting and family relationships

SIGNIFICANCE: The health and welfare of children are greatly affected by caregivers' ability to detect and remove health risks

The term "accident" usually refers to an event afflictive or unfortunate in nature that takes place unexpectedly. Unfortunately, accidents are the leading cause of death for those under the age of eighteen. In 1993 unintentional injuries caused 6,954 deaths of children aged fourteen and younger. The best way to prevent accidents is to reduce risks of danger.

Adult supervision is one of the best means to reduce the threat of accidents. Accidents increase, however, when adults are fatigued, ill, stressed, or rushed (Saturdays between the hours of 3:00 and 6:00 P.M. are the worst accident time). Parental misunderstanding of the capabilities of children also increases the potential for accidents. Infants unable to walk have been known to pull themselves to precarious heights, yank objects down, and reach dangerous things. Safety is no accident. It is the responsibility of caregivers (parents, relatives, baby-sitters, teachers) to identify and remove hazards, to teach children safety rules, and to enforce established safety regulations. A child's life may depend on accident prevention, alert supervision, and accurate responsiveness.

Home Safety. One-fifth of all accidental deaths happen in the home. Burns, poisoning, and drowning are the main causes of accidents. Other major causes include falls, suffocation, and firearms. Burns are not always caused by fire. Children suffer burns when water-heater thermostats are set higher than the recommended 120°F (49°C). Infants may be burned internally when bottles are heated in microwave ovens (which have uneven heating patterns). Burning can occur if caregivers hold a baby and a cup of hot liquid at the same time.

Drowning is the third most common cause of accidental deaths of children in the United States and is near the top of the list in many other countries. Most drownings occur because of failure to provide protective measures around wells, swimming pools, irrigation canals, beaches, lakes, and

After teaching children the rudiments of safety and placing them in a safe environment, there comes a time when the children themselves must be allowed to act on their own. (Cindy Beres)

other bodies of water. Approximately two children die each month in the United States from drowning. In 1995 twenty-nine children died from drowning in buckets and diaper pails. Babies should never be left alone in the tub; a child can drown in the time it takes to answer the telephone.

Most dangerous falls can be prevented. Securely attached safety gates should be installed at the tops of stairways. Throw rugs should not be placed at the tops of stairs, and nonskid material should be placed beneath all rugs. Passageways should be free from clutter. In order to keep infants from falling, a child should never be left on the changing table. There have been at least 1,330 injuries and nine deaths as a result of children falling from changing tables. High chairs, strollers, infant swings, and infant seats can also be hazardous. In

one year seven thousand children were treated for accidents involving high chairs. Children should be secured with waist and crotch straps. Adults should not leave the room, because straps and trays are not adequate safeguards against falling or strangulation. Another hazard involves shopping carts. Children should be strapped into shopping carts and not permitted to ride in the basket or under and at the end of carts. In 1996 sixteen thousand injuries resulted from shopping cart falls in the United States (80 percent of the children were not buckled in, and two-thirds of the injuries were to the head).

Changes are being made because of the dangers of suffocation and choking. Since it was estimated that one child dies every two weeks from strangulation in the cords of window shades and miniblinds, manufacturers were required to meet new safety standards by December, 1997. Owners of older sets were encouraged to cut looped cords, use safety tassels, and move furniture away from windows. From 1985 to 1997 drawstrings on children's clothing caused twelve deaths and numerous near strangulations. Manufacturers have begun to design clothing without drawstrings around the neck and face. Strings and ribbons on pacifier holders should not be longer than seven inches. Recliner chairs are being made with safety features to keep children from getting their heads caught in the foot rest area. Accordion-style baby gates are being replaced with screen and small-grid gates. Federal agencies are promoting electric garage-door safety by encouraging families to use a paper-towel roll to test the reaction of the door each month, since the door should reverse when it touches another object. Parents should install switches six inches or higher and should watch until the door closes completely; they should not allow children to use the remote control or to walk or crawl under moving doors.

Crib safety is also in the forefront. Fifty babies are strangled to death and more than eleven thousand injuries occur each year due to unsafe cribs. A crib should have all necessary parts and be properly assembled before use. The slats should not be more than $2\frac{3}{8}$ inches apart (the same space requirement for bars or diamonds in rails and safety gates). There should be no less than two finger widths between the edge of the mattress and the crib sides and ends. The mattress should also be firm. Babies should not sleep on adult mattresses. In a five-year period more than two hundred babies died, some from suffocation after being placed face down on a soft mattress and others from strangulation after rolling between the mat-

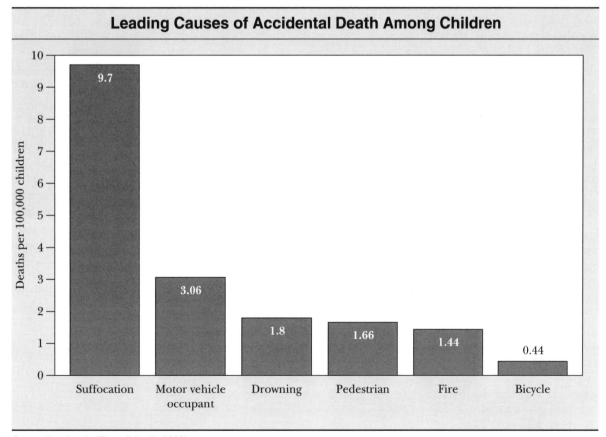

Leading Causes of Accidental Death Among Children

Source: Los Angeles Times (May 5, 1998)

Note: The National Safe Kids Campaign reported these accidents as the leading causes of preventable death among American children younger than age fourteen in 1995.

tress and headboard, footboard, bed frame, or between a mattress and a wall.

Despite many safety innovations, old and unsafe furniture, clothing, and equipment exist. Parents should take appropriate action by bringing items up to current safety standards and removing possible hazards. For example, crib toys should not be suspended across cribs or playpens, toys should not be hung on long strings from the rails, pillows should be removed from infants' cribs, plastic bags and plastic wrap should be kept out of the reach of children, and the doors of all discarded large appliances should be locked or removed.

Choking hazards surround children. Toddlers especially like to stick items in their mouths. The Consumer Product Safety Commission has developed a truncated cylinder test tube (available in stores) to test for items small enough for children less than three years old to swallow. Parents should never underestimate children's ability to swallow objects. At least sixteen deaths have been attributed to choking on baby rattles. When childproofing the home, parents should consider removing small rubber caps on doorstops and tightening all furniture knobs less than $1\frac{3}{8}$ inches in diameter. Foods and items that can cause choking include paper, hardware (screws, nuts, bolts), tacks, small coins, small toys or toy parts, sewing notions (buttons, thimbles, pins), balloons, chunky peanut butter, hard candy, hot dogs, ice cubes, grapes, nuts, popcorn, raisins, raw carrots and crudités, and tough meat or meat chunks.

Firearms and other weapons should be stored out of children's reach. It is important to teach children not to remain in the room with another child who has possession of a firearm. They should leave and immediately notify an adult. Ammunition should be stored in a separate locked container from firearms. Children should also be taught not to play with ammunition. Every gun should be treated like a loaded gun; children should leave it alone.

Fire and Home Safety. About 1,000 children die in residential fires in the United States every year. Smoke detectors are the first line of defense. The risk of dying in a fire doubles without smoke detectors. Detectors should be located on each level of a home, in the basement, and in sleeping areas. It has been suggested that people clean, check, and change the batteries of their detectors each time there is a time change (twice a year). Children should be drilled as to their reactions in case of fire. They should practice escape routes (two ways out of every room), staying close to the floor, testing closed doors before opening them, and meeting at a designated place after escaping. In case children's clothing catches fire, they should be taught to stop, drop, and roll while covering their faces. It is also wise to purchase children's clothing with fireproof labels or clothing made of natural fibers (which will not melt when hot).

It is also important to remove combustible hazards from the home. All fireplaces and heaters should have safety devices to protect small children from getting burned, as well as from causing fires. It is suggested that portable heaters should be turned off before leaving the room or before going to bed. All flammable materials (gasoline, turpentine, paint thinner, oily rags, kerosene, and lighting fluids) should be kept out of children's reach, and gasoline and gasoline-powered equipment should be stored away from the house. Gasoline has a flashpoint of $-50°F$ ($-46°C$). Such items should not be stored in the basement. Pilot lights have been known to inflame the fumes of combustible substances.

Kitchen safety may not only prevent fires, but it also keeps children from getting burned by food, oils, and liquids. Food that is cooking should not be left unattended; ap-

Guns in Homes

According to a poll undertaken by *Prevention* magazine in late 1995, nearly half of 264 children ages ten through seventeen who were interviewed said there were guns in their homes. A quarter of these children said they had access to the guns. The figures provided by children contrasted with information provided by the 731 parents interviewed in the same poll. While 45 percent of parents polled said they had guns in their homes, only 12 percent of them polled said their guns were accessible to their children. Eight percent of the parents said they kept their guns loaded.

Source: USA Today (February 10, 1997).

pliance cords should not hang from counters; handles of pots and pans should never extend over the edge of the range; and thick, dry potholders should be used. It is recommended that ABC fire extinguishers be kept in the kitchen. Control knobs located at the fronts of ranges should be covered with childproof protectors.

Each year, approximately 5,000 residential fires are caused by children under the age of five. Because children as young as eighteen months have lit cigarette lighters, it is imperative to keep all matches and lighters out of reach. All lighters made after July 12, 1994, were required to have child-resistant features. Unfortunately, many imported lighters do not meet these qualifications. It is wise never to use a lighter as a toy or as a form of entertainment.

There were 12,600 injuries related to fireworks in 1994. One-third of the injuries involved children under the age of fifteen. Fireworks are illegal in some states. Many countries do not have laws governing the sale and use of fireworks. Some religions and international traditions make use of fireworks extensively. It is up to caregivers to observe local laws, teach children the dangers of fireworks, and provide supervision.

If children are to be in a house, adults should attempt to childproof it. A variety of inexpensive safety equipment is available. If babies or toddlers are to visit, adults should get down on their level to look for hidden dangers. Outlet covers should be used, chemicals should be locked or stored where they are unreachable, safety latches should be installed, and visible hazards should be removed (poisonous plants, medications, letter openers, scissors).

Children at home alone need special instruction. They should be able to identify who is and who is not a stranger (not every person in a uniform is a policeman), be able to call for help or assistance, be trusted not to get into dangerous situations, and be able to keep callers from realizing that they are alone. All children should be taught to stay away from strangers (not to talk to them, not to take any candy or gifts from them, not to help them find a pet). When strangers stop them, they should immediately fetch their caregivers. Children should also stay away from secluded areas. Caution should be used at home, at the store, at play.

Safety from Poisoning. There are many different types of poisons. Some toxins are inhaled while others are injected, absorbed, or ingested. The most dangerous of the inhaled toxins is invisible, tasteless, odorless carbon monoxide. Improper combustion of fuel-burning appliances releases this silent killer. Detectors are available and should be installed in homes. Although it is not toxic, an inhaled danger for babies is baby powder.

Injected poisons include bites and stings. Children should be taught to refrain from touching animals they do not own (pets, strays, or animals in the yard, such as squirrels, snakes, and chipmunks). Insect and spider bites can be kept to a minimum if repellent is used and caution is exercised, such as checking shoes, skates, and helmets for spiders. Some plants can also cause skin irritation by injecting toxins with thorns, bristles, or fibrous needles (stinging nettle, wood nettle, bunny ears, hops, tread softly). Any animal bites should be examined by a physician for rabies or bacterial infection. The injection of foreign substances can sometimes cause anaphylactic shock. Children who begin to wheeze, swell in the face or tongue, become clammy, or have a rapid pulse and shortness of breath must be taken to a doctor immediately.

Poison ivy, sumac, and oak are usually the most well-known absorbed toxins. The toxic sap urushiol is released whenever the leaves, roots, stems, or flowers are bruised. Touching such plants is not the only way of coming into contact with this poison; contaminated sports equipment or clothing can also spread the resin. Other plants, such as buttercup, cashew, fig, hot pepper, lime, mango, and parsnip, can release irritating sap or cause phytophotodermitis (false sunburn).

Ingested toxins are many. Although food poisoning can cause adults to be ill, it may be fatal to children. Children's small size heightens the danger of food tainted with bacteria, bacterial toxins, or poisonous fungi. For instance, honey and corn syrup are harmless to most people, but they can cause deadly botulism poisoning in infants. According to the Centers for Disease Control (CDC), about 9,000 people (mainly babies, the elderly, or ill people) die from food-borne diseases yearly.

The Poison Prevention Act of 1970 required safety closures on aspirin bottles and products containing aspirin. Most ingested products now have safety closures, but medications are not the only chemical toxins dangerous to children. There are many toxic household products, including aftershave lotion, alcohol and liquors, ammonia, antifreeze, car wax, baby powder, bleach, cologne, correction fluid, cosmetics, deodorizers, detergents, diaper pail deodorizer, dishwasher detergent, disinfectants, drain cleaners, fertilizer, fingernail-polish remover, fuel, furniture polish, gasoline, glue, hair spray, insecticides, iodine, kerosene, lamp oil, laundry products, lighter fluid, lotion, lye, mothballs, motor oil, nail polish, naphtha, oven cleaner, paint, paint thinner, perfume, pine oil, rubbing alcohol, rust remover, shaving cream, shoe polish, solvents, toilet bowl cleaner, tobacco, turpentine, vitamins, water softener, weed killer, and windshield washer solution.

Despite safety closures, many children have ingested toxic levels of vitamins and minerals. Vitamin D poisoning is unfortunately common. Taking supplemental Vitamin D with a high intake of Vitamin D fortified foods can be dangerous, especially during the summer months. One of the most common causes of poisoning occurs with the ingestion of iron supplements or multivitamins containing iron.

There are also many toxic plants which may be found in the home or in the home garden. Some toxic plants include amaryllis bulbs, angel's trumpet, antheriums, autumn crocus, azaleas, bird of paradise pods, bittersweet seeds, bleeding heart, bloodroot, buttercups, caladium, calla lily, castor beans, cherry tree twigs or leaves, chrysanthemums, daffodil and jonquil bulbs, daphne, delphinium, dieffenbachia, elderberry, elephant's ear, English ivy, foxglove (digitalis), holly berries, hyacinth bulbs, hydrangea bulbs and leaves, jack-in-the-pulpit, jasmine, Jerusalem cherry, jimsonweed (thorn apple), lantana, larkspur, lilies, lily of the valley, mistletoe berries, morning glory, mountain laurel, monkshood, mushrooms (some varieties), narcissus bulbs, nightshade, oleander, peach leaves, philodendron, poinsettia, poison hemlock, pokeweed stems and roots, privet, rattlebox, rhododendron, rhubarb leaves, sweat pea seeds, tansy leaves and flowers, tulip bulbs, wisteria seeds and pods, and yew.

Another ingested toxin is found in lead. Lead poisoning is cumulative in the human body (remaining in the bones for up to thirty-two years and in the kidneys for seven). It can cause permanent brain, nervous system, and psychological damage. Paint chips from homes painted prior to 1978, old playground equipment, old cribs, and soils may contain high lead residues that are potential hazards for children under six. Many imported miniblinds contain lead in the plastic. As the plastic naturally deteriorates, it forms lead dust. Washing such blinds does not remove the lead hazard. However, blinds made and sold after July 1, 1997, should be in new cartons marked "new formulation" or "nonlead formula." Many imported products (juices, crayons, ceramic and glazed dishware) contain lead. In some areas, lead pipes or lead solder contaminate the water supply. Water testing and soil testing are available.

Transportation Safety. Whether walking or riding, transportation safety depends on children knowing and obeying safety rules. For example, when walking, they should look both ways before crossing, walk and not run across the street, walk facing the traffic, and cross at crosswalks (not between cars).

Children should never be left alone in cars. Doors should be kept locked and all passengers should be secured with seat belts or safety seats. In order to best protect children in vehicles, the Department of Transportation has advised that all children be buckled up in back seats. This eliminates the risk of injury due to air bags. Children should not use adult seat belts and shoulder restraints until they weigh at least forty pounds. Specific safety rules prohibiting children from screaming, hitting, or opening windows and doors and stipulating that they remain buckled until the car is parked should be established and enforced.

Car safety also includes keeping hard or sharp objects (lollipop sticks, ice cream sticks, pencils) out of children's mouths and away from their eyes in case the car must suddenly stop. Car seats should be covered with a blanket on sunny days to prevent children from burning themselves when they get in. Window shades should be provided if the windows are not tinted.

Three types of transportation are also recreational: in-line skating, skateboarding, and bicycling. In 1996 hospitals reported 356,000 bicycle injuries, 58,000 in-line skating injuries, and 26,000 skateboard injuries. Obeying safety rules, checking the equipment for safety, and wearing protec-

Even children who well understand the wisdom of wearing protective gear while engaging in hazardous activities such as skateboarding may succumb to peer pressure by shunning safety equipment. (Ben Klaffke)

Parents can make their children aware of safety requirements through both instruction and example.
(Skjold Photographs)

tive gear reduces risks. Cyclists should wear helmets, see and be seen, ride with the traffic, and obey traffic laws. Skateboard enthusiasts should wear slip-resistant shoes, helmets, and padding. They should also check for environmental hazards (holes, rocks, bumps, debris). In-line skating fans should wear helmets, elbow pads, knee pads, wristguards, and gloves. They should not skate at night and should be attentive to environmental hazards.

Recreational Safety. Many people have marveled that children ever grow up to be adults, since they play without concern. Children can be taught to be cautious and to obey basic safety rules (waiting their turn, not standing behind swings or at the bottom of slides, not pushing, not putting their heads and feet in exercise rings). Playgrounds should be built with safety in mind. The ground surface should be covered with soft material such as mulch, sand, or bark; all equipment should be well anchored; fall zones should be provided with extrathick soft material (6 to 12 inches thick); adequate space should be established between equipment (6 feet); and all spaces between 4 and 8 inches wide, where a child's head could get caught, should be eliminated.

Adults must also be wary of heat stroke. Children may not realize the danger of staying out too long or getting too hot. Children should be given plenty of water before, during, and after playing. They should also take time out to rest and cool down after vigorous play or in hot conditions. In cold-weather conditions, adults can prevent frostbite and hypothermia by ensuring that children are well insulated from the cold and wet elements of winter. Most children are so involved with play that they do not realize the dangers or passage of time.

In all recreational sports, novice players must be instructed on how to reduce risks. Recommendations at the 1997 International Sports Medicine Congress included training coaches to improve their knowledge and monitoring of sports. Children should participate in sports that are geared to the physical, social, and psychological intensity of their development. Adults should also insist on sportsmanship, the use of proper safety gear, and consideration and safety-mindedness. Goalposts should be anchored to the ground so they will not fall (since 1979 tipping soccer goalposts have resulted in twenty-two deaths).

Water safety is of special interest during vacation times. Swimming pools should be surrounded by a six-foot fence. Caregivers or lifeguards should be present, have a clear view of the pool, and know cardiopulmonary resuscitation (CPR). Children in boats or personal water craft should wear appropriate personal flotation devices (PFD). Children should try the float to make sure it keeps their head and mouth out of the water. Children in boats should never sit on the bow. They might fall in and be hit by the propeller. Many states require that children under the age of sixteen undergo specialized training before riding or driving personal water craft.

Responding to Accidents. The American Red Cross is a nonprofit organization that offers many courses in how to best respond to emergencies. In teaching techniques, they also cover ways to prevent accidents. The courses offered at most local agencies that encourage child safety include first aid and CPR, parenting, baby-sitting, sports safety, and fire or disaster courses. In locations where the American Red Cross or its international sister organizations are unavailable, local hospitals usually provide training. Parents and caregivers should be trained by certified instructors to provide basic first aid, administer CPR, and use the Heimlich maneuver (manual application of upward pressure on the upper abdomen of a choking person to dislodge a foreign object from the windpipe). Quick and correct response to emergencies may influence the quality of children's lives or even make the difference between life and death.

—*Anna Sumabat Turner*

BIBLIOGRAPHY

American Red Cross. *Community First Aid and Safety.* St. Louis: Mosby Lifeline, 1993. Available at local American Red Cross locations, this manual is used to teach safety and basic first aid.

Consumer Product Safety Commission. *The Super Sitter.* Washington, D.C.: Office of Information and Public Affairs, 1997. This pamphlet contains information and statistics; other publications concerning child safety are available on the Internet (www.cpsc.gov).

Lansky, Vicki. *Baby Proofing Basics: How to Keep Your Child Safe.* Deephaven, Minn.: Book Peddlers, 1991. Gives numerous facts and ideas for childproofing children's various environments, such as kitchen, bathroom, bedroom, playground, and car.

National Safety Council. *National Safety Council Accident Facts, 1996 Edition.* Itasca, Ill.: Author, 1996. Contains facts, information, and statistics about accidents.

National Youth Sports Safety Foundation. *Sidelines.* Boston, Mass.: Sidelines, 1997. Quarterly newsletters that address youth sports injuries, prevention suggestions, and news concerning dangers, legislation, statistics, and prevention.

Turkington, Carol. *Poisons and Antidotes.* New York: Facts On File, 1994. Comprehensive and succinct compilation including descriptions, symptoms, and treatments for various animal, plant, and chemical toxins.

See also Baby-sitters; Child abduction; Child abuse; Child Abuse Prevention and Treatment Act (CAPTA); Health of children; Latchkey children; Mothers Against Drunk Driving (MADD); Parental Kidnapping Prevention Act (PKPA); Recreation; Sudden infant death syndrome (SIDS); Youth sports.

Child support

RELEVANT ISSUES: Divorce; Law; Parenting and family relationships

SIGNIFICANCE: Initially a family issue to be resolved through private arrangements or local courts, child support has become a major subject of national discussion and extensive federal legislation that has affected divorce, parenting, and family law

Child support refers to the financial assistance that noncustodial parents are legally required to provide their children under eighteen years of age. Enforcement of child support has become a major problem faced by divorced and never-married custodial parents who are left with considerable financial burden as a result of a possible reduction in their family income or additional expenses incurred by the obligation of raising children by themselves. Increased public awareness of this issue, coupled with dissatisfaction with the welfare system, has elevated child support to a major national problem that has attracted the attention of persons of all political persuasions and from all social classes.

Historical Overview. The origins of fathers' obligation to support their families dates back to the agrarian period in Western civilization, when they occupied a position in the family as heads of households and owners of their wives and children. Patriarchal domination over the family morally obligated men to provide for their families' material needs. In exchange for their support, wives and children provided them with free labor. In cases of divorce or separation, children generally resided with their fathers, because mothers did not enjoy the legal right to own property and establish households of their own. In rare instances in which children lived with their mothers men were not legally obligated to support them.

The agrarian family structure was radically altered during the Industrial Revolution, resulting in the formation of nuclear families. While men worked in factories, mines, and offices, their wives stayed home caring for the children. Although the ultimate authority in the family rested with fathers, mothers managed the household. This power sharing within the family eventually resulted in women gaining legal competence to obtain custody of the children when divorce or legal separation occurred. Women's competence to obtain child custody was first recognized by the English Parliament in 1839. Separated and divorced women were still financially dependent on their former husbands, since they had no incomes of their own. This new situation made it necessary for governments to pass laws requiring men to provide their separated wives and children with continued economic assistance. Although Poor Laws had already transformed men's moral obligation to support their children into a legal one in the seventeenth century, it was not until the nineteenth century that this obligation was widely enforced.

Child Support in the United States. Similar to the British practice, courts in the United States beginning in the nineteenth century awarded custody of children to mothers in cases of divorce or legal separation in the belief that women were more suitable than men to care for children. Ever since, American courts have continued to favor women in custody decisions, in contradiction to the gender-neutral statutory criterion of considering only a child's best interests. Despite this gender bias, courts have never questioned men's obligation to support their wives and children even when the wives were financially independent.

The assumption that wives and children were dependent on men for economic support persisted throughout the first half of the twentieth century. Beginning in the 1970's, in part as a consequence of the women's rights movement, child-support laws have been changed to reflect the belief that both a man's and a woman's income must be considered in determining support obligations. Furthermore, custodial parents' financial status became less of a consideration in ordering child support than the widely accepted moral norm that parents have an absolute obligation to share a portion of their income with their children. Child support came to be considered a legal debt owed to custodial parents rather than financial assistance given by noncustodial parents. Thus, even when custodial parents' income by itself is sufficient to provide the children with an affluent lifestyle, the law requires that noncustodial parents' income, even if below the poverty line, be shared with the custodial parents according to an established formula. The elevation of what was originally an economic need to an absolute moral and legal issue has set the stage for well-publicized court battles involving millionaire and celebrity parents whose children are not necessarily in any real financial need.

AFDC and Federal Intervention in the Family. Prior to the 1970's, child-support obligations were a local matter to be handled by local judges within the framework of a state's family law. However, in 1935 the stage was set for federal intervention when the federal government introduced the welfare program known as Aid to Families with Dependent Children (AFDC). The program's original aim was to assist mothers, whose husbands had died, in caring for their children in their own homes rather than placing them in foster homes or orphanages.

The AFDC program was later extended to include those children whose fathers were alive but did not pay support. These fathers were either

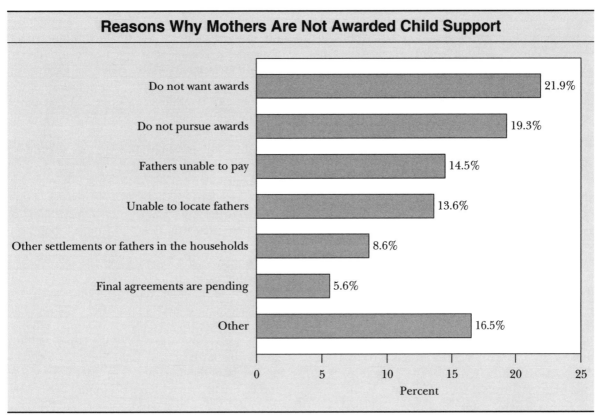

Reasons Why Mothers Are Not Awarded Child Support

Reason	Percent
Do not want awards	21.9%
Do not pursue awards	19.3%
Fathers unable to pay	14.5%
Unable to locate fathers	13.6%
Other settlements or fathers in the households	8.6%
Final agreements are pending	5.6%
Other	16.5%

Source: Bureau of the Census (1990)

unemployed or in prison, or they simply evaded their obligation to pay child support. Some of them moved to other states to evade the law. Existing laws did not permit one state to initiate legal action that would terminate in another. To remedy the situation, the federal government introduced a bill in 1941 making it a federal crime for obligated parents to move across state lines to avoid paying support. The bill never became law. In order to deal with the situation, the state of New York passed the Uniform Support of Dependent's Law in 1949. Within a year, ten other states established similar laws that permitted interstate action. In 1950 the National Conference of Commissioners on Uniform State Laws approved legislation called the Uniform Reciprocal Enforcement of Support Act (URESA), which was eventually adopted in various forms by all states. Although the law helped collection efforts, the states could not keep up with burgeoning case loads because of the accelerated divorce rate and out-of-wedlock births.

By 1950 the AFDC program rapidly grew to become a major entitlement program that imposed a heavy burden on tax payers, and with that the criticism of the program also mounted. Although states permitted custodial parents to sue noncustodial parents for support, collection efforts were not always successful because of the difficulties involved in locating absent parents, establishing paternity, and the additional burden of prosecutors' large caseloads.

Nonpayment of child support by absent fathers emerged as a major public issue in the 1970's when the public continued to voice its complaint about the cost of AFDC. Public outrage was compounded by the fact that an increasing number of women and children who benefited from the program were not orphans and widows, but single mothers and their illegitimate children. Concern was also raised that AFDC contributed to rising illegitimacy.

Federalization of Child Support. In response to the public criticism that the nonpayment of child support imposed a tax burden on the public, the federal government in 1975 passed Title IV-D of the Social Security Act. With the passage of this law, what was until then essentially a local issue became a federal issue. The law established the federal Office of Child Support Enforcement to monitor state child-support programs and a Parent Locator Service to help states, using federal records, to locate absent parents. It mandated the states to establish paternity in never-married cases and required mothers to assist states in tracking down their children's fathers. It also mandated that states enforce child-support laws in order to qualify for AFDC funding. The same year Congress passed the Child Support and the Establishment of Paternity Act, which penalized states that did not vigorously enforce child-support laws.

In 1979 the U.S. Census Bureau started a program to collect data on child-support payments. Later, the introduction of a new law known as the federal Child Support Enforcement Amendments to the Social Security Act of 1984 required states to develop specific numeric formulas to determine the amounts of child support that should be awarded to custodial parents. Additionally, the law required all states to use automatic wage withholding to collect past-due child support, intercept state income tax refunds, and take similar steps to guarantee payment. In 1988 the federal government passed the Family Support Act, which contained provisions for immediate wage withholding and an expedited process for establishing paternity and for closely adhering to the established numeric formula in awarding child support.

A significant development in the history of the enforcement of child support is that the provisions of the Paternity Act were extended to include children who were not on welfare. The extension of publicly funded child-support enforcement measures to nonwelfare cases received support from social workers and other human-service professionals as well as from other social activists who blamed the feminization of poverty on men who failed to support their children.

In later years, the federal government, as part of its ever-increasing efforts to reduce the financial burden of AFDC, has taken numerous measures to assist families in collecting past-due child support. In 1992 Congress passed the Child Support Recovery Act. In an executive order called the Deadbeat Dad Provision, President Bill Clinton in 1995 enabled federal investigators to go after federal employees, including military personnel, who were delinquent in paying child support. In 1996 the Debt Collection Improvement Act was passed.

This act includes provisions that can be used to collect past-due child support. President Clinton, reflecting public sentiments, raised what was originally a financial issue to the level of an absolute moral principle when he declared in a radio address on September 28, 1996: "No one should be able to escape responsibility for bringing a child into the world. That is our first and most fundamental duty." The Clinton years have seen an "unprecedented and sustained campaign" against deadbeat dads, as the president put it.

Enforcement Methods. Methods used for child-support enforcement consist of legal strategies and public shaming. The centerpiece of the legal strategy is income withholding. Unless courts make exceptions, most states require automatic withholding of child support from employees' paychecks regardless of whether or not they are delinquent in their payments. In order to force employers to withhold payments, some states have passed laws providing for the criminal punishment, including imprisonment, of employers who fail to collect and forward payments. In AFDC cases the collected amount is applied to the program cost, while in nonwelfare cases the money is transmitted directly to mothers. Other legal measures include interception of delinquent parents' income tax refunds; placing a lien on their property; accessing their bank accounts; requiring them to post security, bond, or other guarantees; and imposing criminal penalties for nonsupport. Many of these provisions have been attached to the welfare reform legislation of 1996.

In order to assist in establishing paternity, programs have been set up at hospitals to establish the identity of fathers of babies born out of wedlock, and states have made it mandatory for welfare mothers to reveal the identity of the fathers of their children. To help track down "deadbeats," the federal government has created a national data base of delinquent parents. The welfare reform legislation of 1996 includes additional provisions. For example, states can suspend delinquent parents' driver's and professional licenses, and the

---

Who Receives Child Support Payments

In 1990 it was estimated that of approximately 10 million American women heading households from which fathers were absent, about 5.7 million had been awarded child support payments. Only about half of these women, however, actually received the full amounts of the payments due to them. About a quarter of them received partial payments, and another quarter received nothing.

Marital history, education, and race and ethnicity all played roles in child support. For example, 72 percent of women who had been married previously received child support awards, compared to only 24 percent of those who had never been married. Whereas 68 percent of white women received child support awards, only 35 percent of African American women and 41 percent of Hispanic women received such awards. Likewise, 75 percent of women with at least four years of college education received awards, against 37 percent of women who lacked high school diplomas.

Source: Minnesota Children Youth & Family Consortium Electronic Clearinghouse (1922).

---

federal government can deprive them of their passports. Legislation has also been proposed to make it a felony to cross state lines to avoid paying child support. The United States has made arrangements with many foreign governments to enforce U.S. child-support laws in respect to fathers who leave the country to evade the law. Federal agencies have been ordered to deny all government loans to delinquent parents. Plans are also in place to deduct support debts from the pensions of retired government employees and from the fees of those who do business with the government.

In addition to these legal measures, the federal government, in cooperation with state governments, has mounted a vilification campaign against "deadbeats" that is designed to shame them into paying. Pictures and names of delinquent parents are posted in post offices and on states' web pages.

States have begun to take additional punitive measures against deadbeat parents. For instance, Missouri holds car titles of delinquent parents, making it difficult for them to trade in their cars. In Arizona a county sheriff has used a volunteer posse to arrest delinquent parents. Private investigation companies, which have mushroomed all over the country and are helping to enforce the law, collect contingency fees for seeking out parents who owe child support. States such as Florida have attempted to publish the names of deadbeats in newspapers. In Texas a billboard was erected that featured a "Deadbeat of the Week" to humiliate featured parents into paying.

An estimated five percent of parents who owe child support are mothers. There are fewer deadbeat mothers than fathers, primarily because most child-custody awards are given to mothers. However, men have begun to organize to fight against the prevailing perception of sexism in the courts and are demanding child custody. In cases where they have succeeded, mothers have become noncustodial parents who are required to share their income with custodial parents for the care of their children. Delinquent mothers are treated the same way as delinquent fathers. The criminalization of nonsupport has resulted in mothers going to jail.

The Canadian situation is similar to that in the United States. While women complain that support awards are too low and nearly half of them go unpaid, men argue that the justice system is biased in favor of women. The federal government has passed stringent laws to enforce child support in the hopes of relieving the tax burden on the public and alleviating child poverty. Measures that are similar to those in the United States are already in existence to force support payment, such as making driver's and professional licenses conditional on paying past debts and using private companies to track down absent fathers and extract payments. Canadians also have resorted to techniques of vilification. For example, a pressure group called Mothers Against Fathers in Arrears (MAFIA), with placards in hand, has picketed the homes of targeted fathers, usually affluent men.

"Deadbeat Dad" as a Cultural Category. The stringent enforcement measures and the intrusion of the federal government into family matters are not without their critics. Critics argue that the exclusive emphasis on legal measures is fundamentally flawed. They point out that the "deadbeat dad," portrayed as the new villain, is a new cultural myth that ignores reality. "Deadbeat dads" are portrayed as irresponsible, self-seeking, callous, and affluent men who have walked away from their children, willfully exposing them to poverty and misery. The myth of the deadbeat dad is the other side of the myth of the "welfare queen," who supposedly becomes rich and enjoys life at the public's expense. Most deadbeat dads do not correspond to the mythology of affluent fathers who evade the law for egotistic reasons. Critics argue that many deadbeats do not pay because they are not able to. Some deadbeats do not pay because they feel poorly treated by an unfair justice system. Some are estranged from their children as a result of the prolonged fights over custody and visitation rights. Critics point out that these are real problems to be resolved by means other than criminalization of nonsupport. In the view of some critics, the government casts deadbeat dads as scapegoats to appease the public anger against welfare. Others suggest that the crisis of child support points to the slow disappearance of a culture that idealizes the nuclear family. —*Mathew J. Kanjirathinkal*

BIBLIOGRAPHY

Beller, Andrea, and John W. Graham. *Small Change: The Economics of Child Support.* New Haven, Conn.: Yale University Press, 1993. Presents a careful analysis of the economic consequences of child support laws with policy recommendations.

Blankenhorn, David. *Fatherless America: Confronting Our Most Urgent Social Problem.* New York: Basic Books, 1995. Contends that the enforcement of child support is less important than dealing with the more fundamental social issue of the absence of fathers.

Cassetty, Judith, ed. *The Parental Child-Support Obligation.* Lexington, Mass.: Lexington Books, 1983. Collection of basic studies dealing with such issues as the "Sexual Politics of Child Support" and "Reconsidering the Basic Premises of Child Support."

Karause, Harry D. *Child Support in America: The Legal Perspective.* Charlottesville, Va.: Michie Company, 1981. Thorough, well-referenced study of the basic laws affecting child support and the establishment of paternity.

Lieberman, Joseph. *Child Support in America: Practical Advice for Negotiating—and Collecting—a Fair Settlement.* New Haven, Conn.: Yale University Press, 1988. Useful guide for lawyers and government officials involved with child support collection.

Sheets, Virgin, and Stanford Braver. "Gender Differences in Satisfaction with Divorce Settlements." *Family Relations* 45 (July, 1996). Indicates that although women are more satisfied than men with custody, visitation, and property settlements, they are less satisfied with support settlements.

See also Aid to Families with Dependent Children (AFDC); Alimony; Child Support Enforcement Amendments; Children born out of wedlock; Displaced homemakers; Family courts; Family law; Family Support Act; Feminization of poverty; *Gomez v. Perez*; Men's roles; Nuclear family; Paternity suits; Unwed fathers; Welfare.

Child Support Enforcement Amendments

DATE: Enacted on August 16, 1984
RELEVANT ISSUES: Divorce; Law
SIGNIFICANCE: With the passage of the Child Support Enforcement Amendments of 1984, Congress set a goal of establishing an efficient system to find absent parents, establish paternity, obtain support orders, and collect back support

Following a sharp increase in divorce and out-of-wedlock births in the early 1970's, the federal government established the Child Support Enforcement Program to collect money from fathers whose children received welfare. At that time, the collections reimbursed the government and did not go directly to the affected children.

The Child Support Enforcement Amendments of 1984 extended this program to all noncustodial parents and required that each state establish one set of guidelines for determining and modifying child support. These guidelines must take into account all earnings and income of noncustodial parents, define the dollar amounts of support obligations, and provide for the children's health care needs. Courts may deviate from these guidelines in limited circumstances—for example, when the guideline amount would be unjust or inappropriate in particular cases. Individual states vary between judicial and administrative processes, but all must ensure that payments are made to custodial parents. Above all, each state's criteria must take into the consideration the best interests of the children.   —*P. S. Ramsey*

See also Child custody; Child support; Divorce; Divorce mediation; Family courts; Family law; Family Support Act; Paternity suits; Uniform Marriage and Divorce Act (UMDA).

Child Welfare League of America (CWLA)

DATE: Founded in 1920
RELEVANT ISSUES: Children and child development; Parenting and family relationships
SIGNIFICANCE: This association is the oldest and largest organization in the United States dedicated to the well-being of vulnerable children and their families

The Child Welfare League of America (CWLA) is an umbrella association of more than nine hundred public and private nonprofit child welfare agencies across the United States, which provide a wide range of services to abused and neglected children and their families. It was founded in 1920 to protect children and bring uniformity to the work and ideals of protective service agencies. In 1921 Carl C. Carstens, general secretary of the Massachusetts Society for the Prevention of Cruelty to Children, was named executive. By the late 1920's the CWLA was developing recommended standards for adoption and foster care. In the late 1960's the league began to focus on services for children in their own homes.

Since its inception, the league and its agencies have taught parents effective and positive ways of disciplining children; they have taught children and young adults to make good choices, including about sex and school attendance; and they have helped to shore up families that are breaking down because of economic, mental, or other stresses. When families cannot be stabilized, league agencies arrange foster care or adoption. The CWLA has adhered to its mission to protect abused and neglected children, although the threats to such children have changed over several decades. By the end of the twentieth century the CWLA included among its concerns homelessness, pediatric acquired immunodeficiency syndrome (AIDS) and human immunodeficiency virus (HIV), alcohol and drug abuse, and the special needs of various ethnic and cultural populations.

The CWLA assists child welfare agencies by training social workers, consulting, sponsoring conferences, setting national and international standards for child welfare practices, and assisting in the review process that accredits agencies. In the 1990's the CWLA began offering guidelines to social workers and others to help them provide services to clients of different cultures, races, ethnic backgrounds, and religions. National experts employed by the league conduct original research to determine the best ways of helping children and families.

CWLA Publications offers books, videos, and other training materials for child welfare professionals and children's books, parenting guides, and other family materials for a general audience. Moreover, the league regularly releases statistical information to local and national media about child abuse and neglect. During the 1996 presidential campaign the CWLA called on the two major candidates to hold a special debate on their plans to improve children's welfare. The league also encouraged network interviewers to ask questions about children's welfare and offered information to voters about candidates' records on children's issues.

Headquartered in Washington, D.C., the league has representatives who appear regularly before Congress to promote federal laws and policies to protect children and strengthen families. It trains members to appear before state and local legislatures and encourages citizens to appeal to public officials for their support. With its long history and large membership, the CWLA has proven to be an authoritative and effective advocate of children's welfare. —*Cynthia A. Bily*

See also Adoption processes; Child abuse; Children's Defense Fund (CDF); Children's rights; Foster homes; Welfare.

Childbirth

RELEVANT ISSUES: Children and child development; Parenting and family relationships

SIGNIFICANCE: The experience of labor, birth, and delivery is experienced by most married couples

Childbirth is the concluding act of reproduction and follows approximately nine months of pregnancy in human females. Approximately 95 per-

cent of all babies are born within two weeks of their expected delivery dates. A baby is born approximately 38 to 42 weeks after the first day of the mother's last menstrual period. About 4 percent of all births occur on their exact due dates.

Contractions. During the last several weeks of pregnancy, the muscles in the uterus begin to expand and contract at irregular intervals—sometimes days or weeks apart. These short, painless contractions, called Braxton-Hicks contractions, may cause expectant mothers to believe that labor has begun. Braxton-Hicks contractions work to strengthen the uterine muscles in preparation for childbirth. The onset of labor is signaled by regular contractions of the uterus. A labor contraction is the tightening and shortening of the muscles in the uterus. Expectant mothers have no control over these contractions. When labor begins, the contractions are usually 10 to 30 minutes apart and last for 30 to 45 seconds. At the end of labor, the contractions are closer together and last from 60 to 90 seconds.

Contractions usually begin at the top of the uterus and move downward, reaching a peak and then becoming weaker. As labor progresses, the contractions become stronger, last longer, and are closer together. During the process, the baby's head is pushed into the birth canal.

Stages of Labor and Delivery. The term "labor" is commonly applied to the process of childbirth. This term is used because of the difficult use of the muscles involved in giving birth. Although some women experience childbirth in a few hours, others may undergo labor for twenty to thirty hours. It is not known what causes the first stage of labor to begin. Investigations have focused on the identification of hormones and other chemical substances that may, either singly or in combination, trigger the birth process.

Several preliminary signs occur toward the end of pregnancy to tell women that labor is approaching. The head of the fetus rotates and "drops" into the pelvic cavity approximately two to four weeks prior to delivery. This "dropping," often called "lightening," allows mothers to breathe easier. Other preliminary signs include a pink vaginal discharge, or the loss of the mucus plug from the cervical opening. Additional signs include diarrhea, stomach upset, and increased Braxton-Hicks contractions. In some cases, the amniotic

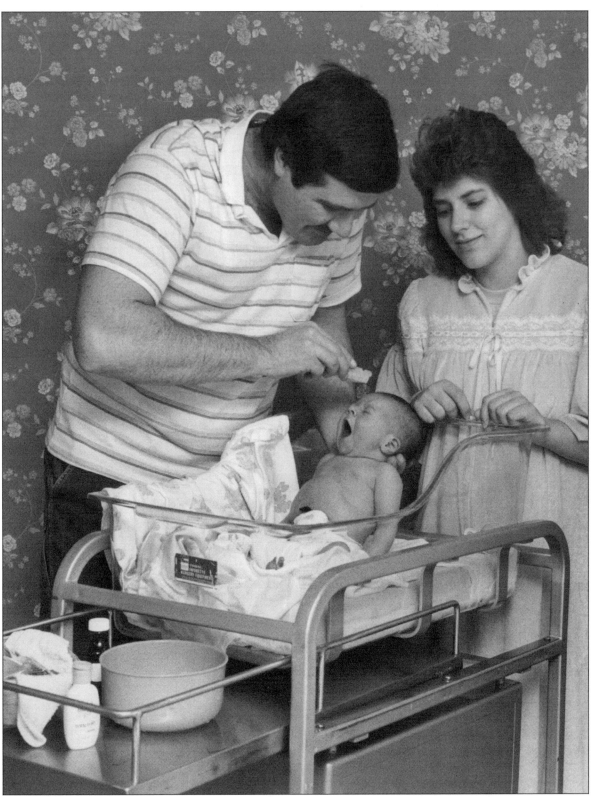

For many, true family life begins only with the arrival of the first child. (James L. Shaffer)

sac breaks before labor begins. Depending on the size of the break in the membranes, there may be a sudden gush of amniotic fluid or a slow leak. In 85 percent of cases, labor begins within twenty-four hours after the amniotic sac breaks. After the amniotic sac breaks, the risk of infection increases.

Labor is usually divided into three parts. When the contractions are ten to twenty minutes apart and at regular intervals, labor is said to begin. The first stage lasts until the cervix is fully dilated to 4 inches (10 centimeters), or the width of the average hand. The first stage is the longest, lasting from a few minutes to a few days. The average duration of the first stage is eight to fourteen hours for women giving birth for the first time and about six hours for women having a second or

third baby. Contractions in this stage help to flatten and open the cervix.

In the second stage of labor, which usually lasts between one and two hours, strong uterine contractions serve to push the baby through the birth canal. The contractions begin at fifteen minutes apart and decrease to two minutes apart. This is the most difficult time during childbirth. The contractions become stronger, last longer, and are closer together. Feelings of fear, discouragement, loss of control, and panic are common. Other difficulties include hot and cold flashes, disorientation, nausea, and vomiting. At the end of this stage, women feel a strong desire to push, comparable to having a bowel movement.

If the baby is in the head-first position, the head advances through the birth canal with each con-

Stages of Childbirth

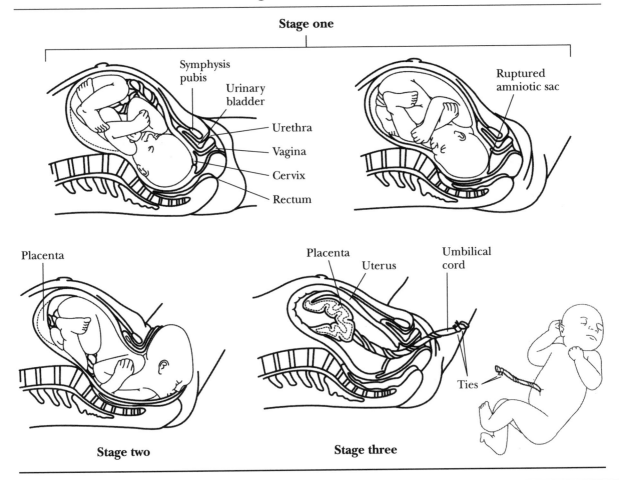

Stage one

Symphysis pubis
Urinary bladder
Urethra
Vagina
Cervix
Rectum

Ruptured amniotic sac

Placenta

Placenta
Uterus
Umbilical cord

Ties

Stage two

Stage three

traction. When one inch of the baby's head is visible, physicians often perform an episiotomy, a surgical incision in the tissue between the mother's vagina and rectum. The episiotomy allows the baby's shoulders and buttocks to pass through the opening without tearing the mother's tissue. The final stage of labor is the expelling of the placenta, often called afterbirth. This stage takes less than one hour in most cases.

In some cases, labor is started by artificial methods. Injections of prostaglandin, oxytocin, or the rupturing of the amniotic sac are methods used to begin the birth process. Labor is usually induced artificially as a response to a prolonged pregnancy or complications such as maternal diabetes, bleeding, excessive amniotic fluid, Rh incompatibility, toxemia, failure of labor to begin within twenty-four hours after rupture of the amniotic sac, or intrauterine fetal death. For the convenience of parents, doctors, or both, labor may sometimes be induced if patients live far from the hospital. Many people oppose the routine practice of inducing labor.

The recovery stage lasts approximately one hour after the complete delivery of the placenta. During this period, the mother and baby are carefully observed for complications of the birth process. The episiotomy and any tears in the vaginal tissue are stitched and repaired. The afterbirth stage and the first hour after birth are considered critical to mother and baby. The mother may experience excessive bleeding.

In the United States, vaginal deliveries account for 84 percent of all births. The remainder of births are performed by cesarean section, often called "C-section." In a cesarean section, an incision is made in the woman's abdomen and uterus while she is under a local or general anesthetic. The baby and the placenta are both removed through this opening. C-sections are used when babies exhibit fetal distress, the mother's health is

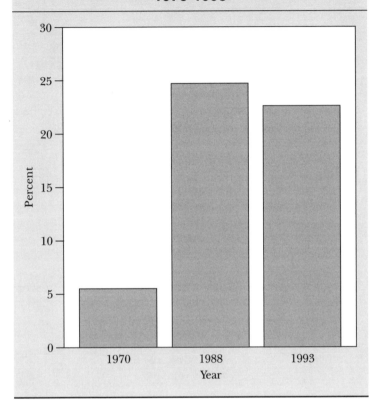

Percentage of Births by Cesarean Section, 1970-1993

Source: Public Citizen

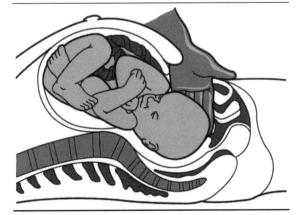

Delivery by Cesarean Section

Several conditions may necessitate the delivery of a baby through an incision in the lower abdomen instead of through the birth canal, including fetal distress or the inability of the baby's head to fit through the mother's pelvis.

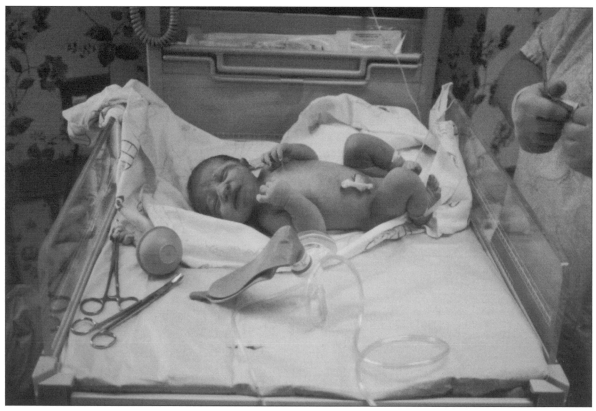

Human babies are among the most helpless of newborn mammals. (Cindy Beres)

at risk, or when the baby is breech. Additional recovery time is required for women after a C-section, because it is considered major surgery.

Childbirth Settings. Most childbirths in North America take place in hospital settings. The hospital environment allows for a large staff to assist in labor, birth, delivery, and the care of newborns. Access to emergency medical care in the event of fetal distress or complications with labor is also available. Labor and birthing rooms are traditionally equipped with comfortable furnishings to accommodate mothers and other family members who are present during birth. Mothers can choose to have their newborns "room in" during the hospital stay. This practice allows newborn babies to be separated from their mothers and fathers for only short amounts of time.

In traditional hospital settings, women are limited to a supine position for most of labor and delivery. Upright positions seem to improve the blood circulation to women's abdominal muscles and increase the oxygen supply to the fetuses. In

addition, when women are upright, the pelvis widens and fetuses have easier access to the birth canal. Pushing is also more effective with the assistance of gravity. There are a variety of ways of achieving upright positions. For example, during labor women can walk around, stand, or squat. Simply changing positions sometimes relieves discomfort. During deliveries, some hospitals use birthing chairs or squatting cushions.

In Canada, many women undergo water births. During water births women experience labor and delivery in a tub of warm water. The baby descends through the birth canal into the warm water. The mother reaches down, takes the baby in her arms, and brings the child to her breast. Birth attendants are nearby, if needed. Mothers report a feeling of excitement and lasting personal empowerment from this experience.

Another alternative to traditional hospital deliveries is the practice of home births. Home births are standard practice in some countries, such as the Netherlands and most of Scandinavia. Professional midwives assist with these births. Certified Nurse-Midwives (CNMs) are registered nurses who have had advanced schooling in prenatal and childbirth care. CNMs work primarily with "low risk" women, or women who are free of conditions that could complicate birth. Certification for nurse-midwives was established in the United States in the 1950's.

Postpartum Depression. Approximately 89 percent of mothers experience a mild state of depression following the excitement and joy of a healthy birth. This is commonly referred to as "postpartum depression" or "baby blues" and is short-lived. A small percentage of women develop long-term postpartum depression that requires professional treatment. Studies suggest that some women also experience post-traumatic stress disorder (PTSD) after childbirth. Pregnancy and childbirth are demanding events requiring that mothers undergo a period of recovery. The rewards experienced during the early months of a new-

born's existence are often combined with major physical and emotional demands. These combined stresses lead some women to experience difficult recovery periods.

Infertility. Approximately 10 to 15 percent of all couples in the United States experience infertility. Infertility is defined as the inability to conceive a child after twelve months of regular intercourse without contraception. Both men and women may be infertile. For example, women may not ovulate or their fallopian tubes may be blocked. Men may produce too few sperm or their sperm may lack adequate motility. Infertility treatments are available. However, couples that have undergone such treatments report that they can be invasive, stressful, time-consuming, and expensive. These factors place enormous stress on couples and the family. Spouses have reported blaming and feeling bitter toward each other in the event of infertility, often leading them to resolve their difficulties by divorcing.

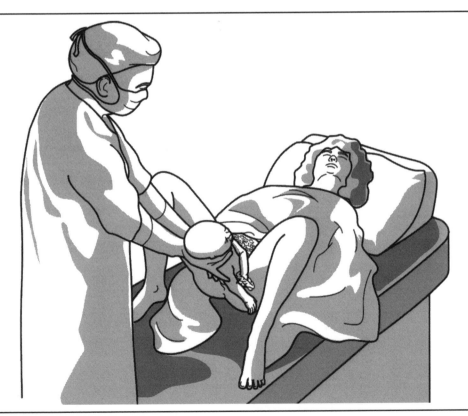

The focus of obstetrics, which is usually practiced with gynecology, is the health of a pregnant woman and her fetus from the beginning of the pregnancy to the time of delivery.

In vitro fertilization is conception outside the body. In vitro fertilization was first introduced to the United States in 1978. An infertile woman, Mrs. Brown, participated in the first successful in vitro fertilization procedure. The standard procedure involves surgically removing the ovum from the mother. The ovum is fertilized in a laboratory with live sperm cells obtained from the father. The fertilized egg is stored in a laboratory solution that substitutes for the uterine environment. The fertilized egg is then implanted in the mother's uterus. Nine months after Brown's in vitro fertilization, she gave birth to her daughter Louise.

Since the first in vitro fertilization, variations of the process have been practiced. One such variation involves the fertilization of a woman's egg with a donor's sperm. The cost of one cycle of in vitro fertilization costs approximately $10,000, and more than one cycle is often required before success is achieved. In another variation of in vitro fertilization, a man and woman contribute sperm and egg, and the resulting embryo is carried by a third party. The third party essentially donates the use of her womb and is considered a surrogate mother. In cases of surrogate motherhood, legal contracts are signed between the infertile couple and the surrogate. The infertile couple usually covers all pregnancy costs incurred by the surrogate, including prenatal visits, vitamins, and hospitalization for labor and delivery. The surrogate is usually paid an additional fee for agreeing to serve as the surrogate mother.

Miscarriages and Stillbirths. A miscarriage, or spontaneous abortion, happens when pregnancy ends before the developing organism is mature enough to survive outside the womb. The embryo separates from the uterine wall and is expelled by the uterus. About 15 to 20 percent of all pregnancies end in a miscarriage, most of which take place during the first ten weeks of pregnancy. Many miscarriages occur without the mother's knowledge, and many involve a fetus that was not developing normally. In past times, it was believed that women could be frightened by loud thunder or abrupt jolts into miscarrying. However, medical science has learned that such shocks are highly unlikely; developing fetuses are well protected. Abnormalities of the reproductive tract and viral or bacterial infections are likely causes of miscarriages. In some cases, severe traumas may lead to miscarriages.

Miscarriages are often accompanied by grief, depression, despair, and feelings of inadequacy. For women who have had one miscarriage, the next pregnancy will most likely be tense. If such women feel that they are capable only of failing, they may project this belief onto the babies they ultimately carry to term. Such mothers may become depressed, rigid, guilty, and afraid of bonding to their babies. Some women miscarry only once, but others experience multiple miscarriages. Few resources are available to women, or couples, who experience miscarriages. Although intervention and emotional support is usually available only to women who miscarry late in pregnancy, miscarriages early in pregnancy can be equally traumatic.

When mothers carry babies to term and the babies are born dead, such births are known as "stillbirths." Stillbirths are highly correlated with mothers who have been abused during pregnancy and with multiple births, such as the birth of twins or triplets. Mothers, fathers, siblings, and other family members who experience stillbirths have special psychological needs. Health care workers spend much time counseling such bereaved families.

Genetic Counseling. Genetic counselors are physicians or biologists who are educated in the field of medical genetics. Genetic counselors are familiar with the kinds of problems that can be inherited, the odds of encountering them, and helpful measures for offsetting some of their effects.

After establishing couples' genetic histories, genetic counselors determine the probability that they will conceive healthy babies. If counselors' findings suggest that couples are likely to have babies with major birth defects, couples must decide whether or not to conceive. The decision to conceive or not is usually based on ethical and religious beliefs. Couples often decide how to balance these factors against the quality of their future children's lives.

—*Lisa Mize*

BIBLIOGRAPHY

Carter, John Mack. *The Good Housekeeping Illustrated Book of Pregnancy and Baby Care.* New York: Hearst Books, 1990. Practical guide to pregnancy, labor, and delivery that largely addresses issues relating to newborns.

Colman, Libby Lee, and Arthur D. Colman. *Pregnancy: The Psychological Experience*. New York: Noonday Press, 1991. Comprehensive look at the stages of pregnancy and postpartum experiences.

Cosslett, T. *Women Writing Childbirth: Modern Discourses of Motherhood*. Manchester, England: Manchester University Press, 1994. Overview of the history of childbirth.

Eisenberg, Arlene, Heidi E. Murkoff, and Sandee E. Hathaway. *What to Expect When You're Expecting*. 2d ed. New York: Workman Publishing, 1991. Provides month-by-month details about what new mothers can expect during pregnancy; discusses miscarriage, labor, delivery, and postpartum depression.

Freeman, E. W., and Karl Rickels. *Early Childbearing: Perspectives of Black Adolescents on Pregnancy, Abortion, and Contraception*. Newbury Park, Calif.: Sage Publications, 1993. Comprehensive look at teenage pregnancy.

Sherr, Lorraine. *The Psychology of Pregnancy and Childbirth*. Cambridge, Mass.: Blackwell Science, 1995. Comprehensive overview of the major psychological changes and challenges that may be experienced during pregnancy, childbirth, and parenting.

Snow, C. *Infant Development*. Englewood Cliffs, N.J.: Prentice-Hall, 1989. Comprehensive overview of infant development with chapters outlining the birth process.

See also Adoption processes; Fertility and infertility; Genetic disorders; *In re Baby M*; Multiple births; Postpartum depression; Pregnancy.

Childhood fears and anxieties

RELEVANT ISSUES: Children and child development; Parenting and family relationships

SIGNIFICANCE: At all stages of emotional development, normal as well as exaggerated childhood fears require that parents support children, complicating parent-child interactions

Fear plays a protective role in human emotion, helping humans to avoid danger. Human beings depend more on learning than on instinct, however. Reasonable and specific fears can give way to less focused and more potentially disabling anxieties. Children's fears are related to the potential dangers to which they are most vulnerable at each stage of development. Additionally, children's stages of cognitive development influence commonly experienced anxieties, as comprehension or incomprehension of life events affects the perception of danger.

Developmental Stage and Anxiety. Newborns experience only two innate fears: fear of loud noises and fear of falling. Separation anxiety emerges at about six months, when children have formed a strong attachment to a parent figure. While separation can arouse distress throughout the life span, protest and clinging are most evident in children from six months until three years of age. Children develop competing motives for exploration as they become more mobile, showing their insecurity when they are tired, ill, or emotionally threatened, such as when they are jealous of other children. In the same age period, stranger anxiety is common, evoking behavioral reactions that vary in intensity from screams of terror in the most frightened children to simple wariness to seeking a parent's presence and approval. This age group is characterized by intense dependency on parents as well as by an inability to predict adult behavior. The sharp increase in communication skills in three-year-olds may account for the typical decrease in anxiety reactions.

Children's fears between ages one and three focus on protecting their physical integrity in a world they are just coming to know. Fears of being washed down a bathtub drain, sucked into a vacuum cleaner, or flushed down a toilet are all common. Fear of the dark increases in children between ages three and five. Nightmares are more frequent in preschool-aged children than in older children or adults and are more likely to involve monsters.

Fears in Maturing Children. As children mature, their fears become more realistic, their anxieties based more on the lack of knowledge of the actual likelihood of feared events. Fear of natural disasters and fear of being victimized by crime increase during the elementary-school years. Fear of ridicule and fear of failure in school increase during adolescence.

Family life can be governed by children's fears. Infants who protest against being left with a babysitter induce guilt in parents and can influence when mothers return to work. Toilet training can be disrupted by normal toddler fears. Children who fear the dark or awaken with nightmares disrupt their parents' and siblings' sleep as well as their own. Resistance to school attendance is a frequent result of children's anxieties, especially in transition years, such as during kindergarten, first grade, or the beginning of middle school. The fear may be fear of separation, ridicule, or failure. Disciplining children who act out of anxiety or who may fear some aspect of the discipline itself poses a dilemma. Psychologists recommend setting very short "time out" periods for toddlers who still have strong fears of separation.

Helping Fearful Children. Understanding that most childhood fear and anxiety is normal is a first step to helping children cope. Benjamin Spock's classic *Baby and Child Care* (1945) advises parents on the range of normal childhood fears and appropriate parental responses. Most recommended responses by Spock and others are noncontroversial, while some approaches have engendered debate among experts in child development.

Children, especially of preschool age, benefit from predictable routines. They like to sit at the same place at the table, have meals or baths at the same time, and follow bedtime rituals. Rituals involve a variety of activities unique to each family, such as putting a stuffed animal to bed first. The most frequent component of such rituals is the bedtime story (more often songs for infants). Children often prefer to hear the same story over and over. Predictability in an unpredictable world provides reassurance.

Children's expressions of fears can be met with physical and verbal reassurance. Touch and hugging are basic to children's emotional security even when, as they grow older, they begin to deny it. Older children may prefer an arm around the shoulder to a hug, but touch remains vital.

Since so much anxiety is a by-product of incomprehension, the answer to fear may be to promote understanding of the feared object or event. Toddlers can watch their parents flush the toilet. Parents of older children can verbally explain events,

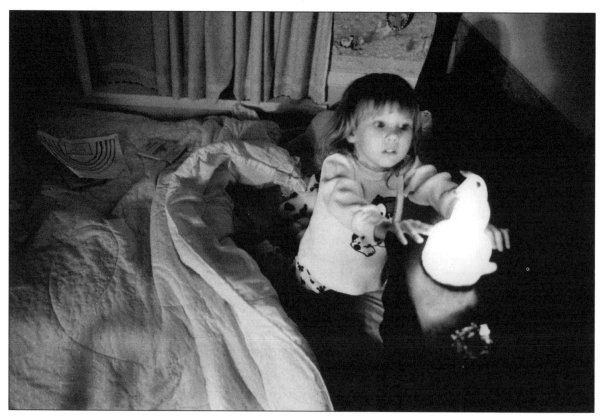

Fear of the dark is especially pronounced in children between the ages of three and five. (Long Hare Photographs)

Even harmless behaviors such as stepping to avoid cracks are manifestations of childhood anxieties. (Ben Klaffke)

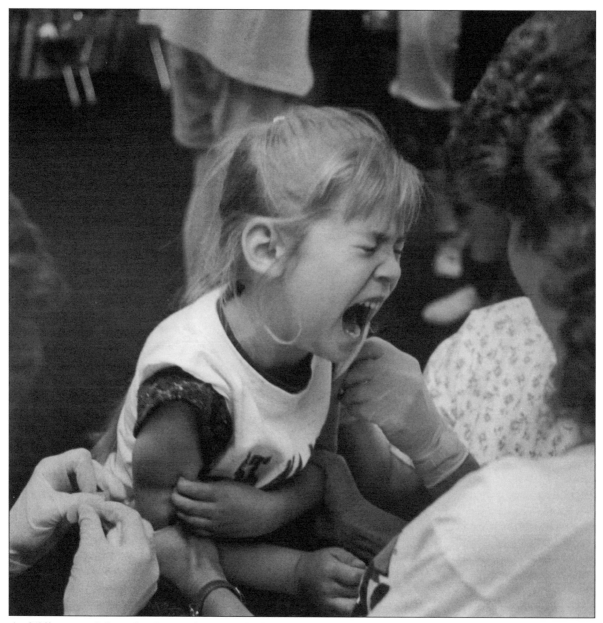

A child's natural fear of pain may become indelible if the child's parents insist that something likely to be painful "will not hurt." (James L. Shaffer)

such as hurricanes, and provide children with age-appropriate books on feared subjects.

Disagreements over Dealing with Fear. Children's fiction has historically revolved around children's fears. Classic fairy tales involve not only monsters but also wicked stepmothers and creatures who willfully harm or even eat children. Experts disagree about how explicit such fictional portrayals should be. Bruno Bettelheim's classic *The Uses of Enchantment* (1975) is an extended argument for the therapeutic value of fairy tales that deal graphically with children's fears. Other experts believe that such stories can induce or exacerbate fear.

There is also disagreement about the appropriate response when children's anxiety reactions create a disciplinary problem or inconvenience others. Generally, experts agree that children's fears should not be allowed to interfere with children's own development. Thus, children who fear baby-sitters will not overcome that fear if their parents decide they should never go out; children who fear school nonetheless must attend school. There is disagreement over how much reassurance to provide fearful children at bedtime. Psychologists commonly advise parents to teach infants to sleep in their own beds, with ever-shorter transitions between waking and sleeping times. Some experts, however, advocate the "family bed," arguing that in many cultures children continue sleeping with mothers or both parents for the first several years of their lives. While there is genuine disagreement on this issue, experts typically concede that parents' preference and household needs should govern decision making in such matters.

The most difficult decision parents may face involves determining whether outside intervention is necessary. Even among siblings there is a wide range of normal child behavior. Moreover, the ever-changing stages in any child's development, as well as transient disruptions owing to life events such as a move, a new sibling, or a divorce, only blur the picture.

Intervention. Reports of fear and anxiety among school-age children increased dramatically between the 1980's and 1990's. This trend can most likely be attributed to the increase in information children received about the dangers in their world. It is worth noting that interventions designed to protect children from harm may have created a different problem in place of real dangers.

Most anxiety problems in children are transient. However, anxious children are predisposed not only to anxiety disorders as adults but also to other problems, such as substance abuse disorders. In childhood, severe anxiety not only may disrupt family life but also may create significant problems for children at school, leading to possible misdiagnoses of attention-deficit hyperactivity disorder or behavior disorders. Severe anxiety can also lower a child's performance on standardized and classroom tests.

A variety of interventions exist. Cognitive-behavioral psychotherapy has been notably suc-cessful with children as well as adults. Family therapy and play therapy (for younger children) may be useful, especially in cases where a traumatic event has occurred. Pharmacological interventions exist, although medications do pose hazards involving potential side effects.

Mary Pipher in *The Shelter of Each Other: Rebuilding Our Families* (1996) argues for the protective and nurturing role of the family in successful child development. She highlights the role of family stories and rituals in strengthening all family members. She takes issue with the social forces undermining today's family. Interventions at the societal level require restoring a set of values which allow the family to function effectively.

—*Nancy E. Macdonald*

BIBLIOGRAPHY

Bettelheim, Bruno. *The Uses of Enchantment.* New York: Alfred A. Knopf, 1976.

March, John S., ed. *Anxiety Disorders in Children and Adolescents.* New York: Guilford Press, 1995.

Pipher, Mary. *The Shelter of Each Other: Rebuilding Our Families.* New York: G. P. Putnam's Sons, 1996.

Sarafino, Edward P. *The Fears of Childhood: A Guide to Recognizing and Reducing Fearful States in Children.* New York: Human Sciences Press, 1986.

Spock, Benjamin, and Michael B. Rothenberg. *Dr. Spock's Baby and Child Care.* New York: Simon & Schuster, 1985.

Wicks-Nelson, Rita, and Allen C. Israel. *Behavior Disorders of Childhood.* Englewood Cliffs, N.J.: Prentice Hall, 1991.

See also Bedtime reading; Child rearing; Emotional abuse; Emotional expression; Imaginary friends; Mental health; Separation anxiety; Spock, Benjamin; Stranger anxiety.

Childhood history

RELEVANT ISSUES: Children and child development; Parenting and family relationships

SIGNIFICANCE: How children experience childhood depends on a variety of factors, including cultural beliefs, class, gender, ethnicity, and the general historical stage of society

Any discussion of the history of childhood requires an answer to two questions. Do specific

Although children are no longer seen as "miniature adults," as they were in colonial times, an important part of early childhood education is mimicking adult behavior. (James L. Shaffer)

societies, in this case, the United States and Canada, historically recognize childhood as a separate developmental state? How have parents historically responded to this developmental state? At first glance, these questions may seem silly or even redundant, because all mammals go through a period of infancy and immaturity before reaching adulthood. Human beings are born as small and very weak creatures that require care and feeding by the adults in their lives. While they are still dependent on breast milk, infants biologically progress to toddlers by gradually shifting to a more varied diet. After four years of age, children increasingly become more self-sufficient. By their early teens, they reach puberty (sexual maturity). Not all societies, however, necessarily view biology as the dominating factor in marking developmental stages.

Definitions of Childhood. The psychologist Jean Piaget defined childhood as a series of developmental stages, each with its own characteristics, needs, and limitations. Historians postulate that this has not always been true. Few historians fail to acknowledge that infants need care to survive, but scholars argue over the cultural significance of childhood. For instance, some question the mothering instinct as a myth, postulating that it does not have a significant impact on the lives of children. Philippe Aries is the definitive advocate of the view that childhood before the seventeenth century was not perceived as a distinct phase. Children were seen as only miniature adults, largely ignored by the adults in their world. Only their smallness was seen as a vital difference. After the seventeenth century, Aries argued, parents viewed children as different from adults, in need of more protection, more directed discipline, and education. In other words, children progressed from "tiny adult to different, not fully developed innocents." Aries derived his conclusions from studying Western Europe, extrapolating from this to the rest of the Western world. In substantiating his theory of generalized indifference, he cited the close proximity in which the family members lived, the stylized clothing that children wore, which resembled that of their parents, and a lack of specific nurturing.

An interesting case study of this viewpoint is Puritan New England in the seventeenth century. After infancy, children wore clothing that duplicated that of their parents, and their daytime chores mimicked the gender duties of their adult counterparts. For reasons that remain historically unclear, in this Northern freehold society children were often "bound out" to be raised by other families. It has been suggested that this was motivated by the notion that emotionally unattached strangers could better raise children in a "godly" way than their natural parents. Like most societies of the seventeenth century, corporal punishment of children and adults was accepted practice.

Indifference or Cruelty. The willingness of older societies to mete out severe punishments and "switchings" to children has led historians to elaborate on Aries' concepts and suggest that childhood was not just tempered by general indifference, but also by cruelty. Among the proponents of this view are Edward Shorter and Lloyd DeMause. Shorter views the history of childhood as one of abuse gradually leading to the enlightenment of the sixteenth century, while DeMause asserts that the abandonment mode lasted until the thirteenth century and the ambivalent mode until the seventeenth century. Lawrence Stone, on the other hand, argues that it was not until the eighteenth century that significant change occurred and that even such change still failed to significantly lessen acts of punishment and violence toward children in efforts to curb their will.

Not every society chose to discipline children by corporal means. Native Americans did not hit their children. Many tribes saw the parental role as strictly one of nurturing, while discipline was left to maternal grandparents or maternal uncles. Children were taught by example and sometimes ostracism. Crying children, for example, were left alone on their cradle boards in the woods for a time or had water poured into their noses. Native American children were fewer in number than European children who came to the shores of North America. Taboos and extended nursing often allowed Native American women to bear only four children, unlike their Anglo-European counterparts. Interestingly, when Canadian fur trappers penetrated the wilderness of the inner continent, they often took native brides to ensure their trade status. Like Europeans, these women bore children every two years for twenty years.

The seeming indifference to the death of children in the early centuries of American life is cited as historical evidence that cruelty played a role in child raising. Women generally bore eight or more children and often saw half of them die before they reached the age of five. This loss was seemingly absorbed by the parents with little emotional upheaval, although the parental custom of having photographs of their children taken after death might suggest a different interpretation. This historical view must consider the medical problems and childhood diseases that quickly winnowed the population of children. The mortality rate remained consistently high until the advent of vaccinations and antibiotics in the twentieth century. Mothers, like children, also died with alarming frequency—one in thirty births resulted in maternal death.

The phenomenon of "murdering mothers"—in other words, mothers who committed infanticide—is cited as further historical evidence of cruelty in raising children. Infanticide certainly existed, as did abandonment, but infant mortality was generally blamed on mothers regardless of whether or not they acted out of volition. Among enslaved African Americans the infant death rate was more than 50 percent. Some children were smothered by their mothers to save them from a life of slavery, but many more died because of their mothers' poor nutrition and a workload that sent them back to the fields only four weeks after giving birth, which took an enormous toll on their health and ability to lactate.

Educational Changes. As children began to be recognized as innocents, their freedom was

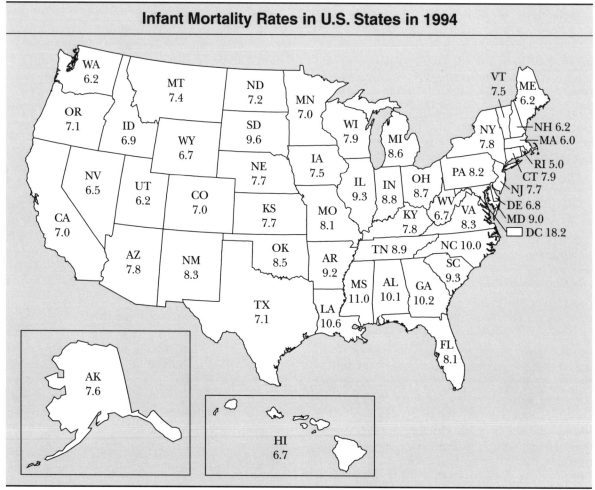

Infant Mortality Rates in U.S. States in 1994

Source: U.S. Bureau of the Census, *Statistical Abstract of the United States: 1997.* Washington, D.C.: GPO, 1997.
Note: Deaths of children under one year of age per 1,000 live births.

School is a primary focus in the lives of most children. (James L. Shaffer)

sharply circumscribed as institutionalized modes of education became the focus of their lives. Aries acknowledges that this change first took place in the lives of young boys, but in the Protestant American colonies girls were gradually taught reading, writing, and arithmetic through the legislation of schools by 1650. Much of this educational change was reinforced by John Locke's 1692 writings on education that outlined the role that education could play in the lives of children.

Education became a barometer establishing the existence of childhood as a separate and distinct developmental phase. Several historians assert that this acknowledgment of childhood existed throughout history, although disease and culture may have sharply defined societies' abilities to act

upon it. Many scholars assert that parents' letters and diaries provide evidence that they have always loved their children. One outspoken scholar who defends this view is Linda Pollack, who sees little difference in parental modes between the sixteenth and nineteenth centuries except for those influenced by social and technological changes. Other scholars, such as Karin Calvert, state that childhood cannot be interpreted as a single entity. Child rearing has differed from class to class; middle- and upper-class children have generally received more careful treatment than working-class children. In her study of the material artifacts of childhood, Calvert discovered that the middle class began to focus on children and children's articles by the end of the nineteenth mainly because of the growth of technology and the separation of spheres.

For Anglo-Americans, changes in technology, urbanization, and nascent industrialization led to the gradual separation of spheres, in which men worked 5.5 days a week and women stayed home to raise their children. Technological advances granted mothers more freedom from chores, as did their ability to procure outside help from nannies and maids for child raising. The new religious definition of women as primarily "mothers" and guardians of virtue, rather than as "Eves", or sexual temptresses, allowed mothers to curb their productivity. Native-born white women in the United States limited their production of offspring to only four in the nineteenth century based on the notions of self-control and passionlessness. These women stocked their nurseries with cradles and toys. For the first time society had enough leisure time to develop a culture of childhood. Aries and his school generally see artifact evidence such as cradles, jumpers, and perambulators as proof that childhood was now viewed as a developmental phase. In this way, middle-class consumerism becomes a barometer for the whole society's view.

A close look at the various nineteenth century views of childhood demonstrates, however, that class, status, and ethnicity sharply defined how children experienced childhood. The historical culture of Native American children was devastated by the coming of the Anglo-Europeans. On the Central Plains the Native Americans had suffered severe losses by 1890 and the Battle of Wounded Knee. Protestant missionaries opposed the traditional child-rearing methods of Native Americans and were determined to further erode their culture by removing their children from reservation lands and placing them in mission schools. Native American author Zitkala-Ša (Gertrude Simmons Bonnin) remembers that Anglo-Europeans, intending to quickly rid Native American children of their heritage, cut off their hair—a humiliating and terrifying experience, as was the corporal punishment meted out to them and the inhospitable dormitory rooms in which they were quartered. By the time such children returned to their families, they were both unfamiliar with their own heritage and unable to meet the expectations of the dominant culture.

Cultural Differences and the Immigrant Experience. In much the same way, African American children found that their childhood experiences were sharply circumscribed by their status and their ethnicity. The children of slaves took their status from their mothers, since many of their fathers were free white men who chose not to acknowledge their offspring. The children of slaves were raised in the slave quarters by older "aunties" or "uncles" until they were about seven years old, when they were put to work on the plantations or in the houses. Since marriage was not legally recognized for slaves, children's actual parents had little opportunity to protect or even raise them. Frederick Douglass remembers that his mother held him in the middle of the night only a few times during his entire childhood, because she lived on another plantation and was not allowed to see him. At plantations with absentee owners, such as the Good Hope plantation, strong family units and nurturing existed. In some ways the lot of African American children improved after emancipation; they could not be sold, but their social status remained low and the threat of violence from whites was overwhelming. African American children often had to work when they were young to help support their families. By the twentieth century, African American communities had evolved in the North, but working or single parents were often absent during the day. Poverty, corporal punishment, lack of education and medical care, violence, and crime often led to angry and fear-laden childhoods, such as that described by Richard Wright in his book *Black Boy*.

The nineteenth and early twentieth centuries were eras of large-scale immigration to American shores from such diverse countries as Norway, Ireland, Russia, Italy, Japan, and China. Families from Northern Europe were generally more easily accepted into the fabric of American life than those from other regions. Often Scandinavian immigrants booked passage to Ellis Island and then took trains to Scandinavian towns in the Midwest. Once they had established themselves, the cultures of their homelands served as a foundation for their children, who grew up surrounded by supportive communities. Many other children, such as those from Ireland, immigrated first to Canada and later to the United States. Despised because they were Roman Catholics, they were often greeted with signs reading, "No Irish need apply." In some areas, such as Boston, strong Irish ghettos developed and "bossism" flourished. Children raised in this situation lived in unsanitary and crowded tenement housing with the constant fear of disease. Parents generally worked to support their large brood of children. The children either helped with the work at home or took jobs in the mills or mines by the age of seven to support the household. In many cases ethnic gangs of Irish, Italians, and Jews waged "turf" warfare. Educating children was a priority, although usually the youngest family member was chosen to receive schooling and was supported by the rest of the family. Even if it took children three years to get through the first grade, because three small boys shared one pair of shoes, immigrant families focused on bettering themselves.

The patterns of Asian immigration often resembled those of European immigration, although Asians generally settled on the West Coast. Many Asian immigrants were male "birds of passage," who intended to earn money at "Gold Mountain," the Chinese nickname for California, and then return to their homelands. In many cases their dreams never materialized. When such laws as the National Origins Act (1924) were enacted, Asian Americans had difficulty in establishing families in their new country. Chinese tongs, or secret fraternal societies, began importing young girls to serve as prostitutes for males in "cribs"; male immigrants outnumbered female immigrants eighteen to one. Japanese immigrants sent away for picture brides from their homeland. Families maintained their native language at home and worked to maintain themselves. Amy Tan describes the pressures of being a Chinese American child in her book *The Joy Luck Club*. Children were expected to succeed, work hard, attend both American and Chinese schools, and retain their traditional respect for their parents and households.

Asian male children had more status then female children and were often better educated. In the Japanese family unit, or *ei*, children respected patriarchal authority and began working at young ages on truck farms or as domestic laborers. This hierarchical system was forcibly broken apart when Japanese Americans were incarcerated in U.S. internment camps during World War II, as Monica Sone describes in her work *Nisei Daughter*.

Growing Middle Class and the Twentieth Century. If life for immigrants and persons of color was difficult, middle-class children's lives improved. Better homes, less crowding, improved sanitation, and fewer children per household led to the more idyllic childhood of prams and baby toys. Children went for walks in the parks and visited new department stores in cities such as New York and Chicago. Education was stressed, as was the task of "raising an upright child," who was to be seen but not heard. Women spent less time with their children, who were placed on schedules, kept in separate cribs instead of the parental bed, and kept in greater seclusion. In other words, as more attention was paid to childhood, children were deprived of liberty. This change in the expectations of childhood may be easily charted through the books of the late nineteenth century. *The Adventures of Tom Sawyer* (1876) by Mark Twain and the *Five Little Peppers* series (1880) by Margaret Sidney depicted typical childhoods. Such stories were an improvement over such medieval fairy tales as Hansel and Gretel and Baba-Yaga—tales of witches that ate children for supper.

Native-born upper-class children lived even more restricted lives than those from the middle class. With the best toys and the best pampering they still saw little of their parents and depended on nannies for their daily nurturing. Many were sent away to boarding school, as was typical for British boys eight years of age and older. This gentility often involved a complete curtailment of children's freedom, as their parents even picked their spouses for them, not unlike during the Middle Ages.

Initially, wealth counted for little on the American and Canadian frontier. A family's ability to survive was vital, and it worked as a unit to retain its land. In the American Southwest Latino children were raised with a strong sense of family responsibility, a product of their Roman Catholic upbringing, but they also had a great deal of freedom to horseback ride and round up animals. The frontier experience described by Laura Ingalls Wilder, with its emphasis on education and a strong Protestant ethic, essentially involved strong child-centered families working toward a common goal.

Frontier boys and girls, like Native American but unlike immigrant children, had time to play.

The views of child development expert Maria Montessori have had a strong impact on modern educational theories.
(R. Kent Rasmussen)

According to child-development experts such as Maria Montessori, playing is vital to children's success. Historian Johan Huizinga believed that play is vital for all humans. Twentieth century middle-class children from the dominant culture have been permitted to play, but their schooling, often beginning at the age of three years old or younger, has absorbed more and more of their time. With the entry of huge numbers of women into the workforce during World War II, a new group of so-called "latchkey" children was created. These latchkey children became more typical as women continued to work outside the home following the war. More and more children were raised in day-care centers in a system reminiscent of the Israeli kibbutz

Scholars have tended to view the world from a "presentist" standpoint—that is, they have felt that the contemporary age is the best. This certainly holds true for scholars in the last half of the twentieth century. However, increased drug use, teenage pregnancy, and a rise in learning defects would suggest that this view might not be entirely justifiable. Certainly, many children in the late twentieth century have been better fed and better educated than their predecessors, but 70 percent of all children have not been raised to maturity in a traditional nuclear family with both birth parents present. Families have often been headed by single mothers living below the poverty line because of high child-care costs and low-paying jobs. Corporal punishment, although it has met with disfavor from pediatricians and scholars, has never been expunged from guidebook on how to manage children. One book, *Parenting for the New Millennium*, has endorsed a notion on the history of childhood reminiscent of Aries and his followers that children are relegated to "silent slavery" as their parents seek to teach them self-discipline and obedience. According to Karen Ryce, children must learn strong decision making, self-esteem, and self-confidence, all skills not taught by a world supposedly built on nurturing.

The history of childhood is the history of what children have experienced in their formative years from infancy to maturity. However, as scholars do not agree on what that experience truly has been, their conflicting theories postulate abused and ignored children, on one hand, and lovingly educated and nurtured children, on the other. The question of the mothering instinct and the role of fathers also enters into the equation. Raising children is the reason why people have families, and their experience is governed by cultural beliefs and pronouncements, class, gender, and ethnicity. Childhood is as old as the human race, but the study of the history of childhood is actually a fairly new area of scholarship compared to the study of warfare. —*Michaela Crawford Reaves*

BIBLIOGRAPHY

Aries, Philippe. *Centuries of Childhood: A Social History of Family Life.* Translated by Robert Baldick. New York: Vintage Books, 1962. An essential touchstone on the entire debate about childhood and its history. Aries, basing himself on studies on France and England, paints a picture of a world before the seventeenth century that neither acknowledges a developmental stage known as childhood nor gives it much room.

Calvert, Karin. *Children in the House: The Material Culture of Early Childhood, 1600-1900.* Boston: Northeastern University Press, 1992. A particularly intriguing work based on primary documentation of material culture from the seventeenth to the early twentieth century, this work looks at how children actually lived and experienced their childhood, while analyzing gender-specific differences of the childhood experience.

DeMause, Lloyd, ed. *The History of Childhood. The Untold Story of Child Abuse.* New York: P. Bedrick, 1988. A fine anthology that is broadly inclusive of the western European experience and includes a range of historical periods from "survivors" of the ninth century to the "home as a nest" of the mid-nineteenth century.

Demos, John. *A Little Commonwealth: Family Life in Plymouth Colony.* New York: Oxford University Press, 1970. A short, readable book that looks into the daily lives of the people of Plymouth plantation in the seventeenth century, examines aspects of courting and sexuality, and successfully investigates material culture.

Pollock, Linda. *Forgotten Children: Parent-Child Relations from 1500 to 1900.* New York: Cambridge University Press, 1983. Based on an examination of several hundred diaries, this work rejects the "pessimistic" version of childhood suggested by Aries and his followers by charting the trends of intrafamilial relationships over a four-hundred year period in the Western world.

Rabb, Theodore, and Robert Rotberg, eds. *The Family in History.* New York: Harper & Row, 1973. A helpful anthology that covers the "investigation" of childhood, discusses the history of family as a multidisciplinary field, and evaluates the status of establishing a history of childhood in America.

Shahar, Shulamith. *Childhood in the Middle Ages.* New York: Routledge, 1992. A discussion of medieval culture that examines the periods of childhood from infancy to adolescence using primary and secondary sources. Essentially debunks the primary thesis of Aries.

Shorter, Edward. *The Making of the Modern Family.* London: William Collins, 1976. A somewhat "presentist" work holding that parents were uninvolved with, and indeed indifferent to, their children before the advent of the modern age, which in the Western world ushered in the nurturing of children.

See also Bonding and attachment; Childbirth; Cultural influences; Educating children; Family: concept and history; Fatherhood; Health of children; Motherhood; Parenting; Puberty and adolescence.

Childless/truncated families

RELEVANT ISSUES: Demographics; Parenting and family relationships
SIGNIFICANCE: "Childless" or "truncated" families are terms applied to married couples who choose to remain permanently childless

Prior to the 1970's permanent childlessness in marriage was treated as if it occurred only on an involuntary basis. Nonparenthood as a deliberately chosen lifestyle was initially brought to public awareness through various articles and books that presented the viewpoints of married couples who voluntarily chose to remain childless. U.S. Bureau of the Census data for 1992 showed that 5 percent of wives between the ages of eighteen and thirty-four years of age did not expect to have children. Despite societal pressures on married couples to have children, more couples have considered the option of not becoming parents because they know how demanding parenthood is and want more time to devote to their marriages.

Few couples decide not to have children prior to marriage. Most couples who choose to remain permanently childless do so after postponing parenthood during their early years of marriage. Most childless couples initially assume that they will become parents but delay parenthood until they finally decide to remain childless. Couples choose to forgo parenthood in order to have more satisfying marital relationships, greater opportunities for personal fulfillment, freedom from child-care tasks and responsibilities, and greater financial security. Women may decide not to have children in order to pursue careers. Childless couples highly value the freedom and flexibility to geographically relocate, change jobs and careers, and to spontaneously pursue interesting endeavors.

The term "child-free couple" is often used instead of "childless couple," which has a more negative connotation. Child-free couples are often negatively stereotyped by society as unhappy, selfish, and frustrated. Research findings indicate that child-free couples tend to report more intense and vital relationships and greater marital happiness than parental couples. —*Marie Saracino*

See also Baby-boom generation; Birth control; Childlessness; Conjugal families; Couples; Reproductive technologies.

Childlessness

RELEVANT ISSUES: Children and child development; Economics and work; Health and medicine; Marriage and dating; Parenting and family relationships
SIGNIFICANCE: Couples and single men and women may be childless by chance, by choice, because they delay having children, because of infertility, because of coercion, or because of a combination of factors

In a society that expects most adults to marry and have children, women and men who are not mothers and fathers may feel different, isolated, misunderstood, and stigmatized. The childless in the United States live in a nation virtually obsessed with reproduction. The United States is strongly prochild and promotherhood.

The childless include those who would like to have children but are physically unable. They also include those who postpone childbearing for pro-

Whatever the reasons North American couples remain childless, they live in a society that makes many of them feel stigmatized. (Dick Hemingway)

fessional or personal reasons and those who have made a conscious choice to forgo parenthood forever. Physicians consider people infertile if they are unable to conceive a child after a year or more of unprotected intercourse or if they are unable to give birth to a live child.

Aside from their childlessness, childless people have little else in common. People are childless by chance or choice; because they have delayed having children; are infertile; or have been coerced, as in the case of those who have been sterilized without their knowledge or consent, such as the mentally retarded or insane. Some women choose not to have children or delay having them for reasons of adventure, romance, spirituality, ambition, art, duty, poverty, terror, or the desire for an education. Men who have opted out of fatherhood often cite a desire to hold risky, unremunerative, or totally absorbing jobs as reasons for not having children. Historically, during economically tough times and stress, women have had fewer or no children for reasons of survival or even as passive resistance to slavery and other forms of oppression.

Attitudes Toward Childlessness. During the twentieth century, parenthood has been considered the result of an individual decision, despite marital status or sexual orientation. It is no longer an economic necessity for women to marry. In fact, the negative stereotypes of single women and men have diminished. Marriage is no longer a requirement for motherhood. The days of being stigmatized for bearing children out of wedlock have waned, and adoption has become an option for single women and men.

Childless adults can live extraordinarily interesting and useful lives. Some do not, feeling instead pain and isolation over not having children. Other adults are willing to sacrifice their health, financial security, and daily routines in a desperate medical quest to have children.

The words used to describe childlessness have changed over time, as have attitudes toward the childless. The childless have gone from being barren to sterile, from sterile to infertile, from infertile to childless, even to child-free. Rarely, however, have these terms applied to men.

The lion's share of the burden of involuntary childlessness falls on women, although men are infertile as often as women. Whether or not a woman has been the infertile partner, she has disproportionately borne the medical, social, and cultural burdens of a couple's inability to have children. Throughout American history, society has had a cultural expectation that all women want to become mothers.

Historians and demographers relate the rates of childlessness throughout history to many complex factors. These factors include economic status, race, religion, health, marital status, the availability of reproductive and contraceptive technologies, and cultural beliefs. Scientists and historians measure childlessness in terms of women; there is virtually no available data on childlessness among men.

History of Childlessness. The rates of childlessness and fertility have varied over the centuries. Fertility rates have declined, while the percentage of women bearing children has increased. In the late nineteenth century the proportion of childless couples, not just smaller families, increased. Studies have shown that among white women born in 1835 who had ever married, more than 7 percent were childless. Until 1855 childlessness had increased slowly; thereafter, it began to increase sharply. In the 1920's, more than 20 percent of white women in the United States were childless at age forty. Of white women born in 1970, nearly 16 percent remained childless. By the 1980's this figure had fallen to 10 percent. African American women show a similar pattern of childlessness.

During most of the nineteenth century the rate of childlessness was low. Among women aged forty to forty-four who have been married, childlessness increased from 10 percent in 1910 to 17 percent in 1940, peaking at 20 percent in 1950. America experienced a dramatic decline in childlessness among younger women during the baby boom following World War II. The rate dropped from 14 percent in 1957 to 11 percent in 1990. The highest rate of lifetime childlessness on record—20 percent—occurred among all women born in the first decade of the twentieth century. These women were of childbearing age during the 1920's and 1930's.

Advancements in birth control technologies made voluntary childlessness possible. These methods included sterilization, the pill, intrauterine devices, safe abortions, implants, and injections. Clearly, some couples took advantage of the opportunity to remain childless.

Children in History. For early Americans, having children was an economic necessity and a matter of community survival. Without children to do the work, households could not function as economically productive units, and communities would have withered and died. They needed children to explore and settle the new nation. Children could also provide comfort and companionship to their parents. Colonial children were reared for the benefit of the household, community, and nation, not for the personal pleasure of parents. Childlessness in colonial times was a heavy burden. Women who died during childbirth left many half-orphans. Society expected childless couples to rear their orphaned nieces, nephews, and cousins.

Colonial women without children suffered from their inability to fulfill the biblical commandment to multiply and contribute to the growth of the community and nation. In Puritan New England it was commonly thought that childlessness signified God's disfavor or his desire to test couples' faith. Prayer and reflection were seen as the only means of dealing with childlessness. Married women who did not have children had a higher likelihood of being accused of witchcraft if they did not seem properly virtuous. Childlessness denied a husband the opportunity to achieve head-of-household status. Landowning farmers especially wanted sons to whom they could pass on their land and who would continue the family name.

During the nineteenth century, infertile couples—the involuntarily childless—turned to the adoption of unrelated children for emotional rather than economic reasons. Being single—or voluntarily childless—also became increasingly popular, in part because independence and industriousness were highly valued and respected.

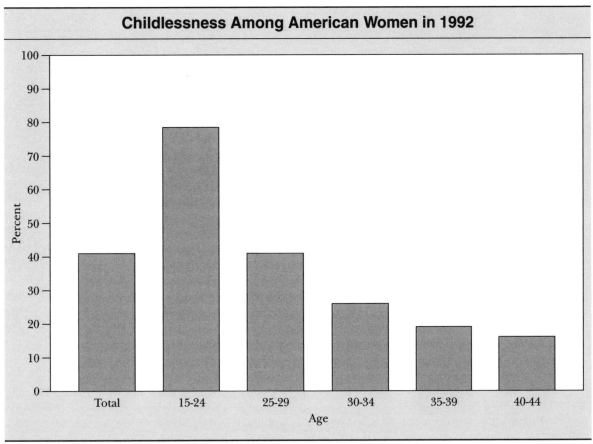

Source: U.S. Bureau of the Census

Childlessness became a new challenge in the nineteenth century. Personal happiness and the quality and number of the future population of the country depended upon the bearing and raising of children. As the century progressed, more men and women elected to lead a single life. Physicians warned women that working and pursuing a college education would make them infertile.

Attacking the Childless. During the late nineteenth and early twentieth centuries, single women like Jane Addams, the social worker and writer who founded Hull House in Chicago, were revered as saints. By the 1920's, however, unmarried women were sneered at as "old maids." Before the twentieth century, it was widely assumed that childless married women were infertile or in poor health. In the twentieth century, voluntary childlessness was promoted as a way of life, in part the result of the suffrage movement and birth control clinics. The progressive 1960's, with its equal rights advances and new workplace opportunities for women, enabled some women to choose alternatives to motherhood.

In 1905, at the height of the wave of European immigration, President Theodore Roosevelt attacked the selfishness of women who refused to have large families. In an address before the National Congress of Mothers, he compared a woman's duty to have a child with a man's duty to fight for his country. His speech was in response to concerns about the millions of immigrants who had much higher birthrates than native-born whites. The white childless became more suspect in the face of "race suicide," and the fertility of the "masses" appeared more dangerous. The stigma surrounding childlessness intensified as the eugenics movement, the first systematic and large-scale movement devoted to improving the human race through scientific breeding, gained momentum. For the first time, infertility emerged as a serious problem facing the nation, and voluntary childlessness became a crime against the citizenry. Childless women were caught in the wave of criticism. The attacks coincided with the fear of racial decline, women's continuing activism (evident in the suffrage movement), increasing divorce rates, and the continuing use of birth control.

Involuntary childlessness was especially tough and painful during the 1940's and 1950's, because the United States was virtually obsessed with having babies. By 1958, the idea that the infertile—particularly women—were to blame for their childlessness was pervasive. Enlightened physicians felt compelled to state publicly that the infertile were no more responsible for their infertility than were individuals afflicted with other diseases and medical conditions.

Attitudes toward the causes of infertility have also changed with time. During the post-World War II era, some psychoanalysts have argued that women's rejection of their appropriate feminine role could make them infertile. Adoption of children, they said, might make such women more likely to conceive. Early twentieth century physicians believed gonorrhea was among the major causes of infertility and that husbands were the cause of their wives' infertility. During the sexual revolution of the 1960's and 1970's women were seen as responsible for their own infertility because of their sexual activities.

Voluntary childlessness increased after the 1960's, but it was a new phenomenon. However, the stigma surrounding the childless did not disappear entirely. What changed in the 1970's was the visibility and the stridency of the voluntarily childless. For the first time, advocates for the childfree argued that voluntary childlessness represented not simply an alternative to parenthood, but a better one for individuals, couples, and the planet.

Americans live in a society that has from the beginning viewed motherhood and parenthood as the goal for most women. Motherhood has been the primary vocation for those who have married. Some childless women believe that the failure to have children is a social impediment barring them from the special club of motherhood. While

A Day for Childless Women

Even women without children have their own annual day of celebration. Unmothers International, based in Montague, Michigan, has declared the first Sunday of May (exactly one week before Mother's Day) to be International Unmothers Day. Its purpose is to remind society that the worth of women need not be measured by motherhood.

women have greater opportunities to pursue careers and educational opportunities, biological maternity remains a critical factor in women's sense of normalcy.

Effects of Childlessness. Studies have shown that involuntarily childless couples differ in how childlessness affects them. Many women believe that infertility is intolerable and identity threatening. They regret not having children. To most husbands, on the other hand, childlessness is disappointing, but not devastating.

Child-free living is a term generally used to designate infertile couples who have decided not to adopt. Childless couples have had two choices if they wished to pursue parenthood. They could adopt or seek infertility treatment. However, neither route has necessarily guaranteed that they will obtain a child because of the lack of adoptable children and the costs involved in treating infertility.

Medical science has sought various "cures" for childlessness. Help has come from in vitro fertilization, hormonal therapies, artificial insemination, and fertility drugs to help women conceive. Increasing numbers of women have sought the help of physicians to alleviate their childlessness. By seeking treatment, couples have made an active choice to confront their childlessness. The best estimates of the effectiveness of such treatments suggest that only 50 percent of infertile couples undergoing medical therapy have achieved pregnancy in the 1990's.

Formerly, women were almost always considered responsible for sterility. They alone were subjected to examinations, tests, and surgical procedures. The truth is, however, that it is often men who are infertile. In perhaps 40 percent of barren marriages, the cause of childlessness may be the result of a deficiency in men's reproductive powers.

Contraception and abortion have simplified the prevention of unwanted pregnancies and the planning of births. The Margaret Sanger Research Foundation was dedicated to providing contraceptive services before shifting its focus to infertility. The Planned Parenthood Federation of America, formerly the Birth Control Federation, worked to guarantee the best available knowledge for preventing conception. It also promoted social and medical measures to make it possible for responsible parents to have children when they want them.

The childless are different. In a child-centered country they have no children. Aside from their childlessness, however, their lives are really no different from that of others. They are brothers, sisters, aunts, and uncles. They hold jobs, have hobbies, and go on vacations. The childless have had a major impact on children's lives as caretakers, children's authors, teachers, and much else.

—Fred Buchstein

BIBLIOGRAPHY

Bartlett, Jane. *Will You Be Mother? Women Who Choose to Say No.* New York: New York University Press, 1994. Portrays women who choose not to have children and live meaningful lives.

Ireland, Mardy S. *Reconceiving Women—Separating Motherhood from Female Identity.* New York: Guilford Press, 1993. Focuses on the acceptance of women as women—whether they are mothers or not.

Lisle, Laurie. *Without Child—Challenging the Stigma of Childlessness.* New York: Ballantine Books, 1996. Presents childlessness in a positive and historical light, exploring the choices women must make about motherhood.

McLaren, Angus. *A History of Contraception—From Antiquity to the Present Day.* Oxford: Blackwell, 1994. The first comprehensive overview of the history of fertility control since Norman E. Himes's *A Medical History of Contraception*, published in 1936.

Marsh, Margaret, and Wanda Ronner. *The Empty Cradle: Infertility in America from Colonial Times to the Present.* Baltimore: The Johns Hopkins University Press, 1996. The first book-length history of infertility in the United States showing how American families and physicians have struggled with infertility.

May, Elaine Tyler. *Barren in the Promised Land: Childless Americans and the Pursuit of Happiness.* New York: Basic Books, 1995. Probably the first history of childlessness, this book covers voluntary childlessness, compulsory sterilization, infertility, and adoption.

Sandelowski, Margarete. *With Child in Mind: Studies of the Personal Encounter with Infertility.* Philadelphia: University of Pennsylvania Press, 1993. Argues that infertile women are unnecessarily perceived as the creators of and martyrs to their childlessness and insists that infertility should be seen as a source of real sorrow.

Thurer, Shari L. *The Myths of Motherhood—How Culture Reinvents the Good Mother.* Boston: Houghton Mifflin, 1994. Analyzes changing expectations for mothers and motherhood and shows that many cherished ideals of parental excellence are about as useless and ephemeral as daily doses of castor oil.

See also Abortion; Adoption issues; Adoption processes; Birth control; Childless/truncated families; Conjugal families; Cult of True Womanhood; Feminist sociology; Fertility and infertility; Genetic counseling; Genetic disorders; Health problems; Menopause; Motherhood; Only children; Reproductive technologies; Sterilization; Surrogate mothers; Test-tube babies.

Children born out of wedlock

RELEVANT ISSUES: Children and child development; Demographics; Kinship and genealogy; Marriage and dating; Parenting and family relationships; Sociology

SIGNIFICANCE: Children born out of wedlock have presented societies with a moral problem from time immemorial and have been a social problem for the last two centuries

Children born out of wedlock are children whose conception and birth does not conform to the institutional rules governing reproduction in a given community or society. Such children have been called bastards, children of nobody, illegitimate children, generic children, and nameless children. Such descriptions blame these children for the circumstances of their birth. They are often treated as outcasts.

Illegitimacy has long been considered a moral problem, and for the last two centuries it has been a social problem. How societies control illegitimacy varies. The moral condemnation of illegitimacy is not universal. Some societies handle children born out of wedlock in a relaxed manner. Others do not. Marriage and the nuclear family—mothers, fathers, children—are almost the only universal social institutions in existence. In no society has the birth of children out of wedlock been the cultural norm. On the contrary, concern for the legitimacy of children has been nearly universal.

Born Out of Wedlock. Nearly one out of three children born in the United States in the 1990's was born out of wedlock, as opposed to one in ten in 1970. In 1991 1.2 million births were illegitimate—the highest number ever reported in the United States. Whereas in 1993 6.3 million children lived with a single parent who had never married, in 1960 this number was 243,000. Not all births classified as nonmarital involve women living alone. More than a quarter of such births involve unmarried parents living together. No typical unmarried parent exists. Contrary to popular beliefs, most women who give birth to children out of wedlock are not teenagers. Teenagers give birth to approximately one-third of all children born out of wedlock. Researchers have found, however, that nonmarital childbearing is higher among the less educated and poor.

The incidence of nonmarital childbearing has been rising for more than five decades. Between 1940 and 1960 this increase, although slow, was unmistakable. Since the 1970's the increase in the number, rate, and ratio of nonmarital births has been dramatic. The increase in the proportion of nonmarital births reflects both an increase in the number of unmarried pregnant women and the increasing rate of nonmarital childbearing. The growing population of unmarried persons is primarily a result of delayed marriages among the large baby-boom generation and higher rates of divorce and separation. The combination of a higher rate of nonmarital childbearing and a larger population of unmarried persons has resulted in a substantial increase in the number and proportion of nonmarital births.

Theory of Illegitimacy. Anthropologist Bronislaw Malinowski produced the most influential sociological theory of illegitimacy. He argued that children born without mature, male protectors were problem children. Marriage is not merely a license for sex, but a contract legitimizing procreation. Each society decides just what makes a birth illegitimate. Later researchers have attributed rising illegitimacy in the United States not to a breakdown of social control, but to a "quiet revolution" in the family. Americans have subscribed less and less to the assumption that children should inherit their status and opportunities in life solely from husband-fathers.

The impact of illegitimacy on children, their families, and society is significant. Despite evidence that illegitimate children are at greater risk of failing to thrive, most children in single-parent families develop normally. Illegitimate infants are often born prematurely and are underweight, in part because unmarried mothers, on average, obtain less prenatal care than married mothers. Young children in single-mother families tend to achieve lower scores on verbal and math achievement tests than young children in dual-parent families. In middle childhood, children raised by single parents tend to have lower grades, more behavior problems, and higher rates of chronic health and psychiatric disorders than children with two parents. Adolescents and young adults in single-mother families are more likely than those with two parents to be unwed parents, high-school dropouts, prison inmates, and jobless people. Evidence shows that the stigma of illegitimacy can turn mothers and children against each other, as such children blame their mothers for giving birth to them out of wedlock. Some children born out of wedlock have low self-esteem and cannot see themselves as capable and competent, lovable and loving, unique and valuable. Such children are much more likely to experience abuse or neglect than other children.

Whereas some Western societies have tried to outlaw premarital sex to ensure the legitimacy of offspring, others permit it while forbidding pre-

Children Born to Unwed Mothers in U.S. States in 1993

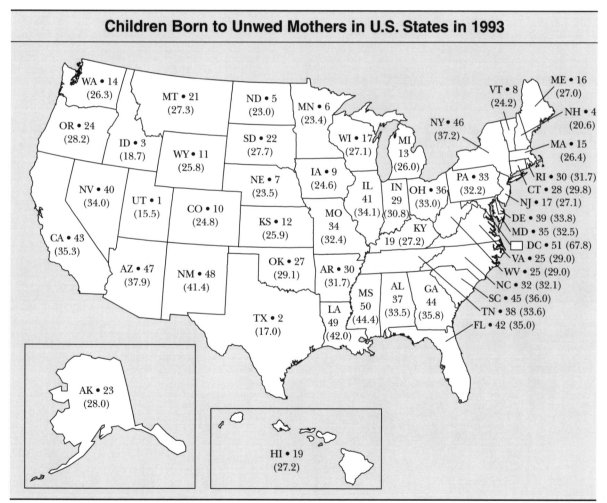

Source: National Center for Health Statistics.

Note: In 1993 31.0% of all children born in the United States had unmarried mothers. This map shows how each state ranks, in ascending order, of births to unwed mothers. Percentages of total births that are out-of-wedlock births are given in parentheses.

marital conception or birth. Societies, however, vary considerably in how strident and effective they are at regulation. For example, among the Mao unmarried women who conceive can be made slaves of the king. The Manchus killed illegitimate infants, in part because they saw no way to legitimate them after they were born. At the turn of the twentieth century the rural Irish condemned nonmarital births. Some women, or couples, who had children born out of wedlock were forced to marry or emigrate to other countries.

Nineteenth century British novelist Charles Dickens is known for books such as Oliver Twist *(1838), about an orphan boy born in a workhouse to an unwed mother.* (Library of Congress)

Many people born out of wedlock are legitimized before they grow up. Their biological parents marry or they are adopted. Of those who remain illegitimate, many suffer social, legal, and financial disadvantages. As late as the 1950's some white unwed mothers avoided the shame of having illegitimate children by moving to states that did not record illegitimacy on birth certificates. However, not all children born out of wedlock pay a heavy price for the circumstances of their birth. Children born to royalty, nobles, and the rich are well treated. If their fathers are rich and powerful, illegitimate children achieve a status of quasi-legitimacy.

The traditional legal, material, and social consequences of illegitimacy vary according to time and place. Abortion and infanticide have been the ultimate consequences of illegitimate conception and birth. The stigma of illegitimacy has driven some unmarried women to commit infanticide. To the Romans, legitimacy meant that women had to be married at the time they gave birth. Under Roman law, children born to unmarried women were *filius nullius*—sons of nobody. Even if the women subsequently married, such children remained illegitimate. Such children could not inherit property and were not entitled to receive support from either of their parents. Children rejected by their fathers were left to die or were enslaved. Until 1836 children born out of wedlock in Scotland were legally prohibited from making wills.

Illegitimacy is a common literary theme, appearing even in the Old Testament. Authors who have written about illegitimate children include Jane Austen, Agatha Christie, Charles Dickens, Fyodor Dostoevski, George Bernard Shaw, William Shakespeare, Leo Tolstoy, and Oscar Wilde. They contrasted illegitimacy to proper marriage, honor, respectability, and security. Children born out of wedlock have been portrayed as shameful villains and as symbols of family greed and dark secrets.

Religious law has also played a significant role in how we view and treat children born out of wedlock. Jews, Roman Catholics, and Muslims are expected to marry within their faith. Roman Catholic and Jewish law and tradition forbid illegitimate men from becoming rabbis or priests. Under Muslim law illegitimate children have no legal fathers, but they can inherit from their mothers.

Evolving Attitudes. America's principle of legitimacy has become less repressive over time. For centuries Western law has been moving away from a definition of legitimacy based strictly on marriage and toward one whereby illegitimate offspring are deprived of fewer rights than previously and biological fathers, regardless of their marital status, have obligations to their illegitimate children. In twentieth century America both middle-class white communities and lower-class African American communities began to treat nonmarital pregnancy and birth less severely than previously. Many other countries have attempted to equalize the rights of legitimate and illegitimate children in the twentieth century, passing laws that make biological fathers responsible for their offspring and guarantee to offspring the rights of support and inheritance, regardless of whether their parents are married or not.

Women have played a significant role in reshaping America's principle of legitimacy into a more restitutive form that makes little distinction between biological and social fatherhood. They have worked to make the treatment of illegitimacy less repressive for women and children, especially in welfare programs, maternity homes, and legal and probate cases on behalf of children. Women have helped focus attention on abstinence and birth control, voluntary abortion, child support from unwed fathers, and the role of government in supporting mothers and children.

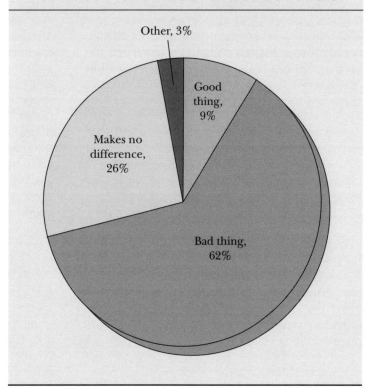

Women's Views on Out-of-Wedlock Births

Other, 3%
Good thing, 9%
Makes no difference, 26%
Bad thing, 62%

Source: The Pew Research Center (1998)

Note: A survey of American women asked whether the trend toward more unmarried couples having children was good or bad for society.

Before World War II illegitimate children were typically considered "children of sin," the products of mentally deficient mothers. Such children were thus tainted and undesirable. Families, states, and communities expected biological mother to nurture and raise their children. Rarely did others want children who were as stigmatized as their parents. Before the 1960's Americans dealt with unwed mothers predominantly by such informal repressive measures as stigmatizing them through rumor and gossip, banishing them to maternity homes, and verbally attacking them.

A 1968 U.S. Supreme Court decision, *Levy v. Louisiana*, held that illegitimate children enjoyed the full protection of the Constitution's equal protection clause. Since this landmark decision, the Court has shown little consistency in interpreting illegitimacy cases. Nevertheless, it has removed many legal obstacles faced by illegitimate parents and children.

Children born out of wedlock have also benefited from changes in law. In 1975 Congress passed a law to improve child support enforcement and establish a federal agency, the Office of Child Support Enforcement (OCSE), that coordinated the work of states and counties in recouping a portion of the monies spent on Aid to Families with Dependent Children (AFDC). AFDC went primarily to female-headed households. All states have passed legislation and set up local agencies to enforce restitution by illegitimate fathers. Before the 1970's the major form of restitution for illegitimate fathers was marrying the mothers to "set things right." Since then biological fathers have been increasingly pressured to help support their children born out of wedlock.

Fathers play a significant role in families and in the lives of their children. Between 1960 and 1990, however, the percentage of U.S. children living apart from their biological fathers more than doubled from 17 to 36 percent. Some researchers have suggested that the decline of fatherhood due to out-of-wedlock births, divorce, and desertion is a major cause of crime and delinquency, teenage pregnancy, deteriorating educational achievement, depression, substance abuse, alienation, and the growing number of women and children living in poverty.

Just as divorce has overtaken death as the leading cause of fatherlessness, out-of-wedlock birthrates are expected to surpass divorce rates in the first decade of the twenty-first century. Substantial evidence exists that children with unmarried fathers face even greater hardships than children with divorced fathers. Research has compellingly shown that fatherhood and marriage are indispensable for the good of children and society.

Prior to the sexual revolution of the 1960's and the Supreme Court's 1973 decision in *Roe v. Wade*, which legalized abortion, extreme shame was attached to illegitimate pregnancies and births among whites and African Americans alike. Unwed mothers were considered deviant. Illegitimate births were a disaster, because they meant a lifetime of stigmatization for mothers and children. They could ruin women's chances of establishing good marriages and a middle-class life. Until the 1960's young, unmarried, pregnant women sometimes attempted suicide, although this rarely occurred in later years. The shame of illegitimacy

extended not only to unmarried mothers, but also to their families and children. Unwed women and their families frequently tried to hide the fact that they were pregnant to avoid being stigmatized and discriminated against by the community.

Unwed mothers sometimes avoided the stigma of having illegitimate children by putting their children up for adoption, having shotgun or rushed weddings, or undergoing illegal abortions. Adoption practices and realities have changed. In the past, dual-parent families adopted many children, especially white ones born to unwed mothers. During the first half of the 1990's only a very small percentage of such infants were put up for adoption. Adoptions in America have traditionally been closed affairs, whereby birth parents and adoptive parents are unknown to one another; but as the stigma of illegitimacy has declined since the 1960's, adoptions have become more open. In earlier decades maternity homes helped unwed mothers put their infants up for adoption. While women were away at maternity homes, where they gave up their babies after they were born, their families fabricated cover stories to explain why their daughters disappeared for months on end. Maternity homes offered salvation to women in trouble and then reentry into the moral community. Few maternity homes accepted African Americans. African American communities organized themselves around mothers and children, while white communities were unwilling and unable to do so, preferring to simply expel them.

The idea of the family is changing, especially because of increased divorce rates, blended families, and single-parent families. Moreover, the laws and societal rules governing reproduction are changing. Insofar as most unwed mothers have been choosing to keep their children, raising children out of wedlock has become more accepted. However, children born out of wedlock remain a moral, as well as a social problem. —*Fred Buchstein*

BIBLIOGRAPHY

Hao, Lingxin. *Kin Support, Welfare, and Out-of-Wedlock Mothers*. New York: Garland, 1994. Explores the causes and consequences of out-of-wedlock childbearing and presents solutions for mothers and their children.

Hendrix, Lewellyn. *Illegitimacy and Social Structures: Cross-Cultural Perspectives on Nonmarital Birth*.

Westport, Conn.: Bergin & Garvey, 1996. Sociologist Hendrix examines the social regulation of illegitimacy and its sanctions.

Laslett, Peter, Karla Oosterveen, and Richard M. Smith. *Bastardy and Its Comparative History: Studies in the History of Illegitimacy and Marital Nonconformism in Britain, France, Germany, Sweden, North America, Jamaica and Japan.* Cambridge, Mass.: Harvard University Press, 1980. The articles in this anthology take a historical look at illegitimacy as a social and moral problem in various countries.

Solinger, Rickie. *Wake Up Little Susie: Single Pregnancy and Race Before Roe v. Wade.* New York: Routledge, 1992. Important history reviewing women, sexuality, race, the ideology of gender and the family, and public policy in the decades after World War II. Focuses on maternity homes, adoption, and African American and white single pregnancy.

Teichman, Jenny. *Illegitimacy: An Examination of Bastardy.* Ithaca, N.Y.: Cornell University Press, 1982. Unravels the notions and ideas behind legitimacy and illegitimacy.

Zingo, Martha T., and Kevin E. Early. *Nameless Persons—Legal Discrimination Against Non-Marital Children in the United States.* Westport, Conn.: Praeger, 1994. Analyzes the U.S. Supreme Court's equal protection birth status decisions from 1968 to 1992.

See also Adoption issues; African Americans; Aid to Families with Dependent Children (AFDC); Alternative family types; Amerasian children; Birth control; Child rearing; Child Support Enforcement Amendments; Childlessness; Children's rights; *Gomez v. Perez*; Inheritance and estate law; Marriage laws; Motherhood; Parenting; Paternity suits; Single-parent families; Teen mothers; Unwed fathers; War brides.

Children's Bureau

DATE: Founded in 1912

RELEVANT ISSUES: Children and child development; Economics and work

SIGNIFICANCE: As the first federal agency dedicated to the welfare of children, the U.S. Children's Bureau reflected and focused national attention on social services for families

The federal Children's Bureau was created in 1912 by President William Howard Taft as part of his administration's efforts to promote family welfare. The bureau's first head was Julia C. Lathrop, an early resident of Jane Addams's Hull House and one of the founders of the nation's first juvenile court. The bureau, a branch of the Department of Commerce, investigated the welfare and mortality of children and, after being moved to the Department of Labor in 1915, enforced child-labor laws. The bureau conduced research into the welfare of children and made recommendations to Congress and other federal agencies based on that research.

Over the next several decades, the bureau was shifted from one department of the federal government to another as federal involvement in family welfare increased and waned. Nevertheless, the bureau continued to play a leading role in drafting and supporting important measures, including the 1921 Sheppard-Towner Maternity and Infancy Act, which created a program to reduce infant mortality. A renewed call to reduce child labor arose in the 1930's, and in 1942 the bureau's Commission on Children in Wartime set age and occupation standards for children called to work in support of the war effort. Throughout World War II the bureau insisted that children's first duty was to receive a solid education, arguing that children should not be encouraged to leave school to work in defense industries. The role of work in children's lives was considered again in the 1960's, when a bureau publication proposed that children work part-time jobs as a solution to the feelings of inadequacy that lead to juvenile delinquency.

Other investigations led to the publication of influential recommendations. In 1937 the bureau issued a report on the effects of the Social Security Act and sponsored the first national conference on housekeeper services. An increase in working mothers during World War II led to the bureau's 1945 policy recommendations known as "Care of Infants Whose Mothers Are Employed." These recommendations sparked a national discussion on child care. This discussion was renewed in the 1960's, when employment opportunities for women and the number of single-parent families increased again and the bureau's Office of Child Development began formulating new standards for child-care institutions. Throughout the 1950's and 1960's the bureau examined adoption and

One of the reasons the Children's Bureau was formed in 1912 was to prevent the exploitation of child labor. (Library of Congress)

custody issues, preparing "Legislative Guides for the Termination of Parental Rights."

In 1969, during the administration of President Richard M. Nixon, the bureau was moved to the Office of Child Development. Its staff was greatly reduced and most of its functions were distributed among other agencies. Although the bureau continued to make public declarations on children's needs, formulating a 1973 Bill of Rights for Foster Children, its influence waned steadily over the next twenty years. In the 1990's the Children's Defense Fund (CDF) successfully filled the place that had once been occupied by the U.S. Children's Bureau, refocusing the nation's attention on child-welfare issues. —*Cynthia A. Bily*

See also Child care; Children's Defense Fund (CDF); Lathrop, Julia C.; Welfare.

Children's Defense Fund (CDF)

DATE: Founded in 1973

RELEVANT ISSUES: Children and child development; Education; Health and medicine; Violence

SIGNIFICANCE: This children's advocacy organization is a recognized national leader in championing numerous issues related to improving the quality of children's lives

The Children's Defense Fund (CDF) was founded in 1973 by civil rights activist and attorney Marian Wright Edelman. Edelman has long served as the organization's president and is nationally known for her work on behalf of children. The organization's mission is to "provide a strong and effective voice for all the children of America." Recognizing that children lack political clout and cannot "speak" for themselves by voting, lobbying, or holding office and that children continue to be

Marian Wright Edelman, the founder and president of the Children's Defense Fund, speaking in Washington, D.C., in 1996. (AP/Wide World Photos)

plagued by inadequate nutrition and health care, societal violence, parental abuse, and political apathy, the CDF accomplishes its mission through a comprehensive array of activities designed to foster national preventive investments in children rather than reactive remediation of these problems. The organization is especially dedicated to the needs of poor, minority, and disabled children.

The CDF publishes a variety of books, reports, and pamphlets, including an annual review on the status of children, an annual report on the U.S. budget, nonpartisan congressional voting records, and a monthly newsletter called *CDF Reports*. As part of its advocacy role, the organization supports research, training, and public education for child advocates, parents, and policymakers. It also hosts an annual national conference and sponsors numerous events and campaigns, such as the "Black Community Crusade for Children," which is designed to empower a new generation of African American leaders and support African American students, and the "Cease Fire!" and "Safe Start" initiatives, which call attention to gun violence and violence in schools and the community. Children who have overcome great difficulties to succeed in school and the community are recognized by the CDF's "Beat the Odds" program, and the organization held "Stand for Children" events in the mid-1990's in opposition to welfare reform, which threatened children's health.

The CDF can claim a number of legislative successes and a large list of contributors and supporters. It maintains an aggressive policy agenda dedicated to enhancing child immunization, nutrition, the Head Start program (an antipoverty program from the 1960's), and child care while reducing infant mortality, adolescent pregnancy, violence against children, and child poverty. As a nonprofit, private organization, the CDF is funded largely by foundations as well as by corporate grants and individual contributions. Although the organization is a visible force politically and lobbies the U.S. Congress and state legislatures, it is nonpartisan and does not accept government funding. The organization is governed by a board of directors and is organized by function into various departments, including communications, development, finance and administration, government and community affairs, and legal matters. It is headquartered in Washington, D.C., and employs more than one hundred persons at its headquarters and state offices in Ohio, Texas, and Minnesota. The CDF is arguably one of the nation's leading advocacy organizations dedicated to children's issues.

—*Robert P. Watson*

See also Child abuse; Child care; Child support; Edelman, Marian Wright; Head Start.

Children's literature

RELEVANT ISSUES: Art and the media; Children and child development; Education

SIGNIFICANCE: Reading books encourages children to think and discuss, expanding their horizons as they learn of peoples and places beyond their own immediate experience

Literature for children and young adults is instrumental in creating meaningful literacy experiences and in giving young readers an opportunity to examine values, build self-esteem, and connect with parents and community. Children's books include picture books for preschoolers and kindergartners, illustrated stories for early elementary-school children, and more mature stories for upper elementary and junior-high-school readers. High-school students often read adult novels with teenage themes. Publishers of children's literature think that they are responsible for providing reading materials that reflect the pluralism of American society.

Literature, including children's literature, began with the oral tradition of families and tribes, leading to folktales and mythology and the tradition of storytellers. Hornbooks (instructional printed sheets on wood) appeared in the 1400's, but the first children's fairytales were *Tales of Mother Goose* by the French writer Charles Perrault, published in 1698. Approximately forty years later John Newberry introduced the idea of literature written specifically for children in Europe and North America. The 1800's saw not only fairy tales by Hans Christian Andersen and the Brothers Grimm (Jacob and Wilhelm) but also the impact of illustrators of children's books, such as Randolph Caldecott and Kate Greenaway. In the 1900's children's literature became thematic, dealing with fantasy, adventure, and real people. Louisa May Alcott's *Little Women* (1868) was based on the experiences of the author's real family.

The earlier parents read to their children, the more likely the children are to become serious readers themselves. (Cindy Beres)

The Nature of Children's Literature. Children's literature includes picture books for young children and preschoolers; fairytales, folktales, and fables; myths and legends; modern fantasy and science fiction; poetry; realistic fiction; historical fiction; multicultural books; and nonfiction, including biographies and information books. Picture books rely heavily on illustrations, such as

Mother Goose books, toy books (alphabet and counting books), and picture storybooks. In evaluating picture books one must consider children's responses to the illustrations and their symbols in terms of their age, cognition, and social development. Wordless picture books rely on humor and require illustrations that accurately tell a story. Wordless books can promote oral language development in children, especially if the topics or subjects appeal to the children. Illustrations must be appropriate to children's experiences. Overcrowded drawings confuse young readers.

Although picture books rely more on illustrations than words, such books nonetheless include elements of imagination, plot, characterization, setting, humor, and style. Typical characters in picture books include animals endowed with human emotions and placed in human situations. Teachers and parents can use picture books to add to children's linguistic and cognitive development, while piquing children's intellectual curiosity about books and reading. Children's self-esteem increases as they build oral and vocabulary skills through easy-to-read books. Interaction between children and texts encourages readers to create new stories and artwork based on books they have read or heard in storytelling sessions.

Traditional tales, such as fictional folktales and fables, and nonfictional myths and legends help children understand the world and universal human rights, providing them with cultural and linguistic awareness of other peoples and places. Traditional folktales are popular with children because of easily identifiable dramatic plots featuring good and evil characters, in which heroes succeed in their struggles and villains are defeated and punished for their bad deeds. Another attractive quality of folktales is animal personification. Themes of folktales include supernatural adversaries such as dragons, helpers such as fairies, ferocious beasts, magical objects, and magical transformations.

Tales encourage young readers to understand relationships and universal values of goodness, mercy, and courage. Jewish folktales, such as those dealing with the Golem (an artificial human being), suggest that wisdom, unselfishness, and sincerity are rewarding values. African American folktales rely on oral and written traditions, often using animals to portray the harsh realities of slav-

A Day for Children's Books

April 2, the birthday of Danish writer Hans Christian Andersen (1805-1875) is commemorated as International Children's Book Day. This annual event is sponsored by the International Board on Books for Young People, which is based in Basel, Switzerland.

ery and introducing the role of the trickster. Such literature encourages storyteller and reader participation. Through such literature children can engage in dramatization and acquire crosscultural understanding by comparing and contrasting folktales from different countries. Parents and other community resources can become storytellers in schools and libraries. Older children can create and illustrate their own folktales.

Fantasy and science fiction encourage children as well as adults to become readers, to suspend disbelief, to understand multiple points of view as presented by the characters, and to affirm human strengths. C. S. Lewis's fantasy saga *Chronicles of Narnia* (1950-1956) and Madeleine L'Engle's *A Wrinkle in Time* (1961) are examples of this type of literature. Teachers and parents can interest their children in fantasy and science fiction through puppet theaters, art projects, and literature webs. The study of science can be interwoven with literature, because many science-fiction books are based on the scientific principles of astronomy, earth science, and technology. Social studies activities can also be interwoven with science fiction, because students can critically analyze social issues, such as cultural differences. Ina R. Friedman's *How My Parents Learned to Eat*, for example, describes a relationship between an American and a Japanese woman, although it has been found to present inaccurate cultural information as well as stereotypical views.

Poetry and Fiction. Poetry provides children with an opportunity to share experiences and feelings while delving into the universal concepts of numbers, colors, and time. It also helps children appreciate language and linguistic differences, expanding young readers' vocabulary. Types of poetry enjoyed by children include nursery rhymes, tongue twisters, concrete poems (shaped into pictures), free verses with little or no rhyme, and haiku (Japanese poetry of three lines). Children's interest in poetry tends to decline as they reach upper elementary grades. This may be attributed to some teachers' apparent lack of interest in sharing poetry with children. Young readers should be encouraged by teachers and parents to read poetry for appreciation and to try writing their own poems. One of the most popular poets writing for children is Shel Silverstein, who writes nonsense and humorous poetry.

Fiction, especially modern realistic fiction that is consistent with lives, issues, and values of real people in modern society, attracts young readers because they can often identify and relate to the problems and issues addressed by such literature. Judy Blume, author of *Are You There, God? It's Me, Margaret* (1970), and other writers have helped young readers learn more about themselves and the world around them. Realistic fiction is often subjected to sharp criticism and censorship because of the seemingly controversial topics it addresses, such as inner-city tensions, sexuality, and conflicts with family values. Themes in modern, realistic fiction include family life (nuclear versus extended families, single-parent families, divorce, and remarriage), child abuse, peer relationships, emotional changes, death and dying, gender roles, disability, and the elderly. "Problem"-oriented books or realistic fiction invite reflection, critical thinking, and decision-making processes. Conse-

quently, the issue of censorship versus the freedom to read is often a challenge more readily associated with realistic fiction.

Stimulating Thought and Discussion. Realistic fiction is often used in bibliotherapy to help children deal with such issues as interpersonal relationships, family disturbances, and physical maturity. Research on children's responses to realistic fiction indicates that readers up to third grade level tend to retell stories literally; fourth and fifth graders tend to identify with the characters in stories; sixth graders interpret characterization; and seventh and eighth graders tend to interpret meaning and have deeper understanding. Researchers advise those who work with literature and children such as teachers, librarians, and parents to create simulations and story webs (with topics and subtopics). For example, *Island of the Blue Dolphins* (1961) by Scott O'Dell can provide opportunities for readers to simulate island survival, in which food and shelter from the elements are scarce, while designing webs of topics: food, subtopic—food chain; shelter, subtopics—weather requirements and materials; geography, subtopics—fresh water, topography, climate. Webbing can be used to guide discussion and encourage decision making.

Realistic fiction helps readers improve self-esteem and cultural understanding by encouraging discussion of gender roles, socioeconomic status, disability, ethnicity, and age. Educators and

---

Children's Books About Divorce and Single Parenting

One trend in children's literature has been publication of realistic fiction about family problems such as divorce. This list is a sampling of popular children's books about divorce and single parenting for all age levels. The self-descriptive titles of many of these books are typical of books on real-life themes for young readers.

- Judy Blume, *It's Not the End of the World* (1982)

- Vera Cleaver and Bill Cleaver, *Ellen Grae* (1967)

- Anne Fin, *Alias Madame Doubtfire* (1990)

- Beth Goff, *Where Is Daddy? The Story of a Divorce* (1969)

- Maria Gripe, *The Night Daddy* (1971)

- Paula Z. Hogan, *Will Dad Ever Move Back Home?* (1980)

- Norma Klein, *It's Not What You Expect* (1973)

- Richard Peck, *Unfinished Portrait of Jessica* (1991)

- Ken Rush, *Friday's Journey* (1994)

- Marilyn Sachs, *The Bears' House* (1971)

- Norma Simon, *I Wish I Had My Father* (1983)

- Muriel Stack, *I Won't Go Without a Father* (1972)

- Judith Vigna, *Daddy's New Baby* (1982)

Once children truly learn to appreciate reading, they will pursue their interest at every opportunity. (James L. Shaffer)

parents can use literature to dispel myths and stereotypes. Even if books portray characters stereotypically, parents and teachers can encourage readers to analyze them and question the validity of characters' behavior. Teachers, librarians, and parents have a responsibility to help children eliminate biased and stereotypical beliefs through questioning, which encourages literal interpretation, inference, evaluation, clarification, and understanding.

Expanded Horizons. Historical fiction allows readers to step into the past by reading about historical facts and dealing with cultural heritage and human relationships. In Laura Ingalls Wilder's books, such as *Little House in the Big Woods* (1932) and *Little House on the Prairie* (1935), children can be encouraged to reenact a typical school day in the life of pioneers. Researchers indicate that children can learn to respect and appreciate history if they can relate to the experiences of characters with whom they may be able to identify.

Multiethnic literature provides children with an opportunity to appreciate and respect the values, traditions, and languages of other peoples inside and outside the United States. It also helps readers to research their own roots and appreciate their own heritage, while broadening their understanding of history, geography, and the arts. In a nation of immigrants, it is imperative that educators and parents encourage children to read accurate portrayals of ethnic groups. Multiethnic literature includes books by and about African Americans, Asian Americans, European Americans, Hispanic Americans, and Native Americans. Multiethnic books can also be by and about immigrants. They can be stories from other countries, written in foreign languages and presented with adjacent translation, and bilingual books. It is important for adults to help children evaluate these materials for historical accuracy, literary merit, and biases.

Nonfiction books include biographies and information books on various subjects, such as art, cooking, geography, pollution, and religion. Information books encourage readers to seek problem-solving strategies. Biographies and informational books must be checked for factual accuracy. Involving children in nonfiction reading enhances their research skills. Biographies can provide posi-

tive role models for children to emulate so that they can strive for success and develop values.

Values in Children's Books. Literature is instrumental in helping individuals understand and value their cultural heritage. Literature also aids children in cognitive, linguistic, personality, social, and moral development. Exposure to literature provides children with the opportunity to discuss family, pets, and the environment, while describing characters and their actions and developing language and social skills. Critical-thinking skills are also practiced as educators and parents encourage children to engage in observing, comparing, classifying, organizing, summarizing, and applying information from independent reading and storytelling. As children go through stages of personality change, they can use stories to help them understand and deal with feelings of insecurity and anger, while learning to respect and appreciate differences in others and maintain pride in their own cultural identity.

Children's self-esteem is heightened as they learn the meaning of responsible citizenship. Children's literature also helps readers understand the importance of collaborative work and community involvement. Stories read aloud or independently not only aid children in social development but also provide guidelines for moral development. Characters in children's books help readers with moral choices in terms of conformity, duty, and conscience. Katherine Paterson's *Jacob Have I Loved* (1980) is an appropriate example of a story that deals with moral choices.

Adults and children must learn and be involved in evaluating the merits of literature using appropriate selection criteria. Educators and parents should be aware that children's reading interests may vary according to gender and cultural backgrounds. Boys tend to show interest in action and adventure, while girls seem to prefer books about emotions and relationships. Children's literature must be nonbiased and nonstereotypical and present multiple perspectives for social significance. Children, like adults, must be encouraged to read not only so that they can acquire knowledge, but also so that they can relax and enjoy themselves. Thus, educators must ensure that literature be accessible to young readers and that schools, libraries, and parents become instrumental in developing reading and literacy habits.

Parental Involvement. Successful reading and literacy programs require parent-teacher cooperation. Parents play an important role in their children's early literacy and reading experiences. Parental selection of appropriate reading materials, daily storytelling and reading time, and conversations about what children have read will affect children's readiness for school and their continued interest in books. Effective teachers must reach out to parents and create a literacy partnership, especially for those families who are culturally different and whose values may differ from school culture. Educators must not impose their literary values on parents, but rather seek a partnership with families that will enhance children's learning environment. Reading and literacy flourish in nonthreatening classrooms in which children's voices are respected and children can bring their personal experiences to bear on their reading and literacy development. Educators, students, and parents must explore their own perspectives on literature, their commonalities and differences, in order to develop meaningful literacy experiences. Shared literacy in social and cultural contexts will encourage children to take an interest in books and to read and write. Parental in-

Although many children are exposed to books in their homes, their systematic introduction to literature begins in the classroom. (James L. Shaffer)

volvement will ensure continuity in students' literacy experiences at school, at the public library, and throughout adulthood.

In the classroom, teachers introduce books from students' different cultures and languages; they encourage children to share, orally or in writing, their personal and family experiences. They design literature webs to facilitate literacy connections, asking children to retell stories from their own perspective and encouraging journaling of their reading experiences. Parents help teachers find books about other cultures and help compile bibliographies of their children's choices. If needed, they can translate stories, take children to the library; and read to and with them at home. Teachers can also send home reading-interest surveys and ask parents to keep logs of the books their children read. For parents who are not fluent in English or who have lower literacy skills, schools may work with libraries in providing adult literacy programs, which improve reading, writing, language, or computer skills. There are communities and schools that offer after-school computer classes for parents and children.

In selecting literature for children, parents and teachers should choose books that appeal to children's interests. To develop positive attitudes toward reading and writing, teachers and parents must work together in finding literature that is appropriate to the age level and reading ability of students. Once children acquire a taste for reading, they will be ready to move to more complex texts and issues. Other outreach efforts include planning literacy projects that involve the entire family, such as creating a children's literature quilt. With many families working long hours, it is also important for schools to form partnerships with community organizations, such as boys' and girls' clubs, to collaborate in after-school literacy programs.

Censorship. Parents and organized groups often censor what children read because they fear that "realistic" subject matter will conflict with parents' religious, social, and political beliefs. Thus, children's books are banned because their themes, characters, and language are considered objectionable by parents and other community members. However, many educators, parents, and writers of children's realistic literature have joined the American Library Association and its Intellec-

tual Freedom Committee in developing guidelines for counteracting censorship. Those who select children's books—teachers, librarians, and parents—should have clear guidelines for assessing reading materials in terms of literary merit, reader appeal, and community concerns. For example, if the theme of a book is drugs, those evaluating it must ask how the author approaches the subject, whether or not the book presents a balanced view, and whether or not it warns young readers about the dangers of substance abuse.

Children's books have often been censored because they are seen as biased and contain sexist and racist ideas and language, racial stereotypes, and derogatory descriptions of culturally diverse groups. Books that discuss sex, describe extramarital relationships, and express un-American ideas have been censored because they raise controversial issues that are seen as undermining the family, society, human relationships, and traditional values. Other books have been censored because they are perceived to have low educational value and objectionable content. Some censored books are branded as "trash"; others are accused of "secular humanism" and blamed for revising values. Books with culturally diverse themes, books dealing with ethnic studies, multicultural education, critical thinking, and ecology have also fallen victim to censorship.

Examples of works that have been censored and, at times, removed from libraries include the Bible, because certain passages are seen as violent; dictionaries, because they contain "dirty words" (the *American Heritage Dictionary* was banned by a school board in Missouri); *The Lorax* (1971) by Dr. Seuss, because it advocates saving trees and forests and offended a community of Oregon loggers; and several Judy Blume books such as *Are You There, God? It's Me, Margaret*, because they deal with such themes as sexual awareness, menstruation, masturbation, and premarital sex. Other censored works have included Alice Childress's *A Hero Ain't Nothin' but a Sandwich* (1973), S. E. Hinton's *The Outsiders* (1967), Robert Cormier's *Chocolate War* (1974), and Eve Merriam's *The Inner City Mother Goose* (1969). *The Diary of Anne Frank* (English trans., 1952) was censored on the grounds that it was a "downer" and Maya Angelou's *I Know Why the Caged Bird Sings* (1970) was censored because it allegedly "preached hatred and bitterness toward

Two of the most famous figures in children's literature, Tom Sawyer and Huck Finn are commemorated in a statue in Hannibal, Missouri, where their creator, Mark Twain, grew up. (R. Kent Rasmussen)

whites." Mark Twain's *Adventures of Huckleberry Finn* (1884) and Katherine Paterson's *Jacob Have I Loved* were censored for containing inappropriate language. Many other examples of censorship cases that have made their way through the courts are listed in the *Newsletter on Intellectual Freedom* by the American Library Association.

—*Maria A. Pacino*

BIBLIOGRAPHY

Cianciolo, Patricia J. *Picture Books for Children*. Chicago: ALA, 1990. Recommends nearly five hundred books for children from infancy through age sixteen and is indexed by author, title, and illustrator.

Donnelson, Kenneth L., and Alleen Pace Nilsen. *Literature for Today's Young Adult*. New York: HarperCollins, 1993. Well-indexed, comprehensive, and detailed book on literature for young people with illustrations and extensive discussion of various titles and themes.

Freeman, Judy. *Books Kids Will Sit Still For*. New Providence, N.J.: R. R. Bowker, 1990. Describes storytelling, reading aloud, booktalks, and other strategies for engaging children in reading and recommends more than two thousand books.

Miller-Lachmann, Lyn. *Our Family, Our Friends, Our World: An Annotated Guide to Significant Multicultural Books for Children and Young Adults*. Providence, N.J.: R. R. Bowker, 1992. Excellent resource for educators and parents that includes annotations of titles, listing strengths and weaknesses, and an author, title, and subject index.

National Council of Teachers of English. Committee on the Elementary School Booklist. *Adventuring with Books: A Booklist for Pre-K-Grade 6*. 9th ed. Urbana, Ill.: Author, 1989. Recommends children's books from early ages through sixth grade, includes bibliography, age and grade levels, and is indexed by author, illustrator, and subject.

Norton, Donna E. *Through the Eyes of a Child: An Introduction to Children's Literature*. 4th ed. Columbus, Ohio: Merrill, 1995. Excellent, comprehensive book on many aspects of children's literature that includes illustrations and recommended titles with extensive discussion, author profiles, and index.

Pilla, Marianne Lano. *The Best: High/Low Books for Reluctant Readers*. Englewood, Colo: Libraries Unlimited, 1990. Recommends more than three hundred titles of recreational books for grades three through twelve and includes bibliographic information and reading levels.

Rochman, Hazel. *Against Borders: Promoting Books for a Multicultural World*. Chicago: American Library Association, 1993. Ideas on curriculum activities for grades six through twelve focusing on the themes of family, friends, and outsiders.

Spredemann Dreyer, Sharon. *The Best of Bookfinder: A Guide to Children's Literature About Interests and Concerns of Youth Ages 2-12*. Circle Pines, Minn.: American Guidance Service, 1992. Recommends more than 650 titles in three volumes, with bibliographic information, age levels, and an extensive index.

Van Orden, Phyllis J. *The Collection Program in Schools*. Englewood, Colo: Libraries Unlimited, 1995. Primarily written for librarians, this book can also be used by teachers and parents for aiding in selecting library materials.

Zvirin, Stephanie. *The Best Years of Their Lives: A Resource Guide for Teenagers in Crisis*. Chicago: American Library Association, 1992. Recommends more than two hundred fiction and nonfiction books for children ages twelve through eighteen and includes bibliographic information, age levels, and annotations.

See also Bedtime reading; Children's magazines; Educating children; Family values; Home schooling; Literature and families; Myths and storytelling; Schools.

Children's magazines

RELEVANT ISSUES: Art and the media; Demographics; Education

SIGNIFICANCE: Children's magazines educate and entertain their readers and reflect the attitudes, ideas, family values, times, and interests of their editors, authors, illustrators, readers, and parents of their readers

American magazine publishers have succeeded in attracting and holding readers aged two to seventeen, despite changing reader tastes, habits, opinions, and circumstances. They have provided publications for children and by children. The best

Illustrations are a crucial part of all children's magazines. (Cindy Beres)

magazines have introduced children and teenagers to the finest writers, illustrators, photographers, and editorial minds of their times. They have educated and entertained. They have given readers the opportunity to tell how they experience the world, not how adults have believed children and teenagers experience it.

The First Magazines. The nation's first periodical for children, *The Children's Magazine*, was published in January, 1789, in Hartford, Connecticut, by printer Barzillai Hudson and his partner, George Goodwin. The new magazine was designed to help readers make the transition from elementary books to more demanding ones. However, it folded with its April issue.

From 1789 through the 1830's the religious, educational, and reform interests of adults and children shaped children's magazines. *The Juvenile Port-Folio and Literary Miscellany*, for example, was founded in 1812 by fourteen-year-old Thomas G. Condie. It is one of the earliest examples of a publication edited by a child for children.

The 1830's marked the beginning of reform-oriented magazines for youth. The *Slave's Friend*, for instance, was founded in 1836 by the American Anti-Slavery Society. By the 1840's organizations such as the American Sunday School Union and American Temperance Union were publishing children's magazines. Besides urging pious conduct, children's magazines frequently condemned slavery, intemperance, the use of tobacco, and other vices. Education became the major editorial focus in magazines published from the 1840's through the Civil War. Publishers sought to ad-

Magazines have played a growing role in classroom education. (James L. Shaffer)

vance the cause of public education and to provide supplementary material for reading instruction, geography, and science.

From 1865 until 1900 secular publications focused primarily on entertainment and amusement. The first modern children's magazine, *Our Young Folks*, appeared in January, 1865, marking the beginning of recreational reading as a desirable end. Its writers advocated rural living, strenuous physical activity, and the virtues of honesty and self-reliance. Contributors included Harriet Beecher Stowe, Louisa May Alcott, and other famous literary figures. *St. Nicholas*, which began publishing in November of 1873, is often considered the best-loved and best-remembered American children's magazine.

All these magazines viewed children as needing adult supervision and guidance. Late nineteenth century editors and writers wanted not only to entertain their readers but also to foster American culture, worldviews, and values. They believed they were educating and influencing the future leaders of America.

Modern Magazines. Magazines since 1900 have done much to segment their audiences and appeal to the varied interests and ages of their readers. They have even targeted readers who want to read only works by other children and teenagers. For example, *Boys' Life*, founded in 1911 by the Boy Scouts of America, sought to mold character and foster self-improvement. *Ranger Rick's Nature Magazine*, published by the National Wildlife Federation, has helped children identify with nature and use natural resources wisely. *National Geographic World*, published by the National Geographic Society, has focused on inspiring readers to learn about natural history, science, and the outdoors.

Many periodicals have targeted specific age groups with unique interests, such as *Field and Stream, Jr.*, which has been devoted to passing on the hunting and fishing tradition to preteen boys and girls. General interest magazines have continued to hold their place. *Highlights for Children*, whose motto is "Fun with a Purpose," has worked to help children be happy, useful citizens, to feel that it is manly or womanly to help their mothers, to be thoughtful and kind to animals and younger children, to read the Bible, to pray, and to go to Sunday school. *Cricket: The Magazine for Children*

has devoted itself to stimulating children's imaginations and their love of fine literature and art. *Merlyn's Pen* has published separate editions of fiction written by teenagers for teenagers. Through Disney character tie-ins and celebrity interviews, *Disney Adventures*, published for children aged six to fourteen, has concentrated on promoting reading as entertainment.

Market Research. Publishers have become more sophisticated in developing magazines. To shape editorial content and design, they have surveyed readers, conducted panel discussions, and established focus groups to determine reader tastes, habits, and opinions.

Reader research has shown that children like magazines. They like having something of their own arrive in the mail with their own name on it and which they can read again and again. In addition, readers want to be engaged and challenged by magazines' content and advertising, much as they want to be entertained when they watch commercials on television. They also want to feel a sense of ownership in a magazine—to know that it is their kind of magazine.

Research has also indicated that children and teenagers consider printed material educational and believable, because they associate reading with school. Parents regard magazines as a bridge to books. This parental seal of approval, coupled with the fact that children like reading magazines, explains why magazines have survived competition from television, cinema, radio, videos, the Internet, and comic books.

Advertising. Advertisers' interest in the purchasing power of children only partially explains the continuing popularity, success, and importance of children's magazines. Well-educated and well-heeled parents and grandparents buy subscriptions to give their children and grandchildren educational advantages. They believe that magazines are important, especially when they reflect their own family and personal values.

Magazines have served two major marketing purposes. First, they have delivered advertising messages to particular audiences of children and teenagers. Second, they have instilled loyalty to products made by companies such as Nintendo and to causes represented by the National Wildlife Federation, National Geographic Society, Consumers Union, and other special-interest organiza-

As children grow older, they tend to switch from children's to adult magazines on their own. (James L. Shaffer)

tions. Some companies, institutions, and organizations have viewed advertising in children's magazines as an investment in the future, hoping to instill loyalty to their products and causes that will last a lifetime. Few children's magazines are sold over the counter or in schools. Most are sold by mail subscriptions.

Periodicals such as *Cobblestone, Calliope,* and *Faces* have carried no advertising. *Sesame Street* magazine itself has not carried advertising, but it has included advertising in an accompanying parents' guide. Instead of advertising, some magazines have allowed corporate sponsorship. For example, *P3* (or *Plant Three*), an environmental magazine, carried a full-page message in its spring, 1991, issue from Patagonia clothing describing the company's commitment to preserving nature.

Publishers have also been aware that new groups of children and teenagers are needed as their readers outgrow their publications. As a result, they must sell their publications over and over again to old and new readers, issue after issue, while adapting to changing readers and times. To meet new competition, magazines must offer a blend of features and departments that readers expect in each issue, as well as features that exceed their readers' expectations. Readers must find their magazines continually interesting, or the magazines will die.

Children's magazines have survived for more than two hundred years because they have met the needs of their readers for advice, assistance, instruction, escape, creative outlets, and entertainment. Some have argued that children's magazines continue to be valued transmitters of family values and cultural heritage, especially in an age when young people are exposed to a great deal of sex, violence, crime, and materialistic behavior in television programs, music, newspapers, and cinema. —*Fred Buchstein*

BIBLIOGRAPHY

Abrahamson, David. *Magazine-Made America: The Cultural Transformation of the Postwar Periodical.* Cresskill, N.J.: Hampton Press, 1996.

Guber, Selina S., and Jon Berry. *Marketing to and Through Kids.* New York: McGraw-Hill, 1993.

Kelly, R. Gordon. *Children's Periodicals of the United States.* Westport, Conn.: Greenwood Press, 1984.

_____. *Mother Was a Lady: Self and Society in Selected American Children's Periodicals, 1865-1890.* Westport, Conn.: Greenwood Press, 1974.

Mott, Frank Luther. *A History of American Magazines.* 5 vols. Cambridge, Mass.: Harvard University Press, 1938.

Stoll, Donald R., ed. *Magazines for Kids and Teens: A Resource for Parents, Teachers, Librarians and Kids.* Newark, Del.: International Reading Association, 1994.

Tebbel, John W., and Mary Ellen Zuckerman. *The Magazine in America, 1741-1990.* New York: Oxford University Press, 1991.

See also Advertising; Childhood history; Children's literature; Entertainment; Literature and families; News media and families.

Children's rights

RELEVANT ISSUES: Children and child development; Economics and work; Law; Violence

SIGNIFICANCE: During the nineteenth and twentieth centuries, when the West achieved industrialization and urbanization, mass manufacturing reduced both pride in craftsmanship and workers' bargaining power, leading to the exploitation of unskilled women and children as cheap laborers who were considered more malleable and less contentious than men

With alienation from skilled labor came alienation from the nuclear family. Rapid urbanization without a social safety net caused many children to fall through the cracks in the system. This resulted in continuous policy debates over the use of child labor as well as debates over the legal rights of children in disadvantaged circumstances.

In the postindustrial world of the late twentieth century, "rights" movements have proliferated. Children's rights came together with social and civil rights in a general antipoverty movement. High divorce rates, feminism, and alternative lifestyles changed the nature of the American family. In this context, children's rights advocates expanded the very notion of children's rights.

Meanwhile, the old debate about child labor became an international issue. In an increasingly integrated world economy, children's and human rights advocates have taken up the cause for children's well-being on a global scale.

Child Labor. In 1790 the first machines to spin cotton were introduced in the United States. These were largely manned by children who were paid thirty-three to sixty-seven cents per week. By the 1820's about half of the cotton textile workers were children under sixteen. Most adults thought it desirable that children be employed in useful work.

By the 1850's, the industrial pace increased, and many states began to pass laws restricting child labor. The richer, unionized industrial states led the way, while the Southern states lagged behind. Connecticut had some form of child-labor law as early as 1842. Vermont was the last New England state to adopt a child labor law in 1867. In 1874 Massachusetts restricted the daily working hours of women and children to ten, and by the 1890's most other states had followed suit. Nevertheless, as late as 1896 Mississippi, Kentucky, Arkansas, and North Carolina had no laws against child labor, and in 1900 about 1.7 million children under the age of sixteen worked full-time. This exceeded the size of the entire membership of the American Federation of Labor at that time.

Existing laws were poorly enforced. In New Jersey, for example, compulsory education laws tried to put some life into child-labor laws. An 1883 act required New Jersey employers to certify that their child laborers had gone to school. The state appointed a single "inspector" for the entire state and the law was observed mostly in the breach.

Progressive Legislation and the New Deal. Sparked by the National Child Labor Committee (1904), nearly every state within a decade banned the employment of children under sixteen and limited the working hours of older children to eight or ten per day. Many states also outlawed night work and dangerous work. All of these laws, however, remained poorly enforced.

The landscape of legal legislation was, however, changing. The "Brandeis brief," which was first employed in *Muller v. Oregon* (1908), a case that involved the exploitation of women workers, became the standard argument for protecting vulnerable workers by means of social legislation. Instead of merely arguing the pros and cons of a law's constitutionality, the brilliant lawyer and later Supreme Court justice Louis D. Brandeis introduced the idea of lawyers including materials demonstrating or denying the economic or social necessities behind laws in question.

This line of reasoning led to the Keating-Owen Child Labor Act of 1916 which, using the extension of federal police powers, barred child-made goods from interstate commerce. By the narrowest of margins, the U.S. Supreme Court in *Hammer v. Dagenhart* (1918) invalidated the act as violating the Tenth Amendment of the U.S. Constitution, arguing that it prohibited rather than regulated commerce. The Court later unanimously reversed itself in *Darby v. United States* (1941).

In another attempt at progressive legislation, Congress passed the Child Labor Act in 1919. This act added a 10 percent federal tax on goods made by child labor. The Court also rejected this attempt to diminish child labor when it ruled in *Bailey v. Drexel Furniture Co.* (1922) that a tax cannot be a penalty. Again, the Court reversed itself in *Mulford v. Smith* (1939), which upheld the constitutionality of the New Deal Agricultural Adjustment Act. This decision declared that the motives of Congress are irrelevant to the validity of legislation. Finally, the 1938 Fair Labor Standards Act formally abolished child labor.

Orphaned, Abused, and Abandoned Children. The problem of orphaned or unwanted children has been around since the dawn of history. Some civilizations have practiced exposure (abandonment) while others have favored infanticide. In New York City, by the middle of the nineteenth century infanticide was common. Birth control methods were primitive and practically unknown, and abortions were dangerous. Unwanted children who survived were treated as adult paupers. Children of all ages were thrown into almshouses with the sick, senile, handicapped, and insane. It was only in the mid-nineteenth century that orphan asylums began cropping up here and there.

Charles Loring Brace believed that all institutions were bad for children. Born to a prominent Connecticut family and educated for the ministry, Brace founded the New York Children's Aid Society in 1853, when he was twenty-seven years old. His philosophy for children was gainful work, education, and a wholesome family atmosphere. His answer was "placing out," or placing children in rural homes out West rather than in institutions. Placing out was not new; it had been practiced in France for centuries. However, Brace insisted that all foster homes should be free of cost and that they should not become a system of indentured servitude. For the next seventy-five years, the New York Children's Aid Society, either through agents or direct requests, learned of towns that were interested in foster children, set up local committees to screen applicants, and brought children and families together. The Society spread to the Midwest, and "orphan trains" became part of American folklore.

According to the Society's records, placing out worked well. Out of a batch of children that went to Indiana in 1859, two became governors: Andrew H. Burke of North Dakota and John Green Brady, a missionary and trader who was appointed governor of Alaska Territory by presidents William McKinley and Theodore Roosevelt. In a 1900 survey the society went through all its records and determined that 87 percent of it placements were doing well.

The celebrated "Mary Ellen" case also broke new ground in child protective services. A horribly abused ten-year-old girl was rescued from a New York tenement in 1874 thanks to the unflagging efforts of a Methodist caseworker, Etta Angell Wheeler. No laws had existed up until that time to remove children from the custody of their parents. Enlisting the help of Henry Bergh, the energetic and sanctimonious founder of the New York Society for the Prevention of Cruelty to Animals (SPCA), Wheeler, Elbridge Gerry, and James Wright founded the Society for the Prevention of Cruelty to Children (SPCC). Cornelius Vanderbilt helped to bankroll the organization. Using a writ of habeas corpus (a legal writ to bring a party before a judge), they succeeded in saving Mary Ellen so that she could live a long, happy, and productive life. The society also fought for child-protection legislation.

Advances in social work, the care of the needy and dependent, and a growing knowledge of child development dovetailed with the Progressive movement. A 1909 White House conference on child development called by Theodore Roosevelt was unanimous in recommending that families should be kept together whenever possible. New state laws provided widow's pensions, sickness insurance, compulsory education, and curbs on child labor—all of which improved children's chances of succeeding in the city.

Children's Rights Expanded. In the latter part of the twentieth century "children's rights" has been an ill-defined term. It invokes debates over everything from school lunches and abortion rights to bicycle helmets and children divorcing parents. In many cases, children's rights has as much to do with adults as children.

The past has been a prelude to a whole array of child-advocacy measures. Potential victims now have a law to protect them from sexual predators. In 1995 New Jersey passed a law ("Megan's Law") mandating that all recently released sex offenders report to the local police for registration. The police must then inform residents, schools, and youth groups of offenders' addresses. More than forty states have passed similar legislation. In 1997, federal lawmakers considered legislation to combat child abuse and neglect and discussed bills called the Early Learning Act of 1997 and Children's National Security Act.

Children have also figured in a renewed debate about their labor rights. The 1938 Fair Labor Standards Act prohibited children from performing "physically hazardous" jobs or jobs that are "detrimental to their health and well-being." However, as of 1996 only four states had set limits on how late teenagers can work. President Bill Clinton and other politicians have called for teen curfews for various reasons, but curfews typically make exceptions for those who work. Such curfews may be illegal. In 1997 the Ninth U.S. Court of Appeals struck down a fifty-year-old San Diego curfew that made it unlawful for people under eighteen to "loiter, idle, wander, stroll, or play" in unsupervised places between 10:00 P.M. and daylight. The court said the law was "quite simply an exercise of sweeping state control irrespective of parents' wishes."

Despite the landmark Supreme Court case *In re Gault* (1967), which held that juvenile courts must afford the same protections to children as are afforded adults under the Bill of Rights, most court decisions still avow that children have lesser rights than adults. In the 1969 decision *Tinker v. Des Moines Independent School District* the Supreme Court ruled that students' right to free speech ends when it "materially and substantially" disrupts the work and discipline of the school. In 1985 the Court ruled in *New Jersey v. TLO* that students have less protection than adults from searches. It opined that students' protection from unreasonable search and seizure must be weighed against schools' right to provide a safe learning environment. Finally, in *DeShaney v. Winnebago County* (1989) the court declared that government may be legally powerless to prevent child abuse, because government may not interfere with the family.

The courts have also been reluctant to allow children to "divorce" their biological parents. A 1993 Florida appellate decision involving a twelve-year-old boy named Gregory Kingsley overturned

One manifestation of the children's rights movement is the recognition that children have the same right to protection from injury as adults. (Dick Hemingway)

his adoption, declaring that because he was a minor he did not have the legal right to sue his mother. This celebrated "divorce" case became the classic case of a "bad" mother who had abandoned her child versus the good family who had adopted him. The story of Gregory K. became the theme of two television films.

Progressive attorneys and advocates became anxious about this new children's rights movement. They were afraid it would function to the detriment of single mothers, particularly those on welfare. They alluded to the work of the nineteenth century Children's Aid Society: "Our history shows that we did break up families and remove children because of economic reasons and because of cultures we did not understand," said Judge Charles Gill of Connecticut, who was the head of the National Task Force for Childrens' Constitutional Rights in 1993. "But we're trying to allay the fears that poor parents will lose their kids."

Children's Defense Fund. Founded by Marian Wright Edelman in 1973, the Children's Defense Fund (CDF) inherited the legacy of the 1960's effort to wage a war on poverty. The organization brought together elements of welfare rights and civil rights, forging a coalition in the name of children's rights. The CDF has defended from budgetary assaults such 1960's Great Society programs as Head Start and the Women, Infants, and

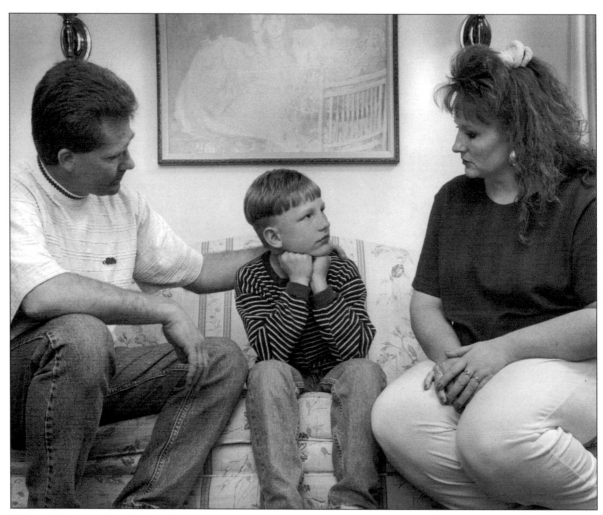

Acknowledgment that children have rights that must be recognized does not mean that parents must abdicate their responsibility for certain important decisions. (James L. Shaffer)

Children Program (WIC). Viewing poverty as a children's issue, the CDF has been very successful in acquiring money for the legislation it has advocated. The organization led a coalition of liberal interest groups that lobbied for a five-billion-dollar child-care bill enacted in 1990. The bill provided grants to states for child care, expanded Head Start education for preschoolers, and offered tax credits to low-income families with young children. Bankrolled by corporate America, the CDF has an estimated annual budget of $9 million and 120 employees. It is one of Washington's best-known and best-connected lobbies.

International Law. In 1989 the United Nations General Assembly passed the Convention on the Rights of the Child. By agreeing to the thirty articles contained therein, nations agree to commit themselves to furnish the basic elements of nutrition, education, and health to all children. In all, 187 of 193 members of the United Nations have ratified the convention. The United States signed the document in 1995, but the U.S. Senate delayed its ratification. Skeptics argued about the convention's provisions that might interfere with the rights of families. Additionally, some people are concerned that the United States might have to pay a disproportionate share of the expenses incurred in furnishing United Nations assistance to nations attempting to comply with the convention.

The United States has taken a stand against worldwide abuses in domestic and overseas sweatshops, particularly in the apparel industry. In 1997 a presidential task force was appointed with representatives from such industry giants as Nike, Reebok, L. L. Bean, and Liz Claiborne, as well as representatives of labor and human rights groups. The task force proposed a code of conduct that would prohibit labor by children under the age of fifteen, limit the workweek to sixty hours, and stop the abuse of workers. The code further calls for companies to hire independent monitors to stop abuses. The task force's recommendations represent a start, but given the vagaries of international enforcement, international children's labor rights have a long way to go. —*Brian G. Tobin*

BIBLIOGRAPHY

DiConsiglio, John. "The Rights Stuff." *Scholastic Update* 129 (February 7, 1997). Reviews Teen's Bill of Rights cases and applicable Supreme Court precedents.

Drinan, Robert F. "Proclaiming the Rights of Children." *America* 175 (August 31, 1996). Clergyman's plea for U.S. ratification of the United Nations Convention on Children's Rights.

Friedman, Lawrence M. *A History of American Law.* New York: Simon & Schuster, 1973. Concise discussion of child labor laws.

Fry, Annette Riley. "The Children's Crusade." *American Heritage* 26 (December, 1974). Sympathetic look at the Children's Aid Society of the nineteenth and twentieth centuries.

Garraty, John A. *The American Nation.* 4th ed. New York: Harper & Row, 1979. Thorough history text that includes explanations of changing attitudes in the United States toward children and the family.

Hall, Kermit L., ed. *The Oxford Companion to the Supreme Court of the United States.* New York: Oxford University Press, 1992. Excellent reference work for exploring relevant Court decisions, including those dealing children's issues.

Healy, Melissa. "Congress Has Kids on the Brain." *San Francisco Chronicle*, June 2, 1997. Explains the rush to embrace legislation on child-related issues.

Herbert, Bob. "A Good Start." *The New York Times*, April 14, 1997. Explores the U.S. presidential initiative to limit overseas child labor.

Kaus, Mickey. "The Godmother." *The New Republic* 208 (Feb. 15, 1993). Critical appraisal of Marian Wright Edelman, founder of the Children's Defense Fund in 1973, which inherited the legacy of the 1960's effort to wage a war on poverty.

Shapiro, Andrew L. "Children in Court—The New Crusade." *The Nation* 257 (Sept. 27, 1993). Comments on the expanding rights of children and the larger implications of this trend.

Stevens, Peter, and Marian Eide. "The First Chapter of Children's Rights." *American Heritage* 41 (July/Aug., 1990). Story of Mary Ellen, a horribly abused ten-year-old girl who was rescued from a New York tenement in 1874, and how, more than a century later, the struggle continues in the fight against child abuse.

See also Age of consent; Child abandonment; Child abuse; Children's Defense Fund (CDF); Curfews; Edelman, Marian Wright; Guardianship;

In re Gault; Juvenile courts; Megan's Law; Parental divorce; Paternity suits; Supplemental Nutrition Program for Women, Infants, and Children; United Nations Convention on the Rights of the Child.

Chinese Americans

RELEVANT ISSUES: Children and child development; Kinship and genealogy; Race and ethnicity

SIGNIFICANCE: Chinese Americans have drawn on a tradition of strong family relationships to help overcome discrimination and become one of the most successful immigrant groups in the United States

Chinese Americans constitute the oldest and largest Asian American group in the United States. North Americans who identify themselves as Chinese are scattered throughout the fifty states and Canada with their largest concentrations in California, New York, Hawaii, Massachusetts, Illinois, British Columbia, and Ontario. According to the 1990 United States census, Americans of Chinese ancestry from China, Hong Kong, and Taiwan numbered more than 1,700,000 persons. More than many other ethnic groups, Chinese Americans have labored to maintain the tradition of strong families and obedience to cultural traditions. While the roles of Chinese Americans underwent great changes after World War II, most of them strongly desire to maintain traditions fostered by obedience to Confucian traditions.

Immigration and Discrimination. Significant Chinese immigration to North America began in response to the California gold rush of 1848-1849. Seven thousand miles across the Pacific Ocean China was a rapidly growing country plagued by foreign domination, political instability, and a weakened dynastic government. Before 1848 political and social stability in China had discouraged emigration to North America.

After news of American "mountains of gold" reached southern China, thousands of Chinese men joined Germans, Irish, Spanish, English, and other immigrants in the hunt for gold in Northern California. San Francisco was soon dubbed Jinshan, or "golden mountain," by newly arrived Chinese settlers. Mainly from southern China, Chinese immigrants were predominantly male. Most hoped to make money and return to their families in China. Like most gold seekers, these settlers became more frustrated than rich.

Reluctant to return home without money, most Chinese accepted positions in various trades that sought workers to offset severe labor shortages in the West. While typically paid less than non-Asian workers, Chinese immigrants were reluctant to return to the political instability and lower wages that awaited them in China. Chinese workers played an important part in the construction of the western section of the transcontinental railroad. Chinese immigrants working on the railroad were so valued for their dedication to hard work that the Central Pacific Railroad began to recruit workers in China. Even after the railroad was completed, immigration from China continued, and newly arrived Chinese immigrants were able to find jobs in factories and farms. Between 1860 and 1880 immigrants from China constituted more than 8 percent of California's population.

Scapegoating Chinese Immigrants. As the North American economy entered a depression in the early 1880's, Chinese immigrants became convenient scapegoats for populist politicians, labor unions, and unemployed non-Asians. In Canadian British Columbia the small Chinese population was blamed by many for the overall economic downturn. In response to growing anti-Chinese sentiments in the West, the United States moved to ban Chinese immigration with the passage of the Chinese Exclusion Act of 1882. The law suspended Chinese immigration and declared Chinese immigrants already in the United States ineligible for citizenship. While Chinese immigrants made up only an estimated 0.002 percent of the American population at the time, the act received wide support and severely limited Chinese immigration into the next century. In 1888 the Scott Act stiffened the 1882 law by prohibiting the entry of Chinese nationals into the United States. The Geary Act of 1892 extended the exclusion of Chinese immigrants by denying habeas corpus rights to persons of Chinese ancestry and requiring all persons of Chinese ancestry to register with local authorities. Immediate deportation threatened those Chinese immigrants who failed to comply with the requirement that they carry official permits. Despite a court challenge by American citi-

A tradition of strong families has helped Chinese Americans to overcome a long history of discrimination. (James L. Shaffer)

zens of Chinese ancestry, the act was upheld by the U.S. Supreme Court. On the West Coast, numerous local laws were passed to limit the growth of Chinese businesses and settlements.

Severely hindered by discriminatory legal codes and racism, Chinese immigrants responded by constructing social structures to serve the needs of their existing population. So-called "Chinatowns" established schools, newspapers, businesses, and cultural institutions. For the most part, Chinese immigrants maintained a willingness to preserve family and cultural traditions despite the racism

Discriminatory laws and mistreatment at the hands of white Americans encouraged early Chinese immigrants to live close together, giving rise to a tradition of "Chinatowns" in most major Pacific coast cities. (Ben Klaffke)

they experienced in North America. The 1906 San Francisco earthquake marked an important milestone in the growth of the Chinese American family. At that time, only 5 percent of the city's Chinese population were female. After the city's birth records were destroyed in the earthquake, thousands of Chinese claimed they had been born in the United States. Unable to refute their applications for naturalization, the U.S. government was forced to grant them citizenship and allow Chinese spouses to immigrate to the United States. After Chinese families were reunited, the traditional Confucian value of obedience and dedication to family remained an important element in Chinese American culture.

The Making of a "Model Minority." As discriminatory practices and laws were overturned in the twentieth century, Chinese Americans moved to integrate themselves into the mainstream of American culture. The U.S. alliance with China in its fight against Japan during World War II served as a major impetus to repeal barriers to immigration. As restrictions on immigration eased, families grew and typically worked hard to obtain educational opportunities for their children. The emphasis on education was so successful that by 1970 56 percent of working Chinese held white-collar jobs, a figure above the national average.

Chinese Americans have generally attempted to maintain ties to their homeland and adhere to cultural traditions. Central to this effort is their use of the Chinese language as part of primary and secondary education. Knowledge of the Chinese language is a valued cultural tradition and a marketable job skill, particularly as North American trade with Asia has grown. In addition to preserving their language, most Chinese Americans observe traditional Chinese festivals. The most significant, the so-called Spring Festival, or Chinese New Year, is widely observed by Chinese Americans. This celebration is based upon the Chinese lunar calendar and is marked by a large family meal on New Year's eve. Children are presented with *hong bao*, red envelopes containing money, and fireworks are often used to scare off evil spirits. In 1993 the U.S. Postal Service issued a commemorative stamp in honor of the Chinese New Year.

Other major festivals include the mid-autumn Moon Festival to celebrate the annual harvest.

Similar to the North American tradition of Thanksgiving Day, this festival celebrates the harvest and the good fortunes of the previous year. This holiday also centers on a large family dinner and is marked by the consumption of moon cakes stuffed with candied fruits. Other major festivals include the Dragon Boat Festival on the fifth day of the fifth moon according to the Chinese calendar. This festival is celebrated with sticky rice cakes and boat races.

As Chinese immigration swelled in the 1980's and 1990's, the role of the family in Chinese culture continued to change. As Chinese Americans became socially and economically diverse and obtained higher-paying jobs, the traditional commitment to the wishes of the family weakened. Because of the economic successes of some Chinese Americans, stereotypes have also undergone radical change. Once denounced as "coolies" for their willingness to work hard for lower wages, many Chinese have been labeled a "model minority" for their perceived overcommitment to financial responsibility, education, and work. While it is significant that many Chinese Americans have college degrees, many of them resent the "model minority" stereotype, because it tends to overlook the discrimination toward Chinese Americans that has persisted in American culture.

—*Lawrence I. Clark*

BIBLIOGRAPHY
Brownstone, David M. *The Chinese-American Heritage.* New York: Facts On File, 1988.
Daley, William. *The Chinese Americans.* New York: Chelsea House, 1995.
Daniels, Roger. *Asian America: Chinese and Japanese in the United States Since 1850.* Seattle: University of Washington Press, 1988.
Hoobler, Dorothy, and Thomas Hoobler. *The Chinese American Family Album.* New York: Oxford University Press, 1994.
Ng, Franklin, ed. *Asian American Encyclopedia.* 6 vols. New York: Marshall Cavendish, 1995.
She, Collen. *A Student's Guide to Chinese American Genealogy.* Phoenix, Ariz.: Rosen Publishing Group, 1996.

See also Ancestor worship; Arranged marriages; Communities; East Indians and Pakistanis; Family: concept and history; Family gatherings and reunions; Filipino Americans; Generational relationships; Japanese Americans; Korean Americans; Pacific Islanders; Southeast Asian Americans; Vietnamese Americans; War brides; Weddings.

Circumcision

RELEVANT ISSUES: Health and medicine; Religious beliefs and practices

SIGNIFICANCE: Male circumcision is a surgical operation that involves the cutting of the prepuce or foreskin covering the *glans penis*

The ages at which males have been circumcised have varied throughout history. The Maya and peoples of eastern Mexico performed circumcisions soon after boys' births, whereas the Jews, Samaritans, and Abyssinians performed them a week after male babies were born. Some peoples delayed the rite until puberty. The earliest forms of circumcision were often extreme. Among the Somali, Masai, and a few Kikuyu of East Africa a cut was made on the upper part of the glans itself, while among the Australian Aborigines a slash was made along the shaft of the penis. The implements used to perform these types of circumcisions ranged from hard stone and sharp metal tools to glass and wooden knives.

Circumcision was common among many primitive peoples. A rite of initiation into tribes or clans, circumcision was also seen as a test of physical endurance, a social distinction, and a preparation for sexual life. In some tribes, women refused to have sexual intercourse with uncircumcised males. The primary significance of circumcision, however, was religious, for among most early peoples all reproductive matters were connected in some way with religion. For example, in ancient Egypt circumcision was restricted to priests and warriors. The British anthropologist Sir James Frazer discovered that the circumcision rite was connected to a belief in reincarnation. Some peoples believed that men's new birth would be facilitated if they could reserve a stock of vital energy for the use of their disembodied spirit by detaching a part of themselves and depositing it somewhere sacred. In ancient times, Semitic circumcision was a sacrifice to the goddess of fertility before it was regarded as a covenant with God.

A common practice among modern Jews and Muslims, circumcision is of fundamental importance to their religions, although it is not regarded as a sacrament. For the Jews, the practice has always been performed in the presence of men and generally in temples or synagogues. Those performing circumcisions, however, have changed from boys' fathers to *mohels*, or trained professionals. During the Roman Empire, Jews were mocked for the rite of circumcision, because the Romans believed that foreskins were cosmetically important for ideal beauty. Indeed, Roman athletic games required competitors to have foreskins that completely covered the glans, and some circumcised athletes from North Africa and the eastern Mediterranean had to undergo operations in which a new prepuce was surgically created. Many early Christians were circumcised, but after controversies flared up in the early Church it was decided that circumcision was unnecessary, especially for converts.

Circumcision became increasingly popular in the United States in the nineteenth century after Sir Richard F. Burton, the English explorer, noted that some physicians believed it discouraged masturbation (onanism). In modern times, however, circumcision in the United States is performed for health reasons by hospital surgeons, especially if males are prone to phimosis, whereby the prepuce is so tightly wound around the glans as to create excessive smegma (calculous deposits), white chancres, impotence, and even cancer. In the light of research into child trauma, the operation has come under new scrutiny, for although Western circumcision has reached a level of medical sophistication that lessens pain and loss of blood, infants are palpably shocked by undergoing circumcision. —*Keith Garebian*

See also Baptismal rites; Jews; Religion; Rites of passage.

Civil marriage ceremonies

RELEVANT ISSUES: Law; Marriage and dating

SIGNIFICANCE: Civil marriage ceremonies are legal ceremonies performed by states in which marrying parties enter into contractual agreements with each other

In the United States a marriage license is necessary in order to enter into a marriage contract.

Civil authorities in each state must be satisfied that the parties entering into this contract are of legal age (have attained the age of consent), are of sound mind, are not currently married to anyone else, and have not been coerced into marrying. If either party has been divorced or has had a mar-riage annulled, documents to this effect must be presented when they apply for the marriage license. Other procedures, such as blood tests, may be required. Couples may elect to have a civil ceremony, which satisfies state requirements, or a religious ceremony under the auspices of a spe-

Civil marriage ceremonies tend to be much less formal than church weddings. (James L. Shaffer)

cific religious sect. In other countries, such as France, a civil ceremony is required before a religious ceremony may take place.

Marriage signifies a change in persons' legal and social status and has serious implications for family life and the safeguarding of traditional values. The civil marriage ceremony is, therefore, a binding contract between two individuals. Fidelity is a requirement of marriage, as are mutual obligations of husbands and wives, including rights to sexual intercourse, property, spousal support, and child support. The state issuing a marriage license is, in effect, a silent third partner to such contracts. The text of the contractual agreement in civil marriage ceremonies is set by law and is not subject to change by the persons entering into the contract. The civil marriage ceremony is usually conducted by state-certified judges, magistrates, or justices of the peace.   —*Jo Manning*

See also Age of consent; Annulment; Common-law marriage; Divorce; Marriage; Marriage laws; Weddings.

Clans

RELEVANT ISSUES: Kinship and genealogy; Parenting and family relationships

SIGNIFICANCE: A key concept in kinship structure, a clan is a group of kin who believe that they are descended from a common ancestor and a group that serves as a basis for mutual aid and a sense of belonging

A clan consists of members who trace their genealogy to a real or mythical common ancestor, although they are unable to specify their actual links to such an ancestor. Furthermore, a clan is a unilineal decent group—that is, membership is always traced from either mothers' or fathers' side. In *Systems of Consanguinity and Affinity of the Human Family* (1871), Lewis Henry Morgan divided clans into two types: patri-clans (membership derived from the male line) and matri-clans (membership derived from the female line).

Clans originate from the fission of large households, which often consist of several generations living under one roof. When households grow and become too large, some daughters or brothers move out and form new households that still retain the name of the original house. Clans can be named after mythical persons, animals, or plants (called a totem). For example, it is common for Native Americans to adopt animals—a bear, an eagle, or a snake—for their clan name. Since members of a clan cannot demonstrate exactly who their common ancestor is, the totem serves as a symbol of continuity and solidarity for group identification, distinguishing one clan from another. It is absolutely forbidden for persons of the same clan to marry one another, for it is presumed that as members of a clan who are descended from a common ancestor, they are all related to one another by direct kinship ties.

Clan membership entails a set of rights and obligations, including mutual support, defense, and the settling of disputes. Because the nuclear family is the most important kinship unit in the United States and Canada, clans in the strict sense of the term do not exist in mainstream North American society. Nevertheless, some clan-like, kin-based associations that offer support to their members can be found in both the United States and Canada. Members of these associations call one another "brother" and "sister." These associations function as gigantic family groups that establish rules for proper behavior while providing nurturance, protection, and a sense of belonging to their members.

An example of a clan-like association may be seen in Los Angeles, which has one of the largest Samoan immigrant communities in the United States. Samoans in Los Angeles draw on their traditional system of *matai* (respect for elders) to deal with modern urban problems. When two unarmed Samoan brothers were killed by a policeman in 1992, clan leaders and elders organized a well-attended community meeting in which they urged young members to be patient. At the same time, they brought a civil case against the officer who killed the brothers and pressed the U.S. Justice Department to initiate a civil rights suit. By combining the strength of the clan with the U.S. judicial system, members of this Samoan community were able to solve the social problem in a viable way.   —*Jian Li*

See also Ancestor worship; Coats of arms; Exogamy; Genealogy; Lineage; Matrilineal descent; Moiety; Muslims; Native Americans; Parallel cousins; Patrilineal descent; Tribes.

The totem poles of Alaska's Tlingit people contain carved and painted representations of clan totems. (Jeff Greenberg/Archive Photos)

Clark, Kenneth

BORN: July 24, 1914, Panama Canal
Zone

Clark, Mamie

BORN: October 18, 1917, Hot Springs,
Ark.
DIED: August 11, 1983, Hastings-on-
Hudson, N.Y.

AREAS OF ACHIEVEMENT: Children
and child development; Education
SIGNIFICANCE: Kenneth and Mamie
Clark conducted pioneering studies indicating that growing up in a
segregated society produces a
negative self-identity in African
American children

Kenneth Clark and his wife Mamie
earned their Ph.D. degrees in psychology from Columbia University
in the 1940's. In the late 1930's and
early 1940's the Clarks conducted
studies on young children's racial
preferences by using black and
white dolls to test the impact of
segregation on the self-awareness,
identity, and self-image of African
American children. Their research
showed that young African American children consistently evaluated
the color white and depictions of
white persons more positively than

Kenneth Clark at the City University of New York in 1970. (AP/Wide
World Photos)

the color black and black persons. The justices of
the United States Supreme Court were influenced
by the Clarks' research in the historic *Brown v.
Board of Education* decision of 1954, when the
Court concluded that segregated schooling for African Americans and whites was inherently unequal, discriminatory, and therefore unconstitutional.

In 1946 Mamie and Kenneth Clark founded
what became the Northside Center for Child Development as an alternative to the harsh, alienat-
ing, destructive child-welfare system of New York
City. The center became a clinic for consultation,
guidance, and therapy for Harlem's youth and
parents. For a time, Kenneth Clark also headed

Harlem Youth Opportunities Unlimited to help
Harlem dropouts. Kenneth and Mamie Clark devoted their lives to helping children cope.

—Alvin K. Benson

See also Educating children; Equality of children; Parenting.

Coats of arms

RELEVANT ISSUE: Kinship and genealogy
SIGNIFICANCE: Coats of arms, or insignia used in
hereditary identification, evolved from the ancient practice of identification of tribes, clans,
and warriors by the use of symbols

The need to identify one group of people from another by visual symbols arose in societies in which most of the population was illiterate. This use of symbols existed in ancient times. The Old Testament refers to the use of symbols to identify the tribes of Israel. For example, the tribe of Judah used the lion as a symbol of recognition. The Vikings used symbols to denote their ships. Also, the ancient clans of Scotland used symbols to distinguish one clan from another. During the Crusades of the Middle Ages, symbols selected by knights were used by their militaries, enabling the armor-clad warriors to distinguish friend from foe during violent hand-to-hand conflicts. The symbols selected by knights often represented significant events in their lives or other outstanding qualities. Knights displayed such symbols on their clothing, especially on their surcoats, or outer tunic garments. This use of symbols gave rise to the term "coat of arms."

Because men of many nationalities were involved in the Crusades, the idea of using symbols (coats of arms) for identification spread readily among the nobility of Western Europe. Because most people, including most of the nobility, could not write, the practice of incorporating coats of arms into the designs of wax seals for stamping important documents became an easy way to communicate and conduct business. Coats of arms were quickly adopted for the same purpose by towns, businesses, and churches.

During the Middle Ages individuals or groups originally selected their own designs for their coats of arms. However, because coats of arms became so widespread, confusion soon arose as duplicative designs flourished. As a result of this situation, it was necessary to supervise the selection of designs. The title of "herald" was used to denote persons who systematically studied symbols and supervised their selection for coats of arms. Thus, the term "heraldry" was used to denote the study of designs used to distinguish individual families and to authenticate official documents. Heraldry also denoted the art of reproducing these designs in picture form. In order to avoid confusion, heraldic terms became precise. In 1484 King Richard III of England established the Herald's College, the purpose of which was to decide who was entitled to wear coats of arms and to select designs.

In modern countries that recognize and gener-

ate a nobility, coats of arms usually depict the ancestry of particular individuals. For persons and families living in countries that do not recognize and generate a nobility but maintain ancestral ties to such countries, it is possible to locate coats of arms for surnames. In addition to family coats of arms, many countries use heraldic symbols on official documents, flags, and seals. Moreover, leaders of countries have official coats of arms.

—Sue Bailey

See also Clans; Family albums and records; Genealogy; Kinship systems.

Codependency

RELEVANT ISSUES: Marriage and dating; Parenting and family relationships
SIGNIFICANCE: Codependency, the altered behavior of persons with chemically dependent and troubled relatives, is characterized primarily by persons' excessive focus on other's needs and neglect of themselves

The basic concept underlying codependency—that the behavior of alcoholics affects the family, particularly spouses—is usually traced back to the founding of Al-Anon Family Groups in 1951. Al-Anon was the first group to extend the Twelve-Step principles of Alcoholics Anonymous (AA) to relationships.

Origin, Development, and Popularization. The term codependency began to be used by addictions treatment professionals in the late 1970's and initially described people affected by chemically dependent persons. The popularity of the term has increased since then, largely due to writers such as Melody Beattie and John Bradshaw, who have produced best-selling books and popular television programs (Bradshaw's series, *Bradshaw On: The Family,* aired on PBS in 1988 and proclaimed codependency the most common family illness). Bradshaw and others extended the dysfunctional behavior which might provoke codependency to include sex addiction, work addiction, chronic physical illnesses, emotional disturbances, eating disorders, gambling, indeed—according to Bradshaw—any force that causes one family member to control others. Beattie notes that parents of children with behavior problems, people in helping professions, and recovering substance abusers can become codependents.

The popularity of the concept of codependency is also linked to the founding of Adult Children of Alcoholics (ACoA) in 1977. Both ACoA and codependency focus on the same behavior; some believe that the term "adult child" is synonymous with "codependent." Al-Anon differs from both ACoA and codependency in interpreting the role of one's past. ACoA and codependency see the past as the root of present problems. Both AA and Al-Anon examine the past only to recognize wrongs done as a result of alcoholism, so that one can make amends.

Codependency books are part of a "recovery" genre which became popular in the late 1980's. Recovery refers to the healing of psychological suffering caused by addiction, whether to chemical substances, processes, or people. Hazelden and Parkside, both drug rehabilitation centers, began publishing recovery books, as did major publishers. In 1997 the Internet-based bookstore Amazon.com carried 149 items on codependency. Many general recovery books either discuss it by name or describe its characteristics. There are numerous bookstores devoted exclusively to codependency and other recovery literature.

The codependency concept has also grown through its adoption by the drug-abuse treatment industry. Substance-abuse treatment centers generally assess and treat family members for codependency. There are outpatient codependency programs, Twelve-Step self-help groups such as Codependents Anonymous (or CoDA, founded in 1986), and counselors who specialize in codependency. Codependency is also included in counseling curricula.

Definitions, Characteristics, Symptoms, and Treatment. The Al-Anon concept of "enabling" means that family members of alcoholics, by intervening and trying to protect alcoholics in areas where they have lost control, unintentionally allow them to continue drinking excessively. Paying unpaid bills and lying to employers about absences from work protects alcoholics from the consequences of their behavior and allows them to deny its destructiveness. This behavior, renamed "caretaking," is the hallmark symptom of codependency.

Beattie states, "A codependent person is one who has let another person's behavior affect him or her, and who is obsessed with controlling that person's behavior." Beattie and others list a wide array of both general and specific symptoms and characteristics of codependency. These include hypervigilance to external cues from troubled persons, repressed feelings, anger and resentment, low self-esteem (manifested by fearing rejection, taking things personally, and getting artificial feelings of self-worth from helping others), obsession (constantly talking and worrying about other persons' problems), controlling (attempting to manipulate others through giving advice, feigning helplessness, or imposing guilt), and poor communication (expressing needs indirectly, trying to say things that will please others). Although Timmen L. Cermak has developed diagnostic criteria for codependency that define it as a personality disorder, most writers caution that these symptoms do not constitute codependency unless they lead to rigid, exaggerated behavior.

Participation in a Twelve-Step group is recommended as the fundamental treatment for codependency. It can be accompanied by the programs of substance abuse treatment centers aimed at families or by private counseling. Beattie offers practical advice on recovery which is quite similar to the Al-Anon literature. She urges codependents to learn to detach from troubling persons or problems, control tendencies to react with urgency and anxiety, stop being rescuers, deal with low self-worth, set personal goals, and communicate clearly and assertively.

Drawbacks of the Concept. In both popular and scholarly evaluations, codependency's critics have been more vocal than its proponents. One of the most prevalent criticisms is that some codependency theorists portray the condition as a disease. Critics counter that although the disease model has been useful in describing alcoholism because it removes the moral stigma, it does not translate well when applied to behavior in relationships. It is unlikely that codependents derive feelings of euphoria from their behavior, as substance abusers do. Calling codependency a disease may either lead people to expect a quick, easy cure or cause them to relinquish responsibility for their problems.

Critics also charge that the concept of codependency is so broad and all-inclusive that it can apply to anyone. Beattie's ten-page list of characteristics, drawn from her own professional experience and from other writings on the topic, has been found to include many contradictions. Grouping persons who were poorly nurtured in childhood with those who live with substance abusers or experience physical abuse is seen as trivializing the suffering of the latter and making it harder to identify those in serious need of help. Furthermore, because of its all-inclusiveness codependency seems to offer overly simplistic explanations and remedies for a complex mix of problems, particularly the dilemmas of caretaking relationships. The recommended Twelve-Step approach may represent overdiagnosis and overtreatment for those whose primary problems are assertiveness, anxiety, or depression. Such persons may be better served by cognitive-behavioral therapy.

Cermak defines as codependent anyone who has been in a relationship with a chemically dependent person for at least two years without seeking help. This definition ignores many studies showing that family members' behavior may be affected but not pathological. Codependency theory also disregards a number of studies showing that people whose families of origin contain persons suffering from addiction do not necessarily exhibit dysfunctional behavior.

The concept of codependency has been further criticized because its suggestion that spouses' and family members' caretaking activities contribute to the continued dysfunction of troubled persons amounts to blaming the victims—particularly women. Moreover, codependency has been seen as focusing on correcting spouses' behavior without holding troubled persons responsible. According to critics, the behavior called "caretaking" could more helpfully be viewed as normal coping mechanisms developed to deal with extremely trying situations. Feminists have charged that codependency's view of health is a male view, since it values separateness rather than connectedness. Codependency, some feminists argue, blames women for doing too much of what they have been socialized to do. Moreover, codependency does not consider the political, economic, and social conditions which contribute to women's caretaking behavior.

Benefits of the Concept. A number of benefits have been linked to the concept of codependency. Although it has been called simplistic, codepen-

dency has succeeded with the public because it presents a way of talking about, understanding, and confronting the emotional pain that comes from being involved with persons who are out of control. The popularity of codependency has been ascribed to other factors as well. One argument is that recovery has taken over the trendiness formerly enjoyed by psychoanalysis, while others see it as a substitute for religion. More specifically, another class of "adult children"—those who did not, as children, receive adequate love and attention—may find a remedy for feelings of spiritual emptiness. Finally, addictions professionals credit the concept with bringing vast numbers of people into recovery.   —*Glenn Ellen Starr*

BIBLIOGRAPHY

Babcock, Marguerite, ed. *Challenging Codependency: Feminist Critiques.* Toronto: University of Toronto Press, 1995.

Beattie, Melody. *Codependent No More: How to Stop Controlling Others and Start Caring for Yourself.* 2d ed. Center City, Minn.: Hazelden Educational Materials, 1992.

Cermak, Timmen L. "Co-Addiction as a Disease." *Psychiatric Annals* 21 (May 1, 1991).

Gordon, Judith R., and Kimberly Barrett. "The Codependency Movement: Issues of Context and Differentiation." In *Addictive Behaviors Across the Life Span: Prevention, Treatment, and Policy Issues,* edited by John S. Baer. Newbury Park, Calif.: Sage Publications, 1993.

Greenberg, Gary. *The Self on the Shelf: Recovery Books and the Good Life.* Albany: State University of New York Press, 1994.

Haaken, Janice. "A Critical Analysis of the Co-Dependence Construct." *Psychiatry* 53 (November, 1990).

Rice, John Steadman. *A Disease of One's Own: Psychotherapy, Addiction, and the Emergence of Co-Dependency.* New Brunswick, N.J.: Transaction Publishers, 1996.

Wegscheider-Cruse, Sharon. *Understanding Codependency.* Deerfield Beach, Fla.: Health Communications, 1990.

See also Al-Anon; Alateen; Alcoholism and drug abuse; Bradshaw, John; Dysfunctional families; Emotional abuse; Recovery programs; Women's roles.

Cohabitation

RELEVANT ISSUES: Marriage and dating; Parenting and family relationships

SIGNIFICANCE: The number of cohabiting relationships, relationships in which partners are not legally married to each other, has been on the rise in the late twentieth century, posing the need to understand and come to grips with this nontraditional form of intimate partnership

Cohabitation is typically viewed as a heterosexual intimate relationship in which two people sexually and romantically involved with each other live together. On a broader level, it can also include lesbian and gay couples who cohabit, yet who are not considered to be married or in a common-law relationship. Cohabiting couples include a subgroup of individuals who are considered to have common-law relationships. Such couples present themselves to others as married in a variety of ways, despite not having legally formalized their relationships. If they end their relationships, they may have to go through a divorce process similar to that for married couples. Even though some governments, organizations, and individuals assume that cohabitation is synonymous with common-law marriage, these terms should not necessarily be used interchangeably. All common-law couples may cohabit, yet not all cohabiting couples live in a common-law relationship or wish to be identified as a common-law couple.

Cohabitation was initially thought to be a college-student phenomenon that emerged in the 1970's. Individuals with lower levels of education, however, cohabited long before college students. Cohabitation increased dramatically during the 1980's and 1990's, with various studies indicating that the numbers doubled in Canada while they doubled or tripled in the United States. By the early 1990's, cohabiting relationships accounted for approximately 10 percent of all families.

Along with an increase in the number of people who cohabit, public attitudes toward cohabitation have also changed, reflecting a shift in morality over time. Before cohabitation became more common, it was considered unacceptable, because it was seen as proof that persons were engaged in premarital sex, an act viewed as wrong and immoral. As attitudes regarding sexuality became more liberal, cohabitation became less stigmatized. Other factors affecting persons' attitudes toward cohabitation include their age, relationship status (not married versus married, widowed, or divorced), occupation status, and their levels of education and religiosity. Interestingly, religious beliefs have not affected individuals' timing of cohabitation after they divorce, nor do they appear to have affected persons' decision to bear children within a cohabiting relationship. In general, nontraditional views regarding family life have been associated with the increase in cohabitation.

As a Step Toward Marriage. Cohabitation takes several forms and means different things depending on the persons or couples involved. Most cohabiting couples in the United States and Canada view cohabitation as a precursor to marriage or a "trial marriage," in which individuals test out their mutual compatibility. Such couples hope to minimize the risk of divorce by developing marriage-like intimacy before contracting a legal marriage. Yet, persons in the United States and Canada who marry after a period of cohabitation have about a 50 percent higher chance of divorcing than those whose marriages do not follow cohabitation. Numerous studies have found that cohabitation before marriage results in less stable marriages, and this relationship is termed the "cohabitation effect."

A closer look, however, reveals that certain cohabitation "histories," not prior cohabitation itself, may be related to higher risks of future divorce. Those who cohabit only with persons whom they eventually marry undergo divorce at similar rates as individuals who have not cohabited with their marital partners (or anyone else) prior to marriage. On the other hand, serial cohabiters (those who have cohabited with more than one partner) show higher rates of divorce.

As an Alternative to Marriage. In addition to being a precursor to marriage, cohabitation may also be an alternative to marriage. Lesbians or gay men may view cohabitation as an alternative to marriage, either because they may not marry legally or because they actively reject the institution of marriage. Heterosexuals may view cohabitation as an alternative because they reject the notion of traditional marriage, have been married previously, or view themselves as too old to marry.

Persons may reject traditional marriage as the

sole acceptable form of a lifelong relationship, viewing it as too constraining or restricting. Some feminists have rejected marriage on the grounds that it is patriarchal in nature and therefore oppressive toward women, and women in cohabiting relationships have been more likely than married women to question traditional marriage. Moreover, the increase in cohabitation appears to have compensated for a corresponding drop in remarriage. Divorced individuals have tended to live with their partners rather than marry them. Finally, older individuals may choose to cohabit because their incomes are inadequate, they fear losing their pensions if they remarry, or they are unwilling to change their wills if doing so is disadvantageous to their beneficiaries. In 1990 approximately 1 percent of those more than sixty years old cohabited, while the "young-old" (those under seventy years of age) were more likely to cohabit than the "old-old." This percentage will likely increase in the future: 11 percent of those between the ages of forty and fifty-nine years old cohabited in 1990, and some of them will continue to cohabit into their later years.

Additional Factors Related to Cohabiting. Some individuals may not think about cohabitation as a precursor or alternative to marriage. They may cohabit purely for companionship or economic reasons. Interestingly, cohabitation has appeared to be an alternative to singlehood for some African American women rather than an alternative to marriage. This might indicate a much more complex view of the benefits of cohabitation, or perhaps of not marrying.

Behaviors and attitudes toward cohabitation are further influenced by geographical location, family policies, age, and sex. Persons' residences may affect their attitudes and behaviors. People in Quebec, Canada, and the Sunbelt region of the United States have had more positive attitudes toward cohabitation and have been more likely to live in cohabiting relationships than people in other geographical regions. This may be due partly to specific legislation regarding cohabitation and common-law relationships, which differs by region and country. Younger persons are more likely than older persons to have positive attitudes toward cohabitation; they have greater opportunities to cohabit and engage in it more frequently, reflecting the norms and experiences of their peers. On the other hand, gender appears to be a factor with older cohabitants. Men more than sixty years of age have been more likely than women of the same age to cohabit, because they have tended to cohabit with younger women. Elderly women have been less likely to cohabit, because they have typically had relationships with men of a similar age. As women reach old age the number of older men decreases because of their higher mortality rates and their tendency to have relationships with younger women.

Characteristics of Cohabiting Relationships. Cohabiting relationships have tended to be relatively short, although about 20 percent have lasted longer than five years. This estimate would be greater if lesbian and gay relationships were included, because analyses have indicated that the longevity and quality of homosexual cohabiting relationships is similar to that of married heterosexuals. Cohabitation has remained an underexplored field, and much more must be learned about the quality, stability, experiences, violence levels, satisfaction, happiness, and commitment of cohabiting relationships. For example, the presence of children is a deterrent toward ending a cohabiting relationship, but little is known about why some people choose to have children within a cohabiting relationship while others wait until marriage.

Late twentieth century statistics have indicated that the numbers of individuals in intimate relationships have not changed significantly over time. Although marriage and remarriage rates have decreased, cohabitation rates have largely compensated for them. Stable union rates in the late twentieth century have signified that individuals have not rejected the notion of marriage, but rather that the nature of marriage has perhaps changed. Typically, cohabiting persons have been presented as being significantly different in their attitudes and beliefs from noncohabiting persons. As cohabitation becomes more common among younger people, however, the differences between those who choose to cohabit and those who choose not to may decrease. —*Áine M. Humble*

BIBLIOGRAPHY

Bumpass, Larry L., James A. Sweet, and Andrew Cherlin. "The Role of Cohabitation in Declining Rates of Marriage." *Journal of Marriage and the Family* 53 (1991).

Chevin, Albert. "As Cheaply as One: Cohabitation in the Older Population." *Journal of Marriage and the Family* 58 (1996).

Cunningham, John D., and John K. Antill. "Current Trends in Nonmarital Cohabitation: In Search of the POSSLQ." In *Under-Studied Relationships: Off the Beaten Track*, edited by Julia T. Wood and Steve Duck. Thousand Oaks, Calif.: Sage Publications, 1995.

Macklin, Eleanor D. "Nontraditional Family Forms." In *Handbook of Marriage and the Family*, edited by Marvin B. Sussman and Suzanne K. Steinmetz. New York: Plenum Press, 1987.

Rice, F. Philip. *Intimate Relationships, Marriages, and Families*. 2d ed. Toronto: Mayfield, 1993.

See also Children born out of wedlock; Common-law marriage; Couples; Domestic partners; Familism; Nannies; Persons of opposite sex sharing living quarters (POSSLQ); Religion.

Coles, Robert

BORN: October 12, 1929, Boston, Mass.
AREA OF ACHIEVEMENT: Children and child development
SIGNIFICANCE: A social psychiatrist and Harvard professor, Coles has explored children's lives in different cultures, classes, races, and economic conditions, winning a Pulitzer Prize for his five-volume series *Children of Crisis* (1967-1978).

As the titles of his books suggest, Coles has explored the lives of children and families in crisis. He began his work in the South in the 1960's, studying the impact of the racial struggle on children and writing about them with extraordinary sensitivity. Coles's literary sensibilities—reflected in several books on writers and on the making of literature and art by children—transforms nearly all his work into storytelling, so that his work conveys the drama and inner lives of his subjects. He has written about migrants, sharecroppers, mountaineers, Eskimos, Chicanos, and Native Americans. However, he has also investigated the lives of privileged children and addressed his concerns about families to society at large. *A Festering Sweetness* (1978) includes Coles's poetry about the lives of African American and Native American children and describes their social environments, marked by poverty and urban violence. He finds much support for his studies of children in their own creativity, as evidenced in *Their Eyes Meeting the World: The Drawings and Paintings of Children* (1992).

Robert Coles at Harvard University in 1981. (AP/Wide World Photos)

Coles is engaged in much more than social theory and sociological analysis. In *The Spiritual Life of Chil-*

dren (1991) and *In God's House: Children's Drawings* (1996) he examines how children—Christian, Muslim, Jewish, and secular—react to the idea of God. How children struggle with moral choice, their reactions to the films they see and the stories they hear, has also been his concern. In *The Moral Life of Children* (1991) he has analyzed what children say about moral conduct in their drawings and conversations and observed their family lives in the United States, Brazil, and in other countries.

In *When Slow Is Fast Enough: Educating the Delayed Preschool Child* (1993) Coles assesses twenty early intervention programs for preschool children in ten states. He calls for a more sensitive, less authoritarian model of instruction that stimulates children's natural and spontaneous, if sometimes slow, development. He pays special attention to the developmental needs of girls in *The Story of Ruby Bridges* (1995) as well as to the reasons why men are responsible for such a disproportionate number of the dysfunctional things that happen in society. *The Trouble with Boys: A Wise and Sympathetic Guide to the Risky Business of Raising Sons* (1995) investigates why boys are prone to violence.

Coles has demonstrated that although children often adopt their parents' moral attitudes, there is a discrepancy between what children actually think and their parents' perceptions of them. There are what Coles calls moral crossroads, which parents can identify and with which they can deal. His method, moreover, extends to at-risk youth and to a concern with teenage parents in *The Ongoing Journey: Awakening Spiritual Life in At-Risk Youth* (1997) and *The Youngest Parents: Teenage Pregnancy as It Shapes Lives* (1997).
                                        —*Carl Rollyson*

See also Child rearing; Childhood fears and anxieties; Cultural influences; Educating children; Moral education; Poverty; Religion.

James P. Comer at Yale University in 1988. (AP/Wide World Photos)

Comer, James P.

BORN: September 25, 1934, East Chicago, Ind.

AREAS OF ACHIEVEMENT: Children and child development; Education

SIGNIFICANCE: The "Comer method" has rehabilitated undisciplined and failing schools and children by teaching mainstream social values, involving parents, and integrating arts and academics, thus fostering interest and self-esteem in students

After receiving his M.D. from Howard University in 1960, James P. Comer found medical practice unfulfilling. He enrolled at the University of Michigan, where he completed a master's degree in public health in 1964. Comer then completed a four-year residency program in psychiatry at Yale University, where he became associate dean of the school's Child Study Center in 1969. In 1968 the center had become associated with the Baldwin and King elementary schools in New Haven, Connecticut. These schools had the lowest test scores in the city, massive student and faculty absenteeism, and an almost complete lack of classroom discipline. After allowing attrition to remove incompetent teachers, Comer worked hard to enlist the cooperation of neighborhood families. As an African American, Comer understood the deep mistrust many of the area's poorly educated African American families had for school methods. Determined to instill pride in the schools' students, Comer instituted a program that taught them explicit techniques of mainstream social behavior, including methods for making polite requests and paying attention to teachers' questions. He also brought the arts to bear on academic subjects, encouraging teachers to combine graphics with literature and mathematics with music instruction. By the late 1970's these teaching techniques helped raise students' achievement above standard grade level. The "Comer method," which remains controversial, has spread to school districts throughout the United States and is supported by funding from a sizable Rockefeller grant.

—Robert M. Hawthorne, Jr.

See also Bethune, Mary McLeod; Educating children; Public education; Schools.

Common-law marriage

RELEVANT ISSUES: Marriage and dating; Parenting and family relationships

SIGNIFICANCE: The laws concerning common-law marriage can affect the property rights, inheritance, legitimacy, and welfare of families based on such marriages

While many people use the term common-law marriage to describe the relationship between any unmarried persons who live together, such usage is not accurate. The legal definition of common-law marriage varies from state to state; however, common-law marriage can generally be defined as a marriage agreed to by both a man and a woman that lacks the benefit of a religious or civil ceremony.

Legal Conditions for Common-Law Marriage. By the late twentieth century only twelve states and the District of Columbia recognized as legal common-law marriages contracted within their borders. These states include Alabama, Colorado, Georgia, Iowa, Kansas, Montana, Oklahoma, Pennsylvania, Rhode Island, South Carolina, Utah, and Texas. In addition to these states, Idaho recognizes common-law marriages that were instituted within its state borders before 1996, and Ohio recognizes those instituted within its state borders before 1991. All of these states require that for a common-law marriage to be valid both partners must agree that they intend to be married, that they have cohabited, or lived together, on a regular basis for a specified period of time, and that they must present themselves to others as married. Cohabitation implies that partners engage in sexual intercourse. However, cohabitation alone is insufficient to establish a legal common-law marriage.

Couples entering a common-law marriage must observe all state regulations concerning marriage. These include the age of each party and consanguinity, or how closely the two are related to each other. No state recognizes common-law marriages between two people of the same sex or bigamous or polygamous relationships. Couples who enter into a valid common-law marriage have all the rights and obligations of legally married couples, including inheritance rights, child support, and workers' benefits. The only way that a common-law marriage can be ended is through legal divorce administered by the courts. Although few states allow common-law marriages to be contracted within their boundaries, nearly every state recognizes that such marriages, once undertaken in states that allow them, are legal. That is, if couples enter common-law marriages in the state of South Carolina and move to North Dakota, the latter state will recognize these marriages as legal and valid.

Historical Background. Although the term common-law marriage sounds as if it were based on the common law of England, it really had its foundations in North America because of two realities of life in the early days of colonization. First, the Puritan dissenters were unable to contract legal marriages in England because only Church of England clergy could perform marriages. Thus, the earliest settlers were not permitted to marry under English law. Second, as settlers moved westward, they frequently lacked contact with clergy for long periods of time. Although these people were considered inside the law because they bought and sold property, entered into contracts, and wrote wills, they found themselves in an anomalous situation with regard to their marriages. Consequently, states, territories, and provinces recognized informal common-law marriages as legal.

In the slave states the concept of common-law marriage was very important both before and after the Civil War. Slaves could not enter into legal marriages or leave property to their children. In fact, their children were not even considered their own property. Once they were freed, however, it became an important issue for them to establish the legitimacy of their children. Thus, an 1868 Alabama law proclaimed that freedmen and women who lived together were married under the law and that their children could rightfully claim themselves as legitimate offspring of these marriages.

Increasing urbanization and communications led to a decrease in the need for common-law marriages. Over time, common-law marriage died out in most locations. At the same time, the states became increasingly involved in regulating who could marry and what constituted a legal marriage. Over the years, most states passed statutes forbidding common-law marriage.

Legal Problems with Common-Law Marriage. Common-law marriage creates many difficult legal situations. Most of these difficulties become manifest when spouses die or when one spouse wants to terminate the marriage. Generally, the other spouse must establish that a valid marriage exists in order for children of the marriage to inherit property or for the first spouse to divorce. Through a provision known as "right of election," a common-law spouse can disregard the provisions of the other spouse's will and take whatever percentage of the estate the state designates as the spouse's portion. For example, a common-law spouse who is expressly excluded from inheritance by the terms of the deceased spouse's will can still claim and collect a sizable portion of the estate if it can be established that a common-law marriage existed.

The burden of proof falls upon the person who wants to establish that a common-law marriage exists. That is, the court does not assume that a common-law marriage exists unless the spouse can present sufficient evidence that the couple agreed together that they were married, lived together as husband and wife, and acted as if they were married. Evidence may include joint tax returns, the assumption of the husband's name by the wife, bank records, conversations between the couple and with others, and the manner in which the spouses introduce each other to other people.

Some of the thorniest issues arise when cohabiting couples from a state that does not recognize common-law marriage visit a state that does. The question is posed of how long couples must be in the common-law state in order to find themselves married in their home state.

Such was the question in a case that received a good deal of notoriety and media attention. Sandra Jennings and actor William Hurt had a long-term relationship that included years of cohabitation and the parenting of a child. Because the couple lived in New York, their union was not considered a common-law marriage. However, when Hurt chose to leave Jennings, she took him to court, claiming that they had contracted a common-law marriage while they lived in South Carolina during the filming of one of Hurt's movies. It was important for Jennings to be able to make such a claim in order for her to be eligible for a portion of Hurt's property under New York's divorce law. In spite of a strong case, Jennings was unable to convince the New York court that Hurt ever considered himself married. In another case, however, a spouse was able to establish the existence of a common-law marriage on the strength of a weekend visit to Pennsylvania. Therefore, it is difficult to predict how courts will interpret the evidence in common-law marriage cases.

Implications for Families. The ambiguity of the law and the unpredictable nature of court decisions can have serious consequences for cohabiting families. Partners may find themselves as spouses in a legally constituted common-law marriage based on conduct during a visit to a common-law state. Likewise, partners who consider themselves married based on cohabitation and consent may find themselves locked out of property or inheritance upon the death of a spouse or the dissolution of the union. The implications for children of such unions are serious; children may suddenly find themselves unable to inherit property or unable to establish themselves as legitimate offspring of a legally constituted marriage. Therefore, cohabiting couples and their families must be clear about the laws governing common-law marriages, not only in their own states, but also in any states they may visit overnight. Ignorance of the law will not prevent courts from determining that a common-law marriage exists or does not exist.

—*Diane Andrews Henningfeld*

BIBLIOGRAPHY

American Bar Association. *Family Legal Guide.* New York: Times Books, 1994.

Ashley, Paul P. *Oh Promise Me but Put It in Writing: Living Together Agreements.* New York: McGraw Hill, 1978.

Friedman, Lawrence. *A History of American Law.* 2d. ed. New York: Simon and Schuster, 1985

Hill, Gerald N., and Kathleen Thompson Hill. *Real Life Dictionary of the Law: Taking the Mystery out of the Law.* Los Angeles: General Publication Group, 1997.

Sadler, Judith DeBoard. *Families in Transition: An Annotated Bibliography.* Hamden, Conn.: Archon Books, 1988.

Samuelson, Elliot D. *The Unmarried Couple's Legal Survival Guide.* Secaucus, N.J.: Carol Publishing, 1997.

See also Cohabitation; Communal living; Domestic partners; Inheritance and estate law; Marriage laws.

Communal living

RELEVANT ISSUES: Children and child development; Parenting and family relationships

SIGNIFICANCE: Communes have had a long history in the United States and have diverged from mainstream society in the way their members relate to questions of sexuality and the rearing and education of children

Since the early years of European colonization the United States has been the site of planned ideal communities and religious isolationist settlements. Unlike every other country in the world, there has been a long history of communal living in the United States. With the prospect of a sparsely populated continent, the European visionary saw the New World as a chance at a new organization of society and family life.

From 1732 until the end of the twentieth century, at least one commune, religious or secular, has been in existence at any given time. Yet, it was not until the 1840's that dozens, sometimes hundreds, of communes simultaneously struggled to form communities distinct from mainstream American society. Another surge of communal growth occurred in the 1890's, but most of the communes of this period did not survive. Only in the 1960's, with the rise of the counterculture, did the number of alternative-lifestyle communes reach into the thousands. Again, many did not survive. However, communes appear to be firmly entrenched in America, with new ones being formed every year, ranging from Hindu ashrams to "urban communes," or large households of unrelated adults sharing the rent and little else.

The planners of early American communes decided how members would live and raise their children. Most of these early communes did not reject the standard nuclear family and the monogamous lifestyle of the community at large. Instead, they built villages for member families to live in, although the isolated communities came to be considered an extended family. Later communes were not planned, and family planning was not considered by their founders. In contrast, the typical founders of communes in the 1960's were young people in revolt against monogamy and nuclear family relationships, and their communes resembled group marriages in which the raising of children was a mutual task. In both forms of communes the nuclear family was disrupted.

Nineteenth Century American Communes. Basing their beliefs on the possibility of a socialist or religious paradise within the boundaries of a controlled community, many commune leaders of nineteenth century America designed and built villages for their followers. Adhering to the beliefs of such utopian socialists as Robert Owen, as did New Harmony in Indiana, and Charles Fourier, as did Brook Farm in Massachusetts, the socialist commune leaders sought a society in which everything was held in common. Breaking away from domestic traditions such as marriage was not part of their socialist ideal. Socialist communities consisted of families or individuals who lived in separate houses but chose to work together.

Religious communes, on the other hand, could choose to treat all their members as relatives, at least nominally. The leaders of such communes were usually seen as fathers, or more rarely, as mothers, with members identifying themselves as their children. Sometimes members took on the leaders' surnames or called female members "sisters" and male members "brothers." To foster religious tenets based on different interpretations of the Bible, family life was often altered to meet what the leaders saw as God's plan for them.

Perhaps the most radical change to occur in family life within a commune was initiated by John Humphrey Noyes when he founded Oneida in New York in 1848. Noyes wanted to create a community in which every man was married to every woman. This plan involved much out-of-wedlock sex. Members were discouraged from seeking monogamous relationships, and couples were kept separate from each other if it was discovered that they favored each other's company. Moreover, child rearing was performed differently from society at large. After children were weaned they were raised separately from the adults, and parent-child affection was discouraged. Because of Noyes's beliefs, children engaged in sex at much earlier ages than in the general society, and they almost always had sex with much older adults. Noyes also controlled the number of births in his struggling community and gradually developed a eugenics program so that only certain couples could have children.

Communes of the 1960's. Communes based on religious or socialistic principles were founded only rarely after 1900, and those that survived usually departed from separatism and unusual family patterns to become thriving businesses that sold manufactured products. New communes did not become common until around 1965, when people of the counterculture ("hippies") saw communes as viable alternatives to the mainstream lifestyle.

Many ideals underlay the creation of separate communes of like-minded adults sharing one another's lives. For quite a few people, farming or small-crafts communities were a means to reject mass manufacturing and processed foods. The "back-to-nature" movement led groups of young people to learn subsistence agriculture and practice natural childbirth. Other ideals included personal freedom from society's oppressors, including the police, politicians, employers, and parents. People who chose to live in communes also tended to believe in "free love," a life free of marriage, while sex with multiple partners was encouraged. Through living with like-minded people, counterculture denizens could aspire to live according to beliefs that rejected the attitudes and morals of mainstream society.

To many founders of communes during the 1960's, monogamy was an oppressive institution that hindered free sexual relations. In turn, this repression of natural drives created parents who oppressed their offspring, denying their children's right to self-expression. These founders of communes made it a priority to reject the nuclear family.

In practice, communes during the 1960's more resembled group-housing arrangements than extended families, because their members tended to be transient and of approximately the same age. Because many more communes failed than succeeded and most barely lasted a year, no long-range plans for alternative family lifestyles could take effect. Also, unlike the highly detailed communities of the 1800's, in which relationships, gardens, buildings, and sexual arrangements were all carefully laid out before their founding, farms or group homes of the 1960's were based on an intent to establish common living arrangements and little else. Since members typically believed in removing oppression and authority, it was difficult to impose rules for farm work and housecleaning. Lacking even simple arrangements for cooking, most communes could not or would not develop plans that accommodated all members' sexual needs, visitors' expectations, and—more important—child-rearing methods.

Child Rearing in 1960's Communes. Since no family planning took place in a typical 1960's commune, the young residents did not usually see themselves as obligatory parents. For back-to-nature enthusiasts, having babies was a natural result of love and unprotected sex, not the requisite products of state-approved marriages. After babies

Communal homes tend to mix elements of both institutional and private family living arrangements. (James L. Shaffer)

were born, they were first cared for solely by their mothers, who often breast-fed them. Later, other members of the commune might have looked after the children, but there was no intention of raising them separately from their parents or relieving the parents of the responsibility of child rearing. In urban communes, or communes in which many adults lived together but did not work or farm together, child care was distributed among commune members. In such cases, many of the adults came together to experience the economic benefits of an extended family that would, as a matter of course, accept alternating child care.

At early ages, children in many communes were perceived to be as responsible as adults. They were allowed to make their own decisions, speak for themselves in community meetings, and contribute a few hours of work each week to the support of the communes. Most communal children were taught at home; a typical basic education was usually not deemed important by most communal parents. Many communal children, for example, did not learn to read early on, and some did not learn to read until they were nine or ten years old. Large, successful communes established schools, yet distrust toward a typical education persisted. Children might have benefited from being schooled outside their communes, but many communes were so isolated that this was impossible. Also, children from communes, who would have been viewed as different by their school peers, might have developed problems attending outside schools.

Advantages and Disadvantages of Communes. The advantages of raising children communally are debatable. Children may benefit from being raised by a group of diverse "parents," as has been the case in most communes. Such children might receive attention and partake in a number of interesting activities. By allowing children to make their own decisions and by having them form relationships with adults, commune dwellers have claimed that such children become independent, confident, persuasive, well-adjusted, and socially adept. Some communes have restricted punishment of children to excluding them from meals or group activities, thus reducing child abuse. Some communal leaders have seen early exposure to sexual relations as beneficial to communal children.

Young children in communes may be disadvantaged if they feel confused by love and authority emanating from several "parents." Children born into communes in which most of the residents do not care for children or do not realize how difficult the responsibility of raising children is may end up being raised solely by their mothers. Furthermore, such children might have to live with their mothers in an unwelcome climate, and their mothers may resent them for making them unpopular in their communes. Children might not receive as much attention or education as they need, because commune members treat them as if they are adults who do not have special requirements or need guidance.

Many people who do not live in communes disapprove of children sleeping in the same room as sexually active adults, listening to adults discuss sex, having sex with one another and with adults before the age at which most children enter school, and taking the same illegal drugs as their elders. Children being raised in households of several adults who are isolated from their age peers might be lonely without having others around who share their interests or hobbies. Although commune members claim to treat children as adults, the children do not usually perform difficult work and participate in group decisions that determine the status of the commune. They also do not participate in group coun-

seling, where adult commune members work out their conflicts.

Teenagers are often considered true adults by the members of most communes, yet they are not given any great responsibility over areas such as farming or cooking assignments. When they are named leaders over activities, they are not taken seriously or obeyed by their elders. Many communes do not last, or the children grow up and move away. In such cases, the children may have problems adjusting to society at large. Commune members tend to live one day at a time and do not plan their children's futures. Hence, once they leave home, such children may not be prepared to attend college, to obtain outside employment, or to participate in other aspects of life outside the commune.

Effects of Communes on Families. Since the 1960's countercultural communes have neither had a radical effect on the nuclear family nor have they affected many people. Some sociologists claim, however, that commune members have had a great effect on their own relatives, because when they become a part of a successful commune they adopt a new family. Becoming involved in the lives of a new "extended family" means that they reduce their activities with their real families. In some cases, commune members have severed all family ties and made a full commitment to the commune. Only in this manner can communes, which are difficult to start and sustain, survive the first few years.

Other sociologists claim that successful communes, particularly religious ones, maintain typical nuclear family relationships while their members develop new identities as believers in the tenets of the commune. Certainly some communes have recommended that their members break old family ties, believing that the nuclear family is oppressive, but throughout history most communes have either maintained families or reverted to the nuclear family after experimenting with alternative lifestyles. Since few communes have been successful, most former commune residents have had to return to conventional lifestyles as they have reentered mainstream life.

Group living, whereby members choose to live together at least part of the time for economic and social reasons, has become a more acceptable lifestyle than communal living. Young college-aged people frequently seek coeducational housing arrangements, and because the average age at which people marry has risen in the late twentieth century, these living arrangements have become more common than they were previously. Moreover, the higher divorce rate has yielded more unattached adults or single parents who accept the idea of group housing to solve the problems of limited budgets and single parenthood.   —*Rose Secrest*

BIBLIOGRAPHY

Foster, Lawrence. *Religion and Sexuality: Three American Communal Experiments of the Nineteenth Century.* New York: Oxford University Press, 1981. Mostly concerned with alternative marriage arrangements in communes, with a brief look at child rearing.

Gardner, Hugh. *The Children of Prosperity: Thirteen Modern American Communes.* New York: St. Martin's Press, 1978. Brief look at the characteristics and trends of modern communes.

Kanter, Rosabeth Moss. *Commitment and Community: Communes and Utopias in Sociological Perspective.* Cambridge, Mass.: Harvard University Press, 1972. Broad study that examines how communal life affects individuals and family relationships.

_____. *Communes: Creating and Managing the Collective Life.* New York: Harper & Row, 1973. Anthology of wide-ranging articles, with sections devoted to family life and child rearing in communes.

Kephart, William M. *Extraordinary Groups: The Sociology of Unconventional Life-Styles.* New York: St. Martin's Press, 1976. Covers the family life of a few well-known religious communes and compares these older communes with those of the 1960's and 1970's.

Oved, Yaacov. *Two Hundred Years of American Communes.* New Brunswick, N.J.: Transaction Books, 1988. History and discussion of family, economic success, and societal roles in many communes.

Raimy, Eric. *Shared Houses, Shared Lives: The New Extended Families and How They Work.* Los Angeles: Jeremy P. Tarcher, 1979. Although a guide for those wishing to found a modern commune, it looks at the problems of shared living.

Veysey, Lawrence. *The Communal Experience: Anarchist and Mystical Communities in Twentieth-Century America.* Chicago: University of Chicago Press, 1973. Thorough analysis of what sustains several communes.

Zicklin, Gilbert. *Countercultural Communes: A Sociological Perspective.* Westport, Conn.: Greenwood Press, 1983. Focuses on the success of communes in the areas of child rearing, labor, and economy.

See also Alternative family types; Equality of children; Extended families; Family: concept and history; Group marriage; Hutterites; Mennonites and Amish; Mormon polygamy; Quakers; Shakers.

Communities

RELEVANT ISSUES: Children and child development; Kinship and genealogy; Parenting and family relationships

SIGNIFICANCE: Communities and families evolve with the changing division of labor of societies and are closely interconnected, so that their patterns of development as well as their futures cannot be separated

Social scientists have observed that there are two universal human organizations—the family and the community. In evolutionary terms, the family preceded the community. A family is a set of people related by blood, marriage, or adoption who form a social unit. The various biological and cultural factors which define membership in a family vary from culture to culture.

Although the term community has been used in a number of ways, it has two basic meanings in the social sciences. A community is a spatial or territorial-based group of people. The term also refers to the sense of cohesiveness or belonging that typically develops among the members of such groups. Communities, like other social groups, differ in terms of the extent to which their members identify with and participate in the life of the community. The influence of community life on families and, in turn, of family life on communities is very real and significant.

Basis and Types of Communities. Although human communities have evolved throughout history, the major reason that people live in communities remains convenience. The multitude of peoples' needs and goals are usually better served if they live in clusters, maintaining some sort of relationship, rather than if they are scattered.

Three basic forms of community can be discerned in human social evolution. These are bands of hunting and gathering peoples, the small villages and towns of horticultural and agricultural peoples, and cities comprised of nonagriculatural specialists. Parallel changes in the basic functions or purposes of the family can also be observed. For about three million years people lived in small bands as hunters and gatherers, roaming a somewhat defined territory in search of food. Population growth remained rather limited as did environmental degradation. These foraging peoples spent about three hours per day in search of food. Work as a separate and distinct activity did not exist. When the population of a band exceeded the ability of a territory to provide sufficient food, the band either divided into two or more bands, with each going its own way, or the whole band migrated to a new territory in search of food.

In bands, human relationships tended to be very personal. Given the small size of bands, everyone knew everyone else. People interacted face-to-face. The division of labor was quite rudimentary and was based on gender and age. Women typically gathered roots, berries, nuts, and other foods, while men hunted. The very youngest and the very oldest did not play the adult roles of either hunters or gatherers.

The basis of solidarity or group cohesion—the genesis of a sense of community—among the members of bands was similarity, especially "likemindedness." Such small homogeneous communities were defined by shared or common characteristics or experiences. Although individual differences did exist, modes of dress and adornment, the range of human experiences, and core beliefs and values were quite similar, as was the fact that people tended to see the world through similar eyes.

Cooperation among residents in close-knit communities can provide low-cost alternatives to formal child-care arrangements. (Hazel Hankin)

In conjunction with the development of rudimentary tools and techniques, such as the digging stick and simple means of irrigation, people began to cultivate plants. Horticultural peoples became more tied to the land and less nomadic. The community gradually became a more or less permanent village. With the domestication of plants and animals—growing crops and raising livestock for human use—a horticultural way of life evolved into an agricultural way of life. Agricultural villages grew into small towns. When the division of labor evolved sufficiently to give rise to nonagricultural specialists, a distinctive type of community, the city, emerged. Although significantly different in many respects from the earliest cities, modern cities are still essentially communities comprised of nonagricultural specialists.

With the growth in size and diversity of cities, people of differing races, ethnicity, religions, and cultural backgrounds have found themselves living and working together. Their differences, not their similarities, have become the primary source of solidarity or group cohesion. Specifically, "functional interdependence" has become the foundation of modern communities. With increasing specialization people have become less self-sufficient or independent and more and more dependent on others. The actions of one person often complement those of others. For instance, few city dwellers raise their own food, make their own clothing, or build their own shelters. Even for their bread they are dependent upon a vast array of other people—from farmers, to shippers to millers to bakers to plastic manufacturers to road builders to supermarket clerks.

Forces Redefining Communities. As cities grew in size and complexity and specialization or the division of labor accelerated, the very nature or character of human relationships began to change. In bands and small villages, people knew

Neighborhood communities play an especially important role for retirees. (Hazel Hankin)

each other, often quite personally and even intimately. Primary (familiar) relationships were the norm. There were no strangers. More impersonal and often limited to a specific task, transaction, or goal, secondary (nonfamiliar) relationships characterize virtually all modern social organizations. This transformation in the very quality of human relationships, from traditional communal life to modern associational life, has redefined the nature of community.

Although most modern relationships are secondary in nature, human beings seem to have a deeply rooted desire to experience personal, even intimate, relationships. Although it is quite possible to find primary relationships within secondary settings—best friends working together in a modern factory, for example—for most people the family remains the primary group. The family is where most people express personal concern for one another and experience various types of intimacy.

The specialization of labor, along with technological breakthroughs such as automation and mechanization, the development of the computer, and new sources of abundant energy, when combined with a shift toward a materialistic lifestyle, has produced an outpouring of material "things." Goods and services of every imaginable type are readily available in the modern marketplace. By the time of the agricultural revolution, increasingly during the Industrial Revolution, and in the modern postindustrial electronic world, the appearance of surpluses that can be bought and sold for a profit created increasing differences between the rich and the poor. The resulting stratification of modern societies on the basis of social class divisions has significantly affected the structure of both communities and families. Differences in lifestyles abound in modern communities. Where people live, with whom they interact, their hopes, dreams, fears, and even their life expectancy are class based. In modern societies such as Canada and the United States, rich communities and poor communities, like rich families and poor families, are significantly different in many respects.

Types of Families. The term "family" is a general category that includes several types of families, each displaying a somewhat different structure and performing somewhat different functions. For example, family may refer to spouses and children or to all persons related by blood and marriage.

The nuclear family is composed of parents and children if there are any. It is the smallest and simplest family type and a building block of other family types. Extended families involve two or more nuclear families and typically three or more generations living together. In the conjugal family, husband-and-wife relationships—a socially defined or recognized tie—are emphasized rather than blood relationships. This type of family revolves around parents and their children and does not form an extended family. It is thought of as synonymous with the nuclear family. In societies that emphasize conjugal relationships, romantic love, individual freedom, and the development of individual personality and individual talents are encouraged. In consanguine families the emphasis is on the blood ties of parents and children or brothers and sisters rather than on the marital or conjugal relationship of husbands and wives. The consanguine family normally forms an extended family. The most important element in this family type is the strong obligation of children to their parents. Obligations to the family or collectivity take precedence over individual freedom and initiative.

Most social scientists believe that as societies change from rural agrarian to urban industrial and eventually to postindustrial societies, the predominant type of family also changes. The trend is for consanguine extended families to gradually be replaced by conjugal nuclear families. Extended families, which might include couples' grandparents, unmarried children, and married children and their spouses and offspring are especially well suited to traditional agrarian settings. Prior to the mechanization of agricultural production, farming was labor intensive. Having large families with many children meant having many hands available to work in the fields. Children were an economic asset. Cultivating the soil, growing crops, and raising livestock were labor intensive activities.

Consanguine extended families are tied to the land, often to the same piece of land for many generations. Customs and traditions often exert a powerful influence in such settings. This large family type, in conjunction with the importance of customs, traditions, and the lifelong emphasis on blood relationships between parents and children or brothers and sisters, provides family members

Many communities bring neighbors together through occasional street parties and activities. (James L. Shaffer)

with a sense of security and stability. This is often missing in conjugal nuclear families. Freedom, romantic love, individuality, and the importance of developing a distinctive personality are seldom emphasized in consanguine extended families.

With the transformation to industrialization and urban living, children were no longer an economic asset. Economic pressures and greater gender equality in the workplace have contributed to many women entering the workforce. The emergence of a type of nuclear family where both parents work eight or more hours a day outside the family has meant that the amount of time parents have to spend with their children has decreased. The nuclear family may be disrupted by divorce and often does not provide the relative security and stability of the larger family types. However, this "streamlined" family type allows for individuality and flexibility in personality development. In addition, this type of family is well adapted to many of the demands of modern fast-paced societies, such as the need for geographic mobility in a shifting job market.

From culture to culture and historical era to historical era, families have not only varied in form but also in function. In the simplest hunting and gathering societies, the family was the basic and in some cases the only social unit. Thus all the needs and demands facing the band—political governance, production and distribution of goods and services, protection of people, as well as religious, educational, and recreational functions—were performed by the family. The family, therefore, was a political, economic, recreational, educational, and religious unit. Driven by many of the historical trends unfolding in modern societies, many of the functions previously performed by the family have at least partially been shifted from the home to the state, the church, the business sphere, and the schools. Even with these significant changes, most families continue to perform a variety of important functions, including having and raising children, providing affection for family members, and spousal sexual relations.

Family Life Cycle. Families, like individuals, have a life cycle. The concept of a family life cycle helps to describe changes in family structure, composition, and activities. The various stages of the conjugal nuclear family are: the formation of the family through marriage, bearing children and rearing them through their school years, the departure of children as they marry and form their own families, and the termination of the family life cycle with the death of the parents.

The average age of husbands and wives at the time of their marriage, the birth of their first child, the marriage of their last child, and the death of the first spouse has varied between cultures and social classes and over time. For example, the postparental period marks the time between the departure from the home of the youngest child and the death of the first spouse. At the turn of the century this period, on the average, was about one year, whereas by the mid-1960's it had increased to approximately seventeen years and by the late twentieth century to more than two decades.

Factors Redefining Family Life. The winds of change sweeping through modern societies have very real, significant and lasting implications for both family and community life. There are numerous indications of a broad-based erosion in close personal relationships in modern families and communities. Trends in social connectedness and civic involvement are closely related. Membership and involvement in civic organizations such as parent-teacher associations, the National Federation of Women's Clubs, the Red Cross, the Boy Scouts, and the League of Women Voters, as well as in fraternal orders such as the Elks, Lions, Shriners, and Freemasons have all declined

In the complex, fast-paced, and, at times, threatening modern world, people spend less time chatting over the back fence, playing cards with friends and neighbors, or bowling in a league each week. Increasing geographic mobility among community members may result in a sense of rootlessness. Facilitating coordinated activities among family members or neighbors can be difficult in societies in which families commonly have two working parents.

Electronic technology has also played an important role in contributing to these trends. Technological developments have fostered the privatization of leisure time. Cable television, videocassette rentals, personal computers, and portable cassette decks have allowed individuals to be entertained in private. The scene of a family huddled together in front of the family television set has been replaced by family members, often alone or in pairs, tuning into their favorite programs on separate television sets throughout the house. Cable television caters to their individual tastes. Voice mail and computer networks also discourage neighbors and family members from creating and maintaining personal relationships. Under such conditions, community and family solidarity has gradually weakened.

Technology has created a gap or opposition between individual interests and the collective interests of families and communities. Donning a virtual reality helmet to be entertained in private is the epitome of this trend toward privatizing and individualizing daily life.

President Bill Clinton described this in his state of the union address of January 25, 1995. "We see our families and our communities coming apart. Our common ground is shifting out from under us. The PTA, the town hall meeting, the ball park—it's too hard for many overwhelmed Americans to find the time and space for the things that strengthen bonds of trust and cooperation among citizens. Too many of our children don't have the parents and grandparents who can give them the experiences they need to build character and strengthen identity." The loss of connectedness at the family, neighborhood, and community levels sets the stage for the decline of connectedness in society at large. One outcome of the loss of associational life is the loss of trust between people. Surveys in the United States, Canada, and other modern Western societies indicate that people have become increasingly disillusioned with politicians and political parties, as evidenced in low voter turnouts.

These changes in the sociocultural climate have contributed to the weakening of social relationships, leaving many individuals increasingly alone. Many people in modern societies must now cope with the reality that no one group will be with them from birth until death. They will move through many neighborhoods, communities, groups, and even families. They will often be alone on their journey.

Modern Family Life. The demographic revolution unfolding in virtually every modern society has had profound consequences for both families and communities. With improved sanitation, nutrition, and medical care, life expectancy has steadily increased in modern societies. Communities are increasingly populated by growing numbers of elderly people. This has important implications for entitlement programs for the elderly such as Social Security and Medicare as well as for planning for community needs.

Other historical trends have also affected the pattern of family life in modern societies. Although most marriages continue to occur along class, racial, and religious lines, individuals' free choice in selecting their spouses has increased somewhat. Interracial marriages, for example, have increased. In contrast, arranged marriages continue to occur in traditional societies. Families in modern societies are less patriarch-dominated. Women's status is more equal, as seen in the fact that both spouses have equal rights of divorce. Kinship is recognized bilaterally—that is, through both the husband's and the wife's lineages. In modern societies neolocality, which occurs when newly married spouses leave their parental homes and establish their own joint residences, has become common. This rule of residence serves to discourage the development of extended families and encourage the isolation of nuclear families. More egalitarian family structures, where husbands and wives more equally share household and family responsibilities, have also become increasingly common.

Most families are constantly challenged by the need to juggle work schedules, day care, school events, the social calendar, housekeeping, and paying the bills. Having the time and energy to carry out family responsibilities, much less participate in neighborhood and community activities, is difficult. High rates of divorce and separation mean that single-parent families have become common in modern societies. This contributes to additional legal, financial, and emotional problems. The fact that many divorcees with children remarry or cohabit means that two different styles of family living, including child-rearing patterns based on differing values and beliefs, must somehow be blended together. This can place additional pressures and stress on both parents and children in blended families.

The pace and significance of the sociocultural changes unfolding in most modern societies have contributed to the prevalent generation gap between parents and children in modern conjugal nuclear families. Although children's journeys through life always present challenges for their

Participation in activities such as the Parent Teacher Association is an important manifestation of community involvement. (James L. Shaffer)

parents, in the modern world children often find themselves embracing lifestyles and values that are utterly beyond their parents' comprehension. Parents who are not computer literate cannot understand their children's infatuation with the Internet. Illegal drug use, premarital sex, and the modes of dress and adornment popular among young people often confuse or anger parents who see these developments as the result of increasing peer pressure.

In modern societies, members of families are continually challenged to maintain honest and open communications, a common identity, and a shared outlook. In hunting and gathering and traditional agrarian societies that are tied to the land, the greatest threat to family solidarity is young people's desire for a different way of life

and the lure of city, for their migration will eventually lead to the demise of the extended family.

The Future of the Family. Given the array of problems continually facing the family, be it the conjugal nuclear or the consanguine extended family, each generation must define the family anew. The ultimate challenge facing family members may well be their attempt to balance individual needs and demands for personal freedom and individual initiative with families' collective needs and demands for security, stability, and continuity.

A variety of public and private efforts have focused on strengthening families and communities by addressing the problems and issues confronting these institutions. Numerous schools, churches, and various charitable organizations have been involved in these efforts. They range from very

At times of emergencies, community members can band together quickly for mutual help and support. (James L. Shaffer)

informal arrangements, such as three or four mothers watching each other's children on a rotating basis to allow them a day or night out, to more formally organized efforts, such as local schools collaborating with neighborhood organizations to create community education centers. Such centers stay open in the evenings, offering family-oriented recreational and educational services. Neighbors have banded together to organize neighborhood watch programs and neighborhood improvement programs. Day-care programs subsidized by employers and churches offer child care both in the community and on the job. Schools provide a range of extracurricular activities to encourage pupils to develop their interests, relationships, and abilities, while government has provided tax credits for children and special financing for neighborhood improvements. —*Charles E. Marske*

BIBLIOGRAPHY

Bowen, Linda, and Sherrill Sellers. *Family Support and Socially Vulnerable Communities.* Chicago: Family Resource Coalition, 1994. Presents three case studies that address family services, child welfare, and problem families as well as the lessons learned from each case.

Coontz, Stephanie. *The Way We Never Were: American Families and the Nostalgia Trap.* New York: Basic Books, 1992. According to Coontz, romanticizing the myth of small-town, middle-class family and civic life from America's past will not solve the social problems facing America in the 1990's and beyond.

McCaleb, Sudia Paloma. *Building Communities of Learners: A Collaboration Among Teachers, Students, Families and Communities.* New York: St. Martin's Press, 1994. Examines parent-teacher, home and school, and community and school relationships and their significance.

Wachter, Mary, and Cynthia Tinsley. *Taking Back Our Neighborhoods—Building Communities That Work.* Minneapolis, Minn.: Fairview Press, 1996. In response to the fragmentation and violence of modern life, the authors explain how communities can respond by working together to achieve mutual goods.

Wiener, Valerie. *Gang Free—Influencing Friendship Choices in Today's World.* Minneapolis, Minn.: Fairview Press, 1995. Examines how teenagers make friends even though most teenagers know little about the true nature of friendship or what it requires.

Wireman, Peggy. *Urban Neighborhoods, Networks and Families: New Forms for Old Values.* Lexington, Mass.: Lexington Books, 1984. Examines the role of families, social interaction, and community life in neighborhood and community development.

Zill, Nicholas, and Christine Winquist Nord. *Running in Place: How American Families Are Faring in a Changing Economy and an Individualistic Society.* Washington, D.C.: Child Trends, 1994. Reviews the changing circumstances of American families with reference to modern social and economic developments.

See also Alternative family types; Blended families; Bonding and attachment; Communal living; Couples; Cultural influences; Family life cycle; Family unity; Family values; Volunteerism.

Community programs for children

RELEVANT ISSUES: Children and child development; Parenting and family relationships
SIGNIFICANCE: Community programs and services designed to augment the values, education, recreation, hobbies, or sports skills of children may play an important role in child development, especially if children lack parental supervision

The socialization of children extends from the bonding process with parents, guardians, siblings, and close relatives through school and social organizations in the community. The social network of children includes relatives as well as child-care givers, day-care staff, other infants, and the staff of various community services. Community programs include educational, recreational, religious, and social group organizations that provide services to promote the welfare of children. These programs may be sponsored by the government, by voluntary nonprofit or for-profit agencies, and by religious associations.

Diversity of Programs. Community activities for children are an intrinsic part of their socialization process. Participation in social activities helps create friendships, teaches skills, and helps youngsters learn to cooperate with others. Services devoted to children's social needs have expanded tremendously since the 1970's. No longer are children simply involved in spontaneous play with their siblings and peers in their neighborhoods, but there are also adult-controlled after-school programs. The expansion of community programs for children is supported as positive extracurricular activities. Such programs encourage participation, learning, and cooperation with peers and community role models. These programs are also perceived as a rationally focused way to orient children to corporate work values. However, these increasingly professionalized activities are also criticized as adult interference with children's play and because social inequities may be replicated in terms of who has access to the more challenging and creative programs.

Families that have economic resources to afford the range of pleasurable and educational entertainment introduce their children to recreational activities such as sports, clubs, video games, computers, arcades, lessons, and camps, along with program staff who have the potential for being important teachers and role models in children's lives. This exposure is perceived as benefiting children's communications skills and their ability to take advantage of resources and access opportunities. For lower-income children, however, the variety of opportunities may not be as easily accessible. While such children may face limitations on their leisure activities, they may also have to deal with more personal and familial stressors than higher-income children. Minority status stressors, family pressures, and health issues are likely to pose additional hurdles for children. However, there are community resources available to such children through schools, churches, family-service agencies, local recreation departments, and other community organizations, such as sororities, fraternities, and cultural groups. Some socially responsible activities are sponsored by corporations.

According to child-development researchers, it is important for children to have social networks that are supportive, stimulating, and challenging and that result in creativity and learning. As more children must care for themselves at least a few hours a day or are supervised by siblings, communities have begun to acknowledge and respond to the need for safe and constructive after-school programs. Regardless of families' income, chil-

dren usually remain unsupervised while their mothers are at work.

History of Community Programs. The role of community programs in the care of children has a long history. In the late nineteenth century, when alcohol abuse and delinquency drew increased attention, settlement houses, parks, gymnasiums, libraries, and recreation programs responded to the absence of safe, constructive places for urban children to play. Mutual benefit and voluntary associations initiated community programs for children, and subsequently government sponsored agencies were also established. Programs to help children included associations for their protection (Society for the Prevention of Cruelty to Children, 1875), settlement-house projects that emphasized group work and recreation for children (Hull House, 1889), and recreation programs that offered access to gymnasiums and sports competitions. As groups attempted to meet the costs of these services, fees were raised and funding was terminated for some programs. Unfortunately, services were reduced or eliminated in lower-income communities while they continued and proliferated in middle-class areas.

Families adjusted to changing economic conditions and the pressures of the times. Both adults worked, children worked, and single parents sometimes worked more than one job. Families in the nineteenth and twentieth centuries often found single mothers, usually widows, connected to extended families, so that child-care arrangements and housekeeping chores were shared. However, children were unsupervised or left in the care of siblings when adults' work needs prevailed.

Modern Child-Care Needs. As in the nineteenth and early twentieth centuries, modern families are also challenged by economic transitions that force mothers into the labor force and away from the home. Some families, because of migration and loss of family, may be isolated from other family members. Separation and divorce may also create disrupted families. In the light of these circumstances, the need for commu-

Many communities have a critical need for supervised after-school activities for children. (R. Kent Rasmussen)

Woodworking class in a Young Men's Christian Association (YMCA) center in New York City's Chinatown. For more than a century, the YMCA has been a major nongovernment provider of youth programs, especially for immigrant communities in large cities. (Hazel Hankin)

nity resources that support family changes have found hearty advocates.

The increasing demands for family participation in the labor force because of individual goals and welfare reform have created the need for after-school programs for latchkey children of all economic groups. Latchkey children are those who have their own keys to enter their homes when their parents are at work. Statistics suggest that about 2.4 million children between the ages of five and thirteen care for themselves or are cared for by other children younger than fourteen years of age for about two hours each day. Moreover, concern for isolated children—those who have few friends and limited opportunities for social contact outside school—and heightened consciousness of the need for recreation to alleviate the causes and consequences of problems facing at-risk children have drawn attention to the need for more accessible children's support networks.

Types of Community Programs for Children. Because of these circumstances, responsibility is being shifted to service organizations to help families lacking the time and energy to supervise their children. Community programs for children are not simply a U.S. phenomenon; Canada, Europe, and some African and Latin American countries have also addressed the need for child supervision, as more women around the world seek education and join the labor force. Programs that offer after-school education, homework assistance, and sports activities have proliferated. Programs are offered in various settings.

Some public libraries offer after-school reading and homework programs. Many schools have opened their doors not only to after-school clubs, sports activities, and homework assistance but also to other services to help parents and reduce their need to travel to different locations. Some high schools offer on-site health services as well as regular activities for adolescents. Museums have listed special offerings on afternoons and weekends. Some day-care centers specialize in evening and overnight programs for children to address parents' need for leisure time. Resorts have also introduced special programs for children in families.

Neighborhood organizations have responded to the expressed needs of community residents. Programs have been implemented to address juvenile crime committed between the hours of 3:00 P.M. and 8:00 P.M. Because these are the hours that many youngsters are unsupervised or without the means to be involved in private activity programs, communities have organized basketball programs and other recreational activities in response to this need. These programs have established significant relationships for children who otherwise might be without adult supervision and organized activities. In cases in which parents are too burdened with their own problems to help students' academic performance, some programs provide homework assistance to children. Urban programs for males, mentoring programs, rites of passage programs in ethnic settings, church programs, and activities in local malls are other examples of community programs for children.

Programs administered by government and voluntary agencies stretch their budgets to pay for professional and community staffs, often recruiting volunteers to provide services for children. The multicultural communities of Canada offer an exciting environment of immigrant traditions and customs, raising children in modern society. Communities have responded in creative ways to address the needs of children in their environments.   —*Gwenelle S. O'Neal*

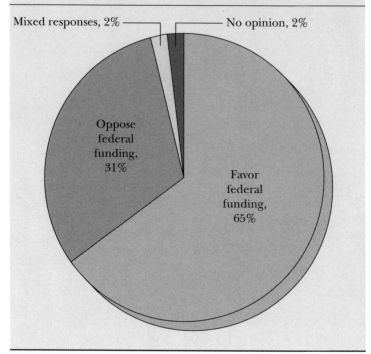

U.S. Public Opinion on Government Funding of Community Programs

Source: CNN/*USA Today*/Gallup Poll
Note: In 1994 a cross-section of Americans were asked if they favored or opposed federal government funding of social programs and such activities as midnight basketball for low-income children.

BIBLIOGRAPHY

Adler, Patricia, and Peter Adler. "Social Reproduction and the Corporate Other: The Institutionalization of After-school Activities." *The Sociological Quarterly* 35 (May, 1994).

Coleman, Mick, Bryan E. Robinson, and Bobbie H. Rowland. "A Typology of Families with Children in Self-Care: Implications for School-Age Child Care Programming." *Child and Youth Care Forum* 22 (February, 1993).

Dowd, Frances. "Public Library Programs for Latchkey Children: A Status Report." *Public Libraries* (September/October, 1995).

McLaughlin, Milbrey W., Merita A. Irby, and Juliet Langman. *Urban Sanctuaries: Neighborhood Organizations in the Lives and Futures of Inner City Youth.* San Francisco, Calif.: Jossey Bass, 1994.

Schultz, L. E., J. Crompton, and P. Witt. "National Profile of Status of Public Recreation." *Journal of Parks & Recreation* 13 (Fall, 1995).

Stone, Rebecca. *Comprehensive Community Building Strategies: Issues and Opportunities for Learning.* Chicago: Chapin Hall Center for Children, 1994.

See also Child care; Child Care and Development Block Grant Act; Hull House; Juvenile delinquency; Latchkey children; Women's roles; Youth sports.